# PROLOGUE TO WAR

*Also by Bradford Perkins*

THE FIRST RAPPROCHEMENT: ENGLAND AND THE UNITED STATES, 1795–1805
CASTLEREAGH AND ADAMS: ENGLAND AND THE UNITED STATES, 1812–1823

# PROLOGUE
# TO
# WAR

ENGLAND
AND THE UNITED STATES
# 1805 - 1812

## BY BRADFORD PERKINS

UNIVERSITY OF CALIFORNIA PRESS

BERKELEY    LOS ANGELES    LONDON

UNIVERSITY OF CALIFORNIA PRESS
BERKELEY AND LOS ANGELES, CALIFORNIA
UNIVERSITY OF CALIFORNIA PRESS, LTD.
LONDON, ENGLAND
© 1961 BY THE REGENTS OF THE UNIVERSITY OF CALIFORNIA
FIFTH PRINTING, 1974
PRINTED IN THE UNITED STATES OF AMERICA
ISBN: 0-520-00996-7
LIBRARY OF CONGRESS CATALOG CARD NUMBER: 61-14018
DESIGNED BY WARD RITCHIE

FOR NANCY

# PREFACE

Relations with England dominated American diplomacy until 1914, if not indeed until 1945. Although unexplored areas in this vast panorama still exist, this book examines a relatively familiar one, the quarrel preceding the second and last war between Great Britain and the United States. In 1941, after examining all available studies of the coming of the War of 1812, Warren H. Goodman observed "the need for a comprehensive work on the subject. . . . In this century, only monographs on restricted phases of the topic have appeared; no recent writer has attempted to correlate and synthesize the various sets of causes." [1] Since that time only A. L. Burt's relatively short analysis and H. C. Allen's even more restricted survey have appeared.

I owe much to the various scholars cited in the footnotes and mentioned in the Note on the Sources. For the most part, however, this study rests upon an examination of manuscript materials, including many not previously used, and upon contemporary newspapers and pamphlets. Most notably, no scholar since Henry Adams has examined more than the most obvious English materials. I have therefore devoted much of my attention to the development of British policy, virtually caricatured by too many American historians.

Previous interpretations and old emphases seem to me inadequate. I believe scholars have overemphasized the tangible, rational reasons for action and, while not ignoring, have given too little heed to such things as national pride, sensitivity, and frustration, although the evidence for this sort of thing leaps to the eye. Emotion, chance, and half choices often mold the relations between states as much as or more than cool reason. Such clearly was true in the years between 1805 and 1812.

In this and a succeeding volume I hope to treat the period from 1805 to 1825 as a whole, organizing my study around a central

[1] "The Origins of the War of 1812: a Survey of Changing Interpretations," *Mississippi Valley Historical Review*, XXVIII (1941–1942), 185.

theme—the American search for national respectability and true independence from Europe, independence far transcending the recognition of an American state in 1783. In an absolute sense, such a search is like the quest for the Holy Grail. The early Federalists rejected it as visionary, Jefferson and Madison sought it but failed, Monroe and John Quincy Adams did not lose sight of the ultimate aim but were prepared to proceed mile by visible mile. Since relations with Britain form the most important part of this theme, I have felt free to mention only in passing other matters, notably relations with Spain and many parts of Franco-American relations, which would have complicated the main story.

I should particularly like to express my thanks to the many persons in England who opened family archives to me. Her Majesty, Queen Elizabeth II, graciously permitted me to make use of material from the Royal Archives at Windsor; Sir Owen Morshead and Robert Mackworth-Young eased my path through this tremendous collection and helped me make the best use of this rare privilege. I have profited greatly from the use of manuscripts of Viscount Castlereagh, the Earl of Harrowby, and Admiral Warren, and I am very grateful to the Marchioness Dowager of Londonderry, the Earl of Harrowby, and Lord Vernon for their helpfulness. George Grenville Fortescue repeated a previous favor by opening the manuscripts of Lord Grenville at Boconnoc, a house so charming that one can easily understand the Opposition leader's reluctance to attend the conflicts of Parliament. Oliver R. Bagot willingly tolerated a family invasion of his home in Westmorland while I examined the papers of Charles Bagot. Major Simon Whitbread and Viscount Sidmouth kindly permitted me to see the papers of their ancestors at the Bedford and Devon Record Offices respectively. For the locating of some of these collections I must thank Miss Coates, the Registrar of National Archives, and I am also grateful to Major Bailey, of her staff, for sharing with me the hours among Spencer Perceval's papers temporarily on deposit with the Register. In this and a subsequent volume I hope that my debt to these persons will become clear.

I also owe thanks to the Public Record Office and the British Museum, where I spent most of a profitable year; to Widener Library, Harvard University, which, with its adjunct the Houghton Library, is an almost perfect working library; to the Manuscripts Division of the Library of Congress; to the American Antiquarian Society, with its unparalleled newspaper and pamphlet collections, only superficially tapped in two summers; and to the always helpful, growing library of my home base, the University of California, Los Angeles. Other libraries, from the shadow of Durham Cathedral to the palatial estate of Henry Huntington, have been equally kind to me, but my major effort has been concentrated in the repositories mentioned above.

For the portraits which grace this volume I am indebted to many persons. Representations of Thomas Jefferson by Rembrandt Peale and of John Randolph by John W. Jarvis appear through the courtesy of the New-York Historical Society. The Pennsylvania Academy of the Fine Arts furnished me with a reproduction of Gilbert Stuart's James Monroe. The portrait of William Pinkney by Charles B. King appears through the kindness of the Maryland Historical Society and the Frick Art Reference Library. The National Portrait Gallery, London, furnished me with photographs of four portraits: Charles James Fox by Karl A. Hickel, Spencer Perceval by George F. Joseph (from a death mask by Nollekens), James Stephen by John Linnell, and Henry Brougham by James Lonsdale. Lord Ashburton and Major Simon Whitbread, respectively, sent me photographs of the portraits of Alexander Baring by Thomas Lawrence and Samuel Whitbread by John Hoppner. The coöperation of Lawrence Gouverneur Hoes and the Frick Art Reference Library made possible the inclusion of John Vanderlyn's portrait of James Madison. Charles B. King's John C. Calhoun appears through the courtesy of the Corcoran Gallery of Art, and the Long Island Historical Society furnished a photograph of the portrait of Henry Clay by an unknown artist. The Boston Museum of Fine Arts supplied a photograph of Gilbert Stuart's portrait of Josiah Quincy. Most of the portraits were selected because they show their subjects in the period covered by this book.

None of the research work on this volume could have been done without the cordial assistance of the University of California and particularly the Social Science Research Council. As a Faculty Research Fellow of the Council from 1957 to 1960, I have enjoyed opportunities for research not often available to a young scholar. I am extremely grateful to Elbridge Sibley and to the Committee on Faculty Research Fellowships for granting to me an opportunity which I hope will be considered well used.

I have also benefited greatly from the assistance of my research assistant, Dr. Elmo Richardson, who has rescued me from numerous errors of fact, and of Mrs. Grace H. Stimson, of the University of California Press, whose patient editorial work resulted in many improvements of the manuscript.

Two eminent diplomatic historians have helped to give this volume any merit that it may have. Samuel Flagg Bemis of Yale University read the entire manuscript, gave me the benefit of his wide learning, and suggested many helpful changes. My father, Dexter Perkins, has frequently rescued me from confusion and despond. His scholarly example remains for me a model, if an unattainable one.

My chief debt is to a patient wife who has shared the burdens and joys of travel and the even more equivocal tasks of organization, composition, and supervision of publication. Neither my severest nor my most charitable critic, she has nevertheless been my most helpful one. To her I dedicate this volume.

BRADFORD PERKINS

September, 1960
Los Angeles, California
Harvard, Massachusetts

# CONTENTS

# ILLUSTRATIONS

Is the Patriotism of 1776 no more? Is it all converted, into Fish, Wheat, Flour, Rice or Cotton, or into the love of profit and of gold? The nation is surely paralized by these sordid motives, or they would speak a language That would operate like thunder and Lightning over the Land and Sea. Britain is our inviterate adversary—France is not so, but pursues her own interest and ambition. Let us dread neither of them, for notwithstanding Their present appearances of power, They are both vitally sink$^g$. While we are Vitally rising in the world.

THOMAS RODNEY, 1808

Mr. Speaker, I would solemnly demand, what is this national honor, this object of ministerial idolatry? Is she one of those infernal deities which can feed on nothing but commercial havoc and national ruin? Does she, like the demons of a Merina's temple, sit abstracted and ferocious, never smiling but on national distress, never propitiated but by human sacrifice? Then she is the last deity that a virtuous and republican people should worship. But this is not her character; she is a beneficent, healing, and curing goddess, allied inseparably to public virtue, prosperity, and happiness. . . . And such, notwithstanding the misdeeds that have been perpetrated in her name, she continues to this day.

THOMAS GROSVENOR, 1813

# CHAPTER

# I

# BELEAGUERED BRITAIN

"Britain and the United States are destined to become . . . the predominating nations of Christendom. . . . Each an incumbrance to the other when together, their severance seems to have been the signal for unequalled progress, and boundless prospects to each; not more in material dominion than in the solid and durable glory of widening the empire of rational thought throughout the world." [1] So wrote Richard Rush, the American minister at the Court of St. James, as he ruminated on the death of George III, long the very symbol of Anglo-American discord. During the 1790's a *rapprochement* had been built upon a recognition of mutual interests, and when George III died in 1820 the Earl of Liverpool and Viscount Castlereagh were laboring to construct a new *rapprochement*. Unfortunately, in the intervening years the "rational thought" in which Rush took pride had too often been thrust aside by emotion and prejudice. A long, serious quarrel took

[1] Richard Rush, *A Residence at the Court of London, Second Series* (2 vols.; London, 1845), I, 277–278.

place, a quarrel climaxed by the American declaration of war upon Great Britain in June, 1812.

This friction really sprang from one simple fact: America chose to be neutral while Britain struggled for her life against Napoleon. To keep the Royal Navy manned for the contest, England forcibly enlisted seamen from American merchant ships. To deprive Napoleon of essential goods, but particularly to preserve or reopen trade with the Continent upon which British prosperity presumably rested, England instituted unprecedented systems of blockade which she called executive Orders in Council. Thus the American seaman lost his liberty, the merchant his ships, and the farmer and plantation owner a market for his grain and cotton and tobacco. On the other hand, England objected that Americans covered French property with their flag or greedily sought to replace Britain in European markets, vitiating the effectiveness of English commercial warfare. The American merchant marine seduced mariners from their duty to the King. Not one of these grievances was new. All existed during the first *rapprochement,* when Federalist sympathy for Britain, the wisdom of William Pitt and his foreign secretary, and the valuing of compromise over confrontation prevented a clash that might as easily have come then as a decade later.

As time passed, the ardors of war and the tribulations of neutrality wore patience thin. The issues became an argument and then a war, for irrational and emotional reasons. Too many Englishmen looked upon the Americans with contempt, insisting that the British government treat these bastard Englishmen as upstart commercial rivals and political incompetents. Too many Americans clung to the Anglophobia of Revolutionary days and desired to underscore the chastisement then inflicted upon England. They were touchily conscious that Britain, like other European powers, regarded America as an unimportant factor in world politics. "Britain never has treated the Americans as an independent nation, and has only acknowledged it in words," the West's premier newspaper declared. The new Republican mood insisted upon the fullness of American rights. When the inadequate weapons of Jefferson and

Madison failed to secure these rights from England, war seemed the only alternative to national humiliation. Realistically, there was less cause for war in 1812 than at other times. However, as Samuel Taylor Coleridge observed (perhaps repenting his earlier writings for Britain's most stridently anti-American paper), "The malignant witchcraft of evil passions reads good men's prayers backward, and . . . the hot heads in both countries . . . make folly beget folly, both the more wrong in proportion as each is right." [2]

From the Jay treaty until 1805, hotheads were kept under fairly successful control. When, dressed all in somber black but intent upon Republican hosannas rather than an obituary or a lament, Jefferson delivered his second inaugural address in March, 1805, he found it possible to pass over foreign affairs with bland, naïve generalities. "With nations as with individuals," the President declared, "our interests soundly calculated will ever be found inseparable from our moral duties, and history bears witness to the fact that a just nation is trusted on its word." [3] Jefferson's view of the moral imperatives and Britain's attack upon American interests soon led to a sharp clash. The happy and prosperous years ended shortly after the beginning of Thomas Jefferson's second term.

For this the polarization of European power was chiefly responsible. Horatio Nelson's guns reaffirmed British supremacy on the sea in October, 1805. For many years thereafter the Royal Navy was almost the only effective instrument in the contest against Napoleon. The black-hulled ships broke up France's overseas trade and were used to foster what commerce Britain could find. That neutrals might suffer in this process troubled Englishmen but little, for, as one pamphleteer put it, "God and nature having put the power of the ocean . . . into our hands, we are fully entitled to exercise that power for our complete security,

---

[2] *Reporter* (Lexington, Ky.), June 21, 1809; Coleridge to Allston, Oct. 25, 1815, Jared B. Flagg, *The Life and Letters of Washington Allston* (New York, 1892), p. 117.

[3] James D. Richardson, ed., *A Compilation of the Messages and Papers of the Presidents* (Washington, 1897), I, 378.

and so as to ensure us the full enjoyment of the naval prosperity consequent upon it." Defensively, the Royal Navy prevented an invasion of the British Isles, permitting England to continue resistance to a despot who brought almost the entire continent of Europe to heel. "Britannia needs no bulwark, / No towers along the steep; / Her march is o'er the mountain-waves, / Her home is on the deep," ran one of the most popular ballads of the day.[4]

If Britain controlled the seas, Napoleon dominated the land. Two months after Trafalgar he crushed the Austrians and the Russians with contemptuous ease at Austerlitz, driving the Hapsburgs to humiliating peace. In October, 1806, he annihilated the Prussians at Jena and Auerstadt. The next spring he bludgeoned back the Russians at Friedland, and in July, 1807, he and Czar Alexander arranged an accommodation at the raft-borne conference of Tilsit. The Third Coalition had gone the way of those before it. "We have no friend, no support, no ally in the world, but our own courage and heroism," the London *Times* proclaimed in the month of Tilsit. Britain was beleaguered, isolated. "If Bonaparte does not by an attempt at Invasion or some other great imprudence give us an advantage," Charles James Fox wrote while a leading member of the British government, "I cannot but think this country invariably and irretrievably ruined. . . . To be Ministers at a moment when the Country is falling and all Europe sinking, is a dreadful situation."[5] Fortunately for Britain, somewhat less pessimistic statesmen were at the head of affairs after 1807.

Englishmen honestly thought that in facing Napoleon's challenge they fought for the entire world. "We conquer but to save," a patriotic poet wrote in 1805, and Robert Southey, a far greater one, called his country "Freedom's own beloved Isle." Politicians

---

[4] Nathaniel Atcheson, *A Compressed View of the Points To Be Discussed in Treating with the United States of America* (London, 1814), p. 26; "Ye Mariners of England," Lewis Campbell, ed., *Poems of Thomas Campbell* (London, 1904), pp. 66–67.

[5] *Times* (London), July 15, 1807; Fox to Grenville, April 18, 1806, Boconnoc MSS (Papers of William Wyndham Grenville, Baron Grenville), Lostwithiel, Cornwall, Cabinet Members. Only in citing manuscript collections not rigorously organized chronologically, or undated materials, do the footnotes include volume names or numbers or folio numbers.

added their amens. England, said James Stephen, was "the bulwark and safeguard of all nations which the ambition of the enemy sought to conquer or destroy." British naval power, said the Earl of Selkirk, was "the last stay of the liberties of the world." This prideful language, these expressions of a savior complex, provoked an American to observe that Britain was worse than France "for she adds to her wickedness the crime of hypocrisy." [6]

More specifically, Englishmen believed that their military forces were defending America, and that in the event of British defeat she would find herself unable to protect her shores against Napoleon. "The Alps and the Apennines of America are the British Navy," wrote the *Times*. "If ever that should be removed, a short time will suffice to establish the head-quarters of a Duke-Marshal at Washington, and to divide the territory of the Union into military prefectures." In parliamentary debate over the War of 1812, the Earl of Liverpool rebuked the United States for failing to appreciate the "security and protection" England afforded. America, he said, "ought to have looked to this country as the guardian power to which she was indebted, not only for her comforts, not only for her rank in the scale of civilization, but for her very existence." [7]

The sharp contrast between British political isolation and the omnipotent power of the Royal Navy produced a very harsh policy toward neutrals. "The sea is ours, and we must maintain the doctrine—that no nation, no fleet, no cock-boat shall sail upon it without our permission," the London *Courier* declared in 1811. Many Englishmen believed the holy crusade against Napoleon required Britain to exploit to the full her one effective available weapon. England must show no weakness that would encourage her enemy and increase neutral demands. She must use the naval power God had given her to break up the trade Napoleon carried

<hr>

[6] "Battle of the Baltic," Campbell, *op. cit.*, p. 76; "Ode Written during the War with America," *The Poetical Works of Robert Southey* (New York, n.d.), p. 368; *Hansard*, XXI, 1139; XIV, 349; Rush to John Adams, Aug. 8, 1812, Lyman H. Butterfield, ed., *Letters of Benjamin Rush*, II, American Philosophical Society, *Memoirs*, Vol. XXX (1951), pp. 1157–1158.

[7] *Times*, Dec. 16, 1811; *Hansard*, XXIV, 585–586.

on under neutral flags. "We had much better be at open hostility with both America and Prussia," wrote "A True Englishman" in 1806, "than suffer them, as they do, to prostitute their flags to supply the enemy with the 'sinews of war.' " [8] Followers of Fox, Grenville, and Grey often warned that British obduracy might indeed drive America into the war. Their opponents, who occupied the seats of power after 1807, offered limited concessions to preserve American neutrality. But strident nationalists objected to any sign of weakness, even apology for the *Chesapeake* affair. When war came, some of the ministry's critics blamed it on too-great tenderness in the past. On the whole, Englishmen felt that the situation required an unyielding policy toward neutrals.

Relations with the United States, the chief neutral, attracted far less attention, or at least less thought, than they deserved. Major issues, among them the conduct of the war, the treatment to be accorded Ireland, and the political implications of George III's renewed insanity, displaced American affairs from the center of the political scene. So too did titillating but less important matters like the sale of army commissions by the Commander in Chief's mistress and the raising of prices at Covent Garden. In 1809 Lord Auckland, an Opposition expert on American affairs, considered them "the least regarded & ill understood" major issue. More than a year later the *Times*, which did not particularly like America but understood the controversy's importance, wrote in discouragement: "There is certainly a great apathy in the public mind, generally, upon the questions now at issue between us and our *quondam* colonies, which it is difficult to rouse, and perhaps useless to attempt." [9] This neglect played no small part in the coming of Anglo-American war.

The American Revolution did not make Englishmen respect their victorious colonies. On the contrary, some dreamt of a chance to even the score and many others suggested that America's visible faults were owing to a premature separation from the mother

[8] *Courier* (London), Jan. 21, 1811; A True Englishman, *The War As It Is, and the War As It Should Be* (London, 1806), p. 30.

[9] Auckland to Grey, Nov. 27, 1809, Charles Grey, Second Earl Grey, MSS, The Prior's Kitchen, Durham University, from 1st Ld. Auckland; *Times*, March 1, 1811.

country. On the whole, America was considered an infant among nations—uncouth, argumentative, boasting, essentially weak and entirely dependent upon Britain, ungenteelly grasping in commercial affairs. The British view, like all caricatures, contained a germ of truth. Candid Americans admitted that their own country's assertiveness invited the British reaction. We have "monopolized with so little reserve every attribute of freedom, heroism, intelligence, and virtue," Benjamin Silliman said, "that we cannot be surprised if other countries, should be somewhat reluctant to concede, what we so indecorously demand." Be that as it may, the fact remains that America was, as the *Edinburgh Review* observed in 1812, "less popular and less esteemed among us than the base and bigotted Portugeze, or the ferocious and ignorant Russians." [10] Even comparatively friendly journals like the *Edinburgh Review* took an extremely patronizing attitude toward the United States and its culture as a whole.

London's most nationalistic newspaper wrote in 1811:

Pre-eminently is America advantageous to Great Britain, and Great Britain is scarcely less than *necessary* to America, if the gradual formation of a learned class and of a natural gentry, if the growth of arts and sciences . . . if a stimulus for agriculture, if commerce and commercial cities that alone supply the stimulus, if union, if safety, if national independence be rightly placed among the necessities of a young and free country. It is British capital, which directly or indirectly, sets half the industry of America in motion: it is the British fleets that give it protection and security.

[10] Benjamin Silliman, *A Journal of Travels in England, Holland, and Scotland* (2d ed.; 2 vols.; Boston, 1812), II, 338; *Edinburgh Review*, XX (1812), 460. Characteristic of the British attitude is the following paragraph written to his mother by Augustus John Foster, then a young attaché but later a somewhat more appreciative minister: "They & we are now the Two rivals in what has always given Power wherever it has extended, Commerce, but I trust that still & for a long time we shall maintain the immense superiority that we do now. They are next us in the Race, but in nothing else are they near us. We drove them into being a Nation when they were no more fit for it than the Convicts of Botany Bay, tho I must say that their leader Washington was a great Character, and one or two others whom the Tumult of the Day drove from their Counters. but since that, Interest and speculation seems to have taken fast hold of the whole Country to the Exclusion of every generous Feeling. . . . the Character of a Gentleman is very rare to be found indeed here, but what has surprised me the Character of an Honest Man of Principle is . . . full as rare." Foster to Lady Elizabeth Foster, Dec. 1, 1805, Augustus J. Foster MSS, Library of Congress.

Although at this time hoping for peace, the *Courier* often felt the young nation needed a thrashing before it would appreciate these truths. The Earl of Sheffield argued that firmness alone could check "that spirit of encroachment, that indiscriminate thirst of gain, that sordid jealousy" that fouled America's attitude toward her parent and protector.[11] Time and again British nationalists warned the United States that war would not be unpopular, and America's British friends admitted this. British opinion would have supported a far more rigorous policy toward the United States than the one actually adopted.

Britain considered the American Constitution inadequate to the requirements of government, the nation weak in material strength and in will, and the Republican leaders sycophants of France through sympathy or through fear. The absence of aristocratic influence, even the most liberal Englishmen thought, condemned America to excesses and imbalance. "The mail takes twelve passengers, which generally consist of squalling children, stinking negroes, and republicans smoking cigars," the Irish poet, Tom Moore, wrote at the beginning of the century. "How often it has occurred to me that nothing can be more emblematic of the *government* of this country than its *stages*, filled with a motley mixture, all 'hail fellow well met,' driving through mud and filth, which *bespatters* them as they *raise* it, and risking an *upset* at every step." Even the *Edinburgh Review*, which did not, like Moore, hate America, believed she prospered in spite of rather than because of her Constitution. "It has the appearance . . . rather of an experiment in politics, than of a steady permanent government," the magazine commented. Provisions encouraging party spirit (notably the presidential election) and federal-state conflict would have to be altered before America achieved real strength.[12]

As early as 1806 Jefferson complained that his country's love

---

[11] *Courier*, July 29, 1811; John B. Holroyd, Earl of Sheffield, *Strictures on the Necessity of Inviolably Maintaining the Navigation and Colonial System of Great Britain* (new ed.; London, 1806), pp. 317–318.

[12] Moore to Mrs. Anastasia Moore, June 13, 1804, Lord John Russell, ed., *Memoirs, Journal, and Correspondence of Thomas Moore* (8 vols.; London, 1853–1856), I, 161–162; *Edinburgh Review*, XII (1808), 469–478.

of peace had "begun to produce an opinion in Europe that our government is entirely in Quaker principles." The President hoped that American vigor would destroy this impression, but his policies and those of his successor merely encouraged it. The almost total absence of military preparation, the empty sound and fury after the *Chesapeake* affair, the disreputable flight from the Embargo, successive huckstering legislation designed to find an alternative to war—all these convinced England of America's weakness. Eight months before war finally came, the *Times* pronounced the United States totally incapable of offensive warfare, and a few months later John Quincy Adams observed that the British "will yield nothing in Negotiation, because they have formed a settled opinion that America will not, perhaps that she cannot undertake a War, against England." [13] If war came, the British believed, they would determine the time and the place.

On the other hand, Jeffersonians appeared sufficiently pro-French to give Napoleon aid short of war. Rejection of the Monroe-Pinkney treaty, the proclamation of 1807 banning Royal Navy ships from American ports, and slight differences between the demands made upon France and those made upon Britain as conditions of raising the Embargo all reinforced this British conviction. It became, a pro-American pamphleteer in London complained, "not less general, I had nearly said universal,—than erroneous." As time passed and as the Republicans' obvious dislike of Napoleonic autocracy became too obvious to ignore, some explained the American bias in terms of greater fear of Napoleon than of Britain. William Cobbett, for example, declared that the Americans detested France more than England but had been encouraged to press claims against Great Britain by ministerial weakness. George H. Rose, sent to America on a special mission at the end of 1807, summed up this feeling when he wrote: "Though Mr. Jefferson's Sympathy with the internal policy of France can no longer exist, His Antipathy to her Rival is unabated; and though

[13] Jefferson to Thomas Cooper, Feb. 18, 1806, Thomas Jefferson MSS (Coolidge Collection), Massachusetts Historical Society; *Times*, Oct. 28, 1811; Adams to Abigail Adams, March 30, 1812, Adams Family MSS (microfilm), Massachusetts Historical Society, Vol. CXXXV.

he may view Bonaparte with little of affection, he certainly does it with considerable awe." Even Opposition leaders like Lord Grenville and Opposition journals frequently complained of American bias for France. Only a few important figures, among them Henry Brougham, Alexander Baring, and the American-born pamphleteer George Joy, steadfastly repudiated this accusation. On the whole, the British people shared the opinion of Robert Southey, who described the Republicans as the "Vile instruments of fallen Tyranny" after Napoleon's exile to Elba.[14]

Englishmen usually corresponded with Americans who were Federalists (or merchants, much the same thing), Federalist newspapers reached Britain more rapidly and in greater number than those of their opponents, and, as the American minister at London complained, Federalist pamphlets alone were reprinted in Britain. Thus Britain entertained illusory expectations of a Federalist return to power and received news that confirmed the impression of American weakness and Republican Francophilia. When a long diatribe against the Embargo by Timothy Pickering reached England in the spring of 1808, a member of the Cabinet exulted: "This letter . . . will prove a great embarrassment to the opposition, and particularly to Lord Grenville, in his promised motion for the recall of the Orders in Council." As predicted, Grenville's motion failed to get off the ground. The Republicans complained that Federalist attacks were almost treasonable, and William Cobbett, who with characteristic unpredictability shifted from violent opposition to forthright support of the American cause, warned Pickering and his confreres that they played into the hands of those in Britain who most hated the United States.[15] Nevertheless, the flow of Federalist material to England continued. One-sided

---

[14] George Joy to Grenville, n.d., enclosed in Joy to Samuel Whitbread, Feb. 24, 1809, Samuel Whitbread MSS, Southill Park, Biggleswade, Bedfordshire; *Cobbett's Political Register* (London), XIII (1808), 114; Rose #10 to Canning, secret and confidential, Feb. 6, 1808, Foreign Office Archives, Public Record Office, FO 5/56; "Ode Written during the War with America," *Works of Southey*, p. 367.

[15] William Pinkney to Madison, private, Dec. 21, 1807, William C. Rives Collection, Library of Congress; Harrowby to Countess of Harrowby, April 28, 1808, Dudley Ryder, 1st Earl of Harrowby, MSS, Sandon Hall, Staffordshire; *Cobbett's Register*, XX (1811), 397–398.

news helped confirm England's unfavorable portrait of the Americans.

At no time did a powerful phil-American clique develop in either house of Parliament. When Charles James Fox, Lord Grenville, and their lieutenants urged compromise with the United States, they seldom argued in terms of affection for America. Followers of the Cabinet that issued the Orders in Council were more vindictive than the ministers, and the great mass of floating members (nearly half the House of Commons) was almost equally hostile. The temper of the Commons thus forbade important concessions to America. Many pensioners and placemen sat in the House, boroughmongers controlled a third or more of the votes, other and sometimes less important issues reduced the American question to second rank, and at the time of many important divisions the number of absentees (sometimes as many as two-thirds of the membership) would have scandalized even the American Congress. In 1809 Jefferson expostulated that the British government, compared at least with others since the age of Walpole, was "the most corrupted & corrupting mass of rottenness which ever usurped the name of government." [16] Bad though it may have been, and arrogantly unconcerned as it was with American affairs, this Parliament and this system of government carried the war against Napoleon to a victorious conclusion.

In the persons of the aged and presumably vindictive George III and, after his final attack of insanity, his allegedly more liberal son, the Prince Regent, royal influence played an important part in British politics. The Crown powerfully influenced, if it did not control, the election of at least a hundred members of Parliament, and the sovereign played an active role in the construction of new ministries. After William Pitt's death in 1806 George III reluctantly accepted the Ministry of All the Talents, which included his old foe, Charles James Fox. The next year the weight of the Crown was thrown against the government and it fell from power. The King supported the ministry that followed, and in general

<hr />

[16] Jefferson to William Lambert, Sept. 10, 1809, Thomas Jefferson MSS, Library of Congress.

he approved its policies. But he did not oppose the Talents because he objected to their comparatively mild American policy, and he neither sought to encourage nor enthusiastically praised the rigid line adopted by their successors. The Prince Regent, who took over the powers of the sovereign in 1810 and 1811, was thought more liberal than his father, primarily because in his youth he had consorted with Fox. Americans hoped the Regent would return the heirs of Fox to power, and on several occasions American diplomats at London thought they detected conciliatory tendencies in his conversation. But the Prince of Wales supported the ministry of Spencer Perceval and did not urge him to repeal the Orders in Council. After Perceval's assassination the Regent made no effort to secure a pledge of repeal from the politicians arranging a new ministry. As far as American affairs were concerned, the selfish, lazy Prince Regent played no more important a direct part than his father.

Pitt's survivors, who defeated the Ministry of All the Talents in 1807, maintained themselves in power from then onward. William Pitt had an undeservedly unfavorable reputation in the United States—the Philadelphia *Aurora* congratulated America on the death of this "offence to God and to man" [17]—but in his last months British policy toward the United States became more harsh. Most of Pitt's successors, like him devoted to vigorous prosecution of the war, unlike him failed to see the advantages of at least a partial understanding with the most important maritime neutral; they also pushed aside the comparative economic liberalism that had been their master's. A notable exception was Earl Bathurst, a quietly unobtrusive and efficient protégé of Pitt's who served for a long time as president of the Board of Trade and often occupied the Foreign Office ad interim. More than any other Pittite, Bathurst recognized the importance of preserving American neutrality, if only for economic reasons.

Encouraged by American weakness, angered by the way neutral trade enriched the United States and eased pressure upon

[17] *Aurora* (Philadelphia), March 21, 1806. This obituary notice also described Pitt as "the English *Robespierre*" and "the late execrable *prime minister* of England."

France, devoted to the strengthening of British commerce, most Pittites advocated a harsh policy toward Americans. Their leader, Spencer Perceval, was always eager for battle with his parliamentary enemies and ready to face any Napoleonic challenge. His piety, simplicity, and uncompromising view of the war made him very popular in Commons. Perceval was also stubborn and intolerant of criticism, and his ideas, particularly in the commercial field, often simplified Pitt's almost to the point of caricature. Perceval opposed toleration of American trade with the West Indies and sponsored the Orders in Council of November, 1807. His system received enthusiastic support from lesser members of the faction, perhaps most consistently from George Rose, a statistics-laden veteran at the Board of Trade, and from Daniel Stuart, editor of the *Courier*, one of the most important and certainly the most anti-American journal in London. Although cabinet colleagues sometimes doubted the wisdom of Perceval's policies, the force of his opinions and his strength in Parliament defeated major challenges until 1812.

The transformation of the Pitt party, which had helped to construct Anglo-American understanding in the 1790's, is best illustrated by the Earl of Liverpool. Although his father, the first earl, was a bitter enemy of the United States and its trade, as a young man Liverpool loyally supported Pitt's policy of conciliation. In 1801 he became foreign secretary, and while at Downing Street he presided over the most moderate American policy Britain adopted in the first forty years of American independence. Liverpool earned a reputation as a friend of the United States, and in 1807, when the United States returned the Monroe-Pinkney treaty for modifications, Secretary of State Madison expected Liverpool, now again in the Cabinet, to support the changes America desired.[18] The weakness and the apparent Francophilia of the Jeffersonian regime caused Liverpool to abandon his early attitudes. He supported the Orders in Council, and minimized the dangers of American retaliation. In 1810 he wrote:

[18] Madison to Monroe and Pinkney, May 20, 1807, Department of State Archives, National Archives, Instructions, All Countries, Vol. VI.

The Situation of Affairs in America appears to us here to be as little likely to lead to any amicable settlement, as they have been at any time for the last three or four Years. It is a Satisfaction, however, to reflect, that the Cause of our Country appears to gain ground in many parts of the United States, and if some material Change should not occur in the System of the Government, the result will probably be, the Separation of the Eastern from the Southern States. This Event, whenever it takes place, (and it will take place at no very distant period) will have the effect at least of securing the British Possessions in North America, from any Danger arriving from Foreign Aggression.[19]

Liverpool was essentially a pragmatist, and when after the War of 1812 he felt British interests best served by reconciliation he loyally supported the policies of his subordinate, Castlereagh. In the critical years before the war the facts seemed to him to justify a more rigorous policy. In similar fashion many Pittites abandoned the policies followed by their leader in the 1790's.

Essentially a disciple of Pitt, and in his own mind the most logical heir, was George Canning. Canning served as foreign secretary from 1807 to 1809. Thereafter, thanks to his own arrogance and a quarrel with Castlereagh, he was out of the government and often opposed it in Parliament. The Americans regarded Canning as their worst enemy, a not surprising attitude in view of the language Canning allowed himself to use in his diplomatic correspondence and speeches. Canning considered America a perversion of republicanism; in 1813 he asked sarcastically, "Who would have expected to have seen this favourite child of freedom leagued with the oppressor of the world?" and added, "In the republic of America we look for the realization of our visions of republican virtue in vain." [20] Nevertheless, Canning, along with Bathurst, attempted to preserve American neutrality by modifying the Orders in Council, and in 1812 he supported the Opposition attack upon the entire system. Although he paid too little attention to

[19] Liverpool to Sir James Craig, April 4, 1810, MSS of the first and second Earls of Liverpool, British Museum (Add. MSS 38190–38489, 38564–38581), Add. MSS 38323.
[20] *Hansard*, XXIV, 640–642.

American sensibilities, the policy he favored was closer to the old Pitt tradition than the policy actually followed.[21]

Also somewhat apart from orthodox Pittites stood the tiny faction called "the Saints." These evangelicals supported the Ministry of All the Talents because it opposed the slave trade, but most of them later backed Perceval's ministry. By far the most important for Anglo-American relations was James Stephen, a sturdy, obstinate, argumentative lawyer of the West Indian interest, and a man possessed of almost equal hatred of Napoleon and Jefferson. In 1805 Stephen's polemic, *War in Disguise; Or, the Frauds of the Neutral Flags,* touched off attacks upon American commerce. In succeeding years his pen and voice stirred up feeling against the United States. Stephen, who knew Perceval well and frequently advised him on maritime policy, was popularly supposed to be the father of the Orders in Council. He defended them vehemently until the very end, when he absented himself from the House of Commons to avoid listening to the announcement of suspension. As a faction, however, the Saints took no consistent position on American policy. One of them, William Wilberforce, philosophically apportioned the blame for friction equally between the two countries. His desertion of the Orders in Council played an important part in their demise.

Between the government's supporters and that large group most conveniently called the Opposition wandered a number of factions. Viscount Sidmouth, very unpopular with the country but in firm command of some twenty votes in Commons, had presided over the liberal American policy of Liverpool (then Lord Hawkesbury) as head of the ministry from 1801 to 1804. Americans considered him a friend, and in 1812 he did decline to enter the Cabinet until assured that the Orders in Council would be changed.

---

[21] Years later an American minister at London described Canning as "sarcastic as well as logical in debate, and sometimes allowing his official pen to trespass in the former field; but in private circles, bland, courteous, and yielding." Richard Rush, *A Residence at the Court of London,* ed. Benjamin Rush (3d ed.; London, 1872), p. 236. Many years passed after Canning's first foreign-secretaryship before such a balanced estimate was possible.

But Sidmouth did not like the Americans nor did he fear them. Neither he nor his followers participated actively in any but the closing debates over the orders. Marquis Wellesley, who headed another faction, was arrogant, ambitious, untrustworthy, and lecherous. Wellesley acted as though he were still a virtually independent sovereign in India, and he tended to look upon Americans as a slightly superior breed of the type he had defeated in the Mahratta wars. Except when forced while foreign secretary to turn his attention to American affairs, the marquis ignored them. He shared, however, the general prejudices of Sidmouth.

The uneasy coalition of Foxites and Grenvilles, backbone of the Ministry of All the Talents and after 1807 the core of the Opposition, unvaryingly supported conciliation of the United States. They numbered approximately as many as the Pittites but were not so attractive to Sidmouths, Wellesleys, independents, and the Crown.[22] After Fox's death in 1806 they lacked effective leadership in the House of Commons. Friction between the two wings frequently deprived them of unity. "Are we not a good deal in the same situation with the poor Spaniards," one of them disconsolately asked, "united in nothing but our dislike of those to whom we are opposed . . . and fighting for the mere sake of fighting without an acknowledged executive Power to direct or controul our exertions?" With some justice a semiofficial American newspaper praised the Opposition as commanding "the best talents and the purest . . . patriotism of England," [23] but they were steadily worsted by less able but better-organized, more determined men.

For this Lord Grenville, an intelligent man but a poor party leader, was largely responsible. Although Grenville did not favor absolute surrender to American demands (on impressment, for example), he frequently spoke proudly of the policy he had followed as foreign secretary under Pitt and urged a similarly moderate approach. He and his principal commercial adviser, Lord Auckland, favored liberal treatment of American trade, and they

[22] For a careful estimate of factional strengths in the Parliament of 1807 see Michael Roberts, *The Whig Party, 1807–1812* (London, 1939), pp. 333–345.
[23] George Tierney to Whitbread, Dec. 29, 1808, Whitbread MSS.

bitterly attacked the Orders in Council for risking Britain's share of it. "With the friendship of America," Grenville wrote in 1809, "we might rest a husbanding & defensive system on the basis of an extensive commerce, & so might still survive the storm. Without such a resource what hope have we?" Grenville's personal failings made him ineffective in forwarding his views. In power, he stressed the probable unfavorable consequences of any new departure. In opposition, he avoided as much as possible "the irksome & hopeless duties of Parliament," gloomily concluding that the government occupied a nearly impregnable position.[24] Throughout, he clung to a conviction that Napoleon could not be defeated, that Britain's days of glory had passed. Grenville's loss of fire, his decline since the fall of his cousin's ministry in 1801, was a catastrophe for Anglo-American comity.

Whereas Grenville had an undeserved reputation as an Americanophobe, his political ally, Charles James Fox, was remembered in the United States as a friend of the Revolutionary struggle. Whatever Fox really thought of America per se in the closing years of his life (and he neither wrote nor spoke on the subject), he did favor a conciliatory policy toward her as best for Britain, and he opposed monopolistic, mercantilist trade policies of the sort that challenged America. The Foxite paper, the London *Morning Chronicle,* probably the most widely read in the kingdom, consistently took a pro-American line; Cobbett once suggested that the editor, James Perry, acted as though he "had a general retainer from the Americans." [25] Fox's nephew and protégé, Lord Holland, steadily supported conciliation. He once summarized Foxite doctrine, a combination of economic liberalism and political sympathy, in the following words:

In every friendly intercourse between two countries, there was . . . always a mutual advantage: but this reciprocity of interest was most remarkable, as it existed between the united states of America and Great Britain. . . . The republican institutions of America, like those of every govern-

[24] Grenville to Grey, May 26, 1809, Grey MSS; Grenville to Auckland, Sept. 16, 1810, William Eden, Baron Auckland, MSS, British Museum (Add. MSS 34412–34471, 45728–45730), Add. MSS 34458.
[25] *Cobbett's Register,* XII (1807), 182.

ment in which a true spirit of freedom prevailed, contained energies which were capable of being called forth to meet any difficult crisis that might occur. . . . Nothing therefore could appear . . . worse policy than to wish to see any thing like disunion among the people of the United States. Indeed, the more powerful and the more wealthy they became, the better it would be for this country. As they became more populous, the customers for our manufactures would become more numerous, and increase of riches would only give them increased means of consumption.[26]

Lord Howick, Fox's successor as factional leader in 1806, shared with Holland a dislike of monopolistic ambition. While favoring "the utmost limit of reasonable concession," he nevertheless distrusted the Jeffersonian regime, saying that "in the language and the conduct of the latter Government, enough has appeared to create a well-founded doubt, whether this policy, however carefully pursued, would have been successful." [27] His father's death transferred Howick to the House of Lords as Earl Grey in 1807, a crippling blow to him and his party, for Lord Henry Petty and Stephen Ponsonby, who attempted to fill the shoes of Fox and Howick, failed dismally. Not until Henry Brougham secured a seat in 1810 did the Opposition find an effective leader, and even then only on the single issue of the Orders in Council. This able, offensively ambitious Scot marshaled the troops that brought down the orders in 1812, but he never achieved the parliamentary primacy that once belonged to Fox.

Although they never attained the lead in Commons, Alexander Baring and Samuel Whitbread most forcefully presented the two strains of Opposition argument against the ministry's American policy. Whitbread, a self-made man in the brewing business, was stout, uncultured by the standards of British aristocracy, and often violent in debate. He was also probably the most extreme republican in Parliament, and his attitude sometimes embarrassed Grey, whose sister he had married. He was almost the only member of Parliament who praised America without reservation. In 1812

[26] *Hansard*, IX, 806–807.
[27] Grey to Grenville, Jan. 3, 1808, Charles Grey, *Some Account of the Life and Opinions of Charles, Second Earl Grey* (London, 1861), p. 190.

he said that she was "extremely popular" with him and that he looked upon her Revolution "with reverence and admiration." In 1813, after war began, he declared, "If truth must be spoken, . . . America had always been in the right, . . . until, by the declaration of war she had changed her situation." [28] Whitbread's political arguments for America were paired by Alexander Baring's emphasis upon the value of her trade. Baring, who married a Federalist senator's daughter and whose banking house had heavy investments in the United States and handled the accounts of many American merchants as well as of the United States government, worked more than forty years for peace between the two countries. Although often attacked as a self-seeker interested only in the profits of Baring Brothers & Company, his devotion to liberal principles went further than that. None could deny that his writings and his parliamentary speeches were, with the possible exception of Brougham's, which began somewhat later, the most effective statement of the argument that British prosperity depended upon the fostering of American trade.

Most Englishmen agreed with Baring that commercial considerations, not theories of government, were the most important aspects of Anglo-American relations. Should America's trade be encouraged, even if it flowed to Britain's enemies or to neutrals, so that the United States could purchase larger amounts of British goods with her profits and perhaps, with her shipping, supply Great Britain with an indirect outlet for her own manufactures? Or should Britain consider the Americans commercial rivals whose prosperity must be checked, whose expanding commerce could only cut into British trade, destroy the benefits of empire, and weaken economic warfare against the archdevil of the Tuileries? Over these questions Englishmen contended throughout the Napoleonic wars.

Baring, Brougham, and many of the Opposition of course answered the first question with an unequivocal affirmative. The banker argued that England should encourage American trade with any nation whatsoever, since the Americans usually used the

[28] *Hansard*, XXI, 771; XXIV, 632.

proceeds of European sales to purchase British manufactures. The Americans carried on an extensive trade in English goods, penetrating with these cargoes to ports of the Continent where English ships could not go; to strike at American shipping was to destroy the best means of evading Napoleon's Continental System. Baring considered America more valuable as a neutral than she would be as an ally. The *Edinburgh Review* agreed, saying that "the neutrality of the new world is our best safeguard from the subjugation of the old. While America covers the ocean with her ships, England may defy the conqueror of Europe;—she will trade, in spite of him." Like Baring, Brougham stressed that American prosperity really benefited Britain: "Can any but the veriest driveller in political science, doubt for a moment that her gains are our gains; . . . that the less she traded with other nations, the less she will trade with ourselves; and that to confine her foreign commerce to her trade with England, would be to diminish, if not to destroy this trade also." In stressing the importance of exports to America, the Opposition spoke the language of the comparatively new, politically undervalued manufacturing interests. It challenged traditional economic theory, which held that one nation's commercial gains were another's losses, and minimized the plausible claim of shipping and colonial interests that they would be harmed by the growth of American shipping and exports. Finally, as Lord Melville once reasonably pointed out, the benefit of expanded trade was mutual. America, too, might be asked to make concessioons to secure it.[29]

Until 1811 and 1812, when a massive depression forced a reassessment, most Englishmen repudiated the arguments of Baring and Brougham, clinging stubbornly to maxims of the past. They looked upon America as a many-tentacled rival. Her ships plied the oceans as replacements for British merchantmen, capturing,

[29] Alexander Baring, *An Inquiry into the Causes and Consequences of the Orders in Council; and an Examination of the Conduct of Great Britain towards the Neutral Commerce of America* (London, 1808), pp. 153–156 and *passim; Edinburgh Review*, XIV (1809), 475; Henry Brougham, *Orders in Council; Or, An Examination of the Justice, Legality, and Policy of the New System of Commercial Regulations* (2d ed.; London, 1808), p. 57; *Hansard*, XII, 797.

as one indefatigable English conservative complained, nineteen-twentieths of the carriage between the two countries as well as increasing shares of the traffic between Europe and outlying parts of the globe.[30] America undermined British colonies in the Caribbean by producing competing crops on her own Southern plantations and by carrying to Europe the produce of non-British islands in that tropical sea, and then America had the temerity to ask for freedom to trade with British territories as well. When Fox and Grenville proposed legislation to regularize American trade with English colonies, Lord Mulgrave grumpily objected that "the great advantage of possessing colonies, was the enjoyment of an exclusive trade with them." Finally, traditionalists argued that America eagerly replaced Britain in European markets, striking a blow at English commercial prosperity and relieving economic pressure upon Napoleon. In sum, the conservative nationalists believed that shipping and commerce lay at the root of England's greatness. These must be encouraged—and encouraged too by application of the traditional remedies of restriction, regulation, and stifling of competition. "The commerce is connected with the strength and glory of England," one pamphleteer's peroration read, "and he who respects the strength and glory of England, will contemplate her Navigation and Colonial System, but with the sentiment . . . —ESTO PERPETUA." [31] In wartime this system might be extended by the application of naval power.

Those who argued in this fashion usually had their way from 1805 to 1812. Except for the brief Ministry of All the Talents in 1806 and 1807, British governments sought not to foster trade but to monopolize it. To solve Britain's problems, increased pressure upon American neutral commerce often suggested itself. For some this was merely a tactical response to the international situation

---

[30] John B. Holroyd, Earl of Sheffield, *The Orders in Council and the American Embargo Beneficial to the Political and Commercial Interests of Great Britain* (London, 1809), pp. 14–16.

[31] *Hansard*, VI, 1035; Jerome Alley, *A Vindication of the Principles and Statements Advanced in the Strictures of the Right Hon. Lord Sheffield* (London, 1806), pp. 89–90.

or a projection of the feeling that, in resisting Napoleon, Britain was defending the entire free world. For others it had the broader purpose of restricting American growth and her rise to the first rank of powers. British policy combined about equal parts of monopolistic mercantilism and a desire to strangle Napoleon. And although the British system included far more concessions to American sensibilities than is usually recognized, even basically Anglophile citizens of the United States, like Rufus King, complained against the monopolistic implications of English policy. In 1811 Henry Clay declared that "the real cause of British aggression, was not to distress an enemy but to destroy a rival." [32] As Clay suggested, England had rejected the analyses of Baring, Brougham, and the *Edinburgh Review.*

Few people in England or America fully understood the two nations' commercial interdependence. The Earl of Sheffield, who wrote pamphlets bearing the lengthy but explanatory titles of *Strictures on the Necessity of Inviolably Maintaining the Navigation and Colonial System of Great Britain* and *The Orders in Council and the American Embargo Beneficial to the Political and Commercial Interests of Great Britain,* erroneously argued that the United States was or could almost painlessly be made absolutely subordinate and dependent upon Britain in the commercial sphere. (Jefferson equally fallaciously thought his country could wield the whip hand.) Pessimists and alarmists, among whom Baring must sometimes be included, were wrong when they asserted that America could without difficulty ride out the storm of commercial restriction while Britain would be grievously harmed. (In the same fashion, many Federalists spoke of the impossibility of challenging the strong, resilient economy of Britain.) Anglo-American trade had multiplied rather than contracted after separation of the two nations in 1783, and each country was the best customer of the other. Neither could afford to toss away cavalierly this huge trade.

The British West Indies, the colonial area trading most extensively with the United States, did indeed seem at America's

[32] *Annals,* 12th Cong. 1st sess., pp. 599–601.

mercy. Despite efforts to encourage alternative areas of supply, the islands drew most of their foodstuffs and cooperage materials from the United States. From 1801 to 1805 they annually imported nearly $6.5 million worth of American goods; after 1807 commercial restrictions reduced this traffic, but in a twelve-month period in 1810–1811, when trade was comparatively free, more than $4.5 million worth of American provisions flowed to the British colonies. The Americans believed that the West Indies need for food provided an obvious way of bringing pressure upon the entire empire. "If we shut up the export trade six months the Islands would be starved," a Republican commercial expert wrote in 1806; ". . . the West India islands are dependent on it [the United States] for the necessaries of life, both for the white and black population."[33] In seeming confirmation of this analysis, colonial governors frequently found it necessary to suspend the Navigation Acts so that American ships might bring grain and other goods to the British islands.

On the other hand, America's role in the Caribbean strengthened the arguments of British restrictionists. Beginning about 1805, a huge oversupply of coffee and sugar developed in world markets. Exports from British colonies fell off, to the dismay of plantation owners, financiers, and the shipping interest. To reduce competition the British government attempted to eliminate or at least restrict the quantity of cotton, sugar, and coffee the Americans carried away in exchange for cargoes they brought, but this was only a minor aspect of the problem. The chief challenges to British interest lay in the explosive development of American cotton exports and the steady growth of American traffic in French and Spanish colonial goods imported into the United States and then reshipped to Europe, where they entered into competition with British colonial produce. In 1806 and again in 1807 American reexports totaled $60 million. British colonialists, shippers, and the politicians they influenced called for action to reduce the pressure

[33] Jacob Crowninshield, "Some Remarks on the American Trade, 1806," ed. John H. Reinoehl, *William and Mary Quarterly*, 3d Series, XVI (1959), 96–97. For an able discussion of the British colonial economy see Lowell J. Ragatz, *The Fall of the Planter Class in the British Caribbean, 1763–1833* (New York, 1928).

of American competition, to which they ascribed the depression of English colonial trade. While this explanation oversimplified the case, there could be no denying that Americans profited tremendously from the reëxport trade, as well as from the increasing export of her own cotton, nor that the loss of these profits would be a serious blow to the United States.[34]

No colonial trade compared in size, of course, with that carried on between the home islands and the United States. Under normal conditions this traffic was the most important branch of commerce for both countries and also the largest single component of international trade. America often purchased roughly one-third of all British exports, including those to the colonies, and usually took more than did the entire continent of Europe. For the Americans this branch of trade was equally important. In 1806 more than $20 million worth of goods produced in America were shipped to Britain, four-ninths of all exports of domestic produce and more than the total trade to either France or Spain, despite the huge reëxport trade to those countries. After passage of the Embargo Anglo-American trade declined, but the portion that continued was far more substantial than is generally recognized.[35]

Politically and economically the most important American commodities shipped to Britain were foodstuffs and cotton. Despite a spectacular expansion of grain production during the Napoleonic Wars, the British Isles could not feed themselves. In 1807 Eng-

[34] Far less important, but still substantial, was America's trade with British India. Despite expiration of the commercial articles of the Jay treaty and thus of the formal basis for Indian-American trade, this commerce continued. The Americans came to have a share of Indian trade approximately half as large as that of the East India Company, and neither the British government nor authorities in India paid much heed to the company's reiterated desires to curb American rivals. In this area, at least, the ministry recognized that both countries benefited from the fostering of trade. On this subject see Holden Furber, "The Beginnings of American Trade with India, 1784–1812," *New England Quarterly*, XI (1938), 235–265.

[35] This and succeeding paragraphs rest on information from widely scattered sources. Perhaps most important are Eli F. Heckscher, *The Continental System* (London, 1922); William Smart, *Economic Annals of the Nineteenth Century*, I (London, 1910); George R. Porter, *The Progress of the Nation*, rev. F. W. Hirst (rev. ed.; London, 1912); Adam Seybert, *Statistical Annals . . . of the United States of America* (Philadelphia, 1818); François Crouzet, *L'Economie Britannique et le Blocus Continental* (2 vols.; Paris, 1958).

land imported 2 million bushels of wheat from the United States and only 1.25 million bushels from all other countries. That year a young British diplomat at Washington wrote, "War with the World America excepted, which is our granary, I think we might maintain, but, I hope we shall not quarrel with our Bread & Butter." Ordinarily American grain did not dominate the British market, primarily because Napoleon often tolerated huge exports from the Continent. From 1800 to 1812 the Americans provided only about one-quarter of all British wheat imports, and the chances of literally starving England into submission by cutting off this trade were slim indeed. Britain, a Federalist critic of Republican economic warfare wrote, "brews into beer more than we ever sell to her, and almost as much as we can spare to the whole world." The prospects of American supplies powerfully affected the price level in Britain, and the British West Indies and later Wellington's Peninsular army required American foodstuffs. It can reasonably be asserted, however, that the Anglo-American grain trade was most important as a means of disposing of an American surplus, not as a source of British supply.[36]

May the same be said of American cotton exports? From 1805 until the declaration of war in 1812, America annually exported more than 46 million pounds of her cotton, and at least 80 per cent went to Great Britain. In a good year like 1807 the Americans received more than $13 million from England for cotton alone. Without the British market American plantations would have had no excuse for existence. In theory, an alternate market existed on the Continent, and American farmers often complained that the Royal Navy prevented them from exploiting it. (With more justification, the same complaint was made with respect to tobacco, another important export.) However, despite Napoleon's

[36] Foster to Lady Elizabeth Foster, Nov. 1, 1807, Foster MSS; Cabot to Pickering, Dec. 18, 1808, Henry Cabot Lodge, *Life and Letters of George Cabot* (Boston, 1877), p. 402; Crouzet, *op. cit.*, I, 98–100. Heckscher, *op. cit.*, pp. 337–338, estimates that Britain never imported more than one-sixth of the grain she consumed, and on the average only one-sixteenth. The standard treatment of this topic, from which figures in this paragraph have been taken, is W. Freeman Galpin, *The Grain Supply of England during the Napoleonic Period*, University of Michigan Publications in History and Political Science, Vol. VI (New York, 1925).

efforts to increase European textile production, the Continent never absorbed more than a small fraction of the exports that normally flowed to Britain. For their part English mills depended heavily upon American supplies. Although Americans faced competition from British colonies and other areas, they provided almost exactly one-half of all British cotton imports until the Embargo and made huge shipments of raw cotton spasmodically in later years.

Two factors somewhat eased Britain's dependence upon the United States. In the first place, the glut after 1805 delayed the impact of reduced American supplies. Lord Sheffield even maintained that Britain "benefitted [from the Embargo] by an accumulating inactive stock [of cotton] being called into active demand." Second, the uncertainty of American supplies spurred the development of alternate sources. For example, Britain imported only 3,500 bags of cotton from Brazil in 1808. Thereafter the trade mushroomed almost as rapidly as that with America had a decade earlier, and in 1814 England bought more than 100,000 bags of Brazilian cotton. Thus, although Great Britain found the United States by far the easiest and cheapest source of supply, America was not the only one; the day of "King Cotton," if it ever existed, still lay in the future. The United States, on the other hand, was almost entirely dependent upon England as a cotton market.[37]

Britain most needed the American market for her manufactured goods, particularly since it was precisely these that Napoleon most consistently prohibited entry to the Continent. Down to 1807 the Americans purchased about one-third of all exported British goods, roughly $50 million worth every year. The Embargo reduced but did not eliminate this trade (the proportion of British exports sent to the United States never dropped below 15 per cent). After a revival in 1810, when America purchased $48 million worth of British goods, nearly one-quarter of English exports, the Ameri-

---

[37] Sheffield, *Orders in Council*, p. 21. In addition to the sources cited above, see G. W. Daniels, "American Cotton Trade with Liverpool under the Embargo and Non-Intercourse Acts," *American Historical Review*, XXI (1915–1916), 276–287.

can market finally dried up when nonimportation went into effect early in 1811.[38] In that year the United States imported only $6 million worth of British goods, thus contributing mightily to the deepening of a depression that had already commenced in England. Custom, easy transportation, a viable credit system, and the slow development of American manufactures all conferred upon England a huge market in the United States, a market essential to her prosperity.

Although Britain shipped large quantities of metal goods and pottery, books, and even some cheese and salt across the Atlantic, textiles were the major export. The great expansion of Midland mills had already begun, and particularly during war the chief market for cottons produced in Manchester, Birmingham, and lesser centers lay across the Atlantic. In 1806, for example, Britain sent to America cottons and woolens worth $41 million, more than half her textile exports and nearly one-quarter of all British exports of whatever kind. American citizens needed English cloth almost as much as British factories required a market. Like other branches of commerce, the textile trade demonstrated the two nations' interdependence.

Certain British interests, long especially cherished by Parliament, claimed that America attained prosperity at their expense. "They think our prosperity filched from theirs," Jefferson observed in 1810.[39] Merchants, traders, and plantation owners blamed the West Indian depression on American competition. Shipowners expressed dismay at the rise of the American merchant marine, which, one anti-American pamphleteer claimed, deprived England of an income of $18 million a year.[40] More generally, many Englishmen, bearing the burden of a contest they believed

[38] See Heckscher, *op. cit.*, p. 324, for the percentages. They do not quite agree with the figures Heckscher gives for the value of the trade on page 245. See also Crouzet, *op. cit.*, II, 884, 886.

[39] Jefferson to William Duane, Nov. 13, 1810, Andrew A. Lipscomb and Albert E. Bergh, eds., *The Writings of Thomas Jefferson* (Memorial ed.; 20 vols.; Washington, 1903–1904), XII, 434.

[40] *Journals of the House of Commons*, LXVII (1812), 761, 768; Joseph Marryat, *Hints to Both Parties; or Observations on the Proceedings in Parliament upon the Petitions against the Orders in Council* (London, 1808), p. 20.

a struggle for the world's freedom, felt jealousy rather than gratification when they saw America thriving. Almost all English
travelers commented unfavorably on the acquisitiveness of Americans, the single-mindedness with which they pursued profit. Britons
scoffed when, in his first inaugural address, Jefferson hailed his
country as a "rising nation, spread over a wide and fruitful land,
traversing all the seas with the rich productions of their industry,
. . . advancing rapidly to destinies beyond the reach of mortal
eye." Englishmen pointed out how much America owed to the
Royal Navy, which, by driving Britain's enemies from the seas,
had in effect conferred a huge commerce upon the neutral United
States. "Their own fair Trade has increased immensely & yet,"
Augustus Foster complained, "they would have the carrying all
the French & Spanish. there is not, thanks to our Tars, a single
French or Spanish merchantman that now navigates these Seas—
& these Jews want to navigate for them." Many Americans agreed
that their countrymen pushed too hard, that national interests had
been subordinated to individual greed. "Where interest prevails
& patriotism is little known," a Jeffersonian minister lamented
when Massachusetts protested the Embargo, "we can hope nothing from the latter without some present hopes of the former.
Prosperity has been at the helm & has corrupted us." [41] Extreme
Republicans and British nationalists agreed on one thing, at least.

Nominally, America showed a deficit in her trade with Britain.
But English statistics are unsatisfactory and incomplete, and, as
the Secretary of the Treasury himself pointed out, his reports, based
upon costs at American seaports, included freightage on imports
from Britain but omitted it on exports. The profits of transatlantic
carriage, almost monopolized by the Americans, surely reversed
the theoretical deficit. Furthermore, Americans often transferred
the proceeds of European sales to Britain for expenditure there
(Alexander Baring estimated that three-quarters were so trans-

[41] Richardson, op. cit., I, 321; Foster to Lady Elizabeth Foster, May 3, 1806, Foster
MSS; entry of Jan. 5, 1808, The Diary of William Bentley, D.D. (4 vols.; Salem,
1911–1914), III, 337. The French minister also considered Americans sordidly
materialistic. See Louis M. Turreau de Garambouville, Aperçu sur la Situation Politique des Etats-Unis d'Amérique (Paris, 1815), passim.

ferred); Continental receipts probably financed about one-third of British exports to America. Secretary Gallatin argued, and jealous Englishmen like Joseph Marryat and Nathaniel Atcheson agreed, that the balance of trade actually favored the United States.[42] As a practical matter, whatever the trade balance, both countries benefited from Anglo-American trade. American agriculturists, Yankee shipowners, British capitalists, and Midland workmen owed much to the steady flow of commerce between Liverpool and London on the one hand, and New York, Boston, and Philadelphia on the other.[43]

At a time when the British merchant marine could barely maintain itself, the American maritime service grew steadily, advancing from 558,000 tons in 1802 to 981,000 at the end of 1810.[44] At a time when the trade of the British Empire suffered from the vagaries of war, American trade shot upward. Before the outbreak of Franco-British war the United States never imported or exported goods worth more than $30 million in a single year. In 1807 exports and imports reached $108 million and $138.5 million respectively. At a time when military expenditures multiplied the British national debt, the Americans cut theirs from $83 million in 1801 to $45 million at the opening of 1812. The revenue that made this reduction possible came from increasing customs receipts, the direct result of expanded foreign trade.

Aside from colonial interests, Britons could scarcely object to the increased exportation of goods grown or harvested in the United

[42] Seybert, *op. cit.*, p. 219; Baring, *op. cit.*, p. 153; Norman S. Buck, *The Development of the Organization of Anglo-American Trade, 1800–1850* (New Haven, 1925), pp. 119–130; Marryat, *op. cit.*, p. 20; Nathaniel Atcheson, *American Encroachments on British Rights* (London, 1808), pp. 89 ff.

[43] Liverpool steadily displaced London as the chief entrepôt for American goods and the major port of export, which may explain the comparatively greater hostility of London merchants toward the United States. New York became the leading American seaport before 1800, although Massachusetts owned by far the largest proportion of ships engaged in foreign trade.

[44] The statistical information in this and succeeding paragraphs is drawn from Seybert, *op. cit.*, and United States Bureau of the Census, *Historical Statistics of the United States, 1789–1945* (Washington, 1949). For some purposes, particularly in connection with foreign trade, the Americans used a statistical year beginning October 1 and ending September 30. In such instances, reference here is to the calendar year in which nine months of the commercial year fell.

States. Most went to the British Isles and aided the British economy. Even in 1801–1802, when Europe was at peace and the oceans were open, Britain purchased goods worth twice as much as the American produce shipped to France. In wartime the proportion was even higher; in 1806 the United States exported $20 million worth of her own goods to Britain and only $2.7 million worth to France. Total American domestic exports topped $41 million in 1806 and reached a peak of nearly $49 million in 1807. That year, 64 million pounds of cotton, 1.2 million bushels of wheat, 62,000 hogsheads of tobacco, and large amounts of hemp, beef, corn, and other commodities were shipped abroad. Some of these goods were exported in larger quantities later on—in terms of bulk, the peak of cotton and tobacco exports did not come until 1810—but a falling price level and reduced exports of foodstuffs meant that the peak value of 1807 was not again reached. Still, except during the Embargo, exports remained about double what they had been in the early 1790's. Until at least 1807 the American farmer was correspondingly prosperous.

The reëxport trade expanded even more spectacularly, from an infinitesimal amount in 1791 to $60 million in 1806. In 1806, 47 million pounds of coffee, more than 146 million pounds of sugar, and nearly 2 million pounds of cotton imported into the United States were reëxported to Europe. The government encouraged this commerce by returning, in the form of drawbacks, almost all customs duties levied at the time of the original importation. This trade permitted goods from French and Spanish colonies in the Caribbean, as well as the Île de France and Bourbon, to reach the home country. It cast the protection of a neutral flag over supplies Napoleon woefully needed, frustrating the Royal Navy's efforts to break up French commerce. It contributed to a worsening depression in the British West Indies by providing competitive goods that increased the oversupply in Europe. Britain scarcely benefited at all, for less than 5 per cent of all reëxported commodities went to England and her colonies. Many Englishmen angrily pronounced American merchants and shipowners effectively allied with the Emperor Napoleon.

The passage of time enables us to be dispassionate, to see that Alexander Baring argued correctly when he attempted to convince his countrymen that American prosperity was in effect their own. It is, however, characteristic of the entire period that emotion and not reason governed British attitudes. Faced with prospects so bleak that Lord Grenville virtually turned his back upon office to avoid responsibility for the national humiliation he considered inevitable, consoled only by a conviction that England acted as the defender and, God willing, the savior of the entire world, painfully aware that the Americans—formerly symbols of successful rebellion and now of republicanism—were steadily advancing in wealth and self-esteem, Englishmen understandably allowed themselves to treat the United States in a brusque, cavalier, contemptuous fashion. To say this is not to condone the interruption of American trade, to palliate the brutal attack upon the *Chesapeake,* to justify the forcible seizure of American seamen. In fact, Britain would best have served her own interests if she had done none of these things. But Britain was beleaguered, and those under siege are not likely to allow dispassion and long-range thinking to dominate their policy.

CHAPTER

# II

# REPUBLICANISM
# AND NEUTRALITY

Parliament met in the world's largest city, the metropolitan focus of Anglo-American civilization. By contrast, the American government sat at Washington, a young city considered by most Europeans and not a few Americans almost a travesty of a national capital.[1] Only 6,000 people, settled in straggling little villages along the axis of Pennsylvania Avenue from the Eastern Branch to Georgetown, lived in the District of Columbia. The arrival of 140 congressmen and 34 senators strained the modest capacities of Washington boardinghouses; several congressmen often shared a bedroom, and the dining rooms frequently served as small caucus

---

[1] One British minister, Augustus John Foster, mildly challenged the opinions of other foreign visitors, but his comments are cool enough: "I would not, of course, compare the life we led at the American capital with the mode of spending time in any of the great European cities where amusements are so varied and manners are much more refined, but making allowances for its size and strange position I cannot be so severe in describing it as some travellers have been." Richard B. Davis, ed., *Jeffersonian America: Notes on the United States of America . . . by Sir Augustus John Foster, Bart.* (San Marino, 1954), p. 108.

or committee rooms. For its formal business Congress had to make do with the north wing of the Capitol, completed in 1807. The roof soon leaked, and acoustics in the legislative chambers, particularly the House, were so bad that many a fiery oration escaped the hearing of congressmen distant from the speaker. At no time was Washington more than the political capital of the nation, for, whereas London was also the center of British economic life, in America the commercial cities of Boston, New York, Philadelphia, and Baltimore shared this function. Washington and London symbolized the contrast between republican America, a young nation with a white population of scarcely 5 millions, and aged, ordered Britain, with nearly four times as many people.

Political life in the United States was in many respects simpler than in Britain, where factionalism made the tenure of governments insecure. After 1801 the decline of Federalist strength conferred almost dictatorial powers upon the Republicans, provided they could maintain discipline. In 1805 the Federalists held only one quarter of the seats in each of the houses of Congress, and until the War of 1812 temporarily aided them, their share never much exceeded one-third. For this their own weakness was primarily responsible, for, the Louisiana Purchase aside, the Jeffersonians had accomplished remarkably little. Federalists allowed themselves to become identified with separatism, with disloyal Anglophilia, with supercilious disregard for less successful fellow citizens. Except in Connecticut they had to fight for their political lives, even in the old bastion of Massachusetts. The broad national appeal that once brought them support even in the South evaporated, although a few Southern Federalists remained in Congress even after 1805. Federalism might profit from Jeffersonian mistakes or Republican divisions, but it was sterile; its days of usefulness had passed.

The Federalists lacked leadership as well as a positive program. John Adams' retirement to Quincy removed him from the scene almost as effectively as Aaron Burr's pistol had quieted Hamilton, and the party fell into the hands of lesser leaders neither so well balanced as Adams nor so bold as Hamilton. Rufus King of New

York, whose services during and after the Constitutional Convention entitled him to leadership, rusticated on Long Island, observing the political scene, farming, playing with his nephews and nieces, but rarely attempting to influence the party. In foreign affairs, although an undoubted Federalist, King was a loyal American, judging each issue upon its merits as he saw them and conferring his support upon the administration when he thought it acted wisely.[2] Had Federalism been led to constructive criticism by King or a man of his stamp, it would have had a reason and perhaps a hope for success. Instead, narrow and unreasonable men like Timothy Pickering, Barent Gardenier, and Josiah Quincy took command. Pickering in particular opposed any moderate course; he was described by one critic as possessed of "the stern severity of a Roman Cato" and by an ally as "a perfect hater of democratic fraud and villainy," [3] and this severity and hatred became his most notable characteristics. In the Senate and in pamphlets and newspaper articles he showed himself willing to risk the Union itself if this would advance the cause of Federalism and Great Britain. Barent Gardenier, a New Yorker who led the Federalist clique in the House of Representatives during the Embargo, differed little from Pickering in his political outlook. His successor as file leader wrote of Gardenier, "He is a man of wit and desultory reading, accustomed to the skirmishing and electioneering violence of New York. He brings it all into debate in an honest, unguarded, inconsiderate manner, very well calculated to inflame the party passions opposed to him, but not to make converts." [4] Josiah Quincy, minor-

---

[2] John Quincy Adams also might have been considered for leadership. But, discouraged by the disloyal carping of other Federalists and doubtless also influenced by the treatment accorded his father in 1800, Adams drifted toward Republicanism, and in 1808 he attended the Republican caucus. That his sturdy nationalism and his interest in the rights of American neutral commerce found an easier home in the Republican party is an added condemnation of Federalism in this period. Similarly alienated by Federalism's drift were such persons as William Plumer of New Hampshire and, more slowly, Oliver Wolcott, the ultra-Hamiltonian secretary of the treasury under Adams.

[3] William Plumer to William Plumer, Jr., Dec. 30, 1805, Charles S. Hall, *Benjamin Tallmadge* (New York, 1943), p. 184; Bigelow to Hannah G. Bigelow, Dec. 29, 1810, Clarence S. Brigham, ed., "Letters of Abijah Bigelow, Member of Congress, to His Wife, 1810–1815," American Antiquarian Society, *Proceedings*, n.s., XL (1931), 312.

[4] Quincy to Eliza S. Quincy, n.d., Edmund Quincy, *Life of Josiah Quincy* (Boston,

ity leader in the war Congress of 1811–1812, had prejudices almost equally deep. For tactical reasons he imposed a flexible policy upon the party, but he never admitted the sincerity of the Republicans upon any important issue. From 1805 to 1812 Federalists seldom offered more than carping, negative criticism.

Pessimism and despair largely explain Federalist rigidity. Their enemies' victories convinced them that the people had been seduced by visionary or corrupt politicians. It scarcely occurred to the Federalists, who had usually simply assumed that the people would follow the lead of the virtuous and the wellborn, to try to equal Republican organizational efforts, at least on a national scale. "Neither learning, morals nor wisdom seem any longer to be regarded as objects of public esteem & favour," Rufus King wrote in 1807. King therefore continued in retirement, and active Federalists considered themselves the rear guard of a band of heroes, not the vanguard of a political movement. They opposed as evil almost anything the Republicans supported, to the dismay of some of their number like Noah Webster, who wrote: "There is a way to preserve the confidence of the populace, without a sacrifice of integrity. In morality, an honest man must make no concessions that violate the laws of right. But political measures are rarely connected with moral right & wrong; at least the greatest proportion are mere matters of expedience." By 1811 the habit of rigid opposition against which Webster complained had become a fixation, leading the Federalists to absurd lengths. "Instead of a patriotic opposition to an oppressive government," their congressional leader complained, "they are in great danger of degenerating into a mere faction, ready to quarrel with anything which may endanger, or adopt anything which will promote, party success." [5]

A loosening grip upon the press contributed to the decline of Federalism, particularly since newspaper columns were the princi-

1867), p. 134. Cf. John Randolph: "The gentleman has powers, and of no ordinary cast; and he has certainly given to the House a strong proof of his candor, whatever it may have been of his discretion." *Annals*, 10th Cong., 2d sess., p. 1465.

[5] King to Noah Webster, n.d. [June 30, 1807?], Charles R. King, *The Life and Correspondence of Rufus King* (6 vols.; New York, 1894–1900), V, 35; Webster to King, July 6, 1807, *ibid.*, V, 38; Quincy to Eliza S. Quincy, n.d. [Dec., 1811], Quincy, *op. cit.*, p. 241.

pal vehicles of political propaganda.[6] The Boston *Columbian Centinel* and the *Connecticut Courant* of Hartford spoke the language of Federalist orthodoxy in New England, and lesser journals echoed them. After 1808 the Baltimore *Federal Republican*, managed by a former employee of the Department of State discharged by Madison, carried on a campaign of unequaled viciousness against the administration. On the whole the Federalists were ill served, at least south of the Hudson. Well before the War of 1812 Republican newspapers outnumbered those of their rivals, and a majority of the most important newspapers in the land opposed Federalism even if they did not unwaveringly support Jefferson and Madison. The *National Intelligencer*, edited at Washington by Samuel Harrison Smith, profited from its monopoly of congressional reporting and its important position as administration spokesman to become the most widely read paper in the country. William Duane's *Aurora* often used its energy to attack rival Pennsylvania Republicans, but, as befitted an Irish republican, Duane even more consistently attacked Federalism and Great Britain. At Boston the *Independent Chronicle* carried the war to the enemy so aggressively that the French minister considered it America's most Francophile journal. Only in New York City, where but three of the fourteen newspapers were Republican and the strongest of these, the *Columbian*, was a supporter of Clintonian Republicanism rather than of the administration, was the party in a bad way. Jefferson frequently complained of the public press. Actually Republican papers were better edited and more widely distributed than those of their rivals.[7]

[6] The violence of this propaganda caused frequent complaints of libel. In 1812 Governor Elbridge Gerry of Massachusetts officially declared that 262 libelous articles had been published in the past thirteen months, not counting those directed at foreign governments or individuals or at rival newspaper editors. Republican Gerry declared that only twenty-five of these had appeared in Republican papers. Charles Warren, *Jacobin and Junto, or Early American Politics as Viewed in the Diary of Dr. Nathaniel Ames* (Cambridge, 1931), p. 213.

[7] Isaiah Thomas, *History of Printing in America*, II, American Antiquarian Society, *Transactions and Collections*, Vol. VI (2d ed.; Albany, 1874), pp. 294–304; Louis M. Sérurier to Minister of Foreign Relations, March 10, 1812, Archives des Affaires Étrangères, Correspondance Politique, États-Unis (photostats, Library of Congress), Vol. LXVII.

The great triumvirate at the head of the Republican party explains its success far more than increasing newspaper support or the erosion of Federalism. Thomas Jefferson's simple and often noble ideals, his insistence upon the unique virtue of the American experiment, his sturdy but moderate republicanism, his dislike of pomp and ceremony—these appealed deeply to American citizens. Less loved but widely respected, James Madison admirably conducted the business of the Department of State and loyally supported the efforts of Jefferson, with whom he was in close rapport. Albert Gallatin, similarly devoted, installed at the Treasury the fiscal simplicity required by Republican doctrine and often served as a useful balance wheel to restrain the ardors of his chief. Jefferson and his two lieutenants dominated American politics and American diplomacy. The battles were fought upon issues they pushed to the fore.

Jefferson attracted the blind, even excessive, loyalty of many Republicans. In 1808 an idolatrous clergyman declared: "With the philosopher, the statesman, the patriot Jefferson at the helm, our country assumed an attitude which the angels of God surveyed with approbation, and which excited the rancors of the enemies of Freedom!" [8] Although Federalists attacked him while he lived and some nineteenth-century historians were critical, in our time Thomas Jefferson has become one of the central figures in the American pantheon—Jefferson the democrat, the defender of underdogs, the man of catholic interests, the liberal philosopher, the uniquely perceptive American patriot. Perhaps it is time to reassay the Virginian, at least as chief executive and grand strategist of American diplomacy. Perhaps a half-felt sense of inadequacy caused Jefferson to order that no mention of his presidency be chiseled into the stone that marks his grave.

In 1805 Jefferson had passed the age of sixty, a fact of more than ordinary significance since the story of his life is in part the story of a gradual shedding of youthful enthusiasms. He was tall and carelessly stooped, thin, freckled, grey of hair, somewhat shy

[8] John Foster, *An Oration, Pronounced by Rev. John Foster, on the 4th of July, 1808* (Salem, 1808), pp. 11–12.

and a difficult conversationalist in large groups or with strangers but brilliant and far-ranging when in full flight. As president he adopted informal, democratic protocol at the White House and abandoned the custom of personal appearances before Congress on the ostensible ground that the members might be overawed. The party's rank and file idolized him.

Jefferson considered himself a philosopher, and in a sense he was. But, as Charles Wiltse has observed, Jefferson applied rather than originated theories of human behavior; he was a Locke or a Lenin, not a Hobbes or a Marx. To some at the time—William Plumer, for example—and to others since, he appeared almost too rational and studious. Wiltse comments, "Jefferson's humanity is always of the head rather than of the heart. . . . If he claims equality for all men, it is not because he feels that men are equal, but because he reasons that they must be so." [9] True though this is, it misses another part of Jefferson's thought, the petty prejudices that sometimes influenced him. In 1819 John Quincy Adams, by this time himself a sturdy Republican, came upon a letter written by Jefferson nearly a decade before. Adams commented that the letter was "a mixture of profound and sagacious observation, with strong prejudices and irritated passions. It is a sort of epitome of his political opinions and feelings. Jefferson is one of the great men whom this country has produced, one of the men who has contributed largely to the formation of our national character—to much that is good and to not a little that is evil in our sentiments and manners." [10] Jefferson's correspondence contains many flashes of philosophy, philosophy reflected in the course of action he urged upon the state. But the sage of Monticello never organized his thought in a cohesive whole (how many American political philosophers have?), and he was, far more than he realized, the prey of impulse and emotion. "Eclectic" and "adaptable" are the adjectives best applied to his concepts.

By the time he left office in 1809, Jefferson had modified many

[9] Charles M. Wiltse, *The Jeffersonian Tradition in American Democracy* (Chapel Hill, 1935), p. 5.
[10] Entry of Dec. 27, 1819, Charles F. Adams, ed., *Memoirs of John Quincy Adams* (12 vols.; Philadelphia, 1874–1877), IV, 492.

of his theoretical precepts in the interest of realism as he saw it. Committed to a narrow interpretation of the Constitution, he expanded the activities of the federal government more, at least, than any president between Washington and Jackson. On his own admission he acted unconstitutionally in arranging the acquisition of Louisiana, subordinating theory to national good. The Embargo was of such dubious constitutionality that the Republicans did not permit it to be submitted to the Supreme Court for review. The earnest advocate of republicanism, Jefferson once praised an elaborate pyramidal hierarchy of popular and elected assemblies rising from town meetings of the New England sort to Congress and the president. Later he came, with some justice, to consider the New England gatherings seditious and to doubt the wisdom of Congress, primarily because of "the wonderful credulity of the members . . . in the floating lies of the day, . . . [of which] no experience seems to correct them. I have never seen a Congress during the last 8. years," Jefferson continued, "a great majority of which I would not implicitly rely on in any question, could their minds have been purged of all errors of fact." [11] The minds of Congress and the people could not be purged, and in practice Jefferson fell back upon the theory that the administrators of government were stewards of the people, in whose interests and with whose support the expert, the rational, and the intelligent might govern. The result of these two accommodations of theory to contemporary conditions was government that often differed only in form from that of John Adams.

In the field of foreign policy the contrast between Jefferson and his predecessor became more marked. Jefferson strangely combined idealism and utopianism with pragmatism and cynical craft. He revered international law, interpreting it, however, in a fashion that coincided with American interests, a fairly easy task when the law of nations had not been codified and many of the available authorities had written to defend the rights of small neutrals. Next only to moral law and the general interests of humanity

[11] Jefferson to Madison, March 17, 1809, James Madison MSS, Library of Congress.

39

(which justified the otherwise absurd concept that the American frontier should lie along the Gulf Stream), the President believed that the usage of nations and treaties should govern international relations.[12] Rational application of these should and ultimately must bring an end to quarrels between states. Meantime it was better to insist upon one's rights than to compromise, better to reject, for example, any partial settlement of the problem of impressment until Britain agreed to abandon the practice entirely. Jefferson thus differed sharply from Adams, who never abandoned claims of right but was prepared to compromise them in practice if the United States could profit thereby. In this, too, Jefferson was somewhat in contrast with Madison, whose diplomacy after he became president was more flexible than that of his mentor and friend.

Jefferson could also be an alarmist. In 1803 he seriously considered an alliance with Great Britain, a futile and dangerous project entirely unnecessary to the task of keeping France out of Louisiana. In 1805, with even less reason, he recurred to this plan, only to meet with stubborn opposition in his Cabinet. In 1806 the President procured from Congress, without quite admitting that he was doing so, an appropriation of $2 million to bribe French support in an American quarrel with Spain. Later the President leaped hastily into the Embargo, although the germ of his plan had been in his mind for years. For most of 1808 he clung stubbornly to this measure, so disastrous to American prosperity and inefficacious in coercing Europe, only to abandon it, on the basis of exaggerated reports of impending rebellion in New England, when the Embargo most needed his support. These hasty, ill-digested actions Jefferson justified to himself as part of a larger search for justice and right.

The President recognized that the world did not share his respect for international law. One of the most frequent themes in his correspondence is a protest against the way the din of Napoleonic struggles turned European statesmen from reason to emotion and

12 Wiltse, *op. cit.*, pp. 178 ff.

even idiocy. "I consider Europe as a great mad-house, & in the present deranged state of their moral faculties to be pitied & avoided," Jefferson declared in 1808. In Britain, he believed, "all the bulwarks of morality & right have been broken up." In 1811 he told Kosciuszko, "It would have been perfect Quixotism in us to have encouraged these Bedlamites, to have undertaken the redress of all wrongs against a world avowedly rejecting all regard to right." [13] Unfortunately, many of Jefferson's policies ignored the very emotionalism—to him, lunacy—against which he inveighed. The Nonimportation Act, the Embargo Act, even the attempt to bribe Napoleon might have succeeded in normal times, but they were themselves the fruit of international abnormality.

Jefferson hated war. He felt that the greatest possible American contribution to the happiness of mankind lay not in a military crusade for justice but in the careful preservation of America's position as "the sole repository of the sacred fire of freedom & self-government" at a time when repression swept the world. "Peace . . . has been our principle, peace is our interest, and peace has saved to the world this only plant of free and rational government now existing in it," he declaimed to Kosciuszko. On the other hand, as early as 1806 the President saw the danger of encouraging Europe to believe America treasured peace above all else. "This opinion," he said, "must be corrected when just occasion arises, or we shall become the plunder of all nations." As chief executive Jefferson did little to correct this opinion, but as the War of 1812 approached he became more and more reconciled to the use of force. In May, 1811, he still hoped for peace, but added: "When peace becomes more losing than war, we may prefer the latter on principles of pecuniary calculation." In 1812 he was sure the hour had come: "we are to have war then? I believe so, and that it is necessary. every hope from time, patience & the love of peace is

[13] Jefferson to David B. Warden, July 16, 1808, Thomas Jefferson MSS, Library of Congress; Jefferson to George Gilpin, Sept. 7, 1809, *ibid.*; Jefferson to Tadeusz Kosciuszko, April 13, 1811, Andrew A. Lipscomb and Albert E. Bergh, eds., *The Writings of Thomas Jefferson* (Memorial ed.; 20 vols.; Washington, 1903–1904), XIII, 41.

exhausted, and war or abject submission are the only alternatives left us. I am forced from my hobby, peace." [14] The dualism, the ambivalence in Jefferson's attitude was characteristic of his entire thought, supple rather than stubborn, accommodating rather than principled, ever flexible.

Jefferson never quarreled seriously with his chief subordinates, James Madison and Albert Gallatin. The two Virginians and the Genevese-Pennsylvanian shared broad, general concepts which ran above the crosscurrents of compromise: a deep patriotic nationalism, a vague but nonetheless sincere liberalism, and a desire for peace. Jefferson, *primus inter pares*, never had to impose his major ideas upon unwilling lieutenants. He frequently sought and often accepted the advice of the two secretaries. At first Jefferson polled his Cabinet on all important issues, granting to himself only one vote. Despite usual unanimity the system proved cumbersome and unsatisfactory. During the post-*Chesapeake* flurry of governmental activity, the President substituted consultation with individual members of the Cabinet, and after leaving office he praised this arrangement because it left the president freer to make the ultimate decisions. [15]

Secretary Madison, self-effacing and inevitably cast into the shade by Jefferson's titanic figure, was no mere sycophant. If he seldom took issue with the President, it was because they shared common convictions or because, within a broad conceptual framework, Jefferson permitted his friend to lay out the details of policy. [16] On international affairs James Madison was probably

---

[14] Jefferson's farewell to the citizens of Washington, 1809, Joseph I. Shulim, *The Old Dominion and Napoleon Bonaparte* (New York, 1952), p. 279; Jefferson to Kosciuszko, April 13, 1811, Lipscomb and Bergh, *op. cit.*, XIII, 41–42; Jefferson to Thomas Cooper, Feb. 18, 1806, Jefferson MSS; Jefferson to William Wirt, May 3, 1811, Lipscomb and Bergh, *op. cit.*, XIII, 60; Jefferson to Charles Pinckney, Feb. 2, 1812, Thomas Jefferson MSS (Coolidge Collection), Massachusetts Historical Society.

[15] Jefferson to William Short, June 12, 1807, Lipscomb and Bergh, *op. cit.*, XI, 227; Jefferson to Gallatin, July 10, 1807, *ibid.*, XI, 267–268; Jefferson to Walter Jones, March 5, 1810, *ibid.*, XII, 371.

[16] Irving Brant, *James Madison: Secretary of State* (Indianapolis, 1953), performs valuable service in emphasizing Madison's positive contributions to Jeffersonian diplomacy, but in attempting to restore the balance he perhaps goes too far in the other direction.

better informed than his chief, although his foreign correspondents were far less numerous. Despite the plague of many minor illnesses —Jefferson, too, was not free from frequent migraine headaches —Madison was a tremendous worker, and his contributions to the political success of the Republican party and the development of American policy were scarcely less than those of Jefferson himself.

Differences in age, temperament, position, and reputation made Madison definitely the subordinate of Jefferson until 1809. Madison's mind ran in narrower channels. Although far abler at detailed analysis, he was less decisive, tending always to magnify the dangers of any proposed course. (This served him ill when he became president and lost or discarded Jefferson's guidance.) Federalists called Madison the mere hired attorney of the President, a slander that had a bite of truth within it. An able advocate, a shrewd debater, a master at marshaling facts, down to 1809 the Secretary showed little boldness or originality. In January, 1806, a long pamphlet, the product of several month's labor by the Secretary, was quietly laid on the desks of Congress. It bore the forbidding title, *An Examination of the British Doctrine, Which Subjects to Capture a Neutral Trade, Not Open in Time of Peace.* Characteristically, the pamphlet was anonymous, although the author soon became known. Equally characteristically, it was an overwhelming and in many respects devastating, but almost totally dispassionate, dissection of one aspect of British maritime policy. It was verbose and too complicated for ordinary readers. Above all, the pamphlet contained no suggested remedy for the evil of British insult, and it merited John Randolph's scornful comment: "After all, what does it contain? A remedy for the evil? No; a formal declaration that we are diseased! Sir, we wanted no ghost to tell us that." [17] *An Examination of the British Doctrine,* the chef-d'oeuvre of Madison's secretaryship, properly reflected his strengths and weaknesses.

[17] James Madison, *An Examination of the British Doctrine, Which Subjects to Capture a Neutral Trade, Not Open in Time of Peace* (Philadelphia, 1806), reprinted in Gaillard Hunt, ed., *The Writings of James Madison* (9 vols.; New York, 1900–1910), VII, 204–375; *Annals,* 9th Cong., 1st sess., p. 600.

Yet Madison was not a mere thinking machine. He had pride, ambition, and independence coupled with haunting personal misgivings which no doubt help to explain his frequent illnesses after becoming president. Reserved in official intercourse, in private life he was more sociable than Jefferson. A British diplomat, who during the trying months just before the American declaration of war thought him "rather too much the disputatious pleader," added that, at parties, Madison was "a social, jovial and good-humored companion full of anecdote and sometimes matter of loose description relating to old times, but often of a political and historical interest." [18] Almost without exception, those who knew Madison well liked him. But his compact figure, carefully powdered hair, and neat dress—all in marked contrast to Jefferson—furthered his reputation as a clerkly type of man.

Secretary of the Treasury Gallatin performed somewhat the same function as Madison, acting as an occasional brake upon Jefferson and, in his own special field of finance, as the initiator of detailed policy. Gallatin also served as a channel of informal communication with Congress, partly because he lived nearer Capitol Hill and partly because his brother-in-law, Joseph Nicholson, was until 1807 an important member of the House of Representatives. Although by common consent able and dedicated, Gallatin was not popular. His foreignness offended some Republicans perhaps also jealous of his ability. Some, restive under control but too craven to attack the more powerful Virginia chieftains, took their anger out upon Gallatin. Jefferson, who deeply respected Gallatin and recognized that finance and foreign affairs were closely mingled, unceasingly consulted the Secretary of the Treasury. When they did disagree Gallatin nevertheless devoted his full energies to support of the policy Jefferson desired. In the last eighteen months of Jefferson's administration Gallatin's private voice supported measures looking to war. Commenting on British and French insults, he wrote: "Let those nations pursue what course they please, I feel a perfect confidence that America will never adopt a policy which would render her subservient to

[18] Davis, *op. cit.*, p. 155.

either, and that . . . she will meet with fortitude the crisis . . . which may result from the difficult situation in which she is placed." [19]

With the Republicans enjoying overwhelming majorities in both houses of Congress, the executive, when it bestirred itself, could work its will upon the legislature during most of Jefferson's two terms. John Adams, who had had his difficulties with Congress and clung to much of the old Washington idea of a president above party, complained that "Wisdom and Justice can never be promoted till the Presidents office instead of being a Doll and a Whistle, Shall be made more independent and more respectable; capable of mediating between two infuriated parties," [20] but Jefferson proved that by acting as party leader the president could exert irresistible leverage. Republican floor leaders were chosen and discharged by the president, party caucuses imposed discipline upon legislators (or at any rate most of them), and the administration provided the text of some legislation to be passed by its agents. Until the selection of Henry Clay nearly three years after Jefferson's retirement, the speaker of the House acted merely as one comparatively minor administration spokesman, and the vice-president never established an important position in the Senate. [21] Not a single important piece of Jeffersonian legislation suffered defeat, and serious opposition did not appear until after a schism within Republican ranks brought into the open in 1805 by the proposal to bribe France. The Embargo and its supplements sailed easily through Congress despite the misgivings of many Republicans.

On some occasions the President declined to direct his agents. In 1806, probably because he felt that any American legislation threatening to cut into British exports would bring the ministry to its senses, Jefferson did nothing to indicate to Congress the

[19] Gallatin to Charles Pinckney, Oct. 24, 1808, Albert Gallatin MSS, New-York Historical Society.

[20] John Adams to Rush, July 25, 1808, Benjamin Rush MSS, Library of Congress.

[21] For Jefferson's leadership of Congress see Ralph V. Harlow, *The History of Legislative Methods in the Period before 1825*, Yale Historical Publications, Miscellany, Vol. V (New Haven, 1917), 165–193.

form he wished the legislation to take. The House of Representatives milled in confusion for weeks, and the Non-importation Act that emerged was a jest rather than a serious weapon against England. Similar silence at the White House contributed decisively to the confusion accompanying repeal of the Embargo Act during the last months of Jefferson's regime. Sometimes the President concealed from Congress the reasons for action he had taken or desired the legislators to take. In 1807, for example, he rejected the Monroe-Pinkney treaty without even submitting it to the Senate and, although in private conversations he explained his reasons to some senators, he withheld the treaty and the correspondence relating to it for more than a year.[22] The Embargo message, only one short paragraph, failed to mention several important reasons for adopting this policy. In short, while Jefferson frequently explained his desires to legislators willing to execute them, on other important occasions he drew back into his shell. His choice of times to remain inert proved extremely unfortunate for his party and for the United States.

The President found the management of Congress increasingly difficult during his second term. The Republicans were individualists, more skillful in opposition than in execution. The collapse of Federalism, which had served as a useful focus for their dislikes, actually weakened their vigor. Factionalism developed; New England Republicans showed hostility to their Southern brethren, the Quids professed to be more orthodox than Pope Thomas, and individual feuds and antipathies came into the open. From 1805 to 1808 these difficulties caused debate and delay more often than serious trouble. In the closing months of Jefferson's administration and throughout Madison's reign they often proved unfortunately decisive.

Most Yankee Republicans, even those who came from inland areas, took a far more favorable view of commerce than Southerners. Others who had triumphed by narrow margins over Feder-

---

[22] The documents and correspondence were presented to Congress only in March, 1808, fifteen months after the treaty was signed at London. *Annals*, 10th Cong., 1st sess., pp. 1869–1870.

alist opponents tended to look askance at policies that might permit their enemies to return to power. Not a few, feeling that they had fought the party's most difficult battles and deserved a fair share of influence and power, were jealous of the primacy of their Southern colleagues. Jefferson rewarded several Yankee followers with cabinet positions; in 1805 he made Barnabas Bidwell the administration spokesman in the House of Representatives, and in 1807 General Joseph B. Varnum of Massachusetts became speaker of the House. None of the New Englanders proved particularly helpful. The great Massachusetts merchant, Jacob Crowninshield, who captured Pickering's seat in 1802, died in the spring of 1808 after a long illness which deprived the party of his potentially important services. Bidwell proved a failure as House leader and later an embarrassment, for he decamped to Canada in 1810 when a shortage was discovered in his accounts as county treasurer just at a time when Madison contemplated appointing him to the Supreme Court. "The republicans [here], talk of principles, but seek offices," the Republican governor of Massachusetts told Jefferson in 1808, "they talk of public good, but want places of emolument." [23] Unfortunately, this analysis was only too true.

The most spectacular of the Republican dissidents, John Randolph of Roanoke, owned a plantation fittingly named "Bizarre." Randolph, the most splenetic orator in Congress, a vigorous whip-wielding foe of those who crossed him but courteous and gentlemanly to others, by turns an effeminate boy and an aging man plagued by real and psychosomatic illnesses, led the congressional Republicans during the first years of Jefferson's tenure. In 1805 he broke with the President, thereafter opposing with unique violence almost everything Jefferson supported. In 1811 Jefferson wrote that his former protégé's "exclusion [from Congress] alone would give greater security to our government, than the repeal of the British orders." [24] Randolph's political attitudes were usually the product of his hatreds—for Napoleon, for greedy ship-

[23] James Sullivan to Jefferson, April 2, 1808, Jefferson MSS.
[24] Jefferson to John W. Eppes, March 4, 1811, Thomas J. Coolidge, ed., "Letters of Thomas Jefferson," Massachusetts Historical Society, *Proceedings*, 2d Series, XII (1899), 270.

owners who sought national protection for their filthy and selfish trade, and above all for Jefferson and Madison, who had betrayed the Republican cause as Randolph saw it. These hatreds, plus a feeling of kinship for Britain and fear of the effect of war, particularly as it might strengthen the federal government, made him oppose almost all measures of resistance to Britain. Although his scorn and sarcasm often spurred his opponents to resistance rather than surrender, Randolph was an extremely able debater (when healthy), a masterful parliamentarian, and a very troublesome enemy to the followers of Jefferson.[25]

Nathaniel Macon and James Monroe, two other Republican wheel horses, at times shared Randolph's feeling that Jefferson had abandoned the old party traditions of limited government, a peaceful foreign policy, and the superior importance of agriculture. For personal and political reasons Monroe broke with his fellow Virginians and became a silent but definite anti-Madisonian candidate for the presidency in 1808. Thereafter he drifted steadily away from Randolph, back toward his original allegiance. Nathaniel Macon, speaker of the House of Representatives until 1807, followed somewhat the same path. In 1806 he joined Randolph in opposing resistance to Britain on the issues of the reëxport trade and impressment, partly because he was unwilling that the South should sacrifice for Northern interests and partly because he was convinced that "public force and liberty cannot dwell in the same country." [26] Macon soon abandoned Randolph and resumed support of the administration, perhaps in part because British restrictions began to harm the agricultural as well as the mercantile interest. Without these two veteran Republicans, Randolph and the handful of Tertium Quids, as they called themselves, did not seriously threaten the administration after 1808.

[25] Benjamin Rush expressed a widespread view of Randolph when he wrote: "I have long considered him as a mischievous boy with a squirt in his hands, throwing its dirty contents into the eyes of everybody that looked at him. A kicking or a horsewhipping would be the best reply that could be made to his vulgar parliamentary insolence. It is only because the body which he insults *is what it is* that he has been so long tolerated." Rush to John Adams, April 26, 1810, Lyman H. Butterfield, ed., *Letters of Benjamin Rush*, II, American Philosophical Society, *Memoirs*, Vol. XXX (1951), p. 1042.
[26] *Annals*, 9th Cong., 1st sess., pp. 686–698.

In the Senate, too, there were stirrings of opposition to Jefferson, and Madison later suffered humiliation at the hands of senators who called themselves Republicans. William Branch Giles of Virginia, a congenital opponent of almost everything not suggested by himself, grumbled a great deal against Jeffersonian policy. The President's tactful treatment of Giles and a broken leg that kept the Senator away from Washington in 1805 and 1806 delayed a rupture. After supporting the Embargo in 1807 and Madison's candidacy in 1808 Giles shifted to opposition. Maryland's Samuel Smith, a wealthy merchant, selfish and ambitious, almost always acted as his interests dictated, and his former Federalism made him distrust extreme Republicans. In 1805, commenting on an electoral campaign in Virginia, he wrote, "It is a struggle . . . between those who would carry Democracy to lengths dangerous to civil society, . . . and those whose good sense, talents, & abilities, produce the present state of things & wish to proceed no further in reform." [27] Smith would oppose extremists in his own party, even if it meant temporary alliance with some Federalists.

While schismatics usually could find hallowed party doctrines to justify their rebelliousness, as a responsible national leader Jefferson could not permit himself to be enslaved by antique doctrine. His old prejudices against ocean commerce and native manufacturing gradually softened, although he still gave his greatest devotion to agriculture. In 1809 he wrote, in characteristically simple and mechanical terms:

An equilibrium of agriculture, manufactures & commerce is certainly become essential to our independence. manufactures sufficient for our own consumption of what we raise the raw materials (and no more). commerce sufficient to carry the surplus produce of agriculture, beyond our own consumption, to a market for exchanging it for articles we cannot raise (and no more.) these are the true limits of manufactures & commerce.[28]

A desire for national self-sufficiency and his recognition of the interests of a large nonfarming segment of the population caused

[27] Smith to ———, Dec. 14, 1805, Samuel Smith MSS, Library of Congress, Letter Book 1805–7.
[28] Jefferson to Sir James Jay, April 7, 1809, Jefferson MSS.

Jefferson to shift toward this more realistic view of economic balance.

Jefferson and his followers never abandoned one old Republican ideal, reduction of the national debt as rapidly as possible. Between 1801 and 1812 the government showed a deficit in only one year, 1809. In the best years federal income was nearly double expenditure. In 1806 and 1807 two-fifths of the government's income went to reduce the debt, and in 1808 Jefferson and Gallatin came within half a million dollars of dividing receipts equally between expenditures and debt retirement. Between 1801 and 1812 the Republicans reduced the national debt by $38 million, or about 40 per cent.

Increased customs receipts, not reduced expenditures, really produced the surpluses. Almost no income came from internal taxes, for the hated Federalist excises had been repealed. Despite increased sales of public lands after 1804, income from this source never much exceeded 5 per cent of the government's receipts. The Treasury depended almost entirely upon customs revenue, the fruit of America's prospering foreign trade. Except during the Embargo this ran at about double the Federalist level and made possible the debt retirement so cherished by Jefferson, Madison, and Gallatin.

Republican fiscal policy had unfortunate consequences. Parsimony and retrenchment meant inadequate preparation for war, which reduced American influence and made Madison's task more difficult after 1812. Nearly total reliance upon customs revenues meant serious financial problems whenever trade restrictions or war reduced this income, and the abolition of internal taxes destroyed a potentially broad tax base. Concentration on debt reduction allowed the government to ignore the creation of a federal credit system. Amortization of the debt and government on the cheap were not the prescriptions needed from 1807 to 1812.

"The rage for sinking the national debt a few years earlier," as Robert R. Livingston called it, made Republicans desire to cut the armed forces to the bone, a desire so effectively implemented that in 1806 the navy had only one frigate on active service. In addition,

Republicans considered the armed forces potential agents of despotism. In Macon's words, "It is not . . . an easy matter to raise an army, but it is easier to do this than to get clear of one when raised. . . . I scarcely know which is worst, war or an army without war." [29] Furthermore, the navy seemed a symbol of Federalist involvement in foreign quarrels at the behest of nonagricultural interests. Far more Republican, far cheaper, fully as effective for defense, less likely to involve America in foreign wars, Jefferson thought, was an armada of gunboats which could be manned by skeleton crews until sea militia sprang to arms in an emergency. Whereas U.S.S. *Constellation* had cost more than $300,000, a gunboat cost only $10,000 to $14,000. Jefferson built hundreds. After 1812 they became a macabre monument to his hasty, ill-digested ideas in a field of which he knew little.

Most Federalists and not a few Republicans criticized the gunboat policy. Seaport politicians objected that gunboats and harbor fortifications were inadequate for defense and utterly incapable of carrying war to the enemy. From London, after humiliating experience at the hands of Britain and France, James Monroe wrote: "It is by the means which we have of injuring them only that they regard us, and their regard is proportioned to those means. . . . They are infidels 'till the measure is executed, that we will resort to any other than such as embargoes, which affect us as much as them." [30] Monroe's heretical suggestion that a naval squadron be built failed to move Jefferson, and although Madison refurbished the navy he made no attempt to expand it. During the war session of 1811–12 Republican votes defeated a building program. Traditional sentiments produced these votes, along with a feeling that, it being too late to challenge Britain at sea, a building program might merely encourage her to strike before America accumulated an effective force. [31] The failure to develop military

---

[29] Livingston to Madison, Jan. 8, 1810, Madison MSS; Macon to Nicholson, Jan. 31, 1806, Joseph H. Nicholson MSS, Library of Congress.

[30] Monroe to Randolph, June 16, 1806, Stanislaus M. Hamilton, ed., *The Writings of James Monroe* (7 vols.; New York, 1898–1903), IV, 464.

[31] This argument appealed to Republicans of otherwise different views, among them Jefferson, Joseph Story, and John Quincy Adams. The elder Adams, however,

defenses, like the policy of rigorous financial retrenchment, undermined the effectiveness of American protests before 1812, convinced Britain she need never fear more than an ineffectual war against her, and cost the United States heavily when war came. In precisely those areas most requiring flexibility, Jefferson and his followers proved most rigid.

Federalists accused Jefferson and orthodox Republicans of being sycophants of Napoleon. The truth was far more complicated. Affection for imperial France influenced only a tiny handful of Republicans, certainly not Jefferson himself. If the same was not true of the Federalists and Britain, still the Anglophilia of the bulk of the party and even of many of its leaders, who tended always to be more extreme than their followers, had very real limits. Appealing for national union in 1808 (but also no doubt well aware of the Federalists' reputation for placing British interests ahead of American), Noah Webster rightly stated: "It is a truth beyond controversy that the number of men who would consent to surrender our national rights or succumb to the domination of either power, who would place our independence under the protection of the British navy or our maritime rights under the protection of France is inconsiderable and comparatively of no weight or influence." [32] Views of the rival belligerents were the product of many things, among them the possibility of domestic political advantage, a general desire to preserve isolation and neutrality, a fairly widespread if often naïve appreciation of the balance of power, and finally of differing sympathies. Policy and attitude fluctuated according to news of decisions at the Tuileries or Whitehall, on the rolling field of Austerlitz or the open sea off Cape Trafalgar. Generalization baffled perceptive diplomats, and stupid ones, like France's General Turreau, simply threw up their hands and despaired of firm analysis. "Their System with regard

---

warned Jefferson that national unity and military effectiveness required the construction of frigates. "Without this," he wrote, "our Union will be a brittle China vase, a house of Ice or a Palace of Glass." John Adams to Jefferson, June 28, 1812, Jefferson MSS (misdated at 1813 in Lipscomb and Bergh, *op. cit.*, XIII, 289–290).

[32] Noah Webster (*pseud.* Public Spirit), "To All American Patriots," May, 1808, Harry R. Warfel, ed., *Letters of Noah Webster* (New York, 1953), p. 301.

to foreign countries is to have none," Turreau complained. ". . . it is the events of the day which determine their policies." [33] In truth, American policy combined deep-seated principles with the pragmatism bewailed by Turreau.

Most widely held of these principles was isolationism, already almost a national tradition. Although the undeclared Franco-American war and the Louisiana crisis both temporarily drew America into the European vortex, John Adams and Thomas Jefferson returned to isolation as rapidly as possible. No responsible American wanted an alliance with the Emperor Napoleon, however serious American complaints against Britain, and when the nation proceeded to war with England in 1812 it made very clear that this did not imply any connection with France. A few Federalists wanted to join the British crusade against France; in 1806 Gouverneur Morris, writing to an English friend, bewailed the fact that "you stand alone, and those who ought to side with you keep aloof, are awed, and subdued," and regretted that America had not become "your firm and useful ally." [34] Not many shared Morris' view. The most rabid Anglophiles, even those whose affection for Britain led them to sedition, rarely desired to join England's war. Sympathy and open commerce, but not alliance: such was the high Federalist creed down to 1812.

Almost all Americans shared the President's feeling that, "Kindly separated by nature and a wide ocean from the exterminating havoc of one quarter of the globe; too high-minded to endure the degradations of the others; possessing a chosen country," the United States might best advance her prosperity and security by avoiding connections with Europe. "May God deliver us from the contagious politics, which have convulsed the old world . . . ," a Republican Fourth of July orator declared. "We wish not the deadly embrace of Gallic friendship, or the corrupted influence of the British cabinet; for the moment either become intermingled with our policy, from that moment we may date the defection of

[33] Turreau #5 to Minister of Foreign Relations, Jan. 20, 1806, AAE, CP, E-U, Vol. LIX.

[34] Morris to Marquis of Stafford, Sept. 14, 1807, Anne C. Morris, ed., *The Diary and Letters of Gouverneur Morris* (2 vols.; New York, 1888), II, 500.

our national prosperity and happiness." A Republican campaign committee in New York expressed the same thought by appealing (there is some irony in this) to the wise advice in Washington's Farewell Address. "This is the only true policy," the committee stated, "that American rulers can honestly or providently pursue. The moment we enlist ourselves by sliding even imperceptibly into European politics, intrigue and warfare, we must abandon our peaceful, commercial, and hitherto prosperous system" for full participation in the broils of Europe.[35]

Americans considered their way of life superior to that of Europe. They desired to preserve it by avoiding contaminating contact, not to expand it through aggressive crusading. George W. Campbell, at the time the most prominent congressman from the West, said in 1806, "It would have been well for us . . . if the American flag had never floated on the ocean . . . to waft to this country the luxuries and vices of European nations, . . . to excite the jealousies and cupidity of those Powers whose existence . . . depends on commerce, and to court, as it were, their aggressions, and embroil us in their unjust and bloody contests." [36] Although Federalists and most Republicans rejected such anticommercial views, they shared the isolationist sentiment underlying Campbell's words. All agreed that the United States had a unique character and unique interests best served by peace and withdrawal.

Many Americans believed that the chance to pursue isolationist policies depended upon a balance of power in Europe. They counted upon *La Grande Armée* and the Royal Navy to form a rough equilibrium, not only giving the United States diplomatic leverage but at the same time preventing either France or Britain from turning possibly threatening attention to the United States. As good isolationists, of course, the Americans did not intend to commit their own power to prop up a European balance, but in

[35] James D. Richardson, ed., *A Compilation of the Messages and Papers of the Presidents* (Washington, 1897), I, 323; Estes Howe, *An Oration, Delivered in Worcester, (Massachusetts,) on the Fourth of July, 1808* (Worcester, 1808), p. 13; General Republican Committee, of the City and County of New York, *A Circular Letter, . . . in Vindication of the Measures of the General Government* (New York, 1809), p. 96.

[36] *Annals*, 9th Cong., 1st sess., pp. 706–707.

principle they hoped for one and in fact sometimes tried to exploit it. As Madison later admitted, the United States would not have gone to war against Great Britain in 1812 had the collapse of Napoleon been foreseen.

President Jefferson wrote frequently of America's interest in the balance of power. After Trafalgar and Austerlitz, he commented on the "awful spectacle . . . the world exhibit[s] at this instant. one man bestriding the continent of Europe like a Colossus, and another roaming unbridled on the ocean. but even this is better than that one should rule both elements. our wish ought to be that he who has armies may not have the dominion of the sea, and that he who has dominion of the sea may be one who has no armies. in this way we may be quiet." Such reasoning naturally led Jefferson to hope for a European stalemate. In 1815 he even half regretted the conclusion of the European warfare, writing in language very similar to that he had used a decade before: "we were safe from the enterprise of Bonaparte because he had not the fleets of Britain to bring him here, and from those of Britain because she had Bonaparte on her back, but we have now, the conquerors of Bonaparte to fear, with the fleets of Britain at their willing command." [37]

Most of his countrymen shared Jefferson's basic view. All Federalists prayed for Napoleon's downfall, only a few for the destruction of the French nation. An occasional Republican still hoped for British collapse, notably William Duane, who in 1806 declared that *nothing could more effectually secure and perpetuate the peace and happiness of America than the humiliation of England,* and her reduction to her natural place, among the third or fourth rank of powers in Europe." Most, like Jefferson himself, wished to see Britain chastised, not destroyed. In 1809 Senator Giles even justified war against England on the ground that Amer-

---

[37] Jefferson to Thomas Lomax, Jan. 11, 1806, Jefferson MSS; Jefferson to Campbell, Oct. 15, 1815, George W. Campbell MSS, Library of Congress. For an extended discussion of the Republican leader's position, see Lawrence S. Kaplan, "Jefferson, the Napoleonic Wars, and the Balance of Power," *William and Mary Quarterly,* 3d Series, XIV (1957), 196–217. Kaplan concludes that Jefferson was very interested in the balance of power, that he felt France no real threat to it, and that he unwisely slanted American policy in a pro-French direction.

ica could not seriously increase the threat to British existence, surely a weird argument for war. Minister Turreau believed the principal reason Americans failed to hail Napoleon's struggle to destroy Britain's sea dominion was their belief that it was "necessary to maintain between these two rival Powers, a balance useful to the United States, since otherwise France would obtain on the ocean the same power that She has obtained on the continent." A Federalist journal circulating in the District of Columbia reminded congressmen assembling for the War Hawk Congress that "all parties in times past have agreed to what has been emphatically called the first article of our political creed, as it relates to other nations: —*That as far as our influence extends, it ought to be used to keep them equally balanced; that on this depends the peace and safety of our country.*" [38]

The problem of course lay in the way one viewed the threat to the balance of power. Probably more Jeffersonians than admitted it publicly believed, like the President himself, that Napoleon posed a potentially dangerous threat to the United States.[39] After Austerlitz few Republicans thought a proper balance required further Napoleonic victories, although in 1809 the bitterly Anglophobe *Aurora* declared, "France has fought our battles—had Britain triumphed, we should have been enslaved." For the most part Republicans argued that the collapse of British resistance was "a remote and extremely improbable contingency," as Senator Giles put it.[40] Furthermore, Republicans believed an existing danger must not be subordinated to a distant, shadowy threat. They ac-

[38] *Aurora* (Philadelphia), March 15, 1806; *Annals*, 10th Cong., 2d sess., p. 379; Turreau #23 to Minister of Foreign Relations, Nov. ——, 1806, AAE, CP, E-U, Vol. LIX; *Alexandria Daily Gazette*, Nov. 2, 1811. Perhaps the most elaborate exposition of the balance-of-power thesis will be found in Robert Hare, *A Brief View of the Policy and Resources of the United States* (Philadelphia, 1810). At one point (p. 21) Hare declares that "our security from the oppression of either of the great belligerents, is in any considerable degree dependent on a due balance of their power." Thomas Ritchie's Richmond *Enquirer* also placed great emphasis upon the balance of power.

[39] In this connection see Plumer to Jedediah Morse, Feb. 24, 1806, William Plumer MSS, Library of Congress; *Enquirer* (Richmond), March 11, 1806; Pickering to Rebecca Pickering, Dec. 20, 1806, Octavius Pickering and Charles W. Upham, *The Life of Timothy Pickering* (4 vols.; Boston, 1867–1873), IV, 101.

[40] *Aurora*, July 31, 1809; *Annals*, 10th Cong., 2d sess., p. 378.

cused Federalists of using the balance-of-power argument to condone British crimes, and in some instances this led them to deny
the validity of the argument altogether. In 1810 Henry Clay declared, "I cannot subscribe to British slavery upon the water, that
we may escape French subjugation on land," and during the war
session he scoffed, "We are invited, conjured to drink the potion
of British poison actually presented to our lips, that we may avoid
the imperial dose prepared by perturbed imaginations." [41] In their
inmost hearts, however, Republicans cherished the idea of a European balance that would permit their nation to secure justice and
enjoy peace.

Federalists took a far simpler view. They considered Napoleon
the only real threat to equilibrium. As Fisher Ames expressed it,
"If France dictates by land and sea, we fall without an effort. The
wind of the cannon ball that smashes John Bull's brains out, will
lay us on our backs with all our tired honours in the dirt." Federalists did not minimize the chances of Napoleonic victory, and they
celebrated as their own the triumphs of Nelson and Wellington.
Some even declared that a "triumph over *Great-Britain,* at this
critical moment would be more fatal to us than defeat." [42]

Closely aligned with English thought as they were in so many
areas, the Federalists thus came to accept Britain's own view of
herself as savior of the world. "Who," asked Timothy Pickering,
". . . can . . . see Britain struggling for existence, and magnani-
mously opposing herself to a power which threatens, & with a rod
of iron, to rule the world, and not bid her *God-speed?* Who can
think of 'France lord of the navies as well as the armies of Europe,'
and not contemplate America as one of her provinces?" George
Cabot, arguing that Britain defended "the independence of the
civilized world," pronounced her justified in ignoring the cavils
of those for whom she fought. Scores of Federalist pamphleteers
and speakers echoed the same theme. Timothy Pickering's famous
toast, "The World's last hope—Britain's fast anchored Isle," de-

---

[41] *Annals,* 11th Cong., 1st and 2d sess., p. 581; 12th Cong., 1st sess., p. 600.
[42] Ames to Pickering, Feb. 14, 1806, Timothy Pickering MSS, Massachusetts
Historical Society, Vol. XXVII; *Columbian Centinel* (Boston), Dec. 23, 1807.

livered at a Boston dinner for a British minister recently declared
*non grata* by Madison, drew a roar of approval from its hearers.
John Lowell, a wealthy Boston lawyer whose health forced him
to professional retirement which he used to produce a steady stream
of Federalist pamphlets, repeatedly stressed that "the fall of British independence would destroy all hope of maintaining our own."
Even moderate Federalists like Rufus King, who were prepared
to admit some good in Jeffersonian policy and even to support
limited resistance to Britain, believed England defended the world
against French domination. "If England sink, her fall will prove
the Grave of our Liberties," King declared in 1808.[43]

The truth or falsity of the rival American analyses is not the
important thing. The point is that both parties saw, or forced themselves to see, or believed the people saw, the European struggle
in terms of the balance of power. They did not wish either great
belligerent to secure an unalloyed triumph; in particular, they
did not desire Napoleon to become arbiter of the world. Almost
without exception, Americans thought in terms of the national
interest, which seemed to require rough parity in Europe. This
often led Federalists to oppose any resistance to Britain because it
would make her defense more difficult, and induced so deep a
hatred of Jeffersonian policy that they frequently advised Englishmen how to destroy its effectiveness; nevertheless, a great deal
of Federalist sedition sprang from their view of world politics.

Of course, this view was also deeply colored by the powerful
strain of Anglophilia that ran through Federalism. The governmental structure and the social fabric of Britain seemed to the
Federalists almost models of their kind. Not cool reason but emotion often caused Federalists to proceed from this sympathy to
support of the British military cause. Republicans, on the other
hand, detested Britain and indeed had originally built their party

[43] Samuel E. Morison, *The Life and Letters of Harrison Gray Otis* (2 vols.;
Boston, 1913), II, 21; Pickering to Ames, Feb. 1, 1806, Pickering MSS, Vol. XIV;
Cabot to Pickering, Feb. 17, 1806, Henry Cabot Lodge, *Life and Letters of George
Cabot* (Boston, 1877), p. 353; John Lowell, *An Appeal to the People, On the Cause
and Consequences of a War with Great Britain* (Boston, 1811), p. 35; King to Picker-
ing, Feb. 5, 1808, Rufus King MSS, New-York Historical Society.

almost literally on opposition to England and to apparent British influences in the United States. Their political views bespoke emotionalism as much as did those of Federalists, and in the eagerness of political strife both parties took positions far in advance of those they would have found justified by reason. In 1807, before the worst excesses of partisanship had begun, a federal judge complained, "I think myself sometimes in a Hospital of Lunaticks, when I hear some of our Politicians eulogizing Bonaparte because he humbles the English; & others worshipping the latter, under an Idea that they will shelter us, & take us under the Shadow of their Wings." [44]

Federalists loved Britain largely because she was, in Pickering's words, "the country of our forefathers, and the country to which we are indebted for all the institutions held dear to freemen." America had learned much from British justice, particularly that it must serve the interests of man as well as of the state, and she had learned her lesson so well that many Federalists shared Henry Lee's opinion that Great Britain and the United States were the "only two nations of the many in the world who understand the meaning of liberty, . . . [the] best political blessing of God to man." Federalists considered the English constitution an almost perfect blend of aristocratic leadership and popular government, especially praiseworthy when contrasted with Napoleonic tyranny or the leveling democracy Jefferson was accused of desiring. They believed Britain far more Christian than France, where atheism and Romanism warred for supremacy. In law, in politics, in culture, and in her moral condition England was a model state, blemished at worst by minor defects which time would quickly cure. Old Luther Martin, the Maryland politician who had long ago abandoned his early principles and embraced Federalism, expressed his party's view when he wrote in 1810 to congratulate the English minister, Francis J. Jackson, on his imminent return "to, not a fancied Eutopia, but to a glorious Reality—to a Country, which the Creator in his infinite Goodness disconnected from the rest

[44] Richard Peters to Pickering, Feb. 4, 1807, Albert J. Beveridge, *The Life of John Marshall* (4 vols.; Cambridge, 1916–1919), IV, 6n.

of the World, and destined . . . for the abode and the protection of all that is best, most perfect, most virtuous, most dignified, most noble of the human race,—of all that distinguishes Man from the Brute and from the Daemon." [45] Language could scarcely go further than this, yet many Federalists shared Martin's sentiments.

Hatred of Napoleon was the twin of Anglomania. Federalists saw no redeeming quality in the despot of the Tuileries, and they frequently suggested that he threatened the moral fiber of the entire Christian world. Comparatively mild was a Pennsylvania congressman's assertion that Napoleon was "the great enemy of the liberties of mankind" or even the *Alexandria Gazette*'s claim that he was "one of the greatest tyrants the world ever saw." When warmed to their task, Federalists described the Emperor—and believed what they said—as a "monster, at whose perfidy and corruption Lucifer blushes and Hell itself stands astonished" or a "rival of satan himself in guile and mischief, and his most conspicuous agent here on earth." Just after the declaration of war in 1812, a clergyman in Massachusetts stated that the "contest is no longer between rival candidates for fame, but immediately between Christ and Anti-christ, between Almighty God, and that atheistic Power, who exalts himself above all that is called God." Continuing the Biblical approach to politics, the minister assured his flock that the forces of God would triumph through Britain. "Her banners will wave victorious on the plains of Armageddon, while the blood of her enemies will flow to the horses bridels, and" —this last apparently applied to Mr. Madison—"the flesh of their vassal kings furnish a supper for all the vultures of heaven." [46]

The extravagance of the Federalists' love for England and of their detestation of Napoleon harmed them politically. If the argu-

[45] Pickering to Edward Pennington, July 12, 1812, Henry Adams, ed., *Documents Relating to New-England Federalism* (Boston, 1877), p. 389; Cabot to Pickering, March 12, 1808, Lodge, *op. cit.*, p. 385; Henry Lee to Madison, Aug. 19, 1811, Madison MSS; Luther Martin to Francis J. Jackson, Aug. 29, 1810, Francis James Jackson MSS, Public Record Office (FO 353/58–61), FO 353/59.

[46] *Annals*, 11th Cong., 3d sess., p. 1007 (William Milnor); *Alexandria Gazette*, May 15, 1812; *Annals*, 11th Cong., 3d sess., pp. 1039–1040 (Blaisdell); David Osgood, *A Solemn Protest against the Late Declaration of War* (Cambridge, 1812), p. 13; Elijah Parish, *A Protest against the War* (2d ed.; Newburyport, 1812), pp. 10, 20–21.

ments had been reasonably expressed, the nation might have accepted the theses that Britain had made valuable contributions to the American heritage and that Napoleon offered nothing but a potential threat. The Federalists' emotion-charged words alienated many moderates upon whom they must count if they were to reverse Jeffersonian policy. The depth of their feeling, the hyperbole of their language created the impression that they placed Britain's cause above that of the United States. Sometimes, although not often between 1805 and 1812, the impression reflected fact; more frequently, the dividing line between Anglophilia and treason became blurred. Blunders by Jefferson and Madison presented Federalism with a golden opportunity to recoup. Outside New England the party proved unable to take advantage of it. In 1812 Josiah Quincy, leader of the corporal's guard still fighting in the House of Representatives, wrote his wife that "there is a foolish leaning upon [Great Britain] . . . among some of our friends, which, at the same time that it does little credit to their patriotism, does infinitely less to their judgment. The truth is, the British look upon us as a *foreign nation,* and we must look upon them in the same light." [47] Quincy, who sometimes failed to act upon his own prescription, nevertheless accurately indicated Federalism's major failing.

Federalists often accused their rivals of being pro-French. They brought forward little proof of their assertion. They simply assumed its truth, many of them because they believed that anyone who did not share their own feelings for Britain must be in league with Napoleon. "The obsequiousness of this country to the despot of Europe needs no proof or illustration from me," a Federalist clergyman stated in 1812. "This has been so often proved as to need no confirmation. I might as well prove that the sun shines." With more than a little justice, the *Pennsylvania Republican* hinted that the Federalists' own allegiance to Britain caused them to assume their rivals' connection with France. "The ghost of murdered Banquo was visible, only to the disordered imagination of the guilty Macbeth," this Republican journal noted.[48]

[47] Quincy to Eliza S. Quincy, March 26, 1812, Quincy, *op. cit.*, p. 254.
[48] Parish, *op. cit.*, p. 11; *Pennsylvania Republican* (Harrisburg), Dec. 10, 1811.

The Federalist charge was preposterous, for the old easy parallel —Federalism and Britain, Republicanism and France—had long since ceased to exist. (No more true was the alternate Federalist charge that Jefferson had allowed himself to be cowed into doing Napoleon's bidding.) Turreau and Sérurier criticized the administration's attitude almost as frequently as British ministers did. John Melish, a British traveler who spent a great deal of time in the United States between 1806 and 1811, declared not only that most Americans desired an accommodation with Britain but that, "as to partiality for Bonaparte and the French, it was my sincere opinion, very deliberately formed, that there was none." [49] The undeclared naval war of the 'nineties, and above all the development of imperial rule, had caused Jefferson and his followers to abandon the view of France they took around 1789. In 1810, when Napoleon announced repeal of the French decrees, many Republicans briefly raised their voices to praise him. Such praise was rare and for the most part confined to this particular period of time; especially during the war session did the Republicans assail the Corsican and deny that sympathy for his cause motivated their policy.

Neither Thomas Jefferson nor James Madison had the slightest affection for Napoleon Bonaparte. Jefferson considered Napoleon a great and rapacious despot, the betrayer of a revolution that had once promised so much for human liberty and rational progress. The Republican leader's correspondence abounds with strictures upon Napoleon, and after the Emperor's first abdication in 1814 Jefferson wrote, astonishment mingled with pleasure, "The Attila of the age [is] dethroned, the ruthless destroyer of ten millions of the human race, whose thirst for blood appeared unquenchable, the great oppressor of the rights and liberties of the world, [is] shut up within the circle of a little island in the Mediterranean." [50] Jefferson's lieutenant and successor shared his feelings. Even at the time he welcomed Napoleon's announcement of

[49] John Melish, *Travels in the United States of America, in the Years 1806 & 1807, and 1809, 1810, & 1811* (2 vols.; Philadelphia, 1812), I, 212–213.

[50] Jefferson to John Adams, July 5, 1814, Lipscomb and Bergh, *op. cit.*, XIV, 145.

repeal of the Berlin and Milan decrees, James Madison carefully avoided suggesting that America owed the Frenchman either gratitude or affection.

Since they considered Britain the chief threat to American interests, however, the Republicans often wished Napoleon well. In 1807 William Duane summarized contemporary Republican opinion when he wrote, "Bonaparte, independent of the service he renders mankind by curbing the tyranny of Britain, cannot be an object of regard to us; but as the avenger of neutral wrongs, and the asserter of neutral rights every voice should be raised for his triumph. . . . he is the best negociator we have." Duane wrote before the worst French excesses began, and not many Republicans were so bitterly Anglophobe as he. In the years preceding the War of 1812, Republicans sided only very reluctantly with Napoleon. Without doubt many of them shared the tortured feelings of a Baltimorean who expostulated, "What a cursed Gov$^t$. is that of Gr. Britain, that we cannot wish her success against the worst of Tyrants; and that she damns the best cause by her motives, & her manner of advancing it!" [51]

Although most Republicans considered British policy not only insulting but also a threat to American prosperity, they often reached this conclusion comparatively reluctantly, and the rise of Napoleonic tyranny caused many of them to dream of an accommodation with England. Randolph of Roanoke repeatedly emphasized that the friendly France of 1778 and the republican France of 1793 had been replaced by a vicious enemy whose crimes should cause Americans to forget the Anglophobia that had so long plagued them. John Taylor of Caroline considered France, not Britain, the natural enemy of the United States because of the sharp contrast between their forms of government, America's unwillingness to see Spanish colonies fall under Napoleon's sway, and her destiny to play the role of the Emperor's chief rival should England fall.[52] Taylor steadily favored compromise with Britain,

[51] *Aurora*, June 18, 1807; Nathaniel F. Williams to Story, Dec. 31, 1808, Joseph Story MSS, Library of Congress.

[52] *Annals*, 10th Cong., 1st sess., pp. 1910–1911; John Taylor to Monroe, Nov. 24, 1811, James Monroe MSS, New York Public Library.

and in 1811 he urged his friend Monroe to accept appointment as secretary of state so that he could work for an Anglo-American settlement. Monroe himself definitely favored Britain over France from 1805 until 1811, shifting only toward the end to the War Hawk position.

Nor was it only among the doctrinaire or Quid wing of the party that such sentiments could be found. Jefferson, through negotiations with Britain in 1806, and Madison, in conversations with David M. Erskine three years later, virtually offered to align American policy with Britain, although they asked important concessions in return. Jefferson in particular considered Britain perfidious, selfish, politically corrupt, and tyrannical upon the seas. In 1810, for example, Federalist suggestions that Britain, unlike France, could be trusted to show good faith caused Jefferson to expostulate, "Her good faith! The faith of a nation of merchants! . . . Of the friend and protectress of Copenhagen! Of the nation who never admitted a chapter of morality into her political code!" [53] Nevertheless, both Jefferson and Madison appear to have realized that, however difficult of attainment, an adjustment with England would best serve American interests. The acts supplementary to the Embargo were really pleas to Britain to come to some understanding with the United States. Both presidents dropped the early Republican demand that Britain abandon impressment. From 1808 to 1811 administration policy, if it inclined in any direction, favored Britain over France, and down to the very eve of the declaration of war President Madison hoped against hope for a settlement with England. Even Henry Clay, the future leader of the War Hawks, declared in a famous oration in 1810 that, if accommodation could be had with only one of the belligerents, he preferred that it be with Britain.

It would of course be easy to overemphasize this half-concealed but very real desire for English friendship. Many Republicans considered it unobtainable if desirable; they shared the feeling of John Adams, by this time himself nearly a Republican, that the "deadly wounds . . . inflicted on both sides" had regrettably

[53] Jefferson to John Langdon, March 5, 1810, Lipscomb and Bergh, *op. cit.*, XII, 375.

made reconciliation impossible. "Contempt and disgrace," said Adams, "never can be forgotten by human Nature, and hardly, very hardly forgiven by the sincerest and devoutest Christianity." [54] The legacy of Anglophobia the Republicans had carried with them from the 1790's had by no means disappeared, even though European political events had caused a reorientation of party policy. As American patriots and nationalists, the Republicans chafed under British insult. Unlike so many Federalists, they refused to accept the idea that American interests should be subordinated to those of Great Britain.

There was, furthermore, among some Republicans, if not a majority of the party or its leadership, a bitter, undeviating, unalloyed hatred of the British, a hatred modified neither by time nor by political circumstances. Dr. Benjamin Rush thought that only one-tenth of the American people shared this hatred, and Augustus Foster, the last prewar minister to the United States, said that pure, distilled dislike of Britain was confined to a very few Americans. Still, the sentiment did exist, and episodes like the *Chesapeake* affair often fanned it into flame. The *Independent Chronicle* and the *Aurora* steadily spread anti-British vitriol over the nation. Duane went so far as to declare that only those nations that resisted England could prosper. "The friendship of Britain— is *damnable*," he declared, "it is deadly—it is destructive—her *blessings* are *curses*." Other Republicans asserted that Britain maintained herself on the plunder of war or that, facing a visible doom, she desired to draw a happier part of the world into the same vortex. "Her disposition is unfriendly; her enmity is implacable; she sickens at our prosperity," a War Hawk declared in 1811, summarizing a strain never totally absent from Republican thinking. [55]

The attitudes of the administration party, which was so much

[54] John Adams to Lloyd, March 12, 1815, James Lloyd MSS, Houghton Library, Harvard University.

[55] Rush to Earl of Buchan, July 8, 1811, Butterfield, *op. cit.*, II, 1088; Davis, *op. cit.*, p. 249; *Aurora*, March 17, 1806; A Citizen of Otsego County, *"Union the Bond of Peace," The Origin and Progress of the Present Difficulties between the United States and Great Britain, and France Considered* (Utica, 1809), p. 17; *Independent Chronicle* (Boston), March 23, 1807; *Annals*, 12th Cong., 1st sess., p. 459 (R. M. Johnson).

larger and so much less homogeneous than the Federalists, naturally presented a more complex picture than those of their opponents. Different factions had quite different attitudes, and many individuals, like Jefferson himself, changed position from time to time. As a party the Republicans did not suffer from Anglophobia so deep they desired a war against England. They shared the general national desire for peace and isolation. They took the nation into the War of 1812 as a consequence of specific British actions, policies that threatened American interests and above all challenged the self-respect of the young nation. As patriots, not as Anglophobes, the Republicans cast down the gage of battle.

CHAPTER

# III

## "IS NATIONAL INDEPENDENCE

## A DREAM?"

Neither Yorktown nor the Peace of Paris made American independence secure. During the 1780's the young nation suffered humiliation at British hands while royalist France, midwife at America's birth, treated her as an upstart ingrate and sought to maneuver her as a satellite. Even after the Constitution, many Americans considered the nation an experiment of doubtful permanence. The French Revolutionary wars added to the buffeting America received. France demanded the support of fellow republicans; Britain paid little attention to neutral complaints as she wielded her naval power against her enemy. The Washington administration secured American prosperity by the Jay treaty of 1794, but only at the cost of ignoring or compromising many claims against England and provoking an undeclared war with France which lasted from 1798 to 1800. By 1805 America could look back upon twenty years of increasing prosperity interrupted only by the mild depression of 1797; the Pinckney treaty with Spain in 1795 and particularly the Louisiana Purchase had improved her position; politically and economically she daily gathered strength. These successes had often been obtained at the price of postponing the assertion of many American rights to a later day. This was the part of wisdom, not of greatness.

In May, 1803, Franco-British war recommenced after the interlude of the Peace of Amiens. America soon felt the effects of this struggle *à outrance*. For a decade the United States suffered severely at the hands of European belligerents. Like Holland and Denmark, she found herself treated as a pawn or a shuttlecock by Britain and France. In the autumn of 1807 a ragged group of frontiersmen, gathered in a wretched little town on the Mobile, put their names to a declaration of American rights in which they asked, "Is national independence a dream?" [1] Far-reaching belligerent invasions of American sovereignty, rights, and honor made a negative answer by no means obvious.

Napoleon seldom showed respect for America. So great was his contempt that, as Admiral Mahan has said, he "blinked at the fundamental fact that, while Great Britain ruled the sea, the neutral was the ally of her enemy." [2] Instead of encouraging America's European trade, which would have benefited him directly and perhaps more quickly involved the United States in war with Britain, from 1807 onward he did everything possible to restrict it. John Armstrong and Joel Barlow, the American ministers at Paris, suffered humiliation at the Emperor's hands, either through active rebuke, condescending cynicism, or (if the American was fortunate) silent neglect. On the question of Spanish Florida, which Jefferson and many of his followers wished to acquire for America, Napoleon clearly showed his cynicism. He shifted his attitude—his actions scarcely had the continuity to be called policy —according to interests of the moment and particularly his estimate as to whether the carrot or the stick would prove most effec-

[1] James Caller *et al.*, *The Declaration of the American Citizens, on the Mobile, with Relation to British Aggressions* (Mobile, 1807), p. 1.
[2] Alfred T. Mahan, *The Influence of Sea Power upon the French Revolution and Empire, 1793–1812* (2 vols.; Boston, 1892), II, 355.

tive with the Americans. The Emperor's subordinates frequently urged him to adopt a more friendly policy toward the United States. Napoleon never considered this necessary.

Not only contempt for America but even more an understandable conviction that the British war was an overriding concern caused Napoleon to subordinate his American policy to efforts to cripple England's economy. Deprived of hope at sea by Nelson, Napoleon believed commercial warfare "the only way to strike a blow at England and force her to peace." Specifically this meant "remorseless war against English merchandise," [3] an effort to destroy her export trade, undermine the pound's stability, and sometimes to force her to purchase French goods on very unfavorable terms. In November, 1806, an imperial decree issued at Berlin declared the British Isles in blockade (although Napoleon obviously lacked the naval power to enforce his edict) and prohibited all trade with Englishmen or in British merchandise. Vessels coming from British ports were ordered seized. A little more than a year later a second major decree, this time promulgated at Milan, reinforced and expanded the Berlin Decree. Besides reasserting earlier principles, this declaration announced that ships that submitted to British regulations or allowed themselves to be searched at sea by the Royal Navy would be considered to have lost their neutral character and would therefore be subject to confiscation. Since the great Frenchman dominated most of Europe, this attempt to destroy British trade was quite properly called the Continental System.

The Continental System never completely sealed off Britain. At various times Spain, Sweden, and Russia opened their ports to British goods, and John Quincy Adams rightly observed that the Continental System was somewhat like "an attempt to exclude the air from a bottle, by sealing up hermetically the mouth, while there was a great hole in the side." Furthermore, the states Napoleon dominated had no desire to sacrifice their own commerce to

---

[3] Napoleon to King Louis of Holland, Dec. 3, 1806, *Correspondance de Napoléon I*er (32 vols.; Paris, 1858–1870), XIV, 34; Napoleon to Eugène, Viceroy of Italy, Sept. 29, 1807, *ibid.*, XVI, 66.

serve Paris. Even in Holland, the neighbor of France ruled by Napoleon's brother, huge amounts of smuggling took place. There and elsewhere French officials often connived at violations of the system they were deputed to enforce. Finally, particularly after 1809 but to a degree from the very beginning, Napoleon showed himself willing to permit trade that was nominally interdicted, provided only that his treasury profited or that Britain was deprived of specie. By 1810 the Continental System had become, to quote Adams again, "little more than extortion wearing the mask of prohibition." [4] The drive for commercial advantage which became such an important part of the Continental System made it particularly offensive, since Napoleon forbade to the Americans trade that he actively prosecuted himself.

Despite its weaknesses the Continental System often inflicted serious pain upon Britain. When Napoleon rigorously enforced his policy, as he did for a year following the Peace of Tilsit with Russia in July, 1807, and again from the spring of 1810 until the invasion of Russia in June, 1812, Britain felt the pinch. Her exports to the Continent decreased from a value of more than £16.5 million in 1805 to less than £5.5 million in 1808. Unfortunately for Napoleon, adversity seemed merely to spur the British to greater efforts. Furthermore, as Napoleon should have seen, "the closing of Europe to British commerce could be ruinous to England only if it was accompanied by the closing of the immense American market." [5] It behooved Napoleon to conciliate the Americans, to attempt to weld them to his system.

Instead, the master of the Tuileries struck hard at American

[4] Entry of Dec. 29, 1809, Charles F. Adams, ed., *Memoirs of John Quincy Adams* (12 vols.; Philadelphia, 1874–1877), II, 92; Adams #24 to Secretary of State, Sept. 8/20, 1810, Worthington C. Ford, ed., *The Writings of John Quincy Adams* (7 vols.; New York, 1914–1917), III, 507.

[5] François Crouzet, *L'Economie Britannique et le Blocus Continental* (2 vols.; Paris, 1958), II, 857. This entire paragraph rests heavily on *ibid.*, II, 853–872.

Literature on the Continental System is extensive. In addition to Crouzet's recent volumes, which examine in great detail the impact of Napoleonic policy upon British industry and credit, see particularly Eli F. Heckscher, *The Continental System* (London, 1922); Frank E. Melvin, *Napoleon's Navigation System* (Menasha, Wisc., 1919); Audrey Cunningham, *British Credit in the Last Napoleonic War* (Cambridge, 1910). Their differences in interpretation, however interesting in themselves, are of minor importance for an understanding of Franco-American relations.

trade. The Berlin Decree, which baffled some American merchants and alarmed others, was not seriously enforced against them (nor against the British either, for that matter) until the summer of 1807. Then seizures began, and soon, in the case of the *Horizon,* decided in November, French courts gave their stamp of approval. From that time forward Napoleon dealt harshly with American trade. The Milan Decree aimed fully as much at neutrals as it did at Britain, and the London *Times* even declared: "Its regulations cannot in the slightest degree affect the interests of England. It is exclusively directed against neutrals." [6] In 1808, on the ostensible ground that, since the Embargo confined American ships to port, all ships flying the American flag must really be British ships in disguise, Napoleon ordered the condemnation of any such vessels that appeared in the ports of his dominions. Rapacity, contempt for American retaliation, and anger at postembargo legislation caused him to persecute American commerce for some time thereafter.

Considering his meager naval power, Napoleon captured a remarkable number of American merchantmen. Most of them fell into his hands when they were unwary enough to enter French ports, others were taken by French ships which eluded the British blockade, and some fell prey to Napoleon's satellites. In 1805 and 1806 American losses to Britain far outnumbered those to France. From the end of 1807 onward there was little to distinguish the two foes of American commerce. In an official report in July, 1812, Secretary of State Monroe stated that Britain had seized 389 American vessels since the Orders in Council of November, 1807, orders which, with the *Horizon* decision, opened the most vigorous phase of commercial warfare. Under the Berlin and Milan decrees, Monroe reported, France had seized 307 American vessels. France had also taken 45 ships since allegedly repealing her decrees in 1810, and her satellites were charged with 117 further captures. Monroe had no satisfactory figures on seizures by Spain while she was an ally of Napoleon, but even so his totals showed Napoleon was responsible for the seizure of at least 468 merchantmen. Moreover, the Secretary's report demonstrated that a ship had far better

[6] Jan. 4, 1808.

chances of acquittal or release in a British admiralty court than in a French one.[7]

Napoleon's policy toward American commerce was thus vehemently hostile. Logic seemed to call for an attitude that would encourage Americans to penetrate the British naval wall, bringing raw materials sorely needed by Europe and carrying away manufactures that would profit the Continent and cut into British exports to America. Consistency seemed to require a policy that would lend credence to Napoleon's pose as defender of the rights of neutral commerce. Yet actually the Emperor showed as little respect for America's rights and even less for her political importance than did British leaders. He tried to scourge rather than inveigle America into hostility to England, repeatedly stating that she must suffer at his hands until she effectively resisted English outrages. In effect he attempted to direct the general course of American policy, refusing to admit that the United States had a right to choose passive neutrality.

General Louis M. Turreau, French minister to the United States until early 1811, was a fitting agent of Napoleon. Turreau, who had only a fraction of his master's intelligence, shared with Napoleon contempt for America. The general beat his wife (on at least one occasion to the accompaniment of violin playing by the secretary of legation designed to drown out her cries) and if he never used force with Jefferson and Madison this was the only resource he omitted. The Americans needed no glimpse at his dispatches to know that he considered them selfish, spineless, and incompetent. Ultimately Napoleon replaced Turreau with Louis Sérurier, a more tactful diplomat but almost equally disdainful of

[7] Report of Secretary of State Monroe, July 6, 1812, *American State Papers. Class I. Foreign Relations* (6 vols.; Washington, 1832–1859), III, 583–585. Monroe's figures have often been misconstrued, leading many to say that France alone seized more ships than Britain from 1803 onward or from 1807 to 1812. For this reason it seems advisable to reproduce the following figures drawn from this report.

| *British seizures* | | *French seizures* | |
|---|---|---|---|
| 1803 to orders of 1807 | 528 | 1803 to Berlin decree | 206 |
| After November, 1807 | 389 | Under Berlin and Milan decrees | 307 |
| Total | 917 | After "repeal" | 45 |
| | | Total | 558 |

American worth. Clearly the French monarch and his representatives considered American independence, perhaps not a dream, but at least a limited commodity.

British assaults upon America exceeded Napoleon's in material impact if not in cynicism. Some conflict between Britain and America was inevitable, for, as an English diplomat serving in Washington put it, "The two greatest Commercial Nations in the Globe cannot move in the same Spheres without jostling one another a little; where we were aiming blows at the French Marine, we want Elbow room and these good Neutrals wont give it to us, & therefore they get a few side Pushes which makes them grumble." [8] The Americans, however, felt they were subjected to more than "a few side Pushes." Britain seized hundreds of American merchantmen and interrupted the sale of agricultural produce abroad; she forced American seamen into service under the Union Jack; her Canadian agents intrigued among Indian tribes resident in the United States; she rejected or ignored American protests. From 1805 to 1812 there was scarcely a moment when a storm did not loom over Anglo-American relations. Naval officers, diplomats, legislators, and statesmen plunged into the fray. Newspaper editors and pamphleteers on both sides of the Atlantic added their bit to the cacophony. In 1810 William Cobbett complained that to the real issues there had been added "the greatest curse of all, . . . volumes innumerable written upon the subject. There have been, including both sides, not less than from six to ten able bodied writers, and (what makes the thing more serious) most of them *lawyers*, too, hard at work." [9] Cobbett despaired of renewed amity, and insult and accusation had indeed become almost habitual. In some ways it is surprising that war did not come until 1812.

At no time after the renewal of European war in 1803 did American merchantmen enjoy immunity from British seizure. Secretary Monroe later reported that from 1805 to 1808 the Royal Navy made prize of one American ship every two days. (An American

---

[8] Foster to Lady Elizabeth Foster, Feb. 1, 1806, Augustus J. Foster MSS, Library of Congress.

[9] *Cobbett's Political Register* (London), XVII (1810), 43.

living in England asserted at the time that the real rate was ten per week.) If Monroe's figures are complete, in 1805 and 1806 one of every eight American ships that put to sea, in 1807 two of each nine, and in 1808 more than one in five were seized by the British. After 1808 both the number of seizures and the rate per American venture declined. In no year did Britain seize half as many American ships as she had in 1807, and less than one of every dozen vessels departing from port fell into British hands.[10] But this was only because American shipowners had become more wary or because American law forbade trade with Britain's enemy. As far as the British were concerned, they insisted as forcefully as before upon their right to decide what American trade should be permitted. They insisted that prosecution of the war against Napoleon must take priority over all other concerns.

The British often carried on trade they denied to Americans on the theory that war against France could not be maintained unless the English economy remained strong. Even those Englishmen who deprecated a quarrel with the United States accepted this theory as a truism. Lord Grenville, for example, complained at "the stress w$^h$. Jefferson lays on the supposed unreasonableness of our claim to deprive other nations of a trade w$^h$. we carry on ourselves. . . . We *have* a right to prevent that w$^h$. is injurious to us, & may if we think right relax that right in cases where we think the advantage to ourselves compensates or overbalances the injury."[11] Like that of Napoleon, British maritime policy became heavily tinctured with mercantilist, monopolistic hues.

Contemptuous of a weakling power, jealous of American prosperity, eager for prize money, British naval officers stretched their orders to the limit or beyond. Even James Stephen, spiritual father of the most aggressive attacks upon American commerce, warned from time to time that British commanders must be restrained.

[10] Report of Secretary of State Monroe, July 6, 1812, *ASPFR*, III, 583–585; Macall Medford, *Oil without Vinegar, and Dignity without Price: Or, British, American and West-India Interests Considered* (2d ed.; London, 1807), pp. 101–102.

[11] Grenville to Auckland, Feb. 18, 1806, William Eden, Baron Auckland, MSS (Add. MSS 34412–34471, 45728–45730), Add. MSS 34456.

"These steeds must be well reined in . . . ," he warned the ministry in 1807. "The[ir] spirit is sometimes salutary, however rash or irregular—it may overawe Kings or Cabinets—but in this delicate case we have to do with a democratical society—& with a maritime people too, whose feelings resemble our own." [12] The British government never took action forceful enough to reduce the navy to obedience. No commander who violated American rights, even those rights the Cabinet recognized, suffered real punishment.

British action within sight of the coast particularly irritated Americans. Cruisers mounted an almost continuous blockade until withdrawn a bit in 1812 in a belated effort to lessen American resentment. Off New York, for example, they frequently halted almost every ship leaving the harbor. Sometimes one or two dozen merchantmen awaited British inspection, and even those not sent to admiralty courts for trial often lost a favourable tide, a useful wind, or perhaps even an advantageous market as the result of delay.[13] Even the British consul at New York, who could not be accused of affection for the Americans, urged the navy to exercise restraint. In 1807 the British minister at Washington wrote:

I am persuaded that more Ill will has been excited . . . by a few trifling illegal Captures immediately off this Coast and some Instances of insulting Behaviour by some of His Majesty's Naval Commanders in the very Harbours and Waters of the United States than by the most rigid Enforcement of the Maritime Rights of Great Britain against the Trade of the United States in other Parts of the World. It may easily be conceived to be highly grating to the Feelings of an independent Nation to perceive that their whole Coast is watched as closely as if it was blockaded, and every Ship coming in or going out of their Harbours examined rigorously in Sight of the Shore by British Squadrons stationed within their Waters.[14]

[12] "Coup d'oeil on an American War," n.d. [Dec., 1807], Spencer Perceval MSS (examined while temporarily on deposit at the Register of National Archives, London), 33/99.

[13] Basil Hall, *Fragments of Voyages and Travels* (new ed.; London, 1850), 1st Series, p. 57.

[14] Barclay to Captain John P. Beresford, private, May 28, 1806, George L. Rives, ed., *Selections from the Correspondence of Thomas Barclay* (New York, 1894), pp. 242–243; David M. Erskine #25 to Canning, Oct. 5, 1807, Foreign Office Archives, Public Record Office, FO 5/52.

David M. Erskine here touched upon one of the central reasons that British assaults aroused more resentment than those of France.

Americans also complained strenuously against British admiralty courts. Whereas French judges admittedly acted virtually as agents of the Emperor, British tribunals at least claimed to be free to apply law rather than government policy. Their apparent hypocrisy and the vices of some judges affronted Americans, who described the entire system as one of "lawless plunder." [15] Some American complaints, particularly against Sir William Scott, justice of the High Court of Admiralty, were unjustified,[16] but the system was bad enough without exaggeration. Ships were condemned on trivial evidence, and at least after the *Essex* case in 1805 the burden of proof lay with the owner and not the captor of the ship brought to trial. Furthermore, admiralty courts burdened even innocent shipowners with heavy costs. One writer estimated that from $9 to $13 million worth of American property was always awaiting trial by British courts. Another pointed out that court costs frequently reached $5,000 per case, and even as much as $2,000 or $3,000 when the case was dismissed in early stages. Still a third critic estimated that in fees, loss of market, and immobilization of ships admiralty courts cost American shipowners several million dollars yearly. Alexander Baring declared that captains of the Royal Navy always carried appeals to higher courts, hoping to force shipowners into compromise simply to escape the toils of British law. Privateersmen, Baring claimed, often brought into port ships that had violated no British decree whatsoever, extorting from the owner $500 or $600 as the price of not taking the case to court.[17] Such practices flourished because captors were seldom

[15] George Joy, *The Dispute with America, Considered in a Series of Letters from a Cosmopolite to a Clergyman* (London, 1812), p. 27.

[16] Rare praise of Scott by those friendly to American claims is to be found in *ibid.*, p. 28; William Lyman to Madison, Jan. 14, 1806, Consular Letters, London, Department of State Archives, National Archives, Vol. IX; and, by an Englishman, in Alexander Baring, *An Inquiry into the Causes and Consequences of the Orders in Council; and an Examination of the Conduct of Great Britain towards the Neutral Commerce of America* (London, 1808), p. 75n. Baring declared that Scott tried "to distribute that real justice which unfortunately is not always within his reach."

[17] Medford, *op. cit.*, p. 102; Jacob Crowninshield, "Some Remarks on the American Trade, 1806," ed. John H. Reinoehl, *William and Mary Quarterly*, 3d Series, XVI

burdened with more than a share of court costs, even when they lost a case.

Federalists often pointed out, with justice, that America gained as well as lost from the efforts of belligerents, that by driving French ships from the seas Britain had fostered the development of the American merchant marine, that if only one ship of three escaped interception the merchant's balance would show an over-all profit. Fisher Ames once complained that his fellow Americans reacted too emotionally to British assaults upon their commerce. "We have hated those most who oftenest make us feel our impotence. The British have done this, by their searches of our vessels, even while our trade became a monopoly in consequence of British naval triumphs," he expostulated. Ames misunderstood public opinion, which reacts more often to humiliation than to material hurt. British regulation of American commerce could no more be tolerated by a self-respecting nation than similar activities by Napoleon. The British Orders in Council, John Quincy Adams observed, "strike at the very root of our independence." [18] In this sense they were most deeply resented in the United States.

Until 1805 British assaults upon American commerce were relatively moderate, compared at least with those to follow. Attacks begun in that year reflected a broad national determination to step up the pace of war against Napoleon. This spirit found expression in James Stephen's famous pamphlet, *War in Disguise*. Neutrals and the enemy alone, Stephen argued, profited from British self-restraint, particularly from the *Polly* decision of 1800, which granted the reëxport trade almost complete immunity from seizure when carrying goods, albeit circuitously, from enemy colonies to the metropole. Ship after ship sailed contemptuously past patrolling English vessels, often laden with goods converted only by fraud into nominally neutral property. To deprive Napoleon of the sinews of war and to prevent the United States from sheltering

---

(1959), 114; John M. Taylor to Monroe, Aug. 6, 1806, James Monroe MSS, Library of Congress; Baring, *op. cit.*, pp. 94–95, 95n.

[18] Ames to Quincy, Dec. 6, 1807, Seth Ames, ed., *Works of Fisher Ames* (2 vols.; Boston, 1854), I, 405–406; Adams to Harrison G. Otis, March 31, 1808, Ford, *op. cit.*, III, 200–201.

enemy property under the Stars and Stripes, Stephen urged rigorous execution of the Rule of the War of 1756—the prohibition to neutrals in time of war of traffic closed to them in peace—and complete disruption of the colonial trade, even when carried on through American ports and under the American flag. Such action would have the more than collateral advantage of restoring British shipping and commerce to their wonted preëminence. Basically, as befitted a publication that appeared on Trafalgar day, James Stephen's pamphlet was a clarion call for more aggressive exploitation of Britain's sea dominion, for stronger blows against the enemy —and against neutrals.

Stephen later denied that *War in Disguise* had been written at the Pitt ministry's behest. Only in a technical sense was this denial true, for Stephen submitted his manuscript to Sir William Scott, who in turn showed it to Pitt and then advised Stephen to print it privately, since "if it sh$^d$ carry our Pretensions somewhat higher than the Convenience of Publick Affairs may allow, it will commit Government less" than if it seemed to have "any stamp of Official Communication upon It." Soon after publication, the American minister forwarded a copy of *War in Disguise* to the Secretary of State, commenting, "It is said to be a ministerial work, or rather under its auspices." [19] This was the usual opinion in London. The semiofficial status of *War in Disguise* seemed confirmed when Stephen, whose identity as its author had become known, received from the Pittites a seat in the House of Commons.

Stephen deserved his seat. *War in Disguise,* playing ably upon a growing chord in English sentiment, provided apparent justification for a shift in policy already under way and impressed even Pitt's enemies with its exposition of neutral subterfuges. Thus, for example, the *Edinburgh Review* called it "a pamphlet of great merit" and agreed with Stephen that frauds by neutrals required British counteraction. The London *Times* believed Stephen had

[19] James Stephen (*pseud.* The Author of "War in Disguise"), ed., *The Speech of the Hon. J. Randolph . . . with an Introduction by the Author of "War in Disguise"* (London, 1806), p. xviii; Scott to Pitt, Aug. 25, 1805, Chatham MSS, Public Record Office, Vol. CLXXVI; Monroe to Madison, Oct. 26, 1805, William C. Rives Collection, Library of Congress.

clearly proved that "it was high time to put an end to a system so prejudicial to the commercial interests of the country." Opponents of restrictive measures found themselves overwhelmed. Alexander Baring, who denied that American prosperity had been achieved at British expense, had to admit that this "delusive opinion" was generally held, primarily because the argument had been "too ably illustrated by the author of 'War in Disguise.'" Small wonder that Fox's protégé, Lord Holland, called *War in Disguise* "an abominable & mischievous work." [20]

In 1804 and 1805 Pitt's government, closely in tune with rising public sentiment, increased the rigor of its American policy, and by the time William Pitt died early in 1806 a serious controversy had developed. Refusal to extend commercial articles of the Jay treaty, toleration of renewed impressment, hauteur in dealing with James Monroe, attempts to restrict the trade of American vessels with the British West Indies—all these were parts of a policy Cobbett rightly assailed as "a pretty equal measure of arrogance and imbecility." The greatest American grievance was the *Essex* decision, which marked the end of British tolerance of the reëxport trade. An American War Hawk later described this decision as "the foundation and commencement of the system of vexation and injury under which we . . . [have] suffered." [21] England showed that, without even a bow to American sensibilities, she would alter her rules of maritime behavior as the spirit moved her.

The *Essex* decision replaced the *Polly* decision as the chief guide for British courts. Sir William Scott's *Polly* decision, later communicated to the Americans in even more explicit paraphrase, granted the reëxport trade almost complete immunity from seizure. In effect, the decision stated that landing of goods in America and payment of even the smallest duties neutralized cargo being borne circuitously from the Caribbean to Europe. American reëxports rose from $40 million in 1800, the last year of the first Anglo-

---

[20] *Edinburgh Review*, VIII (1806), 1–35; *Times* (London), Oct. 24, 1805; Baring, *op. cit.*, p. 2; Holland to Fox, Jan. 3, 1806, Charles J. Fox MSS, British Museum (Add. MSS 47559–47601), Add. MSS 47575.
[21] *Cobbett's Register*, IX (1806), 170; Samuel McKee in *American Statesman* (Lexington, Ky.), Sept. 7, 1811.

French war, to more than $60 million in 1805. The Rule of the War of 1756 became virtually a nullity, so unimportant indeed that Alexander Baring later maintained that it was resuscitated "merely because the only remaining neutral had a defenseless commerce." In a series of minor decisions, admiralty courts sought to tighten enforcement of the Rule of the War of 1756,[22] but American merchants ignored these irritants as long as the overwhelming proportion of reëxported cargoes crossed the Atlantic unmolested.

Then, in the spring of 1805, Master of the Rolls Sir William Grant handed down the *Essex* decision of the Lords Commissioners of Appeals.[23] The *Essex'* cargo of wine, bound from Barcelona to Havana but briefly landed in the United States, was condemned although the owners had performed the requirements laid down in the *Polly* case. Grant held that the landing was an attempt to deceive, noted that virtually all duties had been returned as drawbacks, and emphasized that the owners, during the two years' grace given them to collect evidence of a bona fide importation into America, had brought forward no proof. Since Spain had not permitted Americans to share in commerce between the home country and Cuba in time of peace, Grant confirmed the decision of a lower court condemning the *Essex'* cargo. Legalistically speaking, the decision distinguished but did not reverse the *Polly* case. In the earlier decision Scott explicitly upheld the Rule of the War of 1756 and merely stated that landing and payment of duties were but one test of a bona fide importation. In practice, of course, the *Essex*

[22] Baring, *op. cit.*, p. 77; Orby H. Mootham, "The Doctrine of Continuous Voyage" (unpublished M.Sc. [Econ.] thesis, University of London, 1926), p. 38n; C. J. B. Gaskoin, "The Legend of the Essex" (typescript, Gaskoin MSS, London School of Economics), pp. 11–13. Mr. Gaskoin, with whom the author was privileged to have correspondence, died before publishing his valuable work on the *Essex*. His entire manuscript of thirty-two pages is probably the most detailed single examination of this case and its implications. Gaskoin's verdicts are unreservedly hostile to the United States.

[23] The exact date of the decision is still open to question. James Stephen, *War in Disguise; Or, the Frauds of the Neutral Flags* (London, 1805), p. 60, gives the date as May 22, 1805. The only available transcript of this laconic decision is attached to Monroe #35 to Madison, Oct. 18, 1805, Despatches, Great Britain, Vol. XII, where the date is given as June 22, 1805. The earlier date seems more likely, since it alone allows time for news of the decision to have reached captains at sea before the outbreak of seizures early in July.

decision made it much easier to secure condemnation of reëxports. Landing and payment of duties alone would no longer satisfy British courts.[24]

British commanders at first believed they had received license to seize all ships engaged in indirect voyages. Further decisions soon made clear their error, and toward the end of 1805 seizures fell off sharply as American shipowners exercised greater caution or developed shrewder subterfuges to conceal evasion of the arbitrary British rule. In November Monroe reported home, "Our merchants here say that the rule . . . may be easily complied with, & will do no more harm except in the cases that have or may occur before it is known in America: that cargoes may be sold &c [in America before reshipment], & that fact is known and anticipated here by those who make the rule." The number of reported seizures proved exaggerated. In February, 1806, Monroe complained to Fox that 120 vessels had been seized as a result of the *Essex* decision. By August, on the basis of better information, Monroe and Pinkney reduced the figure to 61.[25] Certainly the new rule did not long discourage American merchants, for reëxports dropped only about 1 per cent in 1806.

The decision's real importance lay deeper. In the first place, British courts abandoned the position that the captor must demon-

[24] Sir William Scott, Britain's foremost admiralty judge, loyally applied the principles of the superior court, beginning with the case of the *Enoch* in July. But he obviously believed that it was unsound law and risky politics. In August he urged the Foreign Secretary to turn his attention to the problem and perhaps modify the principle. Scott to Mulgrave, Aug. 9, 1805, Law Officers Reports, FO 83/2204. In October Mulgrave told Pitt that, because Scott was out of sympathy with the new policy, he would be of no help in preparing an answer to Monroe's written protests. Mulgrave to Pitt, Oct. 11, 1805, transcript, Pretyman MSS, Cambridge University (Add. MSS 6958), Vol. XVII. In November and December James Monroe and George Joy, an American in London, both reported to Madison that Scott had only feebly defended the principle when applying it in his own court. Monroe to Madison, Nov. 6, 1805, Rives Collection; Joy to Madison, Dec. 31, 1805, James Madison MSS, Library of Congress. The Pitt government would have done well to have held extensive conversations with Scott on this matter, but Mulgrave preferred to scoff at his opinions.

[25] Monroe to Madison, Nov. 6, 1805, Rives Collection; Monroe to Fox, Feb. 25, 1806, FO 5/51; Monroe and Pinkney to Holland and Auckland, Aug. 20, 1806, and enclosure, *ibid*. The British minister at Washington reported a year later that indirect trade between Spain and her colonies continued to be almost unmolested. Merry #44 to Fox, Sept. 28, 1807, FO 5/49.

strate a prize rightfully his; henceforth the burden of proof lay with the shipowner. Second, the hasty enforcement of the new principle insulted the United States. Many ships sailed from American ports in the spring of 1805 trusting that English practice of five years' standing would be continued. Without warning they were halted and haled into admiralty courts. Such action justified American complaints that the Royal Navy sought plunder for itself rather than strangulation of Napoleon. Federalist merchants struck home when they asserted that "it cannot become the integrity and magnanimity of a great and powerful nation, at once, and without notice, to reverse her rule of conduct." Most important of all, the new departure clearly showed that Britain intended to act without concern for precedent or American sensibilities. In January, 1806, Rufus King noted that although seizures had fallen off "as the Business is fitted to the Rule" there was no assurance Britain would not proceed further and "put an end to . . . [all] Trade in Colonial Articles between the U.S. & Europe." [26] The *Essex* decision ended a comparatively long period of moderate interference with commerce and clearly foreshadowed increasing blows against American trade.

In July, 1805, a week after his return from Madrid and Paris, James Monroe protested the new seizures and then sought an interview with Foreign Secretary Mulgrave to expand upon his grievances. Mulgrave declined a special appointment, writing, "I am not aware of any recent occurrence of so pressing a nature" as to justify one. At a regularly scheduled interview toward the end of August, Lord Mulgrave obstinately defended the Rule of the War of 1756 and made no attempt to explain that the *Essex* principle was not so far-reaching as Monroe feared. The two men "parted as remote from an accord as could possibly be." Subsequently Mulgrave and his under-secretary, George Hammond, blandly insisted that no new principle had been adopted, a statement true only in the most legalistic sense. For the rest of the year Monroe had to be

---

[26] Protest of Boston merchants, *New-York Evening Post*, Feb. 7, 1806; King to Christopher Gore, Jan. 26, 1806, Rufus King MSS, New-York Historical Society, Vol. XI.

content with written protests. Only a hope that Austerlitz would reduce British arrogance and then the prospect of Fox's succession restrained the American diplomat from throwing up his position in disgust.[27]

It would have been easy to explain to the United States the true dimensions of the *Essex* decision. With reluctance, the Jefferson administration might even have accepted the new policy if assured that Britain did not intend to cut off all indirect trade in colonial produce. But the ministry did nothing until March, 1806, when the King's Advocate, Sir John Nicholl, finally prepared a memorandum which the Board of Trade passed on to American merchants. Nicholl, who defended the *Essex* principle and denied that it represented an abandonment of *stare decisis*, admitted the decision had been abused:

Some Vessels were seized which probably would not otherwise have been detained, under a notion that it was illegal for an American ship to convey Colonial Produce from America to Europe; and the misapprehension became so strong, that it was fully believed by many here, and by more in America, that special Instructions to that Effect had been issued by His Majesty's Government, though I believe such a measure never in the slightest Degree entered into its contemplation.

Britain, said Nicholl, sought only to prevent fraudulent evasions of the Rule of the War of 1756, not to cut off the entire reëxport trade of the United States.[28]

Not until May, 1806, nearly a year after the original verdict, did a British judge issue a full-dress amplification of the *Essex* decision. Then, when a new tack taken by the Ministry of All the Talents had in a sense made it superfluous, Sir William Grant chose to elucidate it in the case of the ship *William*. Grant reviewed prior cases, including the *Essex* case, to show the consistency of

[27] Monroe to Mulgrave, July 31, 1805, enclosed in Monroe to Madison, Aug. 6, 1805, Despatches, Great Britain, Vol. XII; Monroe to Madison, Aug. 20, 1805, and enclosures, *ibid.*; "Minute of a Conversation between Mr. Erving & Mr. Hammond," Aug. 30, 1805, *ibid.*; Monroe #35, #39 to Madison, Oct. 18, Dec. 23, 1805, *ibid.*

[28] Sir John Nicholl to Board of Trade, March 20, 1806, Greenwich Hospital Miscellanea, Public Record Office, Adm 80/116.

British courts. He closed by reaffirming that American ships could no longer count on "mere voluntary *ceremonies*" in American ports to protect them. Unlike its predecessor, this decision was well advertised in advance and soon spread before the world. The King's Advocate, doubtless to educate the new ministry to his point of view, secured Lord Auckland's attendance at the Cockpit to hear the decision. The next day Auckland reported to the ministry's leader, "The tendency of that Judgment is to set aside the Pretensions of the Americans to legalize their cargoes by a fictitious landing & reshipping, & by a pretended payment of duties, &c. The Judgment was given with great ability; but will create a *very strong* sensation. That whole subject calls for an immediate & very solemn Consideration." [29] Auckland's concern and that of the British government arose too late to prevent serious friction with America.

Like seizures, the impressment of American seamen increased in 1805 and troubled Anglo-American relations until war came. In coldly economic terms the loss of seamen counted far less than the loss of ships and cargoes, and the recruiting of British seamen by American ships more than balanced the loss of men through impressment. In terms of human right and national self-respect, impressment posed an extremely serious challenge. "This authorized system of kidnapping upon the ocean," as John Quincy Adams called it, condemned Americans to many years service in the Royal Navy, sometimes even to death in a foreign monarch's battles. The American tar could ask aid of "no judge, no jury, no writ of *habeas corpus*." [30] He was forcibly enlisted in the Royal Navy as a result of a decision a boarding officer made as to his citizenship. He knew

[29] Christopher Robinson, ed., *Reports of Cases Argued and Determined in the High Court of Admiralty*, V (London, 1806), 396–397; Auckland to Grenville, May 14, 1806, Boconnoc MSS (Papers of William Wyndham Grenville, Baron Grenville), Lostwithiel, Cornwall, Lord Auckland 1806.

[30] Adams, "Reply to the Appeal of Massachusetts Federalists," n.d., Henry Adams, ed., *Documents Relating to New-England Federalism* (Boston, 1877), p. 178. On the entire subject of impressment, particularly as seen from the American side, the standard work, heavily relied upon here, is James F. Zimmerman, *Impressment of American Seamen*, Columbia University Studies in History, Economics and Public Law, Vol. CXVIII, no. 1 (New York, 1925).

that even if American representatives learned of his detention his release would probably be long delayed. Occasionally a seaman threatened with impressment mutilated himself, cut off his hand perhaps, to destroy his usefulness to the British; often he endured weeks of intermittent flogging before he consented to take up his assigned tasks on an English man-of-war. In the end the Royal Navy usually had its way.

This practice, so evil in its effect upon individual seamen, had even more serious implications for the nation. No state that permitted crews under its flag to be mustered by a foreign officer, that tolerated detention of its citizens by another nation, could seriously maintain a claim to complete sovereignty. When John Adams declared that Jefferson "has not been behind either of his predecessors in his zeal for the liberty of American seamen," the ex-President merely invited criticism of himself as well as of Washington and Jefferson, for protests and half measures satisfied them all. By impressment even more than by seizures Britain challenged America's stature. Replying to Federalist complaints that France treated American commerce as badly as Britain did, a Boston newspaper reminded its readers that "there is another atrocity incident solely to Great Britain, of the blackest and most savage complexion, which would alone convict her of being beyond all comparison to the *greatest aggressor*. We refer to the barbarous THEFTS OF AMERICAN CITIZENS!"[31]

Almost all Britons believed impressment vitally necessary. The number of men in the navy rose from 36,000 in 1792 to about 120,000 in 1805. England's merchant marine lost as many men as it could spare, and large numbers of foreigners had to be enlisted in British service. The *Edinburgh Review* estimated that one-eighth of the navy's seamen were foreigners, and the American consul at London claimed that 15,000 Americans were serving in the Royal Navy, although not all Americans were impressed and many

[31] John Adams, "The Inadmissible Principles of the King of England's Proclamation of October 16, 1807, Considered," Charles F. Adams, ed., *The Works of John Adams* (10 vols.; Boston, 1850–1856), IX, 327; *Independent Chronicle* (Boston), May 27, 1811.

claimed as Americans were British subjects according to English law.[32] To maintain the existing level of manpower and above all to discourage desertion to American merchantmen it seemed imperative to make use of impressment.

Certainly voluntary enlistment could not meet Britain's needs. Service in the Royal Navy was onerous, and able-bodied seamen received only 30 to 35 shillings (about 7 dollars) per month. The Americans paid able-bodied seamen 25 to 35 dollars for service much less painful, and they made strenuous efforts to enlist Englishmen, for America had far too few trained seamen to support her maritime expansion. Thousands of British seamen avoided or deserted service in the Royal Navy by joining the crews of American merchantmen. "The temptation," a class-conscious Englishman observed, "is greater than human Nature, or rather *their* nature can be expected to withstand." [33] These men, patriotic onshore Britains believed, could not be granted immunity from service in the crusade against Napoleon, and the threat of recapture must be held over the heads of other seamen tempted to desert from the Royal Navy to American vessels. Unless impressment continued, the Royal Navy's strength was bound to evaporate.

America's bitterest enemies, James Stephen among them, recognized that impressment humiliated the United States, particularly since naval officers often acted capriciously or cruelly toward crews mustered for their inspection. No responsible Englishman justified the forced enlistment of native Americans, although ministers often permitted Admiralty bureaucrats and naval commanders to evade requests for the release of Americans. On the other hand, nobody of importance save Cobbett favored ending impressment, although in 1806 the Ministry of All the Talents considered sharply limiting impressment in return for firm American commitments on the return of deserters. After criticizing excesses committed by the navy, Sir William Scott declared that "the Right

[32] Christopher Lloyd, ed., *The Keith Papers*, III, Navy Records Society, *Publications*, Vol. XCVI (1955), p. 155; *Edinburgh Review*, XLI (1824), 161; Lyman to Madison, Oct. 23, 1807, Consular Letters, London, Vol. IX.

[33] *Edinburgh Review*, XLI, 160; Jackson to ———, Sept. 22, 1809, Francis James Jackson MSS, Public Record Office (FO 353/58–61), FO 353/61.

itself cannot be departed from; and being as clear in its principles, as it is in importance in its purposes, must neither be surrendered nor enervated by . . . negotiations that may affect its utility." Even Alexander Baring opposed modifications, and the *Edinburgh Review*, otherwise a critic of governmental policy toward America, spoke of the "right which we undoubtedly possess of reclaiming runaway seamen." [34]

Englishmen believed impressment both imperatively required and easily justified. It had existed at least since Queen Anne's reign, most European states either practiced or recognized it, and the Americans had usually protested against specific incidents rather than the general principle since the first impressment of American citizens at the time of the Nootka Sound controversy. Americans did not deny the right of search when applied to goods. How could they question, the *Quarterly Review* asked, that "the right of search for seamen is precisely of the same nature as that for goods contraband of war. It is an instrument, as ancient as the navy itself, . . . perfectly conformable to the law of nations." Englishmen also pointed out that the United States encouraged British tars to forget their duty to king and country ("a damning evidence of American depravity," one magazine called this seduction) and therefore should not complain if press gangs sought to recover them. In 1813 Lord Castlereagh told the House of Commons the ministry insisted upon impressment not for the purpose of acquiring American seamen but for "the much broader and more important one of guaranteeing herself from being deprived of her own." Law and equity justified her, Castlereagh asserted.[35]

Only rarely did Englishmen express nagging doubts about the justice of the practice or justify it in terms of power alone. Never did they suggest that American press gangs might search British ships for wayward American citizens. The *Annual Register* once

[34] Stephen to Liverpool, private and confidential, March 25, 1814, MSS of the first and second Earls of Liverpool, British Museum (Add. MSS 38190–38489, 38564–38581), Add. MSS 38257; Scott to Harrowby, Sept. 20, 1804, FO 5/104; Baring, *op. cit.*, p. 100; *Edinburgh Review*, XX (1812), 455. At the same time both Baring and the *Edinburgh Review* urged great care in the exercise of this undoubted right.

[35] *Quarterly Review* (London), VII (1812), 17–18; *Gentleman's Magazine* (London), Vol. LXXVIII (1807), Part I, p. 180; *Hansard*, XXIV, 601–602.

scoffed at American appeals to "natural law—the principles of morality" since these must be "almost ridiculous" until all nations agreed to observe them; until then Britain must fully exploit her "preponderating power at sea." [36] Although they came close to the truth, such arguments were not used nearly so frequently as they were in justifying new departures in the field of commercial regulations.

Predictably enough, Federalists often accepted British arguments. Sometimes they emphasized that all Europe tolerated the practice or, more hopelessly, that America could not hope to end it even by war.[37] More often, however, they stressed the argument that Britain had a right to recover those who deserted British service. Luther Martin argued that America, by receiving English deserters in her ships, became the aggressor in events culminating in the British attack upon the U.S.S. *Chesapeake*. Dr. George Logan, working for peace as he had during the Franco-American quarrel a decade before, told his friend Madison that the United States had no right to erect "a sanctuary for fugitives," particularly so long as it insisted upon punishing deserters from its own military forces. The *Columbian Centinel* pronounced unjust the "AT-TEMPT to make American merchant ships an asylum for English, Scotch, and Irish runaway seamen," and warned that the recruitment of foreigners not only deprived natives of employment but threatened to involve America in a war for the interest of scum who deserted their own flags for the Stars and Stripes.[38] While there is no indication that such arguments convinced a majority of Americans, Federalists did create doubt in many minds and perhaps delayed exploitation of the impressment issue until just before the declaration of war in 1812.

The American government did not deny Britain's claim to her own seamen. Jefferson and Madison were prepared to tolerate impressment as long as it took place in British ports and was applied

[36] *Annual Register, 1810* (London, 1812), pp. 258–259.

[37] *Columbian Centinel* (Boston), July 25, Nov. 4, 1807.

[38] Luther Martin (*pseud.* Vindex), *The Honest Politician, Part I* (Baltimore, 1808), p. 36; George Logan to Madison, Jan. 10, 1810, Madison MSS; *Columbian Centinel*, Dec. 9, 1807.

solely to British subjects, even though they might be serving in American ships. In 1807 Madison argued with some justice that, since almost all ships eventually visited England, all that was required of Britain was patience.[39] Britain felt that she could not afford patience, and since the 1790's she had been impressing seamen on the high seas. All American governments challenged the legality of this practice. They recognized the right of search when used to seek out contraband or military personnel of the enemy, but they denied that the same right justified search for British seamen. The claimed right was made worse by the means of executing it, Americans declared. "That an officer from a foreign ship should pronounce any person he pleased, on board an American ship on the high seas, not to be an American Citizen, but a British subject, & carry his interested decision on the most important of all questions to a freeman, into execution on the spot," Madison complained, "is anomalous in principle, . . . grievous in practice, and . . . abominable in abuse."[40]

While Britain claimed no right to impress American seamen, she refused to admit that American naturalization relieved an emigrant of obligations to his homeland. An American law of 1802 authorized naturalization only five years after immigration. The United States insisted that naturalization conferred full rights of citizenship, absolving new citizens from former obligations, although, as Federalists and Englishmen frequently emphasized, American courts often denied the right of American citizens to abandon their allegiance and Congress never passed legislation to the contrary. Some Americans, among them Oliver Ellsworth and Rufus King, maintained that naturalization merely doubled a man's obligations. In King's words, "Naturalization when it confers new Rights, does not, and cannot dissolve, old duties—the Performance of which within his own, or a common Jurisdiction, the former sovereign may compel." The United States government, however, maintained the contrary as far as those who as-

---

[39] Erskine #5 to Howick, Feb. 2, 1807, FO 5/52. For a review of American theory on this question, see Zimmerman, *op. cit.*, pp. 19–21, 25–26.
[40] Madison to Joy, May 22, 1807, Madison MSS.

sumed American citizenship were concerned. In doing so it challenged British practice. Thousands of former Englishmen were claimed as citizens by both countries. Many served on ships that might be boarded at any time by British officers, for of the nearly 11,000 naturalized seamen registered with American papers in 1805 an overwhelming majority had been born in Britain. Boarding officers only too often failed to show much concern for niceties of legal theory, particularly in questions of citizenship, and John Quincy Adams was probably fairly near the mark when he claimed that three-quarters of those impressed had been born in America. Still, even officers who exercised restraint were bound to impress seamen claimed by the United States as citizens. Sharply contrasting views of allegiance created a large area in which disagreement was not only possible but inevitable.[41]

These opposing definitions, a tendency on both sides to doctor figures for political purposes, and delayed and incomplete reports make it extremely difficult to establish the precise dimensions of flight from British service on the one hand and impressment on the other. Rough estimates are possible, however. In 1812 the Admiralty claimed that at least 20,000 Englishmen were serving in the American merchant marine. Earlier Gallatin had estimated that about 9,000 Englishmen (English even by American definition) served under the American flag. In other words, about one-half of the able-bodied seamen serving on ships engaged in foreign trade were British. The Secretary of the Treasury calculated that the Americans recruited about 2,500 Englishmen each year.[42]

[41] King to Peter B. Porter [?], Dec. 10, 1811, King MSS, Vol. XIII; report of Secretary of State Monroe, Feb. 19, 1813, *American State Papers. Class IV. Commerce and Navigation* (2 vols.; Washington, 1832–1834), I, 968; John Quincy Adams, *A Letter to the Hon. Harrison Gray Otis . . . on the Present State of Our National Affairs* (Salem, 1808), p. 13; I-Mien Tsiang, *The Question of Expatriation in America Prior to 1907*, Johns Hopkins University Studies in Historical and Political Science, Series LX, no. 3 (Baltimore, 1942), pp. 32–40. Zimmerman, *op. cit.*, pp. 274–275, notes that only 400 applications for release were refused on grounds of British citizenship, but this figure fails to include hundreds who reluctantly accepted the King's bounty after serving some time, or in some other way provided the navy with an excuse for denying discharge. It is impossible to determine with any degree of accuracy how many impressed seamen could actually be claimed as citizens by both nations.

[42] Unsigned memorandum, "Impressment of American Seamen," Feb. 21, 1812,

Although self-imposed American restrictions on foreign commerce reduced recruitment after 1807 and even drove many foreigners, and native Americans as well, back to British employ,[43] it seems a fair guess that except during 1808 and 1809 at least 10,000 English sailors served in American ships. The Royal Navy needed about this many new men every year to maintain its strength at existing levels.

In his last report on impressment, in January, 1812, Secretary of State Monroe claimed that 6,257 Americans had been impressed since 1803. Almost every War Hawk journal printed this figure in boldface type. Yet this was little more than a rough estimate arrived at by totaling applications for the release of impressed seamen made by the American agent at London, the only channel officially recognized by the Admiralty. Monroe's report included only 200 cases not raised at London, entirely omitted 802 applications made by the agents in 1811, and failed to note that no report had been received for the last quarter of 1810. On the other hand the reports, and consequently Monroe's summary, included hundreds of duplicate applications and many others made on a more or less *pro forma* basis without presenting an iota of proof of American citizenship.[44] In a rough way these factors probably canceled one another out, leaving the total number of fairly reasonable applications at about 6,500 but ignoring instances in which a seaman

FO 5/104; Gallatin memorandum, April 13, 1807, Rives Collection; Gallatin to Jefferson, April 16, 1807, Henry Adams, ed., *The Writings of Albert Gallatin* (3 vols.; Philadelphia, 1879), I, 336; Pickering to Jackson, April 8, 1812, Timothy Pickering MSS, Massachusetts Historical Society, Vol. XIV; *Report of the Committee of the House of Representatives of Massachusetts, on the Subject of Impressed Seamen* (Boston, 1813), *passim*; Louis Simond, *Journal of a Tour and Residence in Great Britain, during the Years 1810 and 1811* (2 vols.; New York, 1815), I, 253.

[43] The number of naturalized seamen registered with the American government dropped from 11,000 in 1805 to 1,100 in 1808, the year of the Embargo. In 1809 there were 9,000 registrations. Succeeding years saw a renewed falling off, but the figures are incomplete. Report of Secretary of State Monroe, Feb. 19, 1813, *ASPC&N*, I, 968.

[44] Zimmerman, *op. cit.*, pp. 256, 267; Samuel Taggart, *Mr. Taggart's Address to His Constituents, on the Subject of Impressments* (Washington, 1813), p. 18. The *pro forma* nature of many requests is revealed in various reports by Madison and Robert Smith printed in *ASPFR*, II, 776–798; III, 36–45, 348. Zimmerman, *op. cit.*, p. 266, argues that duplications were unimportant, but this statement is extremely doubtful.

found it impossible to make his plight known to American representatives.

Federalists and Englishmen denied that anywhere near 6,257 Americans had been impressed. Working from Monroe's figures and wringing the errors from them, a Massachusetts congressman purported to show that Britain had impressed far less than 800 bona fide Americans. In 1813 a legislative committee in Massachusetts similarly assailed the official figures, gathered evidence from 51 shipowners purporting to show that only a dozen Americans out of thousands in their employ had been impressed, and even had the temerity to estimate that no more than 100 Americans had been impressed altogether. Federalists also emphasized Britain's willing release of those few Americans impressed by impetuous naval officers and expressed amazement that, when perhaps so large a proportion of American crews was British, there had not been far more vigorous impressment.[45] British claims were less extreme than those of their American friends. Even the Admiralty admitted that approximately 1,000 Americans had been impressed, and in 1813 Castlereagh fixed upon 1,600 or 1,700. After the War of 1812 the British released 1,800 seamen who had been impressed, and this number of course did not include those who had escaped, died, or been released earlier. Since just under 2,000 Americans were ordered released as a result of intervention at London before 1812, we may settle upon 3,800 as the rock-bottom figure, unchallengeable even on the basis of British calculations and British definitions of citizenship.[46] Beyond that it is impossible to go with any certainty, although it may well be that the widely advertised 6,257 actually reflected something near the truth.

The number of seamen impressed might well have been much larger. Because naval expansion virtually ceased after Trafalgar, the practice was not pushed so vigorously as in 1804 and 1805. Furthermore, the Ministry of All the Talents, more phil-American

---

[45] Taggart, *op. cit.*, pp. 18–19; *Report on Impressed Seamen*, pp. 10–11 and *passim*.
[46] Admiralty endorsement on Monroe to Foster, June 8, 1812, FO 5/104; *Hansard*, XXIV, 601–602; Clement C. Sawtell, "Impressment of American Seamen by the British," Essex Institute, *Historical Collections*, LXXVI (1940), 327–338; Zimmerman, *op. cit.*, p. 268.

than its predecessor, kept impressment under fairly tight control for months after coming to power in January, 1806. Even William Lyman, the American agent for seamen, admitted that the situation was improving, and as late as November British negotiators felt it possible to claim that the theoretical problem had ceased to have any real meaning.[47] Finally, by reversing the flow of seamen to American ships, the Embargo checked the fairly heavy impressment that had occurred during most of 1807. For some time press gangs relaxed and the Admiralty quite freely released Americans forced into the Royal Navy.

Federalists claimed that impressment was inconsequential from 1808 until 1812. Reports from London do not bear them out, although in the summer of 1811 Lyman reported that far from being impressed many American sailors were actually "on the beach" in British ports. Requests for release, a rough index of activity, ran at the rate of 750 to 1,000 a year from 1809 onward. In May, 1810, Lyman reported increasing press-gang activity, and his successor later asserted that during that summer impressment had been "carried to an extent beyond all former example," at least in British ports. The new agent, Reuben G. Beasley, protested steadily to the Admiralty during the first half of 1812.[48] Lack of active concern at Washington by no means meant the problem had ended.

The incidence of impressment at any given time simply revealed the degree of the Royal Navy's need. The forced enslavement of even a dozen Americans, any number sufficient to show that honest mistakes were not the sole problem, was in principle as important as the impressment of thousands. Daily mustering of crews under the Stars and Stripes by foreign officers and Britain's unwillingness to negotiate an end to the practice showed the incompleteness of

[47] Lyman to Madison, May 22, 1806, Consular Letters, London, Vol. IX; Holland and Auckland to Monroe and Pinkney, Nov. 8, 1806, FO 5/51.

[48] Lyman to Monroe, Aug. 11, 1811, Consular Letters, London, Vol. IX; Zimmerman, *op. cit.*, p. 256; Lyman to Pinkney, May 10, 1810, Consular Letters, London, Vol. IX; Beasley to John W. Croker, Dec. 19, 1811, Admiralty Papers, Public Record Office, Adm 1/3856; Beasley to Monroe, Jan. 21, Feb. 15, June 25, 1812, Consular Letters, London, Vol. IX. One of the few students to challenge the usual view that impressment declined just before the War of 1812 is Patrick C. T. White, "Anglo-American Relations from 1803 to 1815" (unpublished Ph.D. dissertation, University of Minnesota, 1954), p. 146.

American freedom and, as old John Adams argued, suggested that "the spirits of Lord Bute and Lord George Germain [had] risen again at St. James's." [49]

In March, 1806, Jefferson's friend, Judge John Tyler, wrote to him praising the war against Barbary but adding that "while we go to very great lengths to relieve 200 citizens from the shackles imposed by a barbarous nation, we seem to have doubts about the propriety of emancipating 3,000 now in the hands of Great Britain, who is said to be the most civilized nation in the world. . . . But, by the great God of heaven, I had rather not exist as a man or nation than to suffer such violations of the rights and liberty of our citizens." [50] A few Republican legislators, most notably Robert Wright of Maryland, shared Tyler's feelings to the extent of urging that Britain be coerced into abandoning impressment. For the most part, however, Americans seemed not unwilling to tolerate this national degradation. Certainly from the beginning of 1808 until the War Hawk Congress impressment took a back seat to other complaints against Britain. Americans showed more concern for their prosperity than for national rights or the liberty of seamen.

The administration's wavering course certainly did not add to the nation's dignity. John Adams' administration had worked hard to secure the release of American seamen and attempted to negotiate an agreement with Britain for the reciprocal return of deserters which would have made it possible for England to end impressment on the high seas. While steadfastly refusing to admit the legality of impressment, however, the Federalists never risked national humiliation by making a direct challenge they were unprepared to follow up. Not so Jefferson and Madison. In 1806, having made an agreement on impressment a *sine qua non* of any settlement, they rejected a treaty negotiated by Monroe and Pinkney primarily because it passed over the subject in silence. A few months later, on the other hand, they considered surrendering all British seamen in American employ, or at least those who had served less

[49] "The Inadmissible Principles of the King of England's Proclamation . . . ," Charles F. Adams, ed., *Works of Adams*, IX, 315.

[50] John Tyler to Jefferson, March 25, 1806, Lyon G. Tyler, *The Letters and Times of the Tylers*, I (Richmond, 1884), 211–212.

than two years, if only the British would give up impressment. Figures produced by Gallatin showed the American merchant marine unable to stand the loss of men, and Jefferson and Madison dropped the project.[51] After the *Chesapeake* affair the administration united this attack upon a national naval vessel with the quite different issue of impressment from merchantmen, and for a time refused to consider the issues separately. Only a few months later, in negotiations with a special British envoy, they consented to separate the two.[52] After February, 1808, Jefferson and Madison virtually ignored impressment, except to seek the release of individual seamen. Secretaries of state repeatedly directed William Pinkney, the minister at London, to concentrate on commercial rights rather than seamen, and as late as the summer of 1811 the administration scarcely made anything of impressment in its extensive discussions with a new British minister. The feebleness of Republican leaders encouraged Americans to accept impressment as a price of peace, however galling to national pride.

Britain's policy on seamen and on neutral commerce clearly suggested that she considered America a comparatively inconsequential power. Even the concessions occasionally offered were at best partial recognition of American claims, liberal only in that they offered more than English political opinion desired. Other policies reinforced the impression given by the treatment of American ships and crews. Officials in Canada freely communicated with Indians south of the Great Lakes. These officials did not, as the Americans charged, attempt to provoke the tribes to war with the United States. They did, however, seek to make sure, particularly after the war scare following the *Chesapeake* affair in 1807, that if war came the tribes would not fight against England, and they steadily

[51] Gallatin memorandum, April 13, 1807, Rives Collection; Gallatin to Jefferson, April 13, 16, 1807, Thomas Jefferson MSS, Library of Congress; Madison to Gallatin, April 17, 1807, *ibid.*; Jefferson to Madison, April 21, 1807, *ibid.* In his memorandum Gallatin estimated that 67,000 men were in American crews, 42,000 of them in ships engaged in foreign commerce. He estimated 9,000 of the latter to be British, more than one-fifth of the crews and exactly half of the 18,000 able-bodied seamen, the most important component of the crews.

[52] This development may conveniently be followed in Madison's memoranda of his conversations with George H. Rose, the British envoy, in Gaillard Hunt, ed., *The Writings of James Madison* (9 vols.; New York, 1900–1910), VIII, 1–11.

sought to reduce American influence over Indians resident in the United States. Even the selection of ministers to Washington showed Britain's lack of respect. There appeared at the American capital first an untried youth, then a pair of arrogant professionals who acted more like commanders than negotiators, and finally, after a long and contemptuous interlude, a pleasant enough but inept young man of no particular reputation.

In the face of British hauteur the American nation groped weakly toward effective national sovereignty. Commercial warfare failed to vindicate national rights. By reducing importations from Britain it did contribute to a growing campaign to cast off dependence upon Lancashire. In an amusing reversal, Jeffersonians became apostles of autarky. Almost every presidential message on the state of the union congratulated America on the growth of industry, and President Madison even claimed this increase "more than a recompense" for losses suffered by shipowners and exporters. Some Federalists, on the other hand, so far forgot Alexander Hamilton's teachings as to argue that industry threatened the nation's well-being. "Who that has seen the happy state of society throughout our villages," the *Connecticut Courant* asked, "can wish it to be exchanged for the dissipated and effeminate manners and habits, which extensive establishments of manufactures, never fail to bring in their trains?" [53]

Manufacturing developed slowly. In 1810 there were 269 cotton mills and 153 iron furnaces in the United States, most of them very small. The British Board of Trade occasionally showed concern over the growth of American manufacturing, and in 1811, on the basis of reports from the United States, William Cobbett wrote, "To American commerce, . . . now bid adieu, I think forever." Cobbett was premature. Congressmen affected homespun suits ("more wretched Stuff cannot be conceived," the British minister sniffed),[54] newspapers congratulated the nation, and the census of

[53] James D. Richardson, ed., *A Compilation of the Messages and Papers of the Presidents* (Washington, 1897), I, 484–485; *Connecticut Courant* (Hartford), April 6, 1808.

[54] *Cobbett's Register*, XIX (1811), 558; Erskine to Canning, separate, Nov. 12, 1808, FO 5/58.

1810 reflected increasing interest by adding new statistics on manufacturing. However, although American industrial accomplishments foreshadowed the future, they did not substantially reduce present dependence upon Britain.

In literature and the arts American dependence was even more substantial. Already West and Copley had won respect for American painting,[55] but in most other areas there was little of which to boast. Only the most enthusiastic patriot could claim that such accomplishments as Alexander Wilson's study of American ornithology were more than a beginning. The *Portfolio*, America's first literary magazine, was founded in 1801, but it was a pale copy of English models, pale at least in everything except its criticism of Republicanism. Americans preferred to receive their reading material from Britain, devoured accounts of English travelers in America for information about their own land, and accepted British standards. Samuel F. B. Morse, discussing alleged French influence upon the United States with a member of Parliament, rightly answered that British influence predominated. "As a proof," Morse reported to his parents, "I urged the universal prevalence of English fashions . . . and English manners and customs; . . . the neglect with which they treated their own literary productions on account of the strong prejudice in favor of English works; that everything, in short, was enhanced in its value by having attached to it the name English." [56]

Patriots thought this dependence undignified. Noah Webster and Joel Barlow, one a Federalist and the other a Jeffersonian, agreed that cultural independence was required to reinforce political separation from Britain. "I consider this species of dependence as extremely prejudicial, as it regards our political interest," Webster wrote to Barlow. "In truth, we shall always be in leading strings till we resort to original writers and original principles in-

---

[55] Copley's reputation gained him a commission to paint, for £1,650, a group portrait of the Prince Regent and some friends. The Regent, however, refused to pay Copley, who was left with possession of the portrait. Arthur Aspinall, ed., *The Letters of King George IV*, I (Cambridge, Eng., 1938), 262n.

[56] Morse to Mr. and Mrs. Jedediah Morse, Jan. 1, 1813, Edward L. Morse, ed., *Samuel F. B. Morse, His Letters and Journals* (2 vols.; Cambridge, 1914), I, 90–91.

stead of taking upon trust what English writers please to give us."
In 1806 Webster published the first fruit of his own lexicographical
endeavors, *A Compendious Dictionary of the English Language,*
designed not only to emphasize American language but also, by
questioning the authority of the great Dr. Johnson, to show that
the United States could challenge British scholarship. The next
year Webster's friend Barlow brought out the *Columbiad,* the
culmination of twenty-five years of work to produce an American
epic poem. Robert Fulton, to whom Barlow dedicated his work,
heartily praised the ambitious undertaking: "The poem will be for
ever quoted as proof of American Genius—the printing will shew
our perfection in that art, and the manner in which it is gotten up
. . . will I hope shew the Europeans that there is some taste in
America and will be more." [57] Webster's work was really only an
introduction to later, more important studies, and Barlow's epic
bored many who praised its patriotism; yet these were the major
productions of American writers in the years just before the War
of 1812. A more effective campaign for independence awaited the
end of the war.

British reviews laughed at American cultural pretensions. An
exception was the *Edinburgh Review,* politically the most favorably inclined of all major English journals, which brutally criticized the volumes of Thomas Ashe and other British travelers
hostile to the United States. But even the *Edinburgh Review* generally assailed the work of American writers. A review of Chief
Justice John Marshall's biography of George Washington suggested that such poor treatment of a noble American theme clearly
demonstrated "the poverty of . . . [American] literary attain-
ments." The magazine saw little merit in the *Columbiad,* explained
its faults as the natural consequence of the poet's work in a country
with no literary tradition or audience, and condescendingly added
that, if Barlow worked a few years in Britain, he might aspire to
equality with the lesser English poets. In sum, the *Edinburgh Re-*

[57] Webster to Barlow, Nov. 12, 1807, Charles B. Todd, *Life and Letters of Joel
Barlow, LL.D.* (New York, 1886), pp. 247–248; Fulton to Trumbull, Dec. 16, 1806,
Col. John Trumbull MSS, Yale University Library.

*view* believed that the "destruction of her whole literature would not occasion so much regret as we feel for the loss of a few leaves from an antient classic." [58] Truthful though the comments of the *Edinburgh Review* and her even more strident competitors might be, or perhaps because they came so near the truth, they wounded American sensibilities.

In many ways, then, the young American felt the sovereignty of his nation challenged and her character insulted by Britain. Some challenges suggested an inferiority of status most important in the realm of the spirit. It would be ridiculous to suggest that the impressment of American seamen or the interruption of American trade did not pose a material challenge, to argue that the loss of thousands of men and hundreds of ships had only a symbolic importance. These very tangible pressures played a fundamental part in the coming of war. Still, since the nation could, after all, prosper despite foreign interference, it is most important to recognize the moral implications of the challenges America faced. Britain treated the new republic as if Yorktown had been an incomplete victory. To many, like the citizens on the Mobile, independence seemed almost a dream.

A few months after a British frigate attacked U.S.S. *Chesapeake*, the Speaker of the House of Representatives wrote: "It is highly Interesting to this Nation to remain in a State of peace, if it can be done on honourable Terms; but too much Blood and Treasure have been Expended in the acquisition of our Independence and importance as a Nation, for us to Relinquish the one, or Suffer the Other to be tarnished." Led by an irenic president, the nation chose what appeared to be an honorable alternative to war. Thanks to many things—the weaknesses of Jefferson and Madison, the self-ishness of some citizens, the cowardice and the disloyalty of others—the alternative road led only to further humiliation. "Heretofore," an eager young War Hawk, John C. Calhoun, wrote in 1812, "the conductors of our affairs, have attempted to avoid and remove difficulties by a sort of political management. They thought, that national honor and interest could both be maintained

[58] *Edinburgh Review*, XIII (1808), 148–170; XV (1810), 24–40, 446.

and respected . . . by commercial arrangements and negotiations. . . . This might suit an inconsiderable nation. . . . Experience has proved it improper for us. Its effects have been distrust at home and contempt abroad." [59] These remarks could as aptly have been made in 1805 or 1807 or at any time after Jefferson led the nation to risk its honor by pressing claims that only war could vindicate. Not until Calhoun's day, however, did the truth of these sentiments seem apparent to the President and a substantial part of the Congress. Until then, America sought without success to preserve her honor simultaneously with her peace.

[59] Joseph B. Varnum to Plumer, Dec. 6, 1807, William Plumer MSS, Library of Congress; Calhoun to Dr. James Macbride, Feb. 16 [17?], 1812, Robert L. Meriwether, ed., *The Papers of John C. Calhoun*, I (Columbia, S.C., 1959), 90–91.

# IV

## THE TREATY OF 1806

"Oh, my country! How I leave my country!" With these words, William Pitt died in his rented villa on Putney Heath shortly before sunrise on January 23, 1806. The expiring Chancellor's concern was understandable. He had just received news of Napoleon's crushing victory at Austerlitz. Despite Nelson's success at Trafalgar the war seemed no nearer a victorious conclusion than it had when Pitt drove Henry Addington from power in 1804. As a war leader the great Pitt left much to be desired. Furthermore, he stood alone at the summit of his party. His energetic disciples—Liverpool, Canning, Castlereagh, and Perceval among them—had not yet the prestige to succeed the master. Who, then, was to replace the man who had dominated English politics for a quarter of a century?

While in theory the choice lay with the King, for the moment the answer was virtually forced upon him. No single leader could replace Pitt, but a coalition of Foxites and Grenvilles might. Reluctantly the King turned to his old enemy, Charles James Fox, and to Lord Grenville; from the royal point of view each had dangerous ideas on the Irish issue, but at least they could keep the government going. Within a week the new ministry, dubbed by supporters the Ministry of All the Talents, entered upon its uneasy reign.

All the Talents—a euphemism, and an incomplete euphemism at that. The talented supporters of Pitt had no share in the new government, although the ministry extended feelers to Bathurst and, later in the year, to Canning. The government rested upon the Fox, Grenville, and Sidmouth factions, and in the distribution of offices a balance among these groups was far more important than ability. Grenville, more acceptable to George III than Fox, headed the ministry. Fox took the Foreign Office and installed his able lieutenant, Lord Howick (soon Earl Grey), at the Admiralty. Sidmouth and his conservative friend Ellenborough received cabinet seats. All in all it was not a strong ministry. Grenville was tired, Fox ill, Sidmouth unpopular, and the others were untried.

Most important of all, Fox and Grenville disagreed over almost every major issue of policy except Ireland. How should the war be fought? How financed? How far should Britain go in negotiations with Napoleon? These and other issues could be answered only by compromise, not by real decision. While nothing indicates that Grenville and Fox clashed over American policy, a Pittite pamphleteer was certainly correct in a more general sense when he commented upon the commission appointed to negotiate with Monroe and Pinkney: "The American commission was an epitome of the cabinet; in neither was there a combination, but a collision of talents. Every measure was a compromise. . . . The result was a total want of principle." [1]

At the Foreign Office Fox found only fifteen subordinates to help him face multitudinous problems. Adjustment to Austerlitz and the exploration of chances of peace with Napoleon required most attention, but he could not ignore American relations. Events of the past year, notably the publication of *War in Disguise*, the *Essex* decision, and the implications of Trafalgar, had brought

[1] Thomas P. Courtenay (*pseud.* Decius), *Observations on the American Treaty* (London, 1808), p. 92.

affairs to a pitch unknown since the crisis preceding the Jay treaty. As far as the press of business and the parlous state of his health would permit, Fox had to give attention to the American problem. The fabled friend of American revolutionists, he seemed ideally suited for the task of making a settlement. Beside him stood his colleague, Grenville, architect of the first Anglo-American *rapprochement* a decade earlier.

The beginning was promising. The American minister, James Monroe, informed Washington that he had high hopes of fair treatment from the new secretary, who had even promised to suspend seizures under the *Essex* precedent. Fox's lack of information prevented detailed discussions until April, but even this delay did not discourage Monroe. In the United States the administration permitted its kept journal to inform the people that the "past lives [of the members of the new Cabinet] are a pledge that they will be animated by principles of honor, of justice, and of reciprocity." The British secretary of legation, Augustus Foster, who although he had grown up among the Foxite coterie feared too great concession to the United States, wrote to his mother: "I hope they will keep old England firm; these Wretches speculate on our Debasement, & consequent Compliance with all their unreasonable demands." [2]

The new ministry did not plan to debase itself before Americans. It did see the need for some gestures, some concessions. Symbolically, Fox recalled the minister at Washington, Anthony Merry, who had alienated all but extreme Federalists, and sent in his place David M. Erskine, the thirty-year-old son of the famous liberal lawyer and present lord chancellor. Young Erskine had no diplomatic experience and, at Washington from 1806 to 1809, never showed either perceptivity or strength. His American wife, a chunky damosel somewhat given to unusually deep décolletage, and his father's liberalism (young Erskine had the motto, "Trial

[2] Monroe #40 to Madison, Jan. 28, 1806, Department of State Archives, National Archives, Despatches, Great Britain, Vol. XII; Monroe to Madison, private, March 11, 1806, *ibid.*; Monroe #46 to Madison, April 20, 1806, *ibid; National Intelligencer* (Washington), March 29, 1806; Foster to Lady Elizabeth Foster, May 3, 1806, Augustus J. Foster MSS, Library of Congress.

by Jury," painted on his coach) gained him a favorable reception. He restored good relations between the legation and the American government, partly because, to Foster's disgust, he affected the informality of Jefferson's court, but principally because he did not challenge American positions. The President and the Secretary of State liked Erskine; in this sense he served Fox's purpose.[3]

In another gesture, the new Fox-Grenville ministry introduced legislation to regularize the trade of American ships with the British West Indies. This trade, a direct violation of the Navigation Acts, had been permitted by local executive orders for years because of the wartime shortage of British shipping. In April, 1806, Lord Grenville's friend Auckland, who believed the extension of American commerce should be encouraged, introduced a government bill regularizing and even extending this permission. His proposal soon came under attack from many Pittites who had endorsed similar concessions in the 1790's. George Rose, in particular, spoke at length about the sanctity of the Navigation Acts and the superfluity of conciliating a weak, contemptible nation like the United States. Sir William Grant (now in his politician's role) professed himself willing to meet reasoned arguments or even "the last resort of nations to enforce their will—the thunder of cannon," but he opposed concession to a nation wielding the unfair weapon of economic coercion. Not until July, and after a final session lasting until half past two in the morning, did the ministry secure passage of the American Intercourse Act.[4]

Another, and the most important, of Charles James Fox's gestures to the United States, necessarily disguised because of the growing obduracy of British opinion, fell woefully short of the mark. This was the Order in Council of May 16, 1806, more commonly known as Fox's Blockade, a device designed to supersede

[3] James Hillhouse to Rebecca Hillhouse, Jan. 2, 1807, Hillhouse Family MSS, Yale University Library; entry of March 2, 1807, Everett S. Brown, ed., *William Plumer's Memorandum of Proceedings in the United States Senate, 1803–1807* (New York, 1923), p. 635; Foster to Lady Elizabeth Foster, Nov. 1, 1807, Foster MSS.

[4] Auckland to Grenville, April 17, 18, 23, May 17, 1806, Boconnoc MSS (Papers of William Wyndham Grenville, Baron Grenville), Lostwithiel, Cornwall, Lord Auckland 1806; Grenville to Auckland, May 16, 1806, *ibid.; Hansard*, VI, 595–597, 834–839, 1031; VII, 94–100, 336–347, 686–729, 969–1010.

the *Essex* case as the predominant regulation of neutral commerce. The Foreign Secretary disapproved of the *Essex* decision, not least because it replaced easily applied tests with complicated evidential problems certain to provoke controversy. In the early months of the new ministry seizures declined, either because of quiet hints from ministers or because their reputation as moderates enjoined caution upon naval commanders, but the basic problem still remained.

In the spring of 1806 Fox and Auckland began to search for some device to regularize the position of the American reëxport trade or to replace the *Essex* decision. One suggestion, endorsed if not initiated by the King's Advocate, Sir John Nicholl, was to establish a system of certificates by which British consuls in America could affirm that cargoes from the United States were truly neutral property. By this method, in one stroke the Rule of the War of 1756 would be preserved, yet the Americans could carry on an extensive trade with France in colonial produce. This system smacked too much of the French example and would certainly have been considered an affront by the United States, since it openly demonstrated distrust of American governmental procedures. Thus, although at first the suggestion interested the Cabinet, Lord Grenville soon insisted upon dropping it.[5] The idea of a test of some sort, like that of the *Polly* decision but perhaps more rigorous, survived to arise again during the Monroe-Pinkney negotiations.

This tack temporarily abandoned, the government chose to go ahead with another scheme. It declared the entire northern coast of Europe from Brest to the Elbe under blockade but added that this blockade would be rigorously enforced only from the Seine to Ostend; elsewhere, neutral ships could visit enemy ports if they did not carry contraband or goods owned by the enemy, and if they neither came from nor were bound for other enemy ports. By this

[5] Auckland to Howick, private, May 3, 1806, Charles Grey, Second Earl Grey, MSS, The Prior's Kitchen, Durham University, from 1st Ld. Auckland; Nicholl to Auckland, May 9, 1806, William Eden, Baron Auckland, MSS, British Museum (Add. MSS 34412–34471, 45728–45730), Add. MSS 34456; Grenville to Auckland, May 9, 1806, *ibid.*; Grenville to Auckland, n.d. *ibid.*, Add. MSS 34457, fols. 194–195; Nicholl to ———, n.d., *ibid.*, fol. 198.

measure the government gained praise from some, like the *Times*, who demanded vigorous action against the enemy, for the decree extended the areas under blockade. At the same time Fox and his colleagues intended to imply that the more inclusive but indefinite principle of Grant's decision would not be applied to American ships bound for enemy ports outside the critical zone along the English Channel. As Lord Grenville put it, "With respect to America . . . you open to her for the carriage of Colonial Produce (whether the Enemy's or not, for after *actual* importation into the U.S. they are indistinguishable) not only the ports of the Atlantic & Mediterr$^n$. but also those of Holland & Flanders, & I think in the present state of commerce it will be right so to do." [6]

Unfortunately, although Fox's Blockade succeeded in reassuring Englishmen that its authors intended to fight the war with vigor, it failed in the equally important object of conciliating the United States. Probably because he feared an outcry from his countrymen, Fox withdrew an earlier promise to abandon the *Essex* principle explicitly. In Monroe's words, the new decree "imposed the suspension desired, but in a manner w$^h$. seemed as if it was intended to mask the object from view." [7] This concealed abandonment of the British position satisfied neither American public opinion nor the Jefferson administration. For years the United States had protested against blockades not maintained by cruising squadrons actually in the vicinity. Now, from the very mouth of a ministry nominally friendly, there issued a new order extending blockades over hundreds of miles of coast. Whether Fox's Blockade was ever enforced in the traditional fashion, or whether it remained a purely nominal blockade, became the subject of debate in later years. In 1806 America refused to accept the argument that the new order was simply another decree of the usual type. All but the most partisan Federalists refused to believe that even the Royal Navy could maintain a blockade according to the old standards along such an extensive stretch of coastline.

A fortnight after announcing Fox's Blockade, the British gov-

[6] Grenville to Auckland, n.d., Auckland MSS, Add. MSS 34457, fol. 195.
[7] Monroe #49 to Madison, May 20, 1806, Despatches, Great Britain, Vol. XII.

ernment received jarring news from New York that destroyed any hope, however unfounded, that the new decree would mollify the United States. Within American territorial waters a carelessly aimed shot from H.M.S. *Leander*, fired to warn a vessel that neglected to come to, struck and killed a member of the crew, John Pierce. With Pierce's publicly exposed body to whet their temper, mobs roamed the streets of New York, a British flag was burned, and consul Barclay, who deplored his own navy's action, feared for a time that his house would be burned and he himself seized as a hostage. British officers on shore actually were arrested but subsequently secretly released by city authorities. (The British squadron commander, Captain Henry Whitby, later reported he had been ready to use force to recover them.) Federalist speakers emphasized that Jefferson's neglect of the navy encouraged British insults, but all parties agreed that Pierce must be avenged. The *Aurora* and the Richmond *Enquirer* even talked of a declaration of war.[8]

Had adequate naval forces been available, Jefferson and Madison might have taken strong action. As it was, they felt forced to fall back upon those favorite weapons of Jeffersonian diplomacy, a proclamation and a protest.[9] The President directed the three British ships off New York to leave American waters. To enforce compliance he cut off their supplies. At the same time the administration instructed James Monroe to demand that Britain court-martial Captain Whitby. Then Jefferson and Madison sat back to wait, hoping they had satisfied the minimum demands of American anger and that the British government would offer atonement for Whitby's action.

Fox did his best to meet American expectations. When first reports of the killing reached London, the Foreign Secretary sent

[8] *New-York Evening Post*, April 26, 1806; Barclay to Merry, April 27, 1806, George L. Rives, ed., *Selections from the Correspondence of Thomas Barclay* (New York, 1894), pp. 232–233; Captain Henry Whitby to Captain John P. Beresford, May 6, 1806, enclosed in Beresford to William Marsden, May 19, 1806, Admiralty Papers, Public Record Office, Adm 1/496; *New-York Evening Post*, April 28, 1806; *Aurora* (Philadelphia), April 29, 1806; *Enquirer* (Richmond), May 6, 1806.

[9] Cabinet memorandum, May 1, 1806, Paul L. Ford, ed., *The Writings of Thomas Jefferson* (10 vols.; New York, 1892–1899), I, 315–316.

word to Madison that his government deeply regretted Pierce's death. This attitude contrasted markedly with that of the British press, which blamed the Americans for the incident and virtually dared them to make it a *casus belli*.[10] The ministry ordered Captain Whitby home to face investigation a month and a half before James Monroe presented the formal complaint against him. By this time Fox lay on his deathbed at a ducal establishment in Chiswick. One of his last acts—or one taken in his name—was to inform the American minister that Whitby had been recalled.[11] Unfortunately, this could not wipe away American memories of a fatal invasion of their national waters.

After the beginning of the new ministry, as Fox sought to restore harmony to Anglo-American relations without affronting the unruly brass players under Stephen, a reedy obbligato wafted across the Atlantic from the United States. The notes seemed confused, for the leading wood winds declined to instruct their colleagues, but the central theme of commercial warfare clearly emerged. By cutting off Britain's market, perhaps merely by threatening to do so, America would compel England to accept her demands. This was good Republican doctrine upon which almost all agreed,

[10] Fox #5 to Merry, June 6, 1806, Bernard Mayo, ed., *Instructions to the British Ministers to the United States, 1791–1812*, American Historical Association, *Annual Report, 1936*, III (Washington, 1941), 223. The London *Courier's* comments (June 3, 1806) were characteristic: "If, availing itself, or influenced by that popular feeling, it [the American government] choose to push matters to extremities, we must inform it that Great Britain contemplates a contest with America without dread or dismay."

[11] Marsden to Admiral George C. Berkeley, June 22, 1806, enclosed in Marsden to Sir Francis Vincent, Sept. 6, 1806, Foreign Office Archives, Public Record Office, FO 5/51; Monroe to Fox, Aug. 4, 1806, Despatches, Great Britain, Vol. XII; Fox to Monroe, Sept. 8, 1806, *ibid.*; Monroe #51 to Madison, Sept. 13, 1806, *ibid.*, enclosing the exchange of notes with Fox. Lord Howick, Fox's successor, hoped it would be possible to acquit Whitby without affronting the United States, or at most to convict him on a minor charge. At Monroe's request the trial was delayed to permit witnesses to come from America. When it finally took place in April, 1807, the court-martial held that the charges against Whitby were not proved, to the substantial discomfiture of the United States. In 1808 Whitby even had the effrontery to ask compensation for the sea pay he had lost during the interval between his recall and his acquittal. Howick to Grenville, Sept. 20, 21, 1806, Walter Fitzpatrick, ed., *Report on the Manuscripts of J. B. Fortescue, Esq., Preserved at Dropmore* (10 vols.; London: Historical Manuscripts Commission, 1892–1927), VIII, 345, 350; Monroe #46 to Madison, April 20, 1807, Despatches, Great Britain, Vol. XII; Whitby to Canning, Dec. 15, 1808, FO 5/61.

but the way in which the pressure was to be applied caused serious disagreement. On January 24, 1806, Representative William Gregg of Pennsylvania introduced resolutions for a complete ban on imports from Britain. Not until the middle of April, and then only in emasculated form, did legislation emerge from the congressional mill.

Internal Republican schisms and weak leadership caused the delay, for the Federalists decided to observe silence during the debates.[12] Gregg's resolutions were soon followed by far milder ones introduced by Gallatin's brother-in-law, Joseph Nicholson. The *National Intelligencer* approved first one set and then the other, and rumors flew through Washington that the President preferred Gregg's to Nicholson's, or vice versa. Jefferson, who almost certainly privately favored the less effective but less risky Nicholson resolutions, kept silent. John Randolph rightly complained that "it is not for the master and mate . . . in bad weather, to go below, and leave the management of the ship to the cook and cabin boy." [13]

Since cooks and cabin boys disagreed, this lack of administration leadership became particularly important. Representative Gregg ("a MisRepresentative," Gallatin allegedly called him [14]) argued for a strong course. Such action, he and allies like Jacob Crowninshield argued, would show America's determination far better than half measures, might even cause England to back down before the ban went into effect. In any event, the more powerful the weapon the quicker the cure; Britain would be almost immediately forced to her knees by the sudden loss of the entire American market. To warnings that action of this sort might provoke British retaliation, Representative Gregg replied: "Great Britain is . . . too well

[12] Quincy to Oliver Wolcott, Jr., Feb. 3, 1806, Wolcott Family MSS, Connecticut Historical Society, Vol. XX.

[13] Bayard to Richard Bassett, Jan. 31, 1806, Elizabeth Donnan, ed., *Papers of James A. Bayard, 1796–1815*, American Historical Association, *Annual Report, 1913*, II (Washington, 1915), 165; *National Intelligencer*, March 19, 26, 1806; entry of Feb. 25, 1806, Charles F. Adams, ed., *Memoirs of John Quincy Adams* (12 vols.; Philadelphia, 1874–1877), I, 415; entry of March 8, 1806, Brown, *op. cit.*, p. 446; *Annals*, 9th Cong., 1st sess., pp. 771–772.

[14] Richard B. Davis, ed. *Jeffersonian America: Notes on the United States of America . . . by Sir Augustus John Foster, Bart.* (San Marino, 1954), p. 236.

acquainted with her own interest, to persevere in this lawless system at the hazard of losing customers, whose annual purchases of her manufactures and other merchandise exceeds . . . thirty millions of dollars." [15]

Republicans more cautious than Gregg disputed his predictions. This group included Nicholson, Gallatin's confidant; John W. Eppes, widower of Jefferson's daughter; and Barnabas Bidwell, a new congressman striving with Jeffersonian assistance to secure influence in the House. These men preferred a selective ban, a mild but definite warning to England to mend her ways before the United States proceeded to harsher measures. They argued that it would be far wiser to forbid the importation only of goods that could neither be obtained elsewhere nor be made in America, for the Treasury vitally needed the duties on many British goods and the ordinary citizen required them for himself. A complete ban would harm the United States more than Britain. But the Nicholson group's chief argument was that the United States dared not run the risk of Gregg's policy. Through all of their speeches runs a steady theme of fear, fear either that any demonstration of vigor would prejudice negotiations at London or, worse, that Britain would reply with sterner measures. What Joseph Nicholson and his followers wanted was to demonstrate to their constituents and to Britain, at the least possible cost, that Congress was determined to defend American rights. As the fat, cynical Federalist, Samuel Taggart, put it, the Republicans believed "something must be done, they don't very well know what, but it is above all necessary to vent our indignation against Britain in some way or other." [16] They had no heart for a fight, and in the end Nicholson even proposed to delay action on his own mild resolutions.

The Gregg resolutions, which at least had the virtue of directness, might have attracted broader support had they not collided

[15] *Annals*, 9th Cong., 1st sess., p. 540. The entire debate appears in this volume, pp. 167–878 *passim*, but Senate speeches are rarely reported at length. Specific references are made here only for direct quotations.

[16] Taggart to Rev. John Taylor, March 12, 1806, George H. Haynes, ed., "Letters of Samuel Taggart, Representative in Congress, 1803–1814," American Antiquarian Society, *Proceedings*, n.s., XXXIII (1923), 189.

with a deep prejudice that tortured many veteran Republicans. Even those who believed America pledged to defend commercial interests often regretted it; in George W. Campbell's words, "it would have been better for the American people, if Government had never given protection to commerce, out of sight of our own territory, or beyond the reach of cannon from our own shores." There was something uncomfortable, if not positively sinful, in hazarding the future of an ideal agricultural society to protect commercial interests, particularly since the controversy might be narrowed even further to a contest for the right to carry on a reëxport trade in non-American produce. Crafty merchants, not honest farmers, benefited from such a trade. In vain did New England Republicans point out that it was impossible to exchange the entire agricultural surplus for specie, that merchants were forced to trade much of it for colonial goods they subsequently reëxported to French dominions. For the sake of national honor, Republicans were ready to rally in defense of American rights; they were not ready to budge beyond the Nicholson resolutions unless propelled by administration pressure. "If the President had any plan, which he would assume the responsibility to propose, I have no doubt of his securing a majority to adopt it," wrote a bitter critic of Jefferson.[17] But no word came from the White House.

Against this background congressional Republicans brawled for more than a month. For two weeks in March, after a long delay during which the Republicans found themselves unable to patch up their differences, debate raged in the House of Representatives. On March 5 and 6, John Randolph delivered magnificent if disjointed speeches, each of them more than two hours long, in which he vilified Jefferson and Madison, warned that commercial warfare would lead to armed conflict, and declared himself unwilling to fight for the reëxport trade:

No, sir, if this great agricultural nation is to be governed by Salem and Boston, New York and Philadelphia, and Baltimore and Norfolk and Charleston, let gentleman come out and say so. . . . I, for one, will not

[17] *Annals*, 9th Cong., 1st sess., pp. 706–707; Pickering to King, Feb. 20, 1806, Rufus King MSS, New-York Historical Society, Vol. XI.

mortgage my property and my liberty, to carry on this trade. . . . It is not for the honest carrying trade of America, but for this mushroom, this fungus of war . . . that the spirit of avaricious traffic would plunge us into war.[18]

"This fungus of war"—Republicans flinched at the phrase. But on this occasion, as so often in the future, Randolph's lash drove them to rally together. Gregg's resolutions were beaten on March 13, but by an overwhelming margin the Republican phalanx passed Nicholson's four days later. Randolph himself abstained, and only about a dozen Republican schismatics, sharing his feeling that agricultural prosperity should not be risked to aid the reëxport trade, joined the Federalist band in opposition.

After the success of Nicholson's resolutions, passage of a bill was largely anticlimactic. Presented on March 25, 1806, the bill listed for exclusion precisely those imports Nicholson had originally suggested: some metal goods, cloth made of hemp or flax, high-priced woolens, glass, finished clothing, and sundry other articles including "beer, ale, and porter." The most important imports from Britain—cottons, cheap woolens, iron and steel—did not appear on the list, and the House beat down attempts to add them. In a further demonstration of fear and leaderlessness, the House agreed to suspend the act until November 15 to allow time for further news from England; perhaps even the threat of lost markets would induce British compliance, or perhaps Fox would arrange a settlement. This last weakening of the act evoked from Randolph one of his most famous passages:

Never in the course of my life have I witnessed such a scene of indignity and inefficiency as this measure holds forth to the world. What is it? A milk-and-water bill, a dose of chicken broth to be taken nine months hence. . . . It is too contemptible to be the object of consideration, or to excite the feelings of the pettiest State in Europe. . . . You cannot do without the next Spring and Fall importations; and you tell your adversary so. . . . [It is] a law which . . . cannot be executed, and than the execution of which nothing is further from the minds of its framers.[19]

Randolph's justifiable scorn availed naught. The House approved the bill, and after a brief delay the Senate concurred. Although an

[18] *Annals*, 9th Cong., 1st sess., p. 557.
[19] *Ibid.*, p. 851.

absentee, James A. Bayard, favored the bill, John Quincy Adams cast the only affirmative Federalist vote in either house.[20]

As Adams should have seen, the Nonimportation Act of 1806 was worse than useless. When at last seriously enforced in the spring of 1808, nonimportation became an important ancillary to the Embargo, but the passage in 1806 of weak legislation to take effect only after months of delay was neither an effective act of coercion nor a wise prelude to friendly negotiation. Strong action against Britain required no justification, and an argument could be made for commercial warfare. None could be made for this bill. As Randolph warned, the world's greatest commercial power was unlikely to be impressed by such a gesture. Indeed this posture of feeble defiance strengthened the hands of those in Great Britain who insisted that America was malignantly but ineffectively anti-British. William Plumer, like Adams an independent, analyzed the act far more accurately than his fellow Yankee when he wrote: "It has not sufficient energy to operate on the fears, but may wound the pride, of Great Britain." [21]

The British reaction confirmed Plumer's analysis. Most Englishmen considered the new law a bluff, potentially far more harmful to the United States than to England: "Can the Americans do without our goods? This is to ask: can they go naked . . . ?" Among ministers, only Lord Grenville expressed substantial fear of the act, and his concern sprang from its coincidence with loss of the Prussian market; anxious over its immediate effects, he was at the same time convinced that any ban would be "only temporary because Am$^a$. wants to buy our goods at least as much as we want to sell them." Lord Auckland, the Cabinet's American expert, expressed a more general view when he called the Nonimportation Act a "foolish and teasing measure." [22] And Britain was in no mood to be teased. In May and June, Fox and his undersecretary complained to Monroe. The Foreign Secretary said that

---

[20] Morton Borden, *The Federalism of James A. Bayard* (New York, 1955), p. 7; entry of April 10, 1806, Adams, *op. cit.*, I, 432.

[21] Plumer to John Goddard, April 14, 1806, William Plumer MSS, Library of Congress.

[22] *Cobbett's Political Register*, X (1806), 973; Grenville to Auckland, Sept. 6, 1806, Auckland MSS, Add. MSS 34457; Auckland to Grenville, Nov. 25, 1806, Fitzpatrick, *op. cit.*, VIII, 442.

the law "had the air of a menace, and that it was not agreeable to do things by compulsion." Monroe vainly attempted to convince Fox that the postponed date of implementation showed that America intended no menace. In September the British virtually told the Americans that they could not negotiate seriously while the act hung over their heads. The American representatives, Monroe and Pinkney, then promptly urged their government to push back still further the effective date. Even this did not satisfy Lord Holland, who pressed Monroe to recommend total repeal, since "it is very difficult to yield any thing while such a law is in force or even suspended in terrorem over our heads." [23] Except for Grenville's letter, all the evidence indicates that the threat of non-importation did not spur Britain to concession. On the contrary, both in the short and the long run it had a baneful psychological effect.

Shortly after learning of the Nonimportation Act, Fox derived some solace from information that a special minister had sailed to join James Monroe in full-dress negotiations. Many people in America, even ardent Republicans, preferred renewed negotiations to commercial warfare. In February the Senate called upon the President to give Britain one more chance to demonstrate her reasonableness. Jefferson subsequently denied that he had had anything to do with this resolution. A number of opponents, remembering the uproar when Jay was sent to England in 1794, believed that the administration "had the address behind the scenes to induce . . . the Senate without any direct application from the President to resolve that further negociation . . . is requisite." [24] Senators, among them Samuel Smith of Maryland, then urged Jefferson to appoint a special minister to join Monroe, both to emphasize the importance of the negotiation and because Monroe had a reputation, undeserved at this time, for Anglo-

[23] Monroe #49 to Madison, May 20, 1806, Despatches, Great Britain, Vol. XII; Monroe #50 to Madison, June 9, 1806, *ibid.*; Holland and Auckland to Monroe and Pinkney, Sept. 4, 1806, FO 5/51; Monroe and Pinkney to Holland and Auckland, Sept. 10, 1806, *ibid.*; Madison to Monroe and Pinkney, Dec. 3, 1806, William C. Rives Collection, Library of Congress.

[24] Plumer to Jedediah Morse, Feb. 26, 1806, Morse Family MSS, Yale University Library.

phobia. Here again Jefferson's views are doubtful. He seems to have hesitated before assenting to an appointment bound to affront his loyal friend in London. At last, as the President himself put it in an apology to Monroe two years later, "I found it necessary . . . to yield my own opinion to the general views of the national council, and it really seemed to produce a jubilee among them . . . from a belief in the effect which an extraordinary mission would have on the British mind." [25]

Jefferson's next problem was to choose a joint commissioner or perhaps, as he initially planned, two commissioners. Various names, Burr and Randolph among the most implausible, circulated in Capital rumor mills, and Samuel Smith openly sought the job. But Jefferson concluded that, particularly if the mission should fail, a non-Republican should share the responsibility. The most serious consideration fell upon Rufus King, whose long, successful experience at London and close friendship with English politicians made him a natural candidate. King apparently would accept only if given a free hand, subject only to the normal processes of ratification if he signed a treaty; when Madison informed him that the new commissioner would carry detailed instructions, the New Yorker, who knew from past experience how little freedom this would give him, bowed out.[26]

So, to the astonishment of all, William Pinkney of Maryland received the appointment. The surprise was unreasonable, for Pinkney's background justified his selection. For eight years he had served in London as a member of the Jay treaty commission hearing the claims of American merchants. This service had the advantage of having kept him safely outside partisan struggles at home, although Pinkney was generally believed to be a Federalist. On his return home in 1804 Pinkney almost immediately established himself as a leader of the Baltimore bar. Early in 1806

[25] Jefferson to Monroe, March 10, 1808, Andrew A. Lipscomb and Albert E. Bergh, eds., *The Writings of Thomas Jefferson* (Memorial ed.; 20 vols.; Washington, 1903–1904), XII, 4–5. See also Madison to Monroe, private, March 11, 1806, James Madison MSS, Library of Congress.

[26] Merry #1 to Mulgrave, Jan. 2, 1806, FO 5/48; entry of April 22, 1806, Brown, *op. cit.*, p. 491; Nicholson to Monroe, May 5, 1806, James Monroe MSS, Library of Congress.

he drafted for the merchants of that city a protest against British maritime practice, a memorial so able and so strong that Jefferson decided to send him to London. In the middle of March Pinkney expressed his willingness to serve, and the next month Jefferson nominated him.

Ambition and patriotism probably explain Pinkney's acceptance. He and his wife, the sister of Commodore John Rodgers, had ten children, and in Baltimore he earned about $15,000 a year. As a man largely self-made, William Pinkney well knew what it meant to abandon an extremely prosperous practice. But he was ambitious, and supremely confident that his talents would bring him success in whatever he undertook. His air of self-confidence was compounded by a certain foppishness, so that even Joseph Story, who deeply admired Pinkney, commented, "His first appearance is not prepossessing. He has the air of a man of fashion, of *hauteur*, of superiority, and something, I hardly know what to call it, of abrupt and crusty precision." [27] Pinkney had a great deal to be egotistical about, for he was among the greatest lawyers of his generation.

In 1806 Pinkney worked for an Anglo-American compromise. Doubtless he still believed Napoleon a greater threat than Britain; perhaps he hoped to reconstruct the *rapprochement* his friend King had helped to build a decade before. From 1807 onward, after Monroe's departure and particularly after the *Chesapeake* affair, Pinkney became more bellicose than the administration at home. He loyally executed his superiors' commands, but his correspondence makes it obvious that a more decisive policy would have pleased him better.

Neither Republicans nor Federalists viewed Pinkney in this light at the time of his appointment. Federalists grumbled that he had sold out. Most Republicans failed to see the wisdom of

[27] Story to Samuel P. P. Fay, Feb. 18, 1812, William W. Story, *Life and Letters of Joseph Story*, I (Boston, 1851), 216. There is no adequate biography of Pinkney, although a great deal of information can be found in Henry Wheaton, *Some Account of the Life, Writings, and Speeches of William Pinkney* (New York, 1826), and William Pinkney, *The Life of William Pinkney* (New York, 1853). A sketch by John J. Dolan is in the *Dictionary of American Biography*, XIV, 626–629.

appointing a Federalist to join Monroe. As late as 1808 Republican senators threatened to oppose Pinkney's confirmation as permanent minister, arguing that his Federalist background made him an almost certain Anglophile.[28] Monroe and his supporters considered the appointment a trick inspired by Madison to cut a political rival down to size. "I hope," wrote John Randolph, "that Mr. Monroe . . . will have concluded all matters with the Court of London before that federal interloper P. can arrive to share the honor which does not belong to him." Monroe himself was bitterly disappointed, both from personal pique and because the appointment stymied promising conversations with Fox.[29]

William Pinkney and his family sailed from Baltimore on May 21, 1806. Although he had been selected in March and the Cabinet had outlined his instructions at that time, Pinkney's departure was actually rather precipitate. He had no chance to see Jefferson, who was vacationing at Monticello, before leaving. Favorable winds speeded Pinkney's passage to Liverpool. He nevertheless had twenty-nine days to reëxamine Madison's instructions, all fifteen sheets of them, and perhaps to reread the Secretary's learned disquisition on American rights, which Madison had thoughtfully provided in twelve copies. Pinkney can hardly have been surprised by anything he read, but he must have realized, egotist though he was, that he faced an almost impossible task.

Madison's instructions, drafted after consultation with the President and unanimously endorsed by the Cabinet, listed a dozen items of complaint. For the most part the list was familiar, as indeed it should have been since the instructions largely repeated earlier ones sent to Monroe. In the field of neutral rights, for example, Madison renewed requests Britain had refused before: elimination or at least narrowing of the list of contraband, accept-

---

[28] Gore to King, Aug. 24, 1806, King MSS, Vol. XI; entry of April 19, 1806, Brown, *op. cit.*, pp. 488–489, 491–492; Nathaniel Macon to Gallatin, June 28, 1806, Albert Gallatin MSS, New-York Historical Society; Macon to Nicholson, April 21, 1806, Joseph H. Nicholson MSS, Library of Congress; Pickering to King, Feb. 26, 1808, King MSS, Vol. XII; Jefferson to Giles, Feb. 26, 1808, Thomas Jefferson MSS, Library of Congress (erroneously bound at 1806).

[29] Randolph to James M. Garnett, May 11, 1806, John Randolph MSS, Library of Congress; Monroe to Jefferson, June 15, 1806 (not sent), Monroe MSS.

ance of the doctrine of "free ships, free goods," a return to on-the-spot notifications of blockades, and so on. More original, and a combination of one-sided logic with wild improbability, was the suggestion that Britain recognize the Gulf Stream as the limit of American waters and withdraw her fleet behind it.[30] In his discussion of Anglo-American commerce, Madison offered little that was new, standing behind most-favored-nation status and reciprocal removal of discriminatory legislation, the American position since at least 1794.[31] Since *Essex* seizures formed one of the principal sources of controversy, Madison naturally directed Monroe and Pinkney to seek some compensation for them and for other flagrantly illegal spoliations. But he and Jefferson did not insist upon payment.[32]

Two *sine qua non*'s, intended to prevent further friction, formed the heart of the instructions. One was some limitation on impress-

[30] Almost a year before, the Cabinet had agreed that the United States "ought to endeavor to assume" this position. Entry of July 8, 1805, Ford, *op. cit.*, I, 308. In the instructions the envoys received permission to recede from this position and to seek instead an agreement that American waters extended only to four, or even one, maritime league from the coast. Madison to Monroe and Pinkney, May 7, 1806, Instructions, All Countries, Vol. VI. Monroe and Pinkney adopted this latter position, buttressing it with the administration's argument that it would reduce the number of incidents contributing to discord. But, as British naval officers and Lord Holland pointed out, unless France also accepted the new definition it would in effect grant a zone of immunity to her warships and privateers. Admiral John Markham to Holland [?], Nov. 9, 1806, Greenwich Hospital Miscellanea, Public Record Office, Adm 80/117; Holland to Monroe, Nov. 13, 1806, James Monroe MSS, New York Public Library. In the present discussion, except where otherwise noted, reference is to the instructions cited above.

[31] In the commercial area Madison showed flexibility. If unrestricted most-favored-nation status was unobtainable, he was prepared to accept mere equalization of the burden of charges on ships of both nations. He offered to accept restrictions on the cargoes American ships could carry away from the West Indies after bearing supplies thither. He did not insist upon the opening of British North America. But he did caution Monroe and Pinkney to draft any agreement in such a fashion that, if American ships were not granted entry into Caribbean ports, British ships from the colonies could not demand entry into American ports under the most-favored-nation principle, and he warned that only extensive trading rights would justify the envoys in agreeing to forswear the right of discriminatory legislation to force open the islands. Madison was supremely confident that Britain's own needs "must necessarily produce that effect at no distant period."

[32] Madison laid down extremely detailed specifications here, but his failure to insist upon compensation as a *sine qua non* perhaps suggests that he too had come to realize that *Essex* seizures were not so numerous as the first reports had indicated.

ment, either by substituting for it an agreement for the return of deserters or by arranging to confine the practice to British ports, as Rufus King had sought to do in 1803. As Madison well knew, these limitations would undermine the entire practice, at least in English eyes. "Yet," said the instructions, "so indispensable is some adequate provision for the case, that the President makes it a necessary preliminary to any stipulation requiring a repeal of the act shutting the market of the U. States against certain British manufactures." Similarly, the United States insisted upon more liberal treatment of the reëxport trade as a condition of repeal of the Nonimportation Act. "It is much to be desired," wrote Madison, "that the general principle [of the right to trade freely in colonial goods] in its full extent, be laid down in the stipulation. But as this may not be attainable and as much ought not to be risked by an inflexible pursuit of abstract rights, . . . you are left at liberty if found necessary to abridge the right in practice." In short, the United States would exchange acceptance of the old *Polly* definition of broken voyage (plus perhaps a requirement that goods be reshipped in a different vessel) for British repudiation of the harsher *Essex* restraints. The two *sine qua non*'s really meant that the United States demanded a return to the halcyon days before seizures and impressment became serious problems.[33]

The instructions reflected the constant desire of James Madison and his superior to limit war's impact and to extend commercial intercourse. They spoke the language of the Enlightenment and of the whole career of Thomas Jefferson, its most consistent American spokesman. Naturally American interests would benefit if Britain accepted the proposed regulations, but this is not the sole rea-

[33] A memorandum by Jefferson conveniently summarizes the whole instructions, and shows that the basic outline was settled in March, although the instructions themselves were not prepared until two months later: ". . . we may enter into treaty with England, the sum of which should be to settle neutral rights, not insisting on the principle of free ships, free goods and modifying her new principles of the 'accustomed trade' so as to give up the direct, & keep the indirect commerce between colonies & their metropols, restraining impressmts. of seamen to her own citizens in her own ports, & giving her in commerce the right of the most favored nations without entering into details. Endeavor to get a relinqumt of her right of commerce with our Indians, or insist on security for our people trading with hers. Endeavour also to exclude hostilities within the gulph stream." Entry of March 14, 1806, Ford, *op. cit.*, I, 310.

son Jefferson and Madison advanced them. They deeply believed that restricted warfare and broadened commerce would improve the lot of all men. Philosophically, and from the point of view of abstract justice, there was much to commend the instructions. But, as Abbot E. Smith has commented, "it was less necessary that Madison should have a clear conception of the rights to which the United States was theoretically entitled, than that he should understand the European situation and have a fair notion of what he was likely to get without fighting." [34]

What, then, decided Jefferson and Madison to put these items forward? James Monroe thought them a trap designed to destroy his own political reputation. While this collateral benefit may have crossed Madison's mind it almost certainly was not decisive. Among other things, the President and the Secretary woefully overestimated the impact of nonimportation, blindly convincing themselves that this weapon would bring England to her knees. If the Nonimportation Act was the stick, the proposed commercial treaty was the carrot. Ignoring obvious evidence of British indifference to expiration of the Jay treaty's commercial articles, Jefferson and Madison clung to a conviction that England would recognize, at least ultimately, that she could not maintain her economy without extended American trade. Time, they felt sure, would make these obvious truths visible even to the blind.

Jefferson and Madison expected much from Fox, described by the President as one in whom "I have more confidence than in any man in England." When Fox fell ill the President considered it a crippling blow, for "his sound judgment saw that political interest could never be separated in the long run from moral right, & his frank & great mind would have made a short business of a just treaty." Furthermore, European calamities, so Jefferson reasoned, made good relations with one of the world's few remaining neutrals imperative for Britain. To quote him again, "the change in the ministry & the events of Europe will I think ensure a friendly settlement with her." [35] Jefferson and Madison, who

[34] Abbot E. Smith, *James Madison: Builder* (New York, 1937), p. 254.

[35] Jefferson to Monroe, May 4, 1806, Lipscomb and Bergh, *op. cit.*, XI, 109; Jefferson to Monroe, Oct. 26, 1806, Jefferson MSS; Jefferson to John Tyler, April 26, 1806, *ibid.*

did not want to see Napoleon reign over all Europe, were realistic enough to attempt to exploit his victories for America's benefit.

For other reasons it also seemed unwise to compromise. Napoleon's support in the quarrel with Spain over Florida was so important that it must not be jeopardized by an Anglo-American accommodation, unless that settlement were so favorable that the Florida question shrank to secondary importance. Finally, particularly after the militant declarations of the preceding winter, Jefferson feared the psychological consequences of a retreat: "The love of peace which we sincerely feel & profess, has begun to produce an opinion in Europe that our government is entirely in Quaker principles." [36]

More than two years later, when Jefferson at last released the instructions, some concluded that the administration had intended the negotiations to fail. The French minister reported, "They are long, diffuse and seem equally designed to embarrass the progress of the Plenipotentiaries as to direct them." Later, echoing a frequent Federalist theme, James A. Bayard argued: "Your President never meant to have a treaty with Great Britain. . . . If he had intended it, he would never have fettered the Commissioners with *sine qua nons* which were insuperable." [37] Such criticism missed the point. Madison and Jefferson were not sinister Machiavellians. They believed that Fox would grant American demands. If he did not, they were prepared to wait, confident that time would bring compliance. This fumbling and confused analysis speaks eloquently of the diplomatic ineptness of the President and his chief lieutenant.

Pinkney reached London late in June, 1806. Probably to their mutual surprise, he and Monroe hit it off at once. During the entire subsequent negotiations there is not a hint of disagreement. On the whole, Monroe told Pinkney, the British government's attitude appeared favorable. Fox seemed on the verge of important concessions. Considering his reluctance to promise compensation for

[36] Jefferson to Cooper, Feb. 18, 1806, Thomas Jefferson MSS (Coolidge Collection), Massachusetts Historical Society.

[37] Turreau #14 to Minister of Foreign Relations, May 20, 1808, Archives des Affaires Étrangères, Correspondance Politique, États-Unis (photostats, Library of Congress), Vol. LXI; *Annals*, 10th Cong., 2d sess., pp. 394–395.

seizures largely tactical, Monroe thought England would agree to return to the *Polly* principle and even hoped to reach a settlement on impressment.[38] Less hopefully, on the very day Pinkney reached London Fox fell fatally ill of dropsy, the price finally exacted for a life of dissipation. To the extent that his influence was needed to keep the Cabinet in line (as the Americans erroneously thought), this was a crushing blow.

To replace Fox, the Cabinet asked a young man, Lord Holland, and a diplomatic veteran, Lord Auckland, to take on what Grenville called "a work I fear of no light labor or difficulty." Holland and Auckland accepted with alacrity. At an introductory dinner given by Grenville, Lord Auckland said to the Americans, a note of warning against inflexibility tingeing his courtesy, "I trust we shall be able to do some good to mankind, if your powers are sufficiently extensive." [39]

Holland and Auckland made almost as harmonious a team as Monroe and Pinkney. Holland, Fox's favorite nephew, spoke for his dying uncle's faction in the Cabinet, Auckland for his old friend Grenville. The thirty-three-year-old Holland, already plagued by gout, had no diplomatic experience and none too great a knowledge of public affairs. He tended, his fellow commissioner believed, to proceed without sufficient regard for the necessity of conciliating English pressure groups—manufacturers, shipowners, colonials, the East India Company. On the other hand, as an expansive and friendly littérateur bearing Fox's family name, Holland very favorably impressed the Americans. Auckland, already over sixty, was far more experienced. He had been, among other things, the channel of clandestine peace feelers during the American Revolution, the negotiator of a famous commercial treaty with France, and a long-time member of the Board of Trade. Auckland was the real cutting edge of the commission. On learning of his appointment, Jefferson commented, with his invariable aversion to anyone connected with Pitt or Grenville, that the old diplomat was "too

[38] Monroe to James Bowdoin, June 20, 1806, Monroe MSS.
[39] Grenville to Auckland, Aug. 9, 1806, Auckland MSS, Add. MSS 34456; Monroe and Pinkney #3 to Madison, Aug. 15, 1806, Despatches, Great Britain, Vol. XIV.

much wedded to the antient maritime code & navigation principles of England . . . to make [us] expect either an early or just
result." [40] Actually, Auckland had always worked and would, like
Holland, continue to work for the settlement of Anglo-American
disputes.

Lord Grenville and Fox's successor, Lord Howick, deeply desired to avoid a serious clash with America. On the other hand,
particularly after Fox died, the administration's political weakness
made concession difficult. The service ministries and some important segments of British opinion opposed significant concessions.
As the *Times* put it, "If the Americans have any real ground of
complaint, let them be removed . . . ; it is what is due to them.
. . . But in doing this they cannot expect that we shall surrender
to them the smallest particle of that equitable system of maritime
policy in which we owe our greatness and our prosperity." Grenville and especially Auckland knew the danger of challenging
such sentiment. Furthermore, congressional posturing had irritated them. No doubt Lord Auckland nodded smilingly as he read
the opinion of a friend that "it is absolutely necessary that America
should be taken off the high horse she has lately mounted but in
taking a Lady off her horse care must be taken not to offend her
delicacy or shew her legs." [41]

Negotiations ran on spasmodically from August 23 until the
end of the year. Including intragovernmental discussions as well
as sessions with the Americans, Auckland counted thirty or forty
conferences, and he claimed that one marathon argument with
Monroe and Pinkney lasted seven hours, another took four and a
half hours. After initial exploratory conversations, Fox's final
illness and death (he died on September 13) halted the negotiations. Toward the end of October Auckland and Holland recalled
the subject to the government's attention, and for the next fortnight there was a flurry of activity during which the Americans
agreed to abandon the *sine qua non* on impressment. A second

[40] Jefferson to Monroe, Oct. 26, 1806, Jefferson MSS.
[41] *Times*, June 23, 1806; Lord Temple to Auckland, Aug. 17, 1806, Auckland
MSS, Add. MSS 34456.

hiatus followed, then another brief spurt that arranged the problem of the reëxport trade. Basic agreement was reached by December 6, but not until the last day of the year did the four plenipotentiaries meet at the Foreign Office to sign the treaty.

The negotiators discussed practically every facet of Anglo-American relations except the disputed portions of the Canadian boundary. For the most part, the Jay treaty formulas were repeated with respect to neutral rights and Anglo-American trade. The Americans insisted on an article on trade with India but then accepted a provision somewhat tightening the restrictions on American ships, though not so much as the East India Company desired. By mutual agreement the treaty omitted stipulations on trade with the British West Indies. The sympathetic ministry dared not risk public protest by making a formal concession. On the whole, although Madison and the English commissioners each considered that the other party benefited most from these articles, the discussions confirmed an earlier prediction by Holland and Auckland that "in the Commercial arrangements there will be more detail than difficulty." [42]

In a trifling, tactical concession, the British accepted America's request to extend her territorial waters. Monroe and Pinkney did not press for the Gulf Stream line, and discussion centered on a boundary one or two leagues from shore. Sir John Nicholl, who steadily opposed concession, wrote that the American claim could not "be maintained as a matter of right . . . ; and if it be granted, it should be . . . as a concession depending for its basis upon corresponding concessions," for it would severely handicap the Royal Navy. At the strong behest of its commissioners, the British government finally agreed to a minor extension of American jurisdiction, provided that no third party not extending similar recognition should be sheltered from the Royal Navy by the new line. The British hoped that this concession, although made prac-

---

[42] Holland and Auckland to Howick, Oct. 20, 1806, FO 5/51. Commercial discussions, extensively recorded in various journal entries and copies of letters in Adm 80/117, are summarized in Wilson H. Elkins, "British Policy in Its Relation to the Commerce and Navigation of the United States of America from 1794 to 1807" (unpublished Ph.D. thesis, Oxford University, 1936), pp. 211–246 and *passim.*

tically worthless by the reservation, would have a salutary effect upon the American psyche.[43]

As early as September 6, when Holland met the Americans for a Saturday conference in the nearly empty Foreign Office, the British realized that impressment and the reëxport trade formed the chief American concerns. At that meeting Holland began by re-iterating a request, previously made in a note prepared under the eye of the Cabinet, that the Nonimportation Act be suspended. Monroe and Pinkney immediately asked "with what colour . . . could they call upon Congress to undo what they had done, when nothing but the bare opening of a Negotiation had taken place." Would Lord Holland promise a favorable answer to their demands on impressment and indirect trade? To this Holland replied that, while the American position could not be accepted *in toto*,

> he & his Colleague were sincerely disposed to make any compromise on these two Points that could be devised, consistent with the Dignity and Interests of the two Countries, & that they were losing no time in collecting the Opinions of different Classes of Men, whose information was useful & whose sanction was, in some measure, necessary to secure any concession that might be made . . . from unmerited unpopularity & Misrepresentation.

Holland's answer meant that, within limits which merchants and Admiralty officials would help to establish, he and Auckland, and presumably their superiors, agreed to negotiate on the basis of the American demands. Accepting his assurance at face value, Pinkney and Monroe thereupon replied that they would ask their government to suspend the act, as they soon did.[44]

Holland left the meeting with a clear picture of the American position. He understood that Madison's instructions made agreements on seamen and shipping *sine qua non*'s. He even divined that these instructions were far more inflexible on impressment than on the reëxport trade. The young lord warned Grenville that

---

[43] Nicholl to Howick, Nov. 17, 1806, Adm 80/117; Holland to Auckland, n.d. [Nov. 18–20, 1806], Auckland MSS, Add. MSS 34457, fols. 199–200; Holland and Auckland to Howick, private, Nov. 14, 1806, FO 5/51; entry of Nov. 21, 1806, journal of negotiations, Adm 80/117.

[44] Entry of Sept. 6, 1806, journal of negotiations, Adm 80/117.

"good humour & good will are only to be purchased by very considerable concessions on one or both of these points." [45] On the British side, the story of the ensuing negotiations lies in the construction of these concessions and the checkreins imposed upon Holland and Auckland by the Cabinet. On the American side, it lies in the decision of Monroe and Pinkney to reverse the priority between Madison's two ultimatums and consequently to sign a treaty relaxing the *Essex* principle but silent on impressment.

The British very nearly agreed to end impressment on the high seas. Holland believed the Americans could be trusted, in exchange, to deliver up seamen fleeing from British service. Auckland was more doubtful, being particularly impressed by Admiralty evidence showing that the Americans often induced desertion from British ships and issued fraudulent certificates of American citizenship. Lord Auckland, meeting with Monroe and Pinkney while Holland was in close mourning for his uncle, "insisted much on the Difficulty which this notorious Practice would raise in framing any Article for the due security of the essential Interests of the British Navy. Much conversation ensued on the Subject, but without any satisfactory result." [46] Nevertheless, when the British commissioners, on October 20, submitted a long report to Howick designed to reinvigorate the negotiations made dormant by Fox's death, Auckland joined his young colleague in urging the government to accede to American wishes.

Holland and Auckland believed that Britain, in return for the surrender of her traditional claim to impress on the high seas, would garner substantial advantages. Monroe and Pinkney made no objection to impressment in British ports, and, although this was a concession that the Federalist, King, had refused to make in 1803, "they would probably suffer us to include within these limits the whole extent of the British Channel, though they would not

---

[45] Holland to Grenville, Sept. 6, 1806, Boconnoc MSS, Cabinet Ministers.

[46] Auckland to Howick, Sept. 12, 1806, Grey MSS, from 1st Ld. Auckland; entry of Sept. 22, 1806, journal of negotiations, Adm 80/117. The most detailed treatment of this subject is Anthony Steel, "Impressment in the Monroe-Pinkney Negotiation, 1806–1807," *American Historical Review*, LVII (1951–1952), 352–369.

admit such a construction of jurisdiction to appear on the face of the Treaty." Furthermore, the American commissioners had offered the support of their government and courts "for the recovery of our Seamen, within the limits of their jurisdiction." Holland and Auckland also believed the Americans would permit British captains to stop merchantmen at sea, muster the crew, and require the master (unless he agreed that a suspected man was indeed an Englishman and gave him up) to submit proof to a competent tribunal empowered to punish any captain who did have Englishmen in his crew. Auckland and Holland suggested that the agreement be limited to a short period, after which obvious shortcomings could be corrected or the arrangement dropped. Obviously the British negotiators foresaw many difficulties. On the other hand, they did propose to surrender a practice Britain had insisted upon for centuries, primarily because, in their words, "without some regulation upon it, no permanent or sincere reconciliation with the United States can be expected." [47]

At first the Cabinet reacted favorably. The commissioners received permission to discuss a projet with Monroe and Pinkney and did so in several conversations. Details alone seemed to be holding up agreement. But, on November 2, Howick, whose experience at the Admiralty may have stiffened his position, wrote to Holland: "If the object for which we have hitherto insisted on our rights to impress British Sea Men on the High Seas could be obtained by any more gentle means, nobody would be a more strenuous advocate for such a change than I should. But I cannot satisfy myself that any sufficient security could be devised, & I am certain what is proposed would be none." The next day Sir John Nicholl submitted a report that ringingly vindicated the legality of impressment. On November 4 the Cabinet examined three alternative proposals, one submitted by the Americans and two concocted by Holland and Auckland. The ministers decided not to risk any relaxation of impressment, primarily because they

[47] Holland and Auckland to Howick, Oct. 20, 1806, FO 5/51. Portions of this report are reproduced in Steel, *op. cit.*, pp. 356–358.

doubted that the Americans would execute their part of the bargain.[48]

The next afternoon Auckland and Holland informed the Americans that the Cabinet had decided to break off negotiations on impressment. Loyally executing Madison's instructions, "M$^r$ Monroe & M$^r$ Pinkney entered severally into long & warm arguments for the Purpose of refuting those reasonings on which the right is asserted & intimated that if a satisfactory Article could not be given to them as to this point, all the other Objects of Negotiation were of so secondary a nature that it would not be material to proceed to them." All hope seemed at an end. Two days later, convinced the Americans meant what they said, Lord Auckland urged Grenville to reconsider, arguing that "in the present state of the World . . . even a colourable reconciliation & friendship with the United States would be of an importance infinitely outweighing the Objections to the Article in question after such amendment as it might have admitted." [49] The British government remained adamant, and Auckland proceeded disconsolately to another session that afternoon.

This meeting marked the turning point. To the Britons' amazement, the Americans gave up what had seemed an irrevocable determination. The report of the British commissioners is the fullest statement of the arguments that swayed Monroe and Pinkney. Auckland and Holland emphasized the difficulty of constructing a stipulation

such as would be consistent with the security of a Right essential to . . . our Naval Power, & such at the same time as they & their employers would deem admissable. We urged strongly . . . that it would be neither friendly nor wise to press us further for a stipulation which might be injurious to a Claim from which we cannot depart, & which is at present exercised so as to afford no reasonable cause of complaint. We proposed to them to suspend

[48] Howick to Holland, Nov. 2, 1806, Grey MSS, to Ld. Holland; Nicholl memorandum, Nov. 3, 1806, FO 5/104; entry of Nov. 4, 1806, journal of negotiations, Adm 80/117.

[49] Entry of Nov. 5, 1806, journal of negotiations, Adm 80/117; Auckland to Grenville, Nov. 7, 1806, Boconnoc MSS, Lord Auckland 1806.

or lay aside this part of the Negotiation, by receiving from Us an indefinite but conciliatory statement respecting it; & to proceed forthwith to the other Articles of the Treaty in which we foresee no insuperable difficulty

In the result the American Commissioners gave way to these suggestions, though with some hesitation & reluctance.

The elated Englishmen forwarded to Howick the draft of an official note to the Americans, sufficiently "indefinite but conciliatory," promising that orders would continue to be given "for the observance of the greatest caution in the impressing of British seamen" and inviting the Americans to continue negotiations on other points. The next day, with Howick's approval, they sent the note to Monroe, who transmitted it to Pinkney with a covering note of cautious approval.[50]

The Americans explained their decision to the Secretary of State in a lengthy apologia drafted by Monroe. They argued that the Grenville ministry, which sincerely desired to meet Madison's wishes, dared not risk a public outcry in England. The formal British note, while avoiding the opprobrium of surrender by treaty, had been delivered after cabinet consultation and could be considered as binding as any treaty stipulations. Rather than abandon the chance of gains in other areas, the commissioners had decided to accept a declaration in conformity with the spirit of Madison's demands, particularly since they believed that the Ministry of All the Talents had already restricted the practice. Finally, the ministers reported that, since they had emphasized that they were acting in violation of their instructions, the British government could not be surprised if Jefferson and Madison chose to disavow them.[51] Basically the decision came down to this: the commissioners rejected the high principle of their superiors. They considered impressment, at least as then carried on, a lesser evil than severe limitations on the reëxport trade, national dignity less important

[50] Holland and Auckland to Howick, Nov. 8, 1806, Grey MSS, United States; Holland and Auckland to Monroe and Pinkney, Nov. 8, 1806, enclosed in Monroe and Pinkney #6 to Madison, Nov. 11, 1806, Despatches, Great Britain, Vol. XIV; Monroe to Pinkney, Nov. 9, 1806, Monroe MSS.

[51] Monroe and Pinkney #6 to Madison, Nov. 11, 1806, Despatches, Great Britain, Vol. XIV.

than material profit. Many Americans, both Republicans and Federalists, agreed with them in 1806.

Perhaps none of the proposals on impressment would have ended the issue. The voracious American appetite for seamen and the advantages of service on American merchantmen meant that Englishmen would almost certainly continue to flock to the Stars and Stripes. The British government, however, missed an excellent opportunity to bring the United States to its side and to reduce the vitiating drain of manpower. The margin was narrow. With Holland in the lead, the British nearly made an important concession, only to be restrained by the frowns of civil servants at the Admiralty, by Sir John Nicholl's strident pseudo legalisms, by Howick's doubts, and above all by fear of parliamentary opposition. Even after the Cabinet's decision, Lord Howick tried to construct something effective out of the various projets that littered his desk, and if pressed further the Cabinet might possibly have reversed itself. But the Americans' nerve cracked first, and they accepted the comparatively meaningless note of November 8. In the short run this was a victory for England if not for a ministry sincerely seeking reconciliation, but the triumph turned to ashes, first with Jefferson's decision to reject the treaty and some years later with renewed controversy that played a part in the coming of war.

For various reasons, among them a desire to compensate Monroe and Pinkney for their surrender on impressment, the Cabinet accepted fairly liberal rules for the reëxport trade. The ministry did not feel bound by the *Essex* decision, which had occurred under the aegis of Pitt's government, and it had far less sympathy for British shipowners and colonialists than its predecessor. Although impressment might be defended as an imperative of war, breaking up the reëxport trade smacked too much of commercial selfishness. Even Sir John Nicholl admitted that the requirement of transshipment in America had "for its object considerations more of commerce than of War." The British commissioners also sympathized with the American complaint against "the unsteadiness of our Rules of decision" brought on by elimination of the *Polly* criteria. Nicholl, the captor's losing counsel in that case, agreed that "in order to avoid practical Inconvenience and Litigation, it seems desirable that certain Criteria should be settled, rather than that each Case sh$^d$. depend upon its own Circumstances." [52]

Prior to Fox's death Pinkney and Monroe made it clear that, like Nicholl, they particularly desired to regularize the situation. As Holland and Auckland later reported,

The American Commissioners deny in general the principle of the rule of 1756, but at present they more particularly complain that in the recent detentions we have transgressed the rule laid down by ourselves [in the *Polly* case]. . . .

Thus without actually admitting our right to interfere even with the direct trade between the Colonies of our Enemies and the Mother Country, . . . all that they require of us, is a clear and permanent definition of the circumstances which constitute the difference between a continuous and an interrupted voyage, it being already settled that whatever interrupts the voyage legalizes the trade.

While recognizing that in theory the shipper's intent and not the amount of ceremony in American ports was decisive, the British commissioners nevertheless proposed to meet the American initiative. Sir John Nicholl, mobilized once again, drafted an article requiring that colonial goods be landed in America, warehoused for at least one month, and reshipped in a different vessel; Nicholl did not insist upon the imposition of customs charges in the United States which would equalize the cost of rival British and American shippers.[53] Pinkney in particular strenuously resisted Nicholl's recommendations, and the negotiators had not reached agreement when discussions were suspended in September.

When meetings resumed, impressment at first dominated the discussions. At the end of November, with that subject finally out of the way, Howick circulated through the Cabinet recommendations made by Auckland and Holland. Pinkney's complaints had

---

[52] Holland and Auckland to Howick, Oct. 20, 1806, FO 5/51; Nicholl memorandum, Dec. 15, 1806, enclosed in Nicholl to Auckland, private, Dec. 15, 1806, Adm 80/117.

[53] Holland and Auckland to Howick, Oct. 20, 1806, FO 5/51.

centered on the proposals to require a delay in America and to reship goods in a different ship. Therefore the Cabinet decided to go back to an emphasis upon duty charges, insisting at the same time that only a limited amount of duty be returned on reëxportation. At a long meeting on December 6, and "after much Debate & Doubt," Monroe and Pinkney accepted this proposal in principle.[54] The negotiators eventually agreed upon real charges of 2 per cent on colonial goods and 1 per cent on those from Europe, neither burden particularly onerous.

In effect, the British ministry agreed to retreat from the *Essex* decision to the *Polly* decision, under which American trade had flourished. In practical terms, and omitting all questions of the basic legality of British practices, the Grenville government had made an important conciliatory gesture. Had the treaty gone into effect, British ultras would have complained vehemently; on receiving rumors of relaxation of the *Essex* principle, for example, the *Courier* warned that "in less than three years the carrying trade of this Country will be annihilated.—War, therefore, with America, . . . rather than concession!—War with America rather than the abandonment of the rule of 1756." [55] Moreover, while accepting the British proposal as far as it went, Monroe and Pinkney did not consider it to quiet all other American claims. They believed "the sole Office of this Article . . . [was] to give to certain defined Facts the Effect of breaking the Continuity of a Voyage. . . . It does not . . . determine, or admit . . . that in any Cases, the Voyages . . . will become illegal, if any or all of these Facts should appear to be wanting" [56] Still, because most shipowners would, for their own security, conform to the treaty regulations, the agreement promised to lessen friction and pave the way to continued American prosperity.

Only a few days after agreement on the reëxport trade, the negotiators learned of Napoleon's Berlin Decree. Holland and

---

[54] *Ibid.* and endorsements; Auckland to Grenville, Nov. 28, 1806, Fitzpatrick, *op. cit.*, VIII, 445; entries of Dec. 1, 6, 1806, journal of negotiations, Adm 80/117.
[55] Jan. 1, 1807.
[56] Monroe and Pinkney to Holland and Auckland, Dec. 31, 1806, Monroe MSS, NYPL. No British records indicate that this letter was actually delivered, but the Americans expressed the same reservation orally.

Auckland immediately told the Americans that Britain must now at least reconsider her decision to modify the Rule of the War of 1756, since its rigorous execution might be required to meet Napoleon's edict. Perhaps it would be best to put the negotiations to sleep until it could be determined whether or not the United States intended to resist Napoleon's pretensions. The American pair reacted strongly. They assured the two lords that the United States would resist the new decree and argued that "surely it would be both magnanimous & Wise . . . of Great Britain to presume that the United States would do what they ought to do, & to proceed accordingly as if nothing had happened." The British gave in to this reasoning, but they insisted upon annexing to the treaty an official note reserving to England the right of retaliation against France, as well as nonratification of the treaty, if the Jefferson administration failed to take effective action.[57]

Monroe and Pinkney deemed the declaration a small price to pay for a treaty. The Berlin Decree, which threatened to destroy American commerce, shocked them as much as the British. The Americans seem to have considered Napoleon the greater threat, as they did throughout the negotiations, despite substantial grievances against Britain. They even suggested ways to improve the note by strengthening the passage that contrasted English restraint and the Emperor's sweeping edict, and Lord Holland permitted them to edit the final draft to make it as inoffensive as possible. On the morning of December 31, 1806, the four plenipotentiaries affixed signatures and seals to the treaty, ending what Auckland had earlier described as "our eternal negotiation." [58]

The treaty of 1806 provoked, and continues to provoke, controversy. British nationalists, considering reaffirmation of the Jay treaty's commercial articles a concession to the Americans, argued that Monroe and Pinkney ought to have paid a price for it. They objected that the United States had not surrendered her claim to trade with the British West Indies nor accepted the legality of

[57] Entry of Dec. 9, 1806, journal of negotiations, Adm 80/117.
[58] Auckland to Grenville, Dec. 27, 1806, Boconnoc MSS, Lord Auckland 1806; Holland to Monroe, Dec. 29, 1806, Monroe MSS, NYPL; Holland and Auckland to Monroe and Pinkney, Dec. 31, 1806, FO 5/51; Auckland to Monroe, Dec. 14, 1806, Monroe MSS, NYPL.

impressment nor agreed to end its "war in disguise." The compromise on reëxport trade, one pamphleteer protested, was really "a stipulation, vexatious enough to continue the complaints of America, but too weak to secure the interests of Britain." The treaty's opponents believed that "we have not by our moderation obtained a reciprocity of advantage." [59]

Holland and Auckland answered these assaults in essentially political terms. They believed increasing hostility the only alternative to a treaty, and they asserted that they had paid a small price for reconciliation. Commenting on attacks in the *Courier* and the *Morning Post*, Auckland's secretary wrote to him:

Did you ever see such impudent & barefaced misrepresentations. Concession to America— What concession was made to her except two additional miles of maritime jurisdiction & that so clogged with exceptions as to be merely an empty compliment. In the article on colonial trade greater difficulties were thrown in her way than those specified by Ld Hawkesbury in his letter to Rufus King [formally confirming the *Polly* principle]—& yet the whole article is represented as a boon to America for which we have nothing in return.

Auckland himself argued that the treaty contained not a single "abandonment . . . of any one Claim, or Principle, or right, or Usage, Colonial or Commercial." He trusted however that the treaty would quiet America, "& I feel [this] . . . in the disjointed state of the world to be a Result of great political Importance." [60]

Within a few months—news reached England in April—Jefferson's rejection of the treaty blasted Auckland's hopes. In February, when the President learned that his ambassadors intended to overleap impressment, he and his Cabinet agreed to maintain the *sine qua non* on seamen and to refuse to give up commercial warfare, "the only peaceable instrument for coercing all our rights," as long as this and other issues remained. Jefferson believed "we had better have no treaty than a bad one. it will not restore friendship,

[59] Thomas P. Courtenay, *Additional Observations on the American Treaty, with Some Remarks on Mr. Baring's Pamphlet* (London, 1808), pp. 73, 69, and *passim*.
[60] John Allen to Auckland, Nov. 12, 1807, Adm 80/116; Auckland to Sheffield, Jan. 5, 1806 [1807], Auckland MSS, Add. MSS 45729.

134

but keep us in a state of constant irritation." Failing a treaty stipulation, the two nations might exchange informal promises on seamen. As long as Britain kept her share of the bargain the administration would prevent enforcement of the Nonimportation Act.[61]

On the last day of Congress the British minister received the treaty, which he hastily carried to Madison's office. The Secretary and subsequently the President examined it chiefly to confirm the fact that it omitted impressment, although both also noted with displeasure the annexed note on the Berlin Decree. That evening, when a Senate delegation brought bills for his signature, Jefferson curtly told the legislators he would call no special session since he intended to reject the treaty on his own responsibility. In Jefferson's mind refusal to ratify did not necessarily imply a break with England, and he continued to hope for an informal understanding. The President believed "our best course is, to let the negotiation take a friendly nap"; meanwhile the Nonimportation Act would remain suspended. This moderation annoyed the French warrior-diplomat, Turreau, who reported, "These people here don't take a step forward against England but that they take two backward steps." [62]

For the forward step of nonratification Jefferson and Madison had no regrets. As they examined the treaty at leisure in the spring of 1807, more shortcomings appeared. The administration desired peace and prosperity as much as its agents did, but the price seemed exorbitant. Britain faced national extinction; she, not the United States, should be the suppliant at a time when the Prussian defeat at Jena meant that "no other nation on earth now left . . . can render her the least service." [63] A breach with America, Madison

---

[61] Memorandum of Feb. 2, 1807, Jefferson MSS; Madison to Monroe and Pinkney, private, March 20, 1807, Madison MSS; Jefferson to Monroe, March 21, 1807, Lipscomb and Bergh, *op. cit.*, XI, 167–169.

[62] Jefferson to Madison, April 21, 1807, Lipscomb and Bergh, *op. cit.*, XI, 193; Turreau #13 to Minister of Foreign Relations, April 8, 1807, AAE, CP, E-U, Vol. LX. See also Erskine #8, #10 to Howick, March 6, 28, 1807, FO 5/52. The Administration considered offering a further inducement in the shape of a promise to forbid the enrollment of foreign seamen in American merchantmen, but Gallatin's researches caused the abandonment of this project. See above, pp. 90, 94–95.

[63] *Aurora*, Feb. 21, 1807.

claimed in May, would bring starvation to the Caribbean colonies and loss of the home islands' only certain supply of foreign foodstuffs, and might even throw the United States into the camp of England's enemies, costing her not only her most important economic connection but perhaps the colonies as well.[64]

Moreover, the treaty implied American inferiority perhaps more clearly than that signed by John Jay in 1794 and so bitterly execrated by Republicans. Jay secured compensation for British seizures, but his successors entirely failed to do so and perhaps, by their unaccountable failure to press this point, prejudiced future American claims. Jay's article on trade with India returned, but in tightened form. There was nothing but contemptuous silence toward American requests to share commercial traffic with Britain's colonies in the Western Hemisphere. And, although the treaty rescinded the *Essex* decision, the provisions on the reëxport trade showed deep suspicion of American procedures, exceeded the *Polly* decision (particularly by withholding permission to re-export Asian goods to the West Indies), and seemed to consider toleration of indirect trade as a gift extended by Britain and not a right. Commenting that *"we have not the power of Resistance, and if we had, I fear we would not have the Will,"* Senator Smith at first favored accepting the provision; later this commercial spokesman concluded that, while American traders could prosper under it, the article was too dishonorable to accept.[65] The declaration on Berlin, even as emended by Monroe and Pinkney, affronted their superiors. Jefferson and Madison, who fully recognized Britain's right to retaliate and would have approved reciprocal statements reserving her position and America's, did not like "the form & face chozen" for the unilateral announcement approved at London.

Failure on impressment stirred American sensibilities most of all. Jefferson and Madison knew too well the proclivities of British commanders to believe that general directives would restrain them.

---

[64] Madison to Monroe and Pinkney, May 20, 1807, Instructions, Vol. VI. These instructions contain the fullest official criticism of the terms of the treaty.

[65] Samuel Smith to Madison, March 14, 1807, Rives Collection; Samuel Smith to Madison, April 18, 1807, Samuel Smith MSS, Library of Congress.

As Madison dryly remarked, the "remedy proposed in the Note from the British Commissioners, however well intended, does not inspire the confidence here which gave it so much value in their judgment." National interest, Republicans held, required a formal stipulation, and at least one moderate Federalist believed Jefferson *"absolutely obliged,* if he regards the national honour, to send the Treaty back." In the most important passage in a formal critique sent to London in May, Madison wrote that the President "cannot reconcile it with his duty to our seafaring citizens, or with the sensibility or sovereignty of the nation, to recognize even constructively, a principle that would expose on the high seas, their liberty, their lives, every thing in a word that is dearest to the human heart, to the capricious or interested sentences which may be pronounced against their allegiance, by officers of a foreign Government." [66]

The treaty deprived America of her most effective weapon, so Jefferson and Madison believed, for securing a binding limitation on impressment in the future. Toward the close of the negotiations Lord Auckland succeeded in inserting a ban on "the foolish and teasing measure of non-importation" and others like it. The United States pledged itself to lay down the weapon of commercial warfare for ten years. Since the Republicans were unprepared to fight, this meant that for a decade seamen on American merchant ships must depend solely on protests and exhortation for their defense. This concession capped the general impression of American subordination, an impression that caused the Irish-born editor of the *Aurora* to ask his readers, "Will you abandon your rights? Will you abandon your independence? Are you willing to become colonies of Great Britain?" [67]

[66] Madison to Monroe and Pinkney, Feb. 3, 1807, Instructions, Vol. VI; King to Gouverneur Morris, March 30, 1807, postscript, Charles R. King, *The Life and Correspondence of Rufus King* (6 vols.; New York, 1894–1900), V, 13; Madison to Monroe and Pinkney, May 20, 1807, Instructions, Vol. VI. In the February instructions, Madison had stated that impressments in American waters had "at no time been more numerous or vexatious," but this does not necessarily invalidate the belief, apparently shared by the British and American negotiators in London, that the total number of incidents in all theaters was comparatively low.
[67] March 10, 1807.

In moral terms, Duane's queries answered themselves. But Monroe and Pinkney, faced with political realities, felt that America could not afford utopianism. As Monroe commented, "in all the points on which we have had to press this gov$^t$., interests of the most vital character were involved . . . , at a time too when the very existence of the country depended on an adherence to its maritime pretensions." The envoys signed the treaty when it appeared that Napoleon planned an immediate assault upon neutral commerce. America needed British friendship, both to reinforce pressure on France (which did not implement the Berlin Decree against American commerce until Jefferson rejected the treaty) and to encourage the apparent English drift toward greater rceognition of neutral rights indicated by Fox's Blockade and the disavowal of Whitby. Although "little more than a project," the treaty, Monroe said, started Britain in the right direction. "By arranging our differences in peace with England her merchants would have calculated on its preservation, & embarked most extensively in trade [with us]. . . . The interest in that country for the continuation of peace wo$^d$. have increased daily," forcing any ministry to avoid a clash with the United States.[68]

At least, Monroe and Pinkney argued, they had obtained important immediate advantages, and like the British they had surrendered in principle no claims that could not be reactivated later. While the treaty omitted impressment, the promised restraints and the actual rarity of the practice, which the reduction of rival naval power at Trafalgar might permit to continue, created fairly favorable conditions. Article XI, on the reëxport trade, perhaps imposed more stringent requirements than the *Polly* decision or the King-Hawkesbury exchange of 1801, which made only general reference to duties and drawbacks, but it did destroy the *Essex* decision. With ground rules clearly laid out, American merchants might continue the trade that had already brought so much prosperity.

Considering the comparative power of Britain and America, the

[68] Monroe to Jefferson, Jan. 11, 1807, Feb. 27, 1808, Jefferson MSS; Monroe to John Taylor, Jan. 9, 1809, Monroe MSS.

Napoleonic threat, the later failure of commercial warfare to secure a reasonably speedy victory over England, considering too America's immense material interest in an arrangement with Britain, Monroe and Pinkney seem justified. Nobody can be sure, of course, that ratification of the treaty would have led, as they hoped, to a further reconciliation or even prevented the antineutral proceedings of the ministry that succeeded Grenville's in 1807. But it is even more unreasonable to test the commissioners' hopes against British activities after the treaty failed, to say that the Orders in Council of 1807 or impressment proves that any agreement would at best have been transitory. At worst Britain would have had to make some gestures to preserve a *rapprochement;* at best she might have worked positively to improve it. Monroe and Pinkney not only spoke the traditional accents of American realism; they also opened the door to peace and uneasy friendship. They did these things at the cost of important moral considerations, and Jefferson and Madison expressed more nobly the new nation's aspirations. But if the administration rejected compromise in the interest of idealism and psychological equality, by its future course it condemned itself, lacking the will to vindicate these commendable objectives. Certainly "a quiet nap" could neither long endure nor prove truly restful.

# EMBARGO: ALTERNATIVE TO WAR

Vice-Admiral Sir George Cranfield Berkeley, M.P., owed his appointment as commander in chief on the American station to the Ministry of All the Talents. Grenville, at least, knew Berkeley well enough to have misgivings about his selection,[1] but the admiral's brother commanded a number of votes that marched into the ministerial lobby at division time, as did Berkeley himself between tours of sea duty. Consequently, Howick offered Berkeley the American command. In the spring of 1806 the admiral arrived at Halifax and initiated a steady stream of complaints against the Admiralty, against Jefferson, against the United States, which, with scant regard for normal channels, he forwarded directly to Grenville.[2]

Berkeley believed the United States would back down whenever Britain refused to compromise. In the spring of 1807, in Chesa-

---

[1] Grenville to Thomas Grenville, Oct. 23, 1807, Thomas Grenville MSS, British Museum (Add. MSS 41851–41859), Add. MSS 41852.

[2] See the letters from Admiral Berkeley to Grenville in Boconnoc MSS (Papers of William Wyndham Grenville, Baron Grenville), Lostwithiel, Cornwall, Letters Jan. to Sept. 1806, under the following dates: Feb. 12, 14, April 13, July 29.

peake Bay, a number of deserters from the Royal Navy received protection from local authorities, and many of them even enrolled in the United States Navy. One of these deserters, Jenkin Ratford, a short, swarthy former tailor from London, enlisted on U.S.S. *Chesapeake* and railed at British officers on the quays and streets of Norfolk. Since American authorities refused to return Ratford and the others, one solution alone occurred to Berkeley's unsubtle mind. The admiral "required and directed [his subordinates] in case of meeting with the American frigate the Chesapeake at Sea, and without the limits of the United States to shew to the Captain of her this order; and to require to search his Ship for the deserters." [3] Captain Salusbury P. Humphreys sailed in Berkeley's flagship *Leopard* to carry this fateful order to the ships at Norfolk.

On June 22, a day after Humphreys arrived, the *Chesapeake* stood to sea, bound for the Mediterranean. She was hailed by the *Leopard* and, suspecting nothing, came to. Lieutenant John Meade boarded her to hand Commodore Barron a copy of Berkeley's order and a note from Captain Humphreys expressing hope that peace could be maintained. After fruitless discussion in Barron's cabin, Meade returned to his ship. Humphreys argued further through the hailing trumpet, then fired a shot across the *Chesapeake*'s bow. Finally, as the captain later reported, "conceiving . . . that my Orders would not admit of deviation, I lament to state, that, I felt under the necessity of enforcing them, by firing into the United States Ship." After ten minutes of action (if such a word may be used for a one-sided cannonade), Barron surrendered. A second boarding party from the *Leopard* mustered the American crew and removed four deserters, including Ratford, who was dragged from hiding. [4]

[3] Berkeley to Humphreys, June 1, 1807, enclosed in Berkeley to Marsden, July 4, 1807, Admiralty Papers, Public Record Office, Adm 1/497. For particulars of the provocation for this order and for the subsequent incident, see Henry Adams, *History of the United States during the Administrations of Jefferson and Madison* (9 vols.; New York, 1889–1891), IV, 1–20, and, from the British point of view, Anthony Steel, "More Light on the *Chesapeake*," *Mariner's Mirror*, XXXIX (1953), 243–265.
[4] Humphreys to Captain J. E. Douglas, June 22, 1807, enclosed in Douglas to William Wellesley Pole, June 24, 1807, Adm 1/1729.

Humphreys, who doubted the wisdom of Berkeley's order, executed it moderately. From among the scores of known deserters and Englishmen on the American ship, he took only four. Jenkin Ratford was soon hanged at Halifax. The other three were Americans, two of them Negroes and thus demonstrably non-British, but all three had escaped from the Royal Navy in a British ship's gig. The two Negroes, furthermore, had actually deserted from an American merchantman and enlisted in the Royal Navy in 1806. For his restraint Captain Humphreys, who was placed on half pay in 1808 while Berkeley escaped punishment, received no credit from either government. After all, whether so ordered by his superior or not, and whatever the provocation provided by the *Chesapeake*, called by one English scholar "a kind of fly-paper for picking up deserters and other wandering British seamen," [5] Humphreys had violated American sovereignty. As Niles said, "It is of no importance . . . whether the men were Americans or not—whether they had been impressed or entered the British service voluntarily." [6]

Many British officers, with that paranoid attitude of whining superiority so common among them, chose to believe England the aggrieved party. When their supplies were cut off, certainly a mild enough act of reprisal, commanders in the Chesapeake embarked upon a campaign of petulant interference with American shipping. Berkeley at first believed the American outcry artificially maintained by Jefferson for political purposes, then shifted from a conviction that the Americans would only bluster to a real fear of war, pleaded for reinforcements, and even talked about an anticipatory attack upon New York as a salutary lesson. [7]

Actually, public opinion required no Jeffersonian stimulus. The whole nation demanded satisfaction. In Virginia, militia patrolled the coasts to prevent supplies from reaching British ships. Thomas Ritchie, editor of the Richmond *Enquirer*, abandoned the pen

[5] Steel, *op. cit.*, p. 265.
[6] *Niles' Weekly Register* (Baltimore), Sept. 28, 1811.
[7] Steel, *op. cit.*, *passim*; Berkeley to Bathurst [?], Aug. 13, 1807, Francis Bickley, ed., *Report on the Manuscripts of Earl Bathurst* (London: Historical Manuscripts Commission, 1923), pp. 63–65; Berkeley to Marsden, Aug. 17, 1807, Adm 1/497.

(and the pleasures of his honeymoon) for the sword, and Winfield Scott, a young lance corporal, captured a boat crew that landed to seek provisions. At New York a mob removed the rudder from an English ship, cut the rigging, carried off the sails, and demolished gun carriages. Consul Barclay's house had to be protected by police, and a traveling British diplomat found it wise to adopt an alias. All over the nation, public meetings denounced the British. In Boston the Federalist leadership unsuccessfully attempted to block one town meeting but then, as a measure of political prudence, found it expedient to endorse a second. Two thousand people gathered to hear a youthful Federalist deliver a strident speech in behalf of resolutions pledging support to the national government.[8]

Some Americans urged a declaration of war, and many more expected one. "The probability of war," wrote William Wirt, "is very strong: because it is scarcely presumable that British arrogance & injustice will give us that satisfaction which alone will appease the spirit of this nation—and between the alternatives of war & dishonorable surrender, our countrymen will not long hesitate." But many patriots wished to give Great Britain a chance to make atonement. From Boston Elbridge Gerry reported that "there is no desire here, to engage in a war with Great Britain, if it can honorably be avoided; . . . but if national redress cannot be obtained . . . , peace . . . would cease to be beneficial & honorable." The old Republican wheel horse, Nathaniel Macon, urged restraint, adding, "Peace is everything to us, especially in this part of the nation." Robert R. Livingston, another staunch Republican, agreed that "our national happiness & prosperity depend upon the preservation of peace" and urged one more special mission to London.[9] Rallying, Federalist writers brought out pamphlets that

---

[8] Charles H. Ambler, *Thomas Ritchie* (Richmond, 1913), pp. 42–43; Winfield Scott, *Memoirs of Lieut.-General Scott, LL.D.*, I (New York, 1864), 19–20; Tench Coxe to Madison, July 2, 1807, James Madison MSS, Library of Congress; Richard B. Davis, ed., *Jeffersonian America: Notes on the United States of America . . . by Sir Augustus John Foster, Bart.* (San Marino, 1954), p. 293; Samuel E. Morison, *The Life and Letters of Harrison Gray Otis* (2 vols.; Boston, 1913), I, 276–277.

[9] Wirt to Peachey R. Gilmer, July 18, 1807, William Wirt MSS, Library of Congress; Gerry to Thomas Matthews, July 11, 1807, Elbridge Gerry MSS, Massa-

defended Berkeley's order or at least suggested that Jeffersonian weakness had invited it.[10] Within a month after the attack talk of war had subsided, and at the beginning of September the French minister reported his disgust at the "fear and servile deference" shown toward Britain. The brief flame had burned itself out; the imperatives of honor became passive. Joseph H. Nicholson wrote to Gallatin, his brother-in-law, "The public mind has been suffered to brood so long . . . that I fear its ardor is cooling down. Spirit enough is however left, to blaze, when the constituted authorities will blow the coals." [11]

Initially Jefferson chose to play the part of a damper rather than a bellows. He sought to keep the public conflagration just short of open flame, hoping the heat of anger would force London to settle the *Chesapeake* affair and even abandon impressment. When he received word of Humphreys' brutal attack, the President wrote the governor of Virginia to urge restraint so that Congress, when it met, could have freedom to decide "whether, having taught so many other useful lessons to Europe, we may not add that of showing them that there are peaceable means of repressing injustice, by making it the interest of the aggressor to do what is just." With cabinet approval Jefferson issued a proclamation closing American waters to British warships, a device designed to satisfy the popular demand for action and at the same time reduce the chance of further incidents.[12] The President explained that

---

chusetts Historical Society; Macon to Gallatin, Aug. 2, 1807, Henry Adams, *The Life of Albert Gallatin* (Philadelphia, 1879), p. 362; Livingston to Madison, July 12, 1807, William C. Rives Collection, Library of Congress.

[10] David Everett (*pseud.* An American) *An Essay on the Rights and Duties of Nations, Relative to Fugitives from Justice; Considered with Reference to the Affair of the Chesapeake* (Boston, 1807); Thomas G. Fessenden, *Some Thoughts on the Present Dispute between Great Britain and America* (Philadelphia, 1807); A Gentleman at New-York, *The Voice of Truth; or, Thoughts on the Affair between the Leopard and Chesapeake* (New York, 1807); John Lowell (*pseud.* A Yankee Farmer), *Peace without Dishonour—War without Hope. Being a Calm and Dispassionate Enquiry into the Question of the Chesapeake* (Boston, 1807).

[11] Turreau #43 to Minister of Foreign Relations, Sept. 7, 1807, Archives des Affaires Étrangères, Correspondance Politique, États-Unis (photostats, Library of Congress), Vol. LX; Nicholson to Gallatin, Sept. 10, 1807, Albert Gallatin MSS, New-York Historical Society.

[12] Jefferson to Cabell, June 19, 1807, Andrew A. Lipscomb and Albert E. Bergh, eds., *The Writings of Thomas Jefferson* (Memorial ed.; 20 vols.; Washington, 1903–

"the usage of nations" required him to seek satisfaction before opening hostilities, that delay would permit American ships to return to havens at home, and that—this was good Republican doctrine—"the power of declaring war being in Congress, the Ex[ecutive] should do no act committing them to war, when it is very probable that they may prefer a non-intercourse to war." [13]

As repeated accounts of British arrogance flowed in from Norfolk, Jefferson became more bellicose. He and his Cabinet discussed plans for an attack on Canada, canvassed the financial requirements of war, and planned to use gunboats if the British squadron extended its harassment of shipping. Leaving the final decision until fall, Jefferson departed for Monticello on August 1. There, further news from Europe led him to feel that war was nearly inevitable. Early in September, writing to a member of his Cabinet, he declared that a real settlement with England was unlikely, although if the Baltic were closed to her trade Britain might "temporize with us. But if peace among the *continental* powers of Europe should leave her free in her intercourse with the powers who will then be *neutral*, the present ministry . . . will not in my opinion give us the necessary assurances respecting the flag. In that case, it must bring a war soon, and if so, it can never be in a better time for us." [14]

Four days before the President fled the heat of Washington, Nicholas Biddle, a young friend of Madison's, sailed on U.S.S. *Revenge* bearing instructions to Monroe on the "assurances respecting the flag" required by the United States. "A formal disavowal of the deed, and restoration of the four seamen to the ship from which they were taken, are things of course and indispensable." Failing this, America reserved her right—and here the instructions hinted at war but left the way open to less decisive action

---

1904), XI, 256–257; memorandum of July 2, 1807, Thomas Jefferson MSS, Library of Congress. Jefferson and the secretaries also agreed to mobilize the gunboats, recall naval vessels from the Mediterranean, and send strong instructions to Monroe.

[13] *National Intelligencer* (Washington), July 8, 1807; Jefferson to Thomas M. Randolph, July 5, 1807, Jefferson MSS.

[14] Memoranda of July 26, 28, 1807, Jefferson MSS; Jefferson to Madison, Sept. 3, 1807, Lipscomb and Bergh, *op. cit.*, XI, 358; Jefferson to Jacob Crowninshield, Sept. 3, 1807, *ibid.*, XI, 356–357.

—"to resort to means depending upon the United States alone." The United States required more than a settlement of the *Chesapeake* incident. "As a security for the future, the entire abolition of impressment from vessels under the flag of the United States [not merely from warships] . . . is also made an indispensable part of the satisfaction" demanded. Madison directed Monroe to insist upon this great surrender without even offering, at least initially, any compensatory regulations to discourage the enlistment of British seamen in American ships.[15]

The instructions lay on Madison's desk for three weeks after they were drafted. Perhaps the administration delayed so that the demands could travel in company with reports of angry outbursts from all parts of the Union, thus showing the British government that a united people was ready for war. Even then England was unlikely to be panicked into concession, for the President's proclamation had shown that the executive, at least, still hoped to preserve peace. Far more probably, Jefferson and his subordinates expected to be able to maintain national unity for months and decided to use it as a weapon to force affairs with England to a climax. If the ministry proved stubborn, they believed, the American people would endorse resistance more vigorously than when it could be argued that Berkeley spoke for no one but his cantankerous self. Although not always candid in letters to the obstreperous Philadelphian, William Duane, on this occasion Jefferson probably expressed very nearly his true feelings when he wrote:

Although we demand of England what is merely of right, reparation for the past, security for the future, yet as their pride will possibly, nay probably, prevent their yielding them to the extent we shall require, my opinion is, that the public mind, which I believe is made up for war, should maintain itself at that point. They have often enough, God knows, given us cause for war before; but it has been on points which would not have united the nation. But now they have touched a chord which vibrates in every heart. Now then is the time to settle the old and the new.[16]

[15] Madison to Monroe, July 6, 1807, Department of State Archives, National Archives, Instructions, all countries, Vol. VI.
[16] Jefferson to Duane, July 20, 1807, Lipscomb and Bergh, *op. cit.*, XI, 291.

By October America knew for certain that Britain would not surrender impressment. Although returning congressmen found in the *National Intelligencer* a scarcely cryptic invitation to choose between "a direct resort to war, . . . or . . . a surer reparation through the medium of commercial regulation," Jefferson tended toward the more vigorous course. The first draft of his annual message reviewed British aggressions in language that seemed to invite a declaration of war. Gallatin returned the draft with many changes, warning the President that public ardor had cooled. The final version reprobated British actions in language sufficiently strong to alarm London. Still, the President neither asked for a declaration of war nor suggested that one was inevitable.[17] For more than a month the new Congress remained in uneasy uncertainty.

Among the derelictions charged against Britain by Jefferson, an Order in Council dated January 7, 1807, figured most prominently after the attack on the *Chesapeake*. When Holland and Auckland required the Americans to accept a note reserving the right of retaliation against the Berlin Decree, they spoke of no theoretical contingency. Already the government was at work upon an order forbidding coastal trade between enemy ports. Grenville and Howick calculated that this would strike at French communications and, particularly when garnished with an eloquently belligerent preamble claiming that French action released Britain from the traditional limits of war, would demonstrate at home that the ministry intended vigor. At the same time the government hoped not to interfere seriously with America's transatlantic trade.[18] On both scores the Cabinet miscalculated. Perceval and Castlereagh attacked the declaration as ineffective. After initial hesitation Madison also attacked the order, on the grounds that it directly chal-

[17] *National Intelligencer*, Oct. 26, 1807; Gallatin to Jefferson, Oct. 21, 1807, Jefferson MSS; James D. Richardson, ed., *A Compilation of the Messages and Papers of the Presidents* (Washington, 1897), I, 425–430; *Courier* (London), Dec. 7, 1807; Grenville to Thomas Grenville, Dec. 10, 1807, Thomas Grenville MSS, Add. MSS 41852.

[18] Nicholl to Auckland, private, Dec. 12, 1806, William Eden, Baron Auckland, MSS, British Museum (Add. MSS 34412–34471, 45728–45730), Add. MSS 34457; Auckland to Grenville, Dec. 18, 1806, Boconnoc MSS, Lord Auckland 1806; Auckland to Howick, Dec. 22, 1806, Charles Grey, Second Earl Grey, MSS, The Prior's Kitchen, Durham University, from 1st Ld. Auckland.

lenged American interests (most merchantmen carried cargoes to Europe which could be sold only after calls at several ports); that it had been issued before the American reaction to Napoleon's policy was known; and, more particularly, that, by emphasizing the right of retaliation, it opened the door to an absolute destruction of neutral rights.[19]

Despite the *Chesapeake* affair, the January Order in Council, a royal proclamation reaffirming impressment, the hanging of Ratford, and increased seizures, Congress shrank from a breach. The legislature permitted the Nonimportation Act to go into effect at last; it confirmed Jefferson's expulsion of British ships from American ports; and it debated military preparations at length. But nobody wanted war. Erskine and Turreau agreed that a declaration was highly unlikely. Gallatin felt that Congress was "certainly peaceably disposed." Jefferson pessimistically concluded that the representatives of the people would settle for the Nonimportation Act. He feared this was not enough to coerce Britain but would "end in war & give her the choice of a moment of declaring it." [20] The Jeffersonian strategy of refrigerating the demand for war and then bringing it again to a boil had failed.

Ominous reports soon arrived from Europe. In September Napoleon began to enforce the Berlin Decree against American ships, and Champagny officially informed the American minister that the new decree would be rigorously executed.[21] Shortly after this news reached the United States, London reports indicated that the new British ministry intended to issue regulations of its own. Jefferson expected an announcement forbidding all trade with the Continent and even expressed an approving belief that "it would produce an immediate declaration [of war] here; & that it is the only thing

[19] *Hansard*, VIII, 620–656; Madison to Erskine, March 20, 1807, enclosed in Erskine #11 to Howick, March 30, 1807, Foreign Office Archives, Public Record Office, FO 5/52; Madison to Erskine, March 29, 1807, enclosed in Erskine #12 to Howick, March 31, 1807, *ibid.*; Madison to Monroe, March 31, 1807, Instructions, Vol. VI.

[20] Erskine #25 to Canning, Oct. 5, 1807, FO 5/52; Turreau #4 to Minister of Foreign Relations, Dec. 2, 1807, AAE, CP, E-U, Vol. LX; Gallatin to Hannah M. Gallatin, Oct. 30, 1807, Adams, *Gallatin*, p. 364; Jefferson to Thomas M. Randolph, Oct. 26, 1807, Jefferson MSS.

[21] Champagny to Armstrong, Oct. 8, 1807, AAE, CP, E-U, Vol. LX.

which will." Federalists later claimed that news of the November orders reached America only after the Embargo message had gone to Congress. Although this was true of their text, London papers arriving on December 18 made Jefferson so certain of the general content that he included a description in the first draft of his call for an embargo, only to be dissuaded by the more cautious Madison. All congressmen knew that Britain was preparing to strike. To omit the orders from any list of precipitants of the Embargo, John Quincy Adams later scoffed, was like "laying your finger over the *unit* before a series of noughts, and then arithmetically proving that they all amount to nothing." [22]

Jefferson had totally miscalculated. In June and July he restrained the demand for war, counting on his ability to reinvigorate it if Monroe failed to secure a settlement of the *Chesapeake* affair and an end to impressment. As this unrealistic hope dwindled, the President came more and more to anticipate and perhaps to welcome a war. Down to the very moment of recommending an embargo, the President, although sometimes contradictory, spoke far more favorably and often of war, or at the very least of accepting the gage of battle cast down by Britain. News of enforcement of the Berlin Decree did not alter Jefferson's basic position, and four days before the Embargo message a Republican senator wrote, "(*in confidence*) the man in the Stone House is of opinion that the Die is Cast." [23] But the popular spirit had evaporated, the orators had fallen silent. In July Jefferson could have had war but did not want it; now he probably wanted it but could not hope to get it. He fell back upon the supreme weapon of commercial warfare, a general embargo. The choice was not entirely unpalatable, since if by some chance war should come, the recall of ships and seamen was only prudent. And the efficacy of commercial pressure was an article of faith among Republicans.

[22] Jefferson to Thomas M. Randolph, Nov. 16, 1807, Jefferson MSS; Jefferson to Madison, July 14, 1824, Rives Collection; Adams to Otis, March 31, 1808, Worthington C. Ford, ed., *The Writings of John Quincy Adams* (7 vols.; New York, 1914–1917), III, 201.

[23] Nicholas Gilman to Eustis, Dec. 14, 1807, William Eustis MSS, Library of Congress.

Threats to the British pocketbook had a long, patriotic history in the United States. The first of these, in colonial times, aimed to prevent British sales in America, whereas in 1807 the United States aimed principally to eliminate English sources of supply. This type of pressure had been tried briefly in 1794, prior to the Jay treaty, when an embargo quickly created a serious food shortage in the British West Indies. What had worked in 1794 seemed even more promising now, for Britain had lost much of her European trade. In 1806 Elbridge Gerry argued for an embargo, both to keep American shipping within the protection of its own harbors and to bring pressure to bear upon England. A year later the Richmond *Argus* suggested closing all trade until Europe came to its senses. Robert R. Livingston recommended an embargo "that we may keep what we have at home and daily get more of our seamen & property out of the reach of the piracy of Britain so as to leave, with the debts we owe them, a ballance in our hands to compensate the injuries we may receive." That summer the Secretary of State warned the British minister that, while a *Chesapeake* settlement might prevent war, only a general adjustment could prevent Congress from adopting "very strong Measures of Restraint upon the Intercourse between Great Britain and the United States." [24] For various reasons a general embargo rather than selective pressure upon Britain became Jeffersonian policy in December, 1807. That the Embargo aimed chiefly at England was, however, understood in Washington, London, and Paris.

Like most policy the Embargo reflected many motives, some of them quite indirect. Jefferson, who even in moments of unrelated crisis never lost sight of his Florida objective, doubtless hoped resistance to England would encourage Napoleon to favor American ambitions to the southward. Failure to resist, on the other hand, might cause the French emperor to assail the United States; in the words of the Boston *Independent Chronicle*, "If, by the most humiliating concessions we could avoid a war with England, will

[24] Gerry to Madison, Feb. 19, 1806, Madison MSS; Joseph I. Shulim, *The Old Dominion and Napoleon Bonaparte* (New York, 1952), p. 230; Robert R. Livingston to Madison, July 12, 1807, Rives Collection; Erskine #22 to Canning, July 31, 1807, FO 5/52.

the other nations at war with her be tame spectators of such a compromise?" Later on the President also justified continuance of the Embargo as an experiment, so that "on future occasions our legislators may know with certainty how far they may count on it as an engine for national purposes." [25]

Without any doubt the chief aims of the Embargo were precautionary and coercive. Madison and, as time passed, Jefferson placed great faith in the coercive power of an embargo. Although they thought that total loss of the American market, already constricted by the Nonimportation Act, would hurt Great Britain, they counted most on nothing less than imperial starvation. In the Secretary's view no part of the Empire would escape. "It can no longer be unknown to the most sanguine partizan of the Colonial Monopoly," he said, "that the necessaries of life and cultivation can be furnished to . . . [British Caribbean possessions] from no other source than the United States." The United States supplied vitally needed naval stores. "Lastly it should not be forgotten that the United States are one of the Granaries which supply the annual deficit of the British harvests," a particularly important point when Prussian and French grain might be withheld.[26] Such one-sided calculations minimized American dependence upon trade with Britain, and the whole project rested upon an assumption that England would react rationally. The Adamses, father and son, more realistic than the President, correctly pointed out that in time of war reason often went by the board. The Embargo "affects their interests no doubt," John Quincy Adams noted, "but nations which sacrifice men by the hundred thousands and treasure by the hundred millions in War, for *nothing*, or worse than nothing, pay little attention to their real interests." [27]

Like Senator Adams, Jefferson supported an embargo primarily

[25] *Independent Chronicle* (Boston), Nov. 12, 1807; Jefferson to Gallatin, May 15, July 12, 1808, Gallatin MSS.

[26] Madison to Monroe and Pinkney, May 20, 1807, Instructions, Vol. VI. For a convincing demonstration that Madison had for years advocated commercial coercion, see Irving Brant, *James Madison: Secretary of State* (Indianapolis, 1953), pp. 397–403.

[27] Adams to Ezekiel Bacon, Dec. 21, 1808, Adams Family MSS (microfilm), Massachusetts Historical Society, Vol. CXXXV.

to protect American property. Whether peace or war impended, under existing circumstances "it would be the greatest folly for the Americans to sport their property between the contending powers of Europe." [28] Furthermore, by depriving the belligerents of American merchantmen as targets, an embargo "saves us the necessity of making their capture the cause of immediate war." In time, political developments or the growth of "some sense of moral duty" might change the whole equation. If not, the President by no means intended to maintain terrapin habits forever, wise though a temporary withdrawal into the shell might be. "The alternative," he said, "was that or war. for a certain length of time I think the embargo is a less evil than war, but after a certain time it will not be so. if peace should not take place in Europe, & if both France and England should refuse to exempt us from their decrees & orders, as we shall strenuously urge, it will remain for Congress . . . to say at what moment it will become preferable for us to meet war." [29] The President, through indecision and weakness, later permitted a policy initiated as a temporary precaution to become a semipermanent institution.

Summarizing all the arguments, but giving priority to the precautionary aspect, the *National Intelligencer* stated:

The ocean presents a field where no harvest is to be reaped but that of danger, of spoliation and of disgrace.

Under such circumstances the best to be done is what has been done; a dignified retirement within ourselves. . . .

It is singularly fortunate that an embargo, whilst it guards our essential resources, will have the collateral effect of making it the interests of all nations to change the system which has driven our commerce from the ocean.[30]

As a short-run insulation from danger, the embargo could be justified. If maintained for long it became a craven surrender to European edicts. As time went on, Republican emphasis shifted from

[28] *Independent Chronicle*, Nov. 12, 1807.
[29] Jefferson to John Taylor, Jan. 6, 1808, Jefferson MSS; Jefferson to Major Joseph Eggleston, March 7, 1808, *ibid*.
[30] Dec. 23, 1807.

"dignified retirement" to the originally collateral aim of coercion, a more positive course but also one open to the pragmatic test of success or failure.

On December 17, 1807, Jefferson convened his Cabinet to discuss an embargo message, perhaps, as John Quincy Adams later stated, after conversations with congressional leaders had convinced him that a declaration of war could not be obtained. The ministers unanimously agreed to request a law forbidding the departure of all ships, American and foreign, and the Attorney General transmitted a resolution in this sense to a member of the House for introduction. Overnight Albert Gallatin came to the conclusion that the decision had been too "hastily adopted on the first view of our foreign intelligence," particularly newspaper accounts of the November orders. He urged the President to eliminate controls on foreign ships, fearing retaliation against far more numerous American vessels abroad, and to recommend a definite term for the embargo, for, said the Secretary, "I prefer war to permanent embargo." At a second cabinet meeting Gallatin's first suggestion was adopted, his second refused. In the afternoon Jefferson sent to Congress an extremely short message suggesting an embargo on American ships and goods and, more elliptically, war preparations. With the message Jefferson transmitted the British proclamation on impressment and Champagny's declaration that the Berlin Decree would be enforced, but at Madison's urging the President said nothing of impending British orders. At the Secretary's suggestion, too, the President specifically recommended an embargo instead of simply calling the possibility to Congress' attention.[31]

The Senate rushed the Embargo through in one afternoon. On receipt of the message a committee headed by Samuel Smith withdrew to consider the draft, already prepared, of a bill. The four Republican members had a brief, spirited struggle with John Quincy Adams. Adams objected to the paucity of information

[31] Adams, "Reply to the Appeal of Massachusetts Federalists," n.d., Henry Adams, ed., *Documents Relating to New-England Federalism* (Boston, 1877), p. 188; Gallatin to Jefferson, Dec. 18, 1807, Jefferson MSS; Richardson, *op. cit.*, I, 433; Brant, *op. cit.*, pp. 394–395; Raymond Walters, Jr., *Albert Gallatin* (New York, 1957), pp. 198–199.

Jefferson provided, as well as to the bill's vagueness. In reply Senator Smith brought forward every argument he could think of, in particular urging faith in Jefferson and asserting that an embargo would give the administration an invaluable weapon in negotiations with a special British envoy about to arrive. Incompletely satisfied by Smith's arguments, the Massachusetts independent nevertheless consented to endorse the Embargo, to aid the President and to save commerce from loss. He had no faith in it as more than a short-term device and in February, 1808, called for its repeal.[32]

Having secured unanimity within the committee, Smith reported the bill. By a narrow margin the Senate agreed to suspend the rules requiring three readings on separate days, then turned to a brief, unreported debate on the bill's merits. The bill passed by a vote of twenty-two to six, with six senators absent.[33] Among the minority were two Republicans, William Maclay of Pennsylvania and William H. Crawford of Georgia, who objected not to the Embargo but to overly precipitate action. Four or five hours after Jefferson recommended an embargo, the Senate had done his bidding.

The House of Representatives proved slightly more recalcitrant, as much from indecision, weakness, and lack of leadership as from opposition to the President. Few people respected the Tenth Congress, for, as Senator Adams observed, the legislators repeatedly showed "great embarrassment, alarm, anxiety, and confusion of mind, but no preparation for any measure of vigor, and an obvious strong disposition to yield all that Great Britain may require, to preserve peace, under a thin external show of dignity and bravery." [34] Republican unity had been undermined by a bitter battle to choose a successor to Nathaniel Macon as speaker. Joseph B. Varnum of Massachusetts triumphed by the thin margin of one vote and immediately rewarded his supporters with

[32] Entry of Dec. 18, 1807, Charles F. Adams, ed., *Memoirs of John Quincy Adams* (12 vols.; Philadelphia, 1874–1877), I, 491; Stephen R. Bradley to ———, Sept. 21, 1824, Ford, *op. cit.*, III, 168n–169n.

[33] *Annals*, 10th Cong., 1st sess., pp. 50–51.

[34] Entry of Nov. 17, 1807, Charles F. Adams, *op. cit.*, I, 476.

choice committee assignments. At Embargo time and later, internal frictions weakened the Republican majority's will, even if not enough to bestow success upon the Federalists.

As in the Senate, Jefferson's message was immediately followed by introduction of a bill. Randolph, seeking the lead as usual, quarreled with Benjamin Crowninshield for this honor, and for a time the House engaged in vapid debate. Then the Senate bill arrived. The House, setting aside its own version, rushed through the first two readings of the new bill. Here, too, debates are unreported, but enough opposition developed so that action could not be completed. The next day the House devoted an entire session to the Embargo, and John Randolph vehemently opposed it, perhaps shifting his ground because members emphasized the coercive rather than the precautionary purpose which he alone approved. Timothy Pickering even thought it might be possible to defeat the bill, but over the Sunday recess the administration brought pressure to bear upon Republican legislators. On Monday a solid phalanx of eighty Republicans overwhelmed various mischievous motions, and John Randolph failed to turned the tide with a tearful address not at all in his usual hectoring style. At eleven in the evening the House approved the bill by almost two to one. The forty-two opponents, said the President, were made up of "one half Federalists, ¼ of the little band [Randolph and his coterie], the other fourth of republicans happening to take up mistaken views of the subject." [35] Some of these Republicans, who objected only to Jefferson's furtive methods and his timing, soon supported the system, particularly after the mission of George H. Rose demonstrated that Britain spurned concession. Others drifted in the direction of Federalism without adopting its name. The defection of one Republican out of five, despite alarming news from Europe and heavy administration pressure, should have

---

[35] *Annals*, 10th Cong., 1st sess., pp. 1216–1228; Pickering to Timothy Williams, Dec. 21, 1807, Timothy Pickering MSS, Massachusetts Historical Society, Vol. XXXVIII; Taggart to Rev. John Taylor, Dec. 22, 1807, George H. Haynes, ed., "Letters of Samuel Taggart, Representative in Congress, 1803–1814," American Antiquarian Society, *Proceedings*, n.s., XXXIII (1923), 225; Jefferson to Thomas M. Randolph, Dec. 22, 1807, Jefferson MSS.

warned the administration that the new policy would seriously challenge its command of the loyalties of the American people.

At three in the afternoon the next day, December 22, 1807, Thomas Jefferson signed the Embargo Act. The act was scarcely more than a sketch of policy. Republicans disagreed as to its wisdom or, if they supported it, as to its true purpose. Some, like Macon, considered it valuable for its coercive effect; others, like Wilson C. Nicholas, endorsed it as a means to save American property. Being only vaguely understood, and with no terminal date indicated, the Embargo could appeal to many factions. Those who wanted war supported it as an indispensable prelude; those who wanted peace approved it either as an escape from harsher anti-British action or as a potentially powerful economic weapon that might bring England to her knees. Jefferson had secured his object, had pressured the Congress into passage of the act without revealing his own motives. But if he should fail either to advance to war or to secure British—and French—relaxation of the assault upon American commerce, the President's magnificent feat of legislative dexterity would turn to ashes in his mouth.[36]

The Embargo fell upon the people as a bewildering shock. "We are all much alarmed by the Embargo laid on," a Richmond correspondent wrote Nicholas, "not knowing how to judge of its probable duration, nor the real object for which the measure has been resorted to." Debate in both houses during the winter failed to clarify either of these points. Although urged to issue a public manifesto justifying the Embargo, perhaps rallying the nation behind a clearly defined policy, the administration for months declined to do so. In August, 1808, Jefferson finally composed a form letter to be sent to towns petitioning against the Embargo (he soon had to ask the publisher of the *National Intelligencer* to print 150 copies to save interminable copying). His letter, even then, was hardly revealing.[37]

As a result, unscrupulous Federalists had a field day. They of

---

[36] This verdict coincides, except in shading, with the excoriation of Jefferson in Henry Adams, *History*, IV, 176–177.

[37] Thomas Rutherford to Nicholas, Dec. 27, 1807, Wilson Cary Nicholas MSS, Library of Congress; Jefferson to ———, Aug. 26, 1808 (form letter), Jefferson MSS; Jefferson to Samuel H. Smith, Sept. 9, 1808, *ibid.*

course emphasized the hardships of withdrawal from the ocean, sometimes forecast that Britain would reply with war, and scoffed at the presumed effectiveness of pressure upon England, which, they pointed out, would receive a virtual monopoly of world shipping as compensation for loss of the American market. The most often reiterated argument was the totally fallacious one that Jefferson and his followers, through either fear or sympathy, had obeyed Napoleonic orders. Federalists pointed out that the new law hit Britain far more than France and reminded the people that a request for Minister Armstrong's correspondence from Paris had been refused during the Embargo debate; surely, they cried, something sinister lay behind these facts. So shrill did the accusations of French influence become, and so touchy were the Republicans, that in March Congressman Campbell challenged a persistent tormenter, Barent Gardenier, to a duel in which he seriously wounded the New York congressman.

Campbell's pistol silenced only one critic. For the most part Republicans had to depend upon the less decisive weapon of newspaper editorials. Editors concentrated on two themes, urging the nation to trust a beloved president and, particularly after official news of the November orders fell like a sledge hammer upon Anglophiles, claiming that the Embargo "dashed the philter of pillage from the lips of rapine." In the *Aurora*, Duane brought both themes together when he posed the rhetorical question: "Americans, have you not cause to revere the man whose policy has not only secured you by wise measures from war for three years past, but who has rescued you by a timely and effective measure of energy and prudence, from the fangs of piratical depredation?" Only rarely did administration journals emphasize the Embargo's coercive aspects, and they definitely denied that a desire to strike England more than France had played any part in passage of the measure. "Being one intended . . . chiefly for our own security, even if it should have an unequal operation on the different powers of Europe, should we," the *National Intelligencer* asked, "be under the less obligation to adopt it?" [38] In the spring Jefferson

[38] *Scioto Gazette*, July 19, 1808, quoted in Beverley W. Bond, *The Civilization of the Old Northwest* (New York, 1934), p. 270; *Aurora* (Philadelphia), Jan. 21,

frequently wrote of the Embargo as a temporary measure. But in the summer of 1808 he began to talk of it as a permanent policy and a weapon of coercion.

Successful coercion required the almost unanimous support of the American people, both to enforce self-denial and make it clear to Britain that the United States did not flinch. Here Jefferson was disappointed, for opposition to his policy proved far deeper than he anticipated, thanks primarily to the pressure of economic distress and a broad willingness to believe national honor no less sullied by one-sided trade than by head-in-the-sand withdrawal. All over the country, even in Jeffersonian strongholds, the Hydras of opposition arose. In August, from a vantage point at New York, Gallatin warned his chief that only Virginia, South Carolina, Georgia, and the nearly voteless West could be considered safe. The impending national election, he said, might well go against the Republicans if the Embargo continued. A month later the Secretary of the Treasury more accurately warned that, even if candidates bearing the Republican label formed a majority in the next Congress, the keystone of Republican policy would almost certainly be overthrown, since "there is not patriotism & union sufficient to bear with patience, where there is no stimulus." [39] In the election, using the Embargo as almost their only issue, Federalists tripled their electoral vote of 1804 and doubled their share of the House of Representatives.

Political discontent penetrated most deeply in Massachusetts, only recently redeemed from Federalism. Anglophilia ran deep in the Bay State, as did distrust of Virginia leadership, and many Yankees preferred the risks of wartime trade to embargo. Although Governor Sullivan won reëlection by a narrow margin, at April elections the Federalists recaptured the General Court. The new legislature promptly elected, well ahead of time, a replacement for John Quincy Adams, and Adams, who knew at the time that his

---

1808; *National Intelligencer*, Jan. 4, 1808. For a slightly different conclusion see Lawrence S. Kaplan, "Jefferson, the Napoleonic Wars, and the Balance of Power," *William and Mary Quarterly*, 3d Series, XIV (1957), 200–202.

[39] Gallatin to Jefferson, Aug. 5, 1808, Jefferson MSS; Gallatin to Madison, Sept. 9, 1808, Rives Collection.

vote for the Embargo would probably destroy him politically, equally promptly resigned from the Senate. By summer Governor Sullivan's will had begun to erode, along with that of many loyal Republicans, and Jefferson came to fear an outbreak of rebellion, although in August he was confident that his own supporters and "that portion of the federalists who . . . would not court moblaw would crush it in embryo." [40] It would be nonsense to suggest that all Massachusetts rallied to Federalism. Marblehead and Salem, for example, remained Republican, and in the latter town Joseph Story and William Gray, the state's most prominent shipowner who actually shifted to Republicanism in 1808, successfully led a fight against resolutions denouncing the Embargo. Ezekiel Bacon and Henry Dearborn assured Gallatin that Federalist successes were only hard won and perhaps temporary. Nevertheless, the Embargo resuscitated Massachusetts Federalism. This rebirth encouraged England to resist American claims for redress.

In New York the Embargo destroyed ex-Governor Morgan Lewis' hopes of regaining his post in a three-cornered fight with Clintonians and Federalists. At state elections in April and May, 1808, the Federalists made surprising gains at the expense of both rival factions; in 1809 they recaptured the New York legislature for the first time in a decade. In Jefferson's home state, sentiment stirred in the Tidewater and the back country, and for the first time in many years the Federalists sent a strong minority to the legislature at Richmond. The Republicans actually lost only a few states, partly because many elections took place before Americans felt the full impact of the Embargo. However, the rising Federalist vote, the equivocal Republicanism of many congressmen who saved their seats, and the defeatism of leaders like Sullivan boded ill for the administration.

If the Embargo was considered as a prelude to war, a precaution, or shock treatment of European psyches—Jefferson talked of all these—occasional violations did not much matter. In any event all risk would be borne by the transgressing shipowner. As the coercive emphasis increased in the spring of 1808, becoming the

[40] Jefferson to Gallatin, Aug. 19, 1808, Gallatin MSS.

only possible excuse for the continuation of a policy that had demonstrably failed in its other aims, airtight enforcement of the Embargo assumed new importance. The President devoted most of the energies of his last year in office to this task. Although Albert Gallatin found the entire policy distasteful, he labored with all his might to make the Embargo work, and Treasury agents were by far the most active body thrown into the fray. The Navy Department provided less help, for Robert Smith sent his few ships cruising in often uncoördinated fashion along the coast, once proposed a gallivanting squadron cruise to the Caribbean (nominally to search out Embargo violators in more pleasant climes), criticized the whole scheme on semipublic occasions, and even encouraged the false belief that he himself had opposed it at cabinet meetings in December, 1807.

The success of enforcement fluctuated wildly. In the interval between first news of the Embargo and the establishment of a regulatory system, American shipowners hastily dispatched hundreds of vessels to sea. With the connivance of the collector at New Orleans, forty-two ships escaped from that port alone. Most vessels sailing at this time did not return to American waters during the life of the Embargo. After this outburst the Embargo was comparatively well enforced for some months, as the American people waited to see what lay in store for them. During the summer of 1808 land traffic across the Canadian border, not sailings from the Atlantic coast, posed the chief problem. A few outbursts of lawlessness occurred in the South, some transgressions in Chesapeake Bay and at New York, and substantially more frequent violations in New England. Only at the end of the year, as it became apparent that not war but a long embargo was most likely, and as the political climate became more and more hostile to the whole system, did there arise the last great surge of criminality which destroyed the Embargo and shook its sponsor's reputation. By the time the Embargo became "a mere *brutum fulmen*," as Matthew Carey called it,[41] it had already failed as a measure of rapid coercion.

The most notorious violations took place among vessels nomi-

[41] Matthew Carey, *The Olive Branch, or Faults on Both Sides, Federal and Democratic* (3d ed.; Boston, 1815), p. 37.

nally engaged in coasting trade. Areas contiguous to British possessions developed an unaccountable demand for goods of all sorts, a high proportion of which slipped across the border by land or water. Nineteen thousand barrels of flour reached Passamaquoddy Bay, for example, in the first week of May. Many ships found themselves forced by often imaginary bad weather or constructed circumstance to run to foreign ports for safety, sometimes all the way across the Atlantic. Benjamin Crowninshield once reported two incidents of this sort to Gallatin. The *Commerce,* bound nominally from Massachusetts to New Orleans, called at Havana on the fairly feeble excuse that her water casks were exhausted; while in Cuba, she took on a cargo of sugar. The captain of the *Hope,* on the same course, put in at Havana because of damage to his mainmast, which he claimed had been split by lightning, although Crowninshield sardonically noted that one of the crew had died at Havana, apparently from wounds suffered when he had set off a powder charge in the mast.[42] Against this sort of evasion, the administration fought back. It required heavy bonds for good behavior, and it established a system of licenses limiting the amount of provisions that could be shipped to any particular state. State governors issued the licenses, and Sullivan, for one, proved so liberal that the entire project became ludicrous.

Until autumn, at least, the collateral effects of direct violations counted for more than any relief they gave Britain and France. The Embargo pitted American citizens against one another. The government marched troops to the frontiers, sent gunboats and frigates scurrying up and down the coast, passed law after law and issued directive after directive. And yet violations continued. As a result many Americans came to believe the Republicans had adopted Federalist methods without having the capacity to execute them, while at the same time the violations strengthened the conviction of America's enemies abroad that her republican form of government made any forceful policy impossible. Gallatin, who saw this keenly, wrote in dismay, "I had rather encounter war itself than to display our impotence to enforce our laws." [43]

---

[42] Benjamin Crowninshield to Gallatin, Sept. 23, 1808, Gallatin MSS.
[43] Gallatin to Madison, Sept. 9, 1808, Rives Collection.

In addition to direct violations, important loopholes drained the system of effectiveness. While the Embargo anesthetized American shipping and exports, it did not affect foreign ships or goods. Although the Nonimportation Act banned certain British goods, effective application of this law did not begin until the spring of 1808, and in any event the list of forbidden items was comparatively limited. Throughout the Embargo large numbers of British ships arrived to sell cargoes of English wares, a circumstance that must have made the Embargo even more galling to the owners of vessels tied up at the wharves. Foreign ships had to leave in ballast (or break the law, as many did), and under normal circumstances the voyages would have been unprofitable, but in the absence of American competition they could be made to pay. For some unfathomable reason the administration never secured a law forbidding the exportation of specie, so cash sale was still possible. Consequently, although imports and arrivals from Britain fell off, they by no means ceased. Arrivals at Philadelphia, for example, though dropping by 50 per cent from 1807 to 1808, still continued at a rate about three-quarters of the average of preceding years. Just before learning of repeal of the Embargo, an experienced British civil servant wrote: "Every Article is permitted to enter the American ports as usual. . . . The Americans very good naturedly allow us openly to supply their wants, but will not supply ours in return, except by smuggling." [44]

Six hundred American vessels sailed for foreign ports with the permission of their government. Early in 1808, as Jefferson complained, "the H. of R. were surprised into the insertion [in a supplementary act] of an insidious clause permitting any merchant having *property* abroad, on proving it to the executive, to send a ship for it." [45] Presumably because he desperately needed other powers granted by the bill, the President accepted this rider. The clause encouraged merchants to make perjured declarations which would return a handsome profit, and the administration interpreted

[44] Edward G. Lutwyche to Sheffield, Feb. 25, 1809, Earl of Sheffield MSS, William L. Clements Library. See also Herbert Heaton, "Non-Importation, 1806–1812," *Journal of Economic History*, I (1941), 187.

[45] Jefferson to Cabell, March 13, 1808, Jefferson MSS.

the law to mean that merchants might export American goods to exchange for foreign wares contracted for but not paid for prior to December, 1807. Jefferson and Gallatin did confine most of the operation of this clause to goods from the West Indies rather than from Europe. Nevertheless, it had serious results. In a report covering only the period to the end of September, the President acknowledged that 594 vessels totaling some 87,000 tons had received permission to sail; by December more than 400 of these ships had returned with cargoes which relieved the pressure upon British exporters.[46] Departures continued until January, 1809, just before the entire system collapsed in ruins.

The legislative history of the Embargo, which clearly shows the problems the administration had to face, also demonstrates the gradual rise to predominance of the coercive motive. Within a month after the original act, its deficiencies made necessary a supplementary law extending controls to the coasting trade, fisheries, and whaling, and establishing a complex system of bonds and penalties to give teeth to enforcement. In March Congress passed a second supplement. Its chief purpose was to outlaw exportation to Canada. Thus Congress demonstrated that the protection of ships and seamen and their withdrawal as a possible prelude to war were not the only motives for the Embargo system. In a speech that nearly got him expelled from the House, Barent Gardenier charged that the original act had been "a sly, cunning measure," designed to appear as a precautionary measure but really intended as the first shot in a campaign of pressure on Britain.[47] Actually, the Embargo's supporters appear not to have been so Machiavellian; nobody proposed to follow embargo with war, and the emphasis therefore naturally shifted from precaution to coercion.

When John Randolph twitted his opponents for having attempted "to cure the corns by cutting off the toes," a sturdy Republican replied, "I will cut off the toes, feet, and head too, and perish with the whole nation rather than succumb."[48] Autoamputation

---

[46] *Columbian Centinel* (Boston), Jan. 21, 1809; Richardson, *op. cit.*, I, 458.
[47] *Annals*, 10th Cong., 1st sess., pp. 1653–1657.
[48] *Ibid.*, p. 2136 (D. R. Williams).

continued with an enforcement act which forbade shipments to parts of the United States adjacent to foreign lands unless specifically approved by the President and authorized collectors to take custody of any unusually large stocks in border communities. This act became law on the last day of the session of 1808.

In the summer of 1808, after gathering much information during a visit to New York, Gallatin wrote to the President that "if the embargo must be persisted in any longer," new legislation must be passed to "invest the Executive with the most arbitrary powers & sufficient force" to execute them. He suggested that not a single vessel be permitted to move without presidential approval, that collectors be permitted to seize goods "any where" and to remove rudders and rigging from any suspected vessels, and that "a little army" be collected along the Canadian frontier. These suggestions, perhaps designed as much to shock the President into a reconsideration of his policy as to make the Embargo effective, did not shake the Chief Executive, who replied, "I am satisfied with you that if the orders & decrees are not repealed, & a continuance of the embargo is preferred to war (which sentiment is universal here), Congress must legalize all *means* which may be necessary to obtain it's end." [49]

The fruit of such talk was the last of this series of acts, not passed until January, 1809. The act of 1809, passed over wild Federalist shrieks against tyranny, permitted anticipatory seizures, forbade the loading of ships without permission from federal officials, provided for the arrest of goods traveling toward the border by road, required almost impossible proof of innocence from the owners of ships "blown off course" or "captured" while engaged in coastwise voyages, and authorized an increased maritime force and the use of militia to enforce the laws. This string of restrictions, which came too late to breathe effectiveness into the Embargo, did show the lengths to which Jeffersonians were prepared to go. It also clearly demonstrated the coercive purpose of the system, revealed the pervasiveness of violations, and turned the hitherto largely

[49] Gallatin to Jefferson, July 29, 1808, Jefferson MSS; Jefferson to Gallatin, Aug. 11, 1808, Gallatin MSS.

peaceable opposition of New England into nearly revolutionary remonstrance. Unwittingly, advocates of the Embargo had plunged a knife into its expiring body. All that now remained to be done was to concoct an alternative policy—war or concealed surrender— and total the losses and the gains of the great Jeffersonian experiment.

Some argue that, in one sense at least, the Embargo was clear gain: America did not become involved in war. But did the Embargo preserve peace? Neither Britain nor France ever considered a declaration of war on the United States. War at American initiative was, to put it mildly, highly unlikely; the Embargo cannot be defended as a shrewdly applied Jeffersonian poultice which reduced congressional war fever. Had American ships continued at sea the resulting captures might conceivably have had to be considered a *casus belli*, it is true. The belligerents, however, seized less than 1 per cent of those ships permitted to sail during the life of the Embargo, and in any event for more than three years after repeal America did not make seizures an excuse for war. War immediately after the *Chesapeake* incident was possible, but by the time of the Embargo Act Jefferson had led his people farther from the brink than even he desired. The verdict, "not proved," must be passed upon the claim that the Embargo preserved peace.

As coercion, the Embargo obviously failed. Domestic opposition of course undermined its effectiveness, and Jefferson's enemies were the enemies of national policy determined by Congress. Still, such opposition might have been foreseen. As early as February, 1808, Senator Nicholas' brother warned, "The success of it must depend greatly on the impression which will be made abroad as to it's continuance and I fear the clamour of the federalists and the under tone of Mr. Madison's opponents will give no very favorable idea of our fortitude or perseverance." Yet the intensity of opposition surprised Jefferson. Instead of preparing the way for a graceful withdrawal, he sought to make the Embargo effective by more stringent enforcement. The President tied American prestige to the Embargo's success as a means of extorting European concession, a very risky gamble indeed. John Randolph, expressing for once the thoughts of many, commented: "If it had any opera-tion on the belligerents I could be content to bear its ruinous conse-quences, but in France & England it is equally disregarded." [50]

Napoleon regarded the Embargo complacently. The Royal Navy had already interdicted most transatlantic trade. As for the colonies, which lost an important source of supply, Napoleon did not particularly value the few remaining in French hands. At first the Emperor objected to the Embargo because it fell short of war with England. In the autumn he gave it his blessing, since it fitted in nicely with his Continental System. An official report, largely his own, stated: "The Americans, a people who owe their fortune, prosperity, and almost their existence to commerce, have given the example of a great and courageous sacrifice. They have for-bidden . . . all commerce . . . rather than shamefully submit to the tribute which the English attempt to impose upon the navi-gators of all nations." A short time later, in a message opening the Corps Législatif, Napoleon repeated the same theme. The American representative at Paris reported in August, 1808: "We have somewhat over-rated our means of coercing the two great belligerents to a course of justice. . . . Here it [the Embargo] is not felt, and in England . . . it is forgotten. . . . The Em-peror would prefer to it, a war on our part with G.B., but would prefer it, to any state of things, except that of a war." [51]

In Britain, too, the effect was far less than Jefferson had hoped. Consul Lyman told the President, "Not all the expences and burthens of the war excite so much apprehension or complaint as the want of our commerce," and William Pinkney more moder-ately reported that "the Embargo pinches here." But George H. Rose, on a special mission to the United States, correctly concluded that the Embargo hurt America most, and even David M. Erskine, the regular minister, who was more sympathetic to the United

[50] John Nicholas to Nicholas, Feb. 8, 1808, Nicholas MSS; Randolph to Nicholson, Nov. 13, 1808, Joseph H. Nicholson MSS, Library of Congress.

[51] Champagny, "Report to the Emperor," Sept. 1, 1808, Correspondance de Napoléon Iᵉʳ (32 vols.; Paris, 1858–1870), XVII, 565; message at opening of Corps Législatif, Oct. 25, 1808, ibid., XVIII, 25; Armstrong to Madison, Aug. 30, 1808, Madison MSS.

States, considered the measure ineffective. In England itself, ministers, even in their private correspondence, repeatedly stated that the effect of the Embargo was trifling. The Earl of Sheffield, consistently enough, positively welcomed a policy that aided English shipping, and although the Marquis of Buckingham detested British policy he felt that "the embargo has proved a very impotent and ruinous measure [to the United States], . . . equally insufficient as a measure of offense to us, or of security to her." Of course the loss of American trade could not be totally ignored, but it proved painful rather than catastrophic. In a private memorandum for Perceval written toward the close of the American experiment, James Stephen summarized a point of view fairly generally held: "The intended duress on our commerce has wholly failed, & while America has been more defied & plunged in great interior difficulties by that impotent measure of resentment, we are far more in a condition to despise it than when it was first adopted: the terrors of a suspension of American commerce have vanished from the minds of our Manufacturers & Planters, & our Merchants, are reaping lucrative fruits from our new commercial positions beyond their most sanguine hopes." [52]

Only small, vulnerable areas of the economy were severely affected by the loss of American supplies. Ireland's linen industry, almost entirely dependent upon American flaxseed, suffered as the price bounded up. The most important imports, grain and cotton, were not so deeply missed. Grain shipments from America declined by four-fifths in 1808, and the price of wheat rose sharply. For this rise the Embargo was only partly responsible, and the pressure never became so severe that the government found it necessary, as it had during past shortages, to ban distilling; the Americans

[52] Lyman to Jefferson, Dec. 21, 1808, Jefferson MSS (incorrectly bound at 1806); Pinkney to Madison, private, Sept. 7, 1808, Despatches, Great Britain, Vol. XV; Rose #3 to Canning, Jan. 17, 1808, FO 5/56; Erskine #20 to Canning, June 4, 1808, FO 5/57; John B. Holroyd, Earl of Sheffield, *The Orders in Council and the American Embargo Beneficial to the Political and Commercial Interests of Great Britain* (London, 1809), *passim*; Marquis of Buckingham to Grenville, Feb. 12, 1809, Walter Fitzpatrick, ed., *Report on the Manuscripts of J. B. Fortescue, Esq., Preserved at Dropmore* (10 vols.; London: Historical Manuscripts Commission, 1892–1927), IX, 277; Stephen to Perceval, March 3, 1809, Spencer Perceval MSS (examined while temporarily on deposit at the Register of National Archives, London), 33/44.

even failed to deprive Englishmen of their whisky.[53] Although cotton from the United States had a far larger share of the import market than grain, even here pressure proved ineffective. In the first quarter of 1808 arrivals dropped only slightly, and in the course of the whole year more than 12 million pounds of American cotton reached Britain. This was a far cry from the 44 million pounds imported in 1807, and cotton prices rose steadily to a peak in October, 1808. The huge importations of 1807, which made the drop statistically impressive, had also created an oversupply that could now be absorbed, while non-American sources provided 30 million pounds of cotton to relieve shortages. Few mills closed because of the lack of supplies. The Embargo, Lord Sheffield asserted, "acted the part of a salutary medicine upon a previously diseased body" by reducing a British glut.[54]

Exports, not imports, were Britain's Achilles' heel. Here a combination of unforeseeable circumstance and the American failure to prohibit importations fatally delayed the Embargo's effect. Manufacturers of course suffered, and Baring charged that in Manchester only nine of more than eighty cotton mills were working full time. The share of British exports taken by the United States shrank from one-third to one-seventh, yet more than £5 million worth of British goods still flowed to the United States, embargo or no embargo.[55] At the same time alternative markets opened, particularly the Spanish Empire, where restrictions on trade ended after the Iberian rising against Napoleon in the spring of 1808. The drop in exports to the United States was almost exactly matched by a rise in shipments to other American ports, causing

[53] W. Freeman Galpin, "The American Grain Trade under the Embargo of 1808," *Journal of Economic and Business History*, II (1929–1930), 71–100; Eli F. Heckscher, *The Continental System* (London, 1922), p. 337; Timothy Pitkin, *A Statistical View of the Commerce of the United States* (Hartford, 1816), p. 220; Louis M. Sears, "British Industry and the American Embargo," *Quarterly Journal of Economics*, XXXIV (1919–1920), 105.

[54] Account of Feb. 29, 1809, Rufus King MSS, New-York Historical Society, Vol. XII; Sears, *op. cit.*, p. 100; François Crouzet, *L'Economie Britannique et le Blocus Continental* (2 vols.; Paris, 1958), I, 394–395; Sheffield, *op. cit.*, p. 25.

[55] *Hansard*, XII, 1194; Crouzet, *op. cit.*, I, 308–312; II, 860–861; Heckscher, *op. cit.*, p. 324; Pitkin, *op. cit.*, pp. 223–224; George R. Porter, *The Progress of the Nation*, rev. F. W. Hirst (rev. ed.; London, 1912), p. 479.

the British consul at New York to exult, "The Spanish Colonies in the West Indies and on the Continent of America will now take from our manufacturers all that their Industry can supply; and I am at times in doubt whether a continuance of the American Embargo will not operate beneficially to Britain." Before long the Latin American market became satiated, but in 1808, both psychologically and practically, it cushioned the reduction of exports to Jefferson's America.[56] This, and this alone, was a factor in the equation that the President could not have foreseen. By the summer of 1808 it formed an obvious objection to his policy.

The British West Indies proved less vulnerable to American pressure than expected. Prices of course rose sharply. Flour jumped from $7 to $22 a barrel when news of the Embargo arrived, and by fall reached $40. Although the Embargo worked comparatively efficiently in breaking up trade with English colonies, many ships that sailed to get goods "already owned" in the Caribbean carried grain and flour to exchange for them. The British government mobilized alternative sources of supply and quintupled its exports of flour to the colonies. Jamaica received just about half the normal supply in 1808, and this, though causing severe hardship and eliminating reserve supplies, enabled life to continue. Early in the life of the Embargo, Erskine urged his government to show "the People of this Country that the Threat to starve His Majesty's Islands in the West Indies, is as vain as it is illiberal and disgusting." Canning, Perceval, and company were happy to oblige.[57]

This is not to say that the British government made no efforts to encourage violation of the Embargo. As early as March, 1808, Spencer Perceval proposed only slightly disguised inducements to American lawbreakers, but Canning and Castlereagh briefly dissuaded him with the argument that "the Embargo . . . seems to be working so well for us without our interference, that . . . no

[56] Louis M. Sears, *Jefferson and the Embargo* (Durham, 1927), pp. 284–285; Heckscher, *op. cit.*, pp. 174–175, 245; Barclay to Admiral John B. Warren, private, Sept. 3, 1808, George L. Rives, ed., *Selections from the Correspondence of Thomas Barclay* (New York, 1894), p. 283.

[57] Galpin, *op. cit.*, pp. 91–94; *Monthly Review; or Literary Journal* (London), LIX (1809), 173; Erskine #20 to Canning, June 4, 1808, FO 5/57.

new step should be taken." In April an Order in Council approved neutral trade to the West Indies, even by ships without papers, and also promised that ships engaged in trade approved by Britain would be exempt from seizure even if war should break out. Although phrased in general terms, this order obviously applied exclusively to violators of the American Embargo. William Pinkney considered it "a sneer upon our honor, national and individual," and the Secretary of State, with that hyperbole he favored in diplomatic correspondence, agreed that a "more extraordinary and dishonorable experiment is perhaps not to be found in the annals of modern transactions." Nevertheless the policy continued. Like the local authorities' cynical opening of Halifax to American ships, it tempted shipowners to send their vessels to sea whenever they could evade Gallatin's agents.[58] These British expedients reflected a political desire to speed Republican self-destruction at least as much as a hope to obtain needed supplies.

The Embargo, then, failed as an instrument of coercion, although its continuation a few months longer might have allowed the United States to escape with honor, for early in 1809 the British government began to show interest in the restoration of trade. The Embargo's failure was obvious by the fall of 1808, before the onset of the moral, political, and economic rot that brought down the entire system in ruins. Events of the closing months were dramatic and, for the nation as well as for Jefferson, tragic, but the President's failure predated that climax. He had woefully overestimated British dependence upon American supplies, although the figures were at hand and even hurled in his face by Federalists. He had completely ignored the adaptability of British trade, although its transformations since the outbreak of war in 1792 ought to have been a warning. He had counted upon a rational reaction to pressure, although his own experiences in the American Revolu-

[58] Perceval memorandum, n.d., Perceval MSS, 29/9–10; Canning memorandum, March 28, 1808, ibid., 36/27–28; Castlereagh memorandum, n.d., ibid., 36/29; Henry Adams, History, IV, 327; Pinkney to Madison, private, April 25, 1808, Rives Collection; Madison to Pinkney, July 18, 1808, Instructions, Vol. VII; Erskine #24 to Canning, July 14, 1808, FO 5/58; Warren to Wellesley Pole, July 20, 1808, Adm 1/498.

tion ought to have shown him that faith often overwhelms realism. He had tolerated legislative errors (notably the permission of continued imports in British ships and the rider of March, 1808, permitting American vessels to sail to get goods "already owned") which ripped the heart from the Embargo. In sum, he had permitted a device he had first endorsed as a measure of precaution to become one of economic pressure, and then had not even given this dubious weapon a full chance of success. It is true, as the sage of Monticello later pleaded, that "the rank growth" of violations exceeded everyone's expectations; it is true that nobody foresaw the Spanish rising that opened Latin America to British ships. But neither of these elements was decisive, and some violations at least might have been foreseen.

So, too, could the pain an extended embargo would bring to Jefferson's land. It took no particular wisdom to predict that the farmer and the merchant would suffer blows so deep that only a sparkling diplomatic triumph could compensate for them. Cotton prices fell nearly one-half, bringing ruin to many a planter. "Nothing is now heard of but Bankruptcies which have taken place & more which are apprehended," wrote Senator Nicholas' Richmond agents, and another Virginian wailed, "This Embargo will ruin this state if it continues long." At New Orleans wholesale prices of Western produce averaged 15 per cent lower in 1808 than in 1807, a critical fall for marginal frontier farmers.[59] Shipowners, seamen, and seaboard towns suffered similarly. Five hundred ships lay tied up at New York, and the Embargo caught more than 200 at Savannah. At Salem, Massachusetts, soup kitchens fed 1,200 persons daily and one-fifth of the town was reduced to virtual beggary by the early months of 1809. Even William Gray, a loyal supporter of the Embargo, admitted that his fortune had been reduced one-tenth or more in the first half year of the experiment.

[59] G. W. Daniels, "American Cotton Trade with Liverpool under the Embargo and Non-Intercourse Acts," *American Historical Review*, XXI (1915–1916), 282; Thomas Rutherford to Nicholas, Jan. 8, 1808, Nicholas MSS; John Kelly to William Taylor, Jan. 6, 1808, Nathan Schachner, *Thomas Jefferson* (2 vols.; New York, 1951), II, 863; George R. Taylor, "Prices in the Mississippi Valley Preceding the War of 1812," *Journal of Economic and Business History*, III (1930–1931), 149.

Seamen, both Americans and British fugitives, fled to the English merchant service and even the Royal Navy with the assistance of British consuls, reducing the incidence of impressments in a way Jefferson had never intended.[60] John Trumbull lost his patrons and returned to England; Albert Gallatin lost his customs receipts and found it difficult to balance the budget. In his annual message of 1808, Jefferson found consolation in the stimulus given to American industry, but there is reason to believe that the Embargo, by upsetting the nation's economy, had restrained rather than encouraged American manufacturing.[61]

Northerners and Southerners sometimes argued over the priority of suffering between their sections. Many complaints were politically motivated, aimed either at securing repeal of the Embargo or demonstrating the inanity of Jeffersonianism. The United States was youthful and resilient; it could perhaps afford a year of privation. None of these things alters the essential fact that Jefferson had sacrificed the economic well-being of his country for a phantom, had asked superhuman self-denial from a nation that had perhaps been corrupted by prosperity. "We are almost the only sufferers," expostulated a Marylander; "a *chance of getting a living*, is better than *inevitable starvation*," complained a Connecticut editor.[62] More and more Americans came to share these sentiments, and economic reality supported them.

Nor were economic losses the sole cost. The year of embargo destroyed national unity far more than two years of open warfare with Britain did later on. The nation was forced to fight political battles that had been all but settled before Jefferson's message of

[60] John Lambert, *Travels through Canada, and the United States of North America, in the Years 1806, 1807, & 1808* (3d ed.; 2 vols.; London, 1816), II, 214, 294; James D. Phillips, "Jefferson's 'Wicked Tyrannical Embargo,'" *New England Quarterly*, XVIII (1945), 472; entry of Aug. 12, 1808, *The Diary of William Bentley, D.D.* (4 vols.; Salem, 1911–1914), III, 377; Warren to Wellesley Pole, Sept. 23, 1808, Adm 1/498; Barclay to Captain Bromley, Feb. 15, 1808, Rives, *op. cit.*, p. 274.

[61] Caroline F. Ware, "The Effect of the American Embargo, 1807–1809, on the New England Cotton Industry," *Quarterly Journal of Economics*, LX (1925–1926), 672–688.

[62] Entry of Jan. 5, 1808, *Diary of Bentley*, III, 377; William Patterson to Nicholas, Dec. 1, 1808, Nicholas MSS; *Connecticut Courant* (Hartford), Feb. 17, 1808.

December, 1807. Pickering, the Junto, and their cohorts verged toward sedition. John Quincy Adams, one of the victims, properly observed that "we have too many among us who, to say the least, are ready to let the rights of the country go, provided they can see their political opponents overwhelmed in the same ruin." [63] By stubbornly supporting a policy so harmful to the nation, so unlikely of success, and so conducive to the false charge of French influence, the President at least acted the part of a catalytic agent in precipitating this poison.

In the autumn of 1807 the United States had briefly enjoyed a particularly advantageous tactical position vis-à-vis England. The raft-borne negotiations at Tilsit had joined Prussia and Russia to Napoleon's Continental System, Junot controlled Portugal for his master, and by the Treaty of Fontainebleau Godoy committed Spain to a role as Napoleon's jackal. The attack upon Copenhagen drove Denmark to the French side. Not for the last time in her history, Britain faced a nearly united continent. At the same time, although the Emperor had begun to enforce the Berlin Decree against Americans, the balance of insult clearly lay with the English, as far as the United States was concerned. Never again were conditions so favorable for the exertion of pressure, provided that pressure was effective and not merely self-immolating. Yet Jefferson turned to embargo, partly voluntarily and partly because he had too successfully dampened war sentiment after the *Chesapeake* affair. Within a few months the last remnants of willingness to endorse strong measures disappeared. American sentiment became muddied by Napoleonic insults, notably Champagny's cavalier treatment of Armstrong, the seizure and destruction of American ships, and particularly the Decree of Milan, which reached America early in 1808. In January Turreau fatuously reported that the nation was drifting toward war with Britain, but in May he had to admit that this analysis had been wrong and even claimed that he had never meant it. "A war with that Power would never obtain public assent," he stated, and the administration itself "intends, today more than ever, to stand equally balanced between France

[63] Adams to Giles, Nov. 15, 1808, Ford, *op. cit.*, III, 247.

and England." [64] The tactical moment for pressure had passed. Only a doctrinaire pacifist or an unreasoning Anglophile, both of which Jefferson definitely was not, could take unalloyed pleasure from this.

The Embargo had other unfortunate aspects. It provided an excuse for ineffective military preparations when force was the only language the world understood. According to Senator Adams, the President himself passed word that arming was unnecessary.[65] In any event, after lengthy debates in which members loudly proclaimed their willingness to make any sacrifice for the nation, Congress passed no military bills of any consequence. Second, the Embargo made Europe believe that commercial coercion could be scorned because it would harm the United States more than those against whom it was wielded. Consequently, the British proved far less willing to compromise in the face of renewed economic threats under Madison. Then, too, the policy Jefferson followed during his last year as president convinced Britain of America's essential cowardice. After the *Leopard*'s broadsides, the nation called for war and the administration insisted that Britain must drop impressment. In December the United States settled for an embargo, and the next month, without even waiting to see how this measure would affect England, the administration told Erskine and then the special envoy, George H. Rose, that the *Chesapeake* affair could be settled even if Britain did not agree to cease impressing seamen.[66]

Most important of all, instead of waiting for the Embargo to force British overtures, the Republicans openly sought an escape from their own Frankenstein. "I take it to be an universal opinion," Jefferson wrote, "that war will become preferable to a continuance of the embargo after a certain time." To avoid this catastrophe Jefferson appealed to the reason and the cupidity of the belligerents. In the middle of April, 1808, a report presented by Senator

[64] Turreau #7, #10, #14 to Minister of Foreign Relations, Jan. 30, April 24, May 20, 1808, AAE, CP, E-U, Vol. LXI.
[65] Entry of March 29, 1808, Charles F. Adams, *op. cit.*, I, 524.
[66] Erskine #2 to Canning, Jan. 28, 1808, FO 5/57; Rose #4 to Canning, Jan. 18, 1808, FO 5/56.

Anderson but actually drawn by the Secretary of State recommended that the President be given the power to suspend the Embargo if conditions so warranted.[67] Within a few days this recommendation became law.

Madison quickly instructed Pinkney and Armstrong to use this law as a lever at London and Paris and himself interviewed Erskine. Without entirely giving away American policy, upon which indeed the Cabinet did not settle for another month, he nevertheless made the Englishman understand that the United States would not insist upon repeal of the order of January, 1807, but, on the other hand, would not require France to suspend the municipal regulations forbidding the landing of British goods even when carried in neutral ships. Otherwise the offers were roughly similar: if either power ended actions against American commerce while its rival remained obdurate, the United States would in turn suspend the Embargo in favor of the conceding power and turn a firm face toward the other.[68]

At the end of June Pinkney broached the subject with Canning. The Foreign Secretary at first contented himself with not unfriendly questions, but at their third meeting a month later he asked Pinkney to present his offer in writing. After a long delay during which Pinkney wrestled with various drafts of an official note, a fourth meeting was arranged at which the Secretary received Pinkney's note with cryptic vagueness. Canning then left town for a vacation, and when the American minister went to the Foreign Office to ferret out information he came away with a total blank. He noted uneasily that British spirits had been raised by American opposition to the Embargo, an influx of illegal cargoes from the United States, optimism about the Latin American market, and exhilarating news of Baylen and Vimeiro.[69]

[67] Jefferson to Madison, March 11, 1808, Lipscomb and Bergh, *op. cit.*, XII, 11–12; *Annals*, 10th Cong., 1st sess., pp. 364–368.

[68] Madison to Pinkney, April 30, 1808, Instructions, Vol. VI; Madison to Armstrong, May 2, 1808, *ibid.*; Erskine to Canning, separate and confidential, April 26, 1808, FO 5/57; Erskine #17 to Canning, May 2, 1808, *ibid.*

[69] Pinkney to Madison, private, June 29, 1808, Despatches, Great Britain, Vol. XV; Pinkney to Madison, Aug. 4, Sept. 6, 1808, *ibid.*; Pinkney to Madison, private, Sept. 7, 1808, *ibid.*; Pinkney to Madison, private, Sept. 10, 1808, Rives Collection.

Canning's answer, finally produced on September 23, justified Pinkney's fears. The silent, respectful Foreign Secretary of earlier meetings was replaced by the more characteristic Canning. Britain, he said, unreservedly rejected the American offer, nor could she consent to any important modifications of her system until Napoleon gave prior evidence of weakness by abandoning his decrees. If intended as coercion, Canning declared, the Embargo was unjust, for it should have been directed solely at France, the power whose maritime innovations had forced Britain to retaliate. If, on the other hand, "as it has been more generally represented by the Government of the United States," Canning continued with acutely unpleasant reference to Madison's disingenuous declarations,

the Embargo is only to be considered as an innocent municipal Regulation, which affects none but the United States themselves, . . . His Majesty does not conceive that he has the right or the pretension to make any Complaint of it; and He has made none. But in this light there appears to be not only no Reciprocity but no assignable Relation, between the Repeal . . . of a Measure of voluntary Self-restriction, and the Surrender by His Majesty of his Right of Retaliation against his Enemies.

This sneer was followed by arrogance. While denying that Britain hated the United States or was jealous of her prosperity, Canning demanded respect for English methods on the ground that "the Strength and Power of Great Britain are not for herself alone, but for the world." [70] The Savior stood forth against the Antichrist of the Tuileries.

Early in 1809, when both houses of Parliament weighed what Grenville called "the insulting and sophistical answer written by his Majesty's foreign secretary of state," the Foxite, Grenville, and Sidmouth factions attacked the government. The *Times*, although opining that "Mr. CANNING's late Declaration was a keen and acutely reasoned State Paper," nevertheless found it "repulsive" because it seemed to condemn the country to a continuation of the endurance contest with France. Tierney, erroneously assuming that

[70] Canning to Pinkney, Sept. 23, 1808, enclosed in Pinkney to Madison, Sept. 24, 1808, Despatches, Great Britain, Vol. XV.

THOMAS JEFFERSON
*Portrait by Rembrandt Peale*

JAMES MONROE
*Portrait by Gilbert Stuart*

WILLIAM PINKNEY
*Portrait by Charles B. King*

JAMES STEPHEN
*Portrait by John Linnell*

SPENCER PERCEVAL
*Portrait by George F. Joseph*

the anger provoked by Canning's letter would determine America to continue the Embargo, asked, "Is it not deplorable, sir, that for the sake of a few pointed periods, and well-turned sentences, any individual . . . should do such incalculable mischief . . . ?" But the government had no regrets. Canning scarcely deigned to discuss his American policy, Bathurst sarcastically suggested that the Grenville family knew more than most about the dangers of arousing America, and Liverpool limited himself to a brief statement that America "had shewed no disposition to act properly towards us," since while demanding repeal of the orders she had consented to continuance of France's municipal regulations excluding British goods. Summing up the government's attitude toward "an offer on the part of America to abandon a measure which has been proved to be injurious to no power so much as herself," the *Courier* said, "we cannot allow that necessity calls upon us to depart entirely from our policy towards an enemy, in order that America may be relieved from a burden which she pettishly placed upon her own shoulders." [71]

The act of April, 1808, passed even before coercion had had a fair trial, simply convinced the British that in a contest of wills Jefferson and his people would first give way. At the same time the mere existence of the Embargo made it highly unlikely that a prestige-conscious ministry would offer anything that might be considered a surrender. Bathurst, who believed the Orders in Council no longer desirable, felt that "repealing them in consequence of the American Embargo would be fatal to this Country, and to the friends of this Country in America." All he could suggest was some device like that tried by Fox in 1806,[72] and this was too much for his colleagues, who did not make even a first tentative gesture until it was obvious that the Embargo was dying.

Rebuffed in its pleas to Britain and France, challenged by increasing opposition at home, the administration eddied without purpose in the closing months of Jefferson's regime. Madison

[71] *Hansard*, XII, 18; *Times* (London), Jan. 13, 1809; *Hansard*, XII, 87, 800–801; *Courier*, Feb. 20, 1809.
[72] Bathurst memorandum, July 29, 1808, FO 5/61.

talked alternately about strengthening the Embargo and replacing it with war, either against Britain or against both major belligerents.[73] Gallatin's position was even more complicated. Although formerly opposed to a permanent embargo, he now felt that the policy "having been adopted ought, if there was virtue enough in the eastern people, to be continued." Doubting Yankee virtue, he confessed himself baffled, and the papers from his pen reflect his uncertainty. He presented a report on means to make a permanent embargo effective, prepared for Congressman Campbell a manifesto sternly demanding vigor but leaving open the choice between war and embargo, and capped his labors with a financial statement which seemed to show that the Treasury could stand the shock of war. These apparently contradictory productions are not incompatible: Gallatin favored decisiveness, and he was prepared to support any forthright policy. As he wrote to Jefferson, for himself and the Secretary of State, "considering the temper of the legislature . . . , it would be eligible to point out to them some precise & distinct course. As to what that should be we may not all perfectly agree. . . . I feel myself nearly as undetermined between enforcing the embargo or war as I was on our last meetings. But I think that we must (or rather you must) decide the question absolutely, so that we may point out a decisive course either way to our friends." [74]

The prodding of his two chief lieutenants failed to stir Jefferson into action. The lame-duck President virtually abdicated, merely living out the days until he could depart for the quiet bliss of Monticello. "I think it fair to leave to those who are to act on them, the decisions they prefer, being to be myself but a spectator," he wrote.[75] Ideally speaking, the President would probably have preferred to continue the Embargo. As a compromise with political reality, he favored continuing it for a fixed period, with war to

[73] Madison to Pinkney, Nov. 9, 1808, *Letters and Other Writings of James Madison* (Congressional ed.; 4 vols.; Philadelphia, 1865), II, 425; Erskine #46 to Canning, Dec. 3, 1808, FO 5/58.

[74] *Annals*, 10th Cong., 2d sess., pp. 232–236; undated memorandum, Gallatin MSS, Vol. XV; Henry Adams, *Gallatin*, pp. 412–413; Gallatin to Jefferson, Nov. 15, 1808, Jefferson MSS.

[75] Jefferson to Levi Lincoln, Nov. 13, 1808, Jefferson MSS.

follow unless the European belligerents came to their senses in the interim. But he did not officially communicate these conclusions to Congress, and he allowed the usual channels of executive influence to dry up.

The situation in New England was chiefly responsible for Jefferson's paralysis. There, courts frequently refused to convict those charged with violations of the Embargo. Town after town voted memorials calling for repeal, and the General Court instructed Massachusetts congressmen to work for it. The Enforcement Act of January, 1809, provoked even more stentorian protest. The Massachusetts legislature, proclaiming its loyalty to the union "according to its original purpose," violently attacked the extension of federal power as a breach of the Constitution. "On such occasions," declared the Senate, "passive submission would, on the part of the people, be a breach of their allegiance, and on our part treachery and perjury," while the House proclaimed that "everything which freemen hold dear, is at stake." Governor Trumbull and the Connecticut legislature rallied behind their neighbors.[76]

These inflammatory protests, supported by a rising tide of violence—a mob at Gloucester destroyed a revenue cutter, for example—caused many supporters of the Embargo, including Jefferson, to wonder whether it could be continued without provoking civil war. A flood of inquiries from Washington descended upon John Quincy Adams, and Adams later came to believe that, through his replies warning of the danger, "I was the efficient cause of the substitution of the Nonintercourse for the embargo, which I verily believe saved the country from a civil war." Jefferson himself fixed the responsibility on Joseph Story, who arrived somewhat tardily at Washington as replacement for a dead congressman. Story, a "pseudo-Republican," Jefferson said, convinced Ezekiel Bacon that only a repeal of the Embargo could prevent civil war, and Bacon in turn convinced his colleagues in the House. The President oversimplified. Newspaper reports, letters, and

[76] Walter W. Jennings, *The American Embargo, 1807–1809*, University of Iowa Studies in the Social Sciences, Vol. VIII, no. 1 (Iowa City, 1921), pp. 123–124; Herman V. Ames, ed., *State Documents on Federal Relations* (Philadelphia, 1906), pp. 26–36, 38–42.

travelers from Massachusetts undermined Republican wills. Many congressmen eagerly sought escape from the Embargo throughout the session, although Story may have added his warnings at an important moment. When the President implied, as he did, that he himself was immune from the panic that swept Capitol Hill, he toyed with the truth, for the virus infected him as much as any-one else. In an admission that some honor would have to be jettisoned to keep the nation afloat, he wrote, "We must save the Union; but we wish to sacrifice as little as possible of the honor of the nation." [77]

Joseph Story's course was not quite so clear-cut as legend suggests. A reluctant supporter of the Embargo, he desired to give it a fair trial. On his arrival at Washington in December, 1808, he discovered with surprise that many Republicans wished to continue it indefinitely. On January 4 he wrote home to ask if the amazing rumors of incipient rebellion were true, and at about the same time he received letters informing him that the danger of open resistance had diminished. Story did indeed fear that the new enforcement act would rekindle the crisis in Massachusetts, and he believed it would be very hazardous to continue the Embargo for any substantial length of time. He did not anticipate an immediate revolt, to say nothing of an effective one. Story's open break with his party, maintained despite the pressure of administration whips, contributed much more to defeat of the Embargo than his alleged retailing of rumors of approaching civil war. [78]

The political hazards of stubbornness, hazards made more obvious by Story's disaffection, and the failure to secure European concessions doomed the Embargo. A few congressmen, among them

[77] Adams to Charles F. Adams, Dec. 2, 1828, Samuel F. Bemis, *John Quincy Adams and the Foundations of American Foreign Policy* (New York, 1949), p. 150n; Jefferson to Dearborn, July 16, 1810, Lipscomb and Bergh, *op. cit.*, XII, 398–400; Jefferson to Thomas M. Randolph, Jan. 2, 1809, *ibid.*, XVIII, 258–259.

[78] Story to Joseph White, Jr., Jan. 4, 1809, William W. Story, *Life and Letters of Joseph Story* (Boston, 1851), pp. 174–175; Joseph Story, "Autobiography," *ibid.*, pp. 183–186; Story to Edward Everett, n.d. *ibid.*, p. 187. For the information received from Massachusetts by Story at this time, see particularly the letters of Joseph White, Jr., in the Joseph Story MSS, Library of Congress.

Nathaniel Macon, Speaker Varnum, and Madison's brother-in-law, James G. Jackson, desired to continue it, but these men found few allies. With only two dissenting votes (one was Gardenier's), the House endorsed Campbell's Report, a ringing but meaningless declaration of unwillingness to submit to foreign aggressions. Congress passed the Enforcement Act, but more for reasons of consistency than for devotion to the system, which few people expected to last beyond the spring. The visible confusion and longwindedness of legislators caused Ezekiel Bacon to observe that the debates on the Embargo "might justly be esteemed not the least amongst those many inconveniences which were imputed to it." Most congressmen, wanting to get rid of the Embargo, sought an escape that would not dishonor them. The search was difficult because most of them refused to consider the logical alternative, war. At the end of 1808 Gallatin wrote disgustedly: "A majority will not adhere to the embargo much longer, and if war be not speedily determined on, submission will soon ensue." [79]

As always, the Secretary of the Treasury had a keen eye for congressional currents. On January 24 Wilson C. Nicholas attempted to salvage something from the impending wreck by moving that forcible resistance should, at a date to be fixed by Congress, replace the Embargo. He had always believed, Nicholas said, that "when the embargo failed, we must resort to the valor and patriotism of our citizens. Sir, we have too much reason to believe that the moment is at hand when nothing else can extricate us from our difficulties." Nicholas and others close to the administration proposed June 1 as the date of transformation. A majority was unwilling to wait that long, and more than half the Republicans joined the Federalists in rejecting it. In a last-ditch effort to save the Embargo, George Troup then moved to shelve the entire subject, but only twenty-five members voted with him. The House inserted March 4, fittingly enough the terminus of Jefferson's term, as the date of repeal. Next, it approved the repeal resolution

[79] *Annals*, 10th Cong., 2d sess., *passim;* Varnum to Eustis, Nov. 19, 1808, Eustis MSS; Gallatin to Nicholson, Dec. 29, 1808, Adams, *Gallatin*, p. 384.

by seventy-six to forty. The date was February 3, 1809, a little more than thirteen months after the nation had embarked upon its campaign of privation.[80]

What followed was anticlimax, more closely connected with the birth of the Nonintercourse Act, although the Embargo's enemies feared that some legerdemain would reverse the decision. At several caucuses loyal Republicans pressed the deserters to accept the Nicholas plan. Led by Ezekiel Bacon, for Story had returned home, the dissidents, predominantly from New England and Pennsylvania, held firm. At the end of February the Nonintercourse Act passed, not because it was popular but because it included repeal of the Embargo. In the words of one Northern Republican, "the people, as well as himself, were so heartily tired of the embargo that they would be glad to get anything else in place of it." A few days later Jefferson departed from a Washington to which he never returned, commenting, "Never did a prisoner, released from his chains, feel such relief as I . . . on shaking off the shackles of power." [81]

His most ambitious venture in foreign policy had failed, save only in perhaps delaying the outbreak of war with England—and that, until a less favorable time. The Embargo imposed many of the disadvantages of war on the nation by destroying trade; it secured none of the prospective advantages, such as the conquest of territory or the capture of enemy ships and commerce at sea. Diplomatically, Jefferson failed either to coerce or seduce the European belligerents. Economically, the Embargo proved ruinous at home. Politically, it encouraged fissiparous tendencies in Republicanism and temporarily reinvigorated the most unpleasant forms of Federalism. If Jefferson had acted strongly at the opening of his last Congress, he might have achieved an acceptable substitute for the Embargo. By his inertia he was negatively responsible for its continuation until February, 1809, and for the disgraceful scenes of humiliation and panic which sullied America's reputation for

[80] *Annals*, 10th Cong., 2d sess., pp. 1172–1350.

[81] Brant, *op. cit.*, pp. 478–479; *Annals*, 10th Cong., 1st sess., pp. 1541, 436, 451–452; Jefferson to du Pont de Nemours, March 2, 1809, Lipscomb and Bergh, *op. cit.*, XII, 259–260.

years. In 1810, writing of repeal, Jefferson said, "This is the immediate parent of all our present evils, and has reduced us to a low standing in the eyes of the world." [82] He himself was at least a godparent, for his system and his tactics encouraged the political rebellion of the Tenth Congress. The philosopher-king had asked too much of his people.

[82] Jefferson to Dearborn, July 16, 1810, Lipscomb and Bergh, *op. cit.*, XII, 399.

# VI

## CANNING AND PERCEVAL

Throughout the life of the Embargo the United States confronted, not the compromise-minded ministry of Fox and Grenville, but a new government dedicated to vigorous prosecution of the war against Napoleon. In March, 1807, as a result of unwise, irresolute tinkering with the Irish problem, the Ministry of All the Talents fell from power. Few mourned its passing, even among ministers themselves. A new government under the nominal leadership of the Duke of Portland united Pitt's supporters and others who had served under Addington. The premier himself had little to recommend him save the weakness that made his lieutenants willing to serve under him rather than under one of their own number.

Aside from Portland, the new government represented, far more than its predecessor, a gathering of talents. Four members—Perceval, Hawkesbury, Canning, and young Palmerston—subsequently headed ministries of their own. Castlereagh became perhaps the greatest British foreign secretary, and Bathurst served for many years as an inconspicuous but very capable minister. Of course, these men had to make room for the inevitable baggage of borough-mongering noblemen, and several, notably Canning and Castlereagh, still showed signs of political immaturity. Grenville and Howick naturally remained outside the government, and Sidmouth and Wellesley did not join it for some time. Still, the abilities were there, narrow and rough-honed though they might be. With relatively few changes in personnel, this Cabinet fought the war through to a triumphant conclusion.

Behind the ducal façade, Spencer Perceval was the most influential minister. The expense of a huge array of offspring made him reluctant to abandon his legal practice to become chancellor of the Exchequer. In a transaction loudly criticized by the Opposition, Perceval received an almost unprecedented lifetime appointment as salaried chancellor of the Duchy of Lancaster, and he abandoned the law and the attorney-generalship for an active role in the fight against Napoleon. By nature quiet and courteous, Perceval often flared up into anger when criticized. Habits of the law had bred in him a certain narrowness, but he also had determination, perhaps even stubbornness. With him the anti-Napoleonic crusade took absolute priority. He opposed all but minimum concessions to neutrals, and he never understood America's failure to see that the Emperor threatened world liberties. In his view, the Orders in Council and Wellington's war in Spain were England's two best weapons, and he resolutely refused to abandon either in the face of protests from the United States and from interested British groups.

For the first eighteen months of the ministry's life, this dogged, unobtrusive man had as a colleague the mercurial George Canning, who received the Foreign Office. Canning had had subordinate experience as under-secretary in the Foreign Office in the 1790's, and few in the House of Commons could equal him as an orator. Canning grasped more quickly than his colleague the essentials of a new situation, and he favored decisive action without abandoning flexibility. To the applause of his mentor, Pitt, Channing had married money and position, but his own relatively unpatrician family background kept him out of the Establishment. Many doubted his political stability. By turns a Foxite, a supporter of Pitt, and then a more unyielding Pittite than the ex-Minister himself, Canning had nevertheless negotiated for office with the Ministry of All the Talents, which obviously shared few of the principles of his dead patron.

A diplomatic veteran personally friendly to Canning penetrated to the root of the matter when he wrote, shortly after Canning took office: "Canning possesses the peculiar talent of justifying ably and forcibly all he does . . . and that so rapidly and so eloquently that it is very difficult not to be carried away by what he says. He is unquestionably very clever, very essential to Government; but he is *hardly yet a Statesman,* and his dangerous habit of *quizzing* (which he cannot restrain) would be most unpopular in any department which required pliancy, tact, or conciliatory behaviour." [1] In interviews with William Pinkney, Canning was unfailingly patient and even courteous; in their formal exchange of notes the American often worsted Canning simply because the latter could not restrain his pen. As Lord Henry Petty pointed out, when Canning's notes were published in America "the whole public mind . . . was insulted by his ill-placed irony." William B. Giles, for example, assailed Canning's "prevaricating letters and sophisticated expositions," and later complained that "he chooses to act by tricks and contrivances, . . . by a mental retort, flowing solely from his own visionary mental conceits." Britain, said Giles, had entrusted her affairs to "a parcel of punsters" in "the administration of the energetic, the sarcastic, the facetious, the joking Mr. Canning." [2] The Secretary's official papers and his unrestrained parliamentary oratory affronted the United States nearly as much as his government's policies.

England supported the new ministry primarily because it promised energetic action, for Napoleon's triumphs propelled Britain not in the direction of peace but toward more rigorous warfare.

---

[1] Entry of March 14, 1807, James H. Harris, Earl of Malmesbury, ed., *Diaries and Correspondence of James Harris, First Earl of Malmesbury* (2d ed.; 4 vols.; London, 1845), IV, 375. In a slightly different form, this chapter has appeared in *American Historical Review,* LXIII (1957–1958), 1–22.

[2] *Hansard,* XII, 1208–1209; *Annals,* 10th Cong., 2d sess., p. 371; 11th Cong., 1st and 2d sess., pp. 496–497.

The rights of neutrals were scorned; as William Cobbett put it, in typically forthright language, "Our power upon the waves enables us to dictate the terms, upon which the ships of all nations shall navigate. . . . Not a sail should be hoisted, except by stealth, without paying us tribute." Such thinking produced, among other things, the brutal attack upon Copenhagen; significantly, the Opposition did not present a united front against this aggression. With feeling at such a pitch, it is small wonder that the Portland ministry did not adopt a liberal policy toward, as one conservative journal put it, "a nation that owes to it half the property she possesses, and is destined, to owe to it her preservation from the fate that has attended Continental Europe." [3]

During these years many Englishmen had little respect for Jefferson. "America," one statesman wrote, ". . . is no longer a bugbear; there is no terror in her threats." [4] Down to 1807 words and not deeds seemed to be the rule. Thereafter, evasion, domestic opposition, and its obviously great effect at home vitiated the effect of the Embargo. Although British diplomats sometimes warned that war was possible, they all usually reported the government torn by dissension, Federalism gaining ground, and hostilities unlikely. Even so, the government never treated the Americans so harshly as, for example, it treated the Danes. It desired American neutrality. Although the Cabinet's devotion to rigorous warfare made it avoid self-limiting devices like Fox's Blockade or the Monroe-Pinkney treaty, the ministry did make certain limited efforts to conciliate the United States.

The new ministry, Jefferson complained, included men who were "true Pittites, and anti-American." Madison agreed but did not feel that this doomed the chances of improving the Monroe-Pinkney treaty. Among other things, he considered it possible that "the new Cabinet will be less averse to a tabula rasa for a new adjustment, than those who framed the instrument to be super-

[3] *Cobbett's Political Register* (London), XII (1807), 420; *Leeds Intelligencer*, Dec. 25, 1809.
[4] Sidmouth to Abbot, Oct. 18, 1807, Charles Abbot, Lord Colchester, ed., *The Diary and Correspondence of Charles Abbot, Lord Colchester* (3 vols.; London, 1861), II, 132.

seded." He pressed for some enticing concessions on seamen, and he warned Jefferson that "a final failure of the negotiation must lead to a very serious posture of things." New instructions were therefore dispatched to Monroe and Pinkney toward the end of May, 1807. If Britain wanted a treaty, the instructions declared, she must accept at least six changes in the unratified document; if she preferred broad informal arrangements, the American government would accept them, provided they were equitable and did not tie America's hands. Of the ultimatums, Madison's instructions most emphasized impressment, although he also sought an indemnity for past seizures and at least some modification of the note reserving Britain's right to retaliate against the Berlin Decree. When the Secretary's instructions reached London in July, 1807, his agents immediately asked Canning to resume negotiations.[5]

This request embarrassed Canning. Many supporters of the Perceval government considered the treaty a craven surrender. In the *Morning Post*'s view, "nothing but madness or folly could induce the Americans to refuse their acceptance." George Rose, to whom the Cabinet turned for advice, hostilely dissected the treaty in a long memorandum, and the *Courier* concluded that "it is a Treaty almost entirely in favour of America, with scarcely one stipulation favourable to the commerce of this country—nay, so far from it, that it contains stipulations hostile to it." [6] On the other hand, the agreement promised at least an armistice with America, and British rejection would have outraged the Opposition. Certainly the Foreign Secretary must have felt that by rejecting the settlement Jefferson had unwittingly saved him from a difficult decision. He permitted supplementary articles completed before Grenville's fall to die with their sponsors. At a farewell dinner

[5] Jefferson to Madison, May 1, 1807, Andrew A. Lipscomb and Albert E. Bergh, eds., *The Writings of Thomas Jefferson* (Memorial ed.; 20 vols.; Washington, 1903–1904), XI, 199; Madison to Jefferson, April 24, May 4, 1807, Thomas Jefferson MSS, Library of Congress; Madison to Monroe and Pinkney, May 20, 1807, Department of State Archives, National Archives, Instructions, All Countries, Vol. VI; Monroe and Pinkney to Canning, July 24, 1807, Foreign Office Archives, Public Record Office, FO 5/54.

[6] *Morning Post* (London), April 20, 1807; unsigned Rose memorandum, n.d., FO 95/515; *Courier* (London), Nov. 11, 1807.

to Monroe, whose departure actually was delayed, he offered a fulsome toast to Anglo-American friendship, and a little later he announced (although perhaps insincerely) that had Jefferson approved the treaty the British government would have followed suit.[7] Otherwise, Canning was complacently silent on American affairs.

When the note from Monroe and Pinkney forcibly recalled them to his attention, Canning's first reaction was to seek domestic political advantage. He asked Holland and Auckland the extent of the assurances on impressment the two Americans said they had received. The two lords informed him that, after the formal article was dropped, "it was our private wish to keep that question in a state of presumed negotiation to the close of the war; still however maintaining the unimpaired exercise of the right though carefully avoiding every abuse of it." [8] No political mileage could be made out of this, and Canning certainly did not intend to accept an article on impressment, to say nothing of other changes sought by the Americans. For the rest of the summer he allowed the matter to rest.

Only in October, 1807, did Canning finally bestir himself, composing one of those unnecessarily obnoxious communications that so angered Americans. Some of the excuses for nonratification, he cuttingly observed, "are such as can be Matter of Discussion only between the American Government and its Commissioners; since it is not for His Majesty to enquire, whether . . . the commissioners . . . have failed to conform themselves . . . to the Instructions of their Government." Canning declared that to renegotiate on the basis of the rejected treaty "is a Proposal wholly inadmissible." [9] If there was to be a *tabula rasa*, both sides of the slate must be wiped clean. The *Times* later criticized "the sententious manner in which Mr. CANNING dismisses the . . . mutilated deed," [10]

[7] Canning to Holland, April 2, 1807, FO 5/54; *Times* (London), April 28, 1807; *Courier*, Aug. 11, 1807.

[8] Holland and Auckland to Canning, private, July 28, 1807, Greenwich Hospital Miscellanea, Public Record Office, Adm 80/117.

[9] Canning to Monroe and Pinkney, Oct. 22, 1807, FO 5/54.

[10] Feb. 24, 1808.

but few in Britain suggested that the Foreign Secretary had erred other than in the form of his answer.

Canning broke his silence only after the *Chesapeake* affair had obliterated the treaty as an issue. On July 24, 1807, Admiral Berkeley's dispatches reached Portsmouth, and a courier galloped to London with them. In the Lords that evening, Holland asked for information on "the subject of much discussion, . . . the report of hostilities having actually commenced." Hawkesbury put him off with a conventional expression of the government's desire for peace. Then, along with Eldon, who left the woolsack, he departed for an emergency cabinet session.[11] The ministers decided to disavow and recall Berkeley, but they later gave him a more important command. Although Britain offered compensation for the attack, Canning firmly refused to allow President Jefferson to connect this incident with the general problem of impressment.

In the context of the times these actions were less harsh than they sometimes appear. From the British point of view powerful provocation existed for some action against America, if not for an armed assault upon the United States Navy. Berkeley had of course reported the incidents around Norfolk that inspired his order. The admiral declared that, despite conciliatory efforts on his part, American authorities encouraged rather than discouraged desertion. In addition, the *Chesapeake* enlisted many Englishmen. Doubtless British guesses did not err on the side of moderation, but Berkeley at least claimed that the total was about 150. A later, completely independent estimate provided for the government placed the number at 200 and added that Decatur, who replaced Barron after the attack, had refused to permit 60 or 70 Englishmen to return to the Royal Navy although they desired to do so. Furthermore, the ministry soon learned that three of the four deserters taken from the *Chesapeake* had volunteered for service in the Royal Navy and only one—Jenkin Ratford, an undoubted Englishman—had been impressed.[12] These ameliorating circumstances helped Berkeley escape severe punishment.

[11] *Hansard*, IX, 926–927; *Star* (London), July 27, 1807.
[12] Berkeley to Marsden, Feb. 2, March 23, July 27 (with enclosure), 1807, Admiralty Papers, Public Record Office, Adm 1/497; Warren to Wellesley Pole, March 28, 1808, and enclosure, Adm 1/498.

The fact that the Opposition had appointed the admiral virtually immobilized them. Lord Grenville believed that "there is not in any one writer on the Law of Nations a trace to be found of any claim to search Neutral Ships of War for deserters." While he therefore declined to defend Berkeley in the House of Lords, because of his own responsibility and close ties with Berkeley's brother he followed a very restrained course. On the government side, Bathurst, the admiral's brother-in-law, worked to prevent hasty action, however justified. Bathurst was more interested in saving the admiral and his wife from a winter voyage home than in demonstrating to the American government that Britain disapproved of the assault.[13]

In going as far as it did—that is, in disavowing the attack and reaffirming that Britain did not claim a right to search warships—the government acted contrary to English opinion. Almost every popular journal defended the attack and proclaimed its deathless devotion to the right of search, even when applied to neutral warships. The leading Opposition newspaper, the *Morning Chronicle,* supported later by the *Edinburgh Review,* stood almost alone in arguing to the contrary. Some papers, among them the *Times* and the *Caledonian Mercury,* expressed hope that war could be avoided. But even the *Times* generally defended Berkeley for his forthrightness. "It is impossible an insult and act of manifest injustice like this [seduction]," said the *Times,* "could have been passed over by any British Officer who knew his duty, and left to a tedious and protracted discussion between the two Governments." The *Caledonian Mercury* commented: "We should think it a very great misfortune for this country to have to go to war with America at this time; but we should consider it as a much greater misfortune, if the Government of this country should tamely permit its rights to be violated, or its flag to be insulted by any power whatever." [14]

Other editorial writers, several using the heading "War with

[13] Grenville to Thomas Grenville, Oct. 23, 1807, Thomas Grenville MSS, British Museum (Add. MSS 41851–41859), Add. MSS 41852; Thomas Grenville to Lord Buckinghamshire, Oct. 9, 1807, Richard P. T. N. B. C. Grenville, Duke of Buckingham and Chandos, *Memoirs of the Court and Cabinets of George the III* (4 vols.; London, 1853–1855), IV, 205; Bathurst to Buckinghamshire, n.d., *ibid.,* IV, 211.
[14] *Times,* Aug. 5, 1807; *Caledonian Mercury* (Edinburgh), July 30, 1807.

America," made this language seem moderate. The *Morning Post,* strongly ministerial, argued that the "order of Admiral Berkeley to search the American frigate, appears to have been dictated by the most delicate caution, and to have enjoined nothing which was not fully justified by the extraordinary circumstances of the case." The paper added its trust that "Great Britain will not be . . . scrupulous and delicate about forms in enforcing her maritime rights, when her very existence depends upon the due maintenance of them." The *Courier* declared it time "to pause in our career of forbearance" and added that, if by seducing British seamen "America has offered us an insult, she must either give us ample reparation, or we must go to war." When the Portland government decided to disavow the attack, the *Courier* went along grumpily, warning the Americans to expect more of the same medicine if they did not abandon their career of provocation. Enemies of the regime agreed, notably William Cobbett, who "contend[ed] for the right of searching for deserters, upon the general principle, that the seas are the *dominion* of those who are able to maintain mastery over all that swims upon them." [15]

The still new and insecure government might easily have whipped up support by cultivating such opinion. Instead, the Foreign Secretary acted quickly to minimize the effect of the unfortunate clash. Upon the arrival of Berkeley's preliminary dispatches, he wrote to Monroe, who as yet had received neither instructions nor official information, that "if the British Officer should prove to have been culpable, the most prompt and effectual Reparation shall be afforded to the Government of the United States." Canning then called in George Sansom, spokesman for merchants trading with the United States. He told Sansom—and this information was soon in the papers—that, while he could not predict the future, his first exchanges with Monroe made him hopeful of a settlement. Through Sansom he assured the public that "Ministers will neither compromise the honour of their country, nor give any sanction to a wanton attack upon any other State

[15] *Morning Post,* Aug. 6, 1807; *Courier,* July 27, Aug. 10, 1807; *Cobbett's Register,* XII, 245.

with which we are in amity." [16] This statement, which warned extremists that the Royal Navy might have been at fault, also made it quite clear that the British government did not intend to be rushed into either war or surrender.

It is possible that the Cabinet considered asserting a right to search some foreign warships. The Foreign Office archives contain a long, rather inconclusive memorandum by Sir John Nicholl on this question. Nicholl justified hostile action, perhaps general war and perhaps merely the use of force against a specified ship, toward a state sheltering deserters, but he inclined to the belief that the decision should be made by the government, not by the commander on the spot, "tho even of this there may be possible exception." An equally lengthy memorandum, probably by Perceval, reviews the arguments pro and con but firmly states: "My opinion is clear that it is both most expedient & most right . . . to give up the right of Search of Ships of War." On July 30 Lord Bathurst wrote that, although Berkeley's conduct had been unauthorized, some legal opinion held that the American attitude justified retaliation:

It seems admitted by S$^r$ William Scott and S$^r$ John Nicholl . . . that our right of Search is derived from the circumstance of one of the parties being belligerent; and that the Neutral, by allowing men belonging to the Ships of War of the belligerents to enter into his Service, steps out of his Character of Neutral, by depriving the belligerent of his means of carrying on the War. All this would however have been a fitter subject of remonstrance from this Country, than an Order at once from our Admiral. Large allowances must be made for the provocations which he has for some time receiv'd: and had this arrived after a Victory instead of a defeat in Poland, we should have thought he had acted with great Spirit, and had been fully justified in his Orders.[17]

[16] Canning to Monroe, July 25, 1807, FO 5/34; *Sun* (London), July 30, 1807.
[17] Nicholl, "Principles and Positions Applying to the American Question," n.d. FO 5/104; "Memoranda of heads of arg$^t$ on the Execution of the Right of Search of American Ships of War & Trade," Spencer Perceval MSS (examined while temporarily on deposit at the Register of National Archives, London), 29/31–33; Bathurst to Harrowby, private, July 30, 1807, Dudley Ryder, 1st Earl of Harrowby, MSS, Sandon Hall, Staffordshire. See also Canning to George III, Aug. 2, 1807, Royal Archives, Windsor Castle.

The Cabinet thus reviewed the question before Canning declared to Monroe that His Majesty's government did not claim a right to search neutral warships.

With this question settled, perhaps by default, the Foreign Secretary turned his attention once again to Monroe. Canning apparently decided that delay was the best course, especially after Jefferson raised the issue of impressment. The President's proclamation banning the Royal Navy from American waters seemed to some Englishmen a provocative act requiring a riposte. Doubtless with the recent expedition to Copenhagen in mind, Hawkesbury talked about sending an emissary to America accompanied by a naval force and armed "with full power to commence hostilies" if the United States refused to withdraw the proclamation. Lord Buckinghamshire, a close friend of the Berkeleys, declared that the "inhospitality of M$^r$. Jefferson's proclamation" should be met by an embargo on all American shipping in British ports. For the most part, however, Englishmen rightly regarded the proclamation as an indication that the United States did not plan to rush into hostilities.[18] Canning shared this impression, although he made a great deal of the proclamation in his notes to Monroe, arguing particularly that it would affect the amount of reparation to be tendered.

Canning undoubtedly scored a technical triumph over Monroe. At a meeting on July 29, he agreed that the American would have to hand in a formal note of protest. When Monroe thereupon hastily produced a letter of complaint, on the basis of newspaper reports only, Canning had an opening which, after consultation with the Cabinet, he exploited to the full. His reply, sent four days later, rebuked the envoy for a protest "not brought forward either by the authority of the Government of the United States, or with any precise knowledge of the facts." He added haughtily that,

[18] Hawkesbury to ———, n.d., Charles D. Yonge, *The Life and Administration of Robert Banks, Second Earl of Liverpool* (3 vols.; London, 1868), I, 241–242; Buckinghamshire to Auckland, n.d., William Eden, Baron Auckland, MSS, British Museum (Add. MSS 34412–34471, 45728–45730), Add. MSS 34457, fol. 353; Pinkney to Madison, private, Aug. 13, 1807, William C. Rives Collection, Library of Congress; *Times*, Aug. 10, 1807.

after offering assurances that Britain would not condone Berkeley's action, "I may perhaps be permitted to express my Surprize . . . at the Tone of that Representation which I have just had the Honour to receive from you." The Foreign Secretary, very skillfully anticipating Jefferson's course, emphasized his own agreement with Monroe that the *Chesapeake* affair was "of itself of sufficient Importance to claim a separate and most serious consideration," not mixed with other issues.[19]

Poor Monroe! At the end of August he received James Madison's instructions to unite impressment and the *Chesapeake* affair. After his experiences with the Monroe-Pinkney treaty, he dared not deviate from his orders. He weakly put forward the American position first at an interview and then in a lame, watered-down official note. The Foreign Secretary replied with a strong communication, the fruit of two days' reflection in the country. He firmly declined to link the two issues. He denied that troubles over impressment grew out of British hostility toward America, insisting rather that the similarity of the two peoples caused unavoidable problems. Then, in a very characteristic passage employing phrases he had already used orally and taking advantage of Monroe's incautious admission that citizenship was difficult to determine, Canning wrote that "these Circumstances cannot furnish an argument for the Suspension of the exercises of the right with respect to America, unless it be contended that multiplicity of frauds and difficulty of detection are reasons against Suspicion, or motives for acquiescence." Canning closed by somewhat modifying the harshness of his position, informing Monroe that he would send a special minister to Washington to try to settle the *Chesapeake* problem.[20]

Both parties knew who had won the duel. Monroe abandoned his efforts and, with relief, handed the London mission to William Pinkney. Canning congratulated himself on his success: "If they had taken our atonement by itself, as we offered it, they would have

[19] Monroe to Madison, Aug. 4, 1807, enclosing Monroe to Canning, July 29, 1807, and Canning to Monroe, Aug. 3, 1807, Despatches, Great Britain, Vol. XIII.

[20] Memorandum of conversation with Canning, n.d. [Sept. 3, 1807], James Monroe MSS, Library of Congress; Monroe to Canning, Sept. 7, 1807, Despatches, Great Britain, Vol. XII; Canning to Monroe, Sept. 23, 1807, *ibid.*

appeared to gain something. But they have so managed Matters that we shall now appear to bully them even in making reparation. Nothing could be more advantageous for us than the course which they have taken." [21]

Canning's appointment of George H. Rose as special emissary has sometimes been criticized, largely because Rose's father had a reputation as an Americanophobe. Rose at least was not Canning's first choice. The Foreign Secretary offered the job to Nicholas Vansittart, an important member of the Sidmouth faction. After consulting his political allies, Vansittart declined, primarily because he was to act as a mouthpiece rather than a negotiator, simply reiterating Britain's refusal to join impressment with the *Chesapeake* affair and reasserting her demand that Jefferson withdraw his proclamation. [22] Rose, the second choice, agreed to go.

Canning's instructions to Rose were fully as unrealistic as those Madison had sent to Monroe, and, by the mission, the Foreign Secretary merely sought to gain further delay while American tempers cooled. In January, 1808, Jefferson and Madison agreed to separate the *Chesapeake* and impressment questions, too late to secure the reparation they could once have gained. Canning now insisted that this must be preceded by revocation of Jefferson's proclamation. When, in violation of his instructions, Rose arranged a compromise on this matter, he still had other demands that Canning had instructed him to make. On their rejection, Rose broke off negotiations in March, 1808. By that time, five months after George Canning's official reply to Monroe, the *Chesapeake* issue had been joined by other subjects of complaint more impartially weighted between Britain and France. "The premature fury," wrote Rose, ". . . was too violent to last, the feelings excited are deadened, and it would be difficult to move the Nation to War." [23]

[21] Canning to Lord Boringdon, Sept. 30, 1807, Morley MSS, British Museum (Add. MSS 48218–48301), Add. MSS 48218.

[22] Vansittart to Canning, Oct. 6, 1807, enclosed in Vansittart to Sidmouth, Oct. 6, 1807, First Viscount Sidmouth MSS, County Record Office, Exeter, Devon. See also Auckland to Grenville, Oct. 16, 1807, Boconnoc MSS (Papers of William Wyndham Grenville, Baron Grenville), Lostwithiel, Cornwall, Lord Auckland.

[23] Rose #14 to Canning, Feb. 18, 1808, FO 5/56. For an extended discussion of the Rose mission, showing the inflexibility of Canning's instructions, see Irving Brant, *James Madison: Secretary of State* (Indianapolis, 1953), pp. 404–418.

In many ways, Canning could feel that he had satisfactorily handled the *Chesapeake* affair. At home, he had steered a careful course, one that dampened the initial emotional outburst in Berkeley's favor and yet avoided outright surrender. Diplomatically, he had acted cautiously until it seemed that America again intended to bluster rather than fight. Essentially his policy was delay, and he succeeded in his object. He might, more imaginatively, have used the American retreat on impressment as the path to a settlement, but such a course presupposed greater respect for America and more humility than Britain had. Canning had escaped making an apology and yet had avoided war.

A proclamation recalling British seamen to the Royal Navy, issued in October, 1807, is another indication of Canning's attitude. This document, although often criticized by Americans as arrogant (John Adams later called it "that most atrocious of all violations of the Law of Nations"), undermined anti-American feeling by strongly reaffirming the right of impressment while at the same time publicly stating that Britain did not claim a right to search warships. Cobbett attacked it as a surrender; James Stephen believed it a concession, but a wise one; Vansittart considered it a foolish abandonment of a bargaining point.[24] Thus one cannot accuse Canning and the other ministers of issuing a proclamation which, in the context, was anti-American.

After the possibility of immediate war over the *Chesapeake* had ended, but well before that issue became a nagging, unpleasant memory, the British government proclaimed the Orders in Council of November, 1807. These orders were the Portland ministry's greatest single contribution to eventual war. They ended a short period of comparatively lenient treatment of American commerce signalized by moderation in the High Court of Admiralty. They checked a trend toward Francophobia in the United States, a trend only interrupted by the *Chesapeake* affair, and provided a principal field of controversy between London and Washington in later years. For these Orders in Council George Canning certainly bears

[24] John Adams to Benjamin Rush, Dec. 29, 1812, Adams Family MSS (microfilm), Massachusetts Historical Society, Vol. CXXI; *Cobbett's Register*, XII, 642, 673–683; Stephen, "Coup d'oeil on an American War," n.d. [Dec., 1807], Perceval MSS, 33/98–105; Vansittart to Sidmouth, Oct. 21, 1807, Sidmouth MSS.

a large share of the responsibility. But he was not their author, urged some modifications, and would have preferred a different system.

Long before November, 1807, it was obvious that British action was in the wind. As early as February Perceval, then in opposition, called for a complete interdiction of trade between Europe and the two Indies, and Joseph Marryat's well-received pamphlet, *Concessions to America the Bane of Britain,* argued that the Caribbean colonies' economic plight sprang chiefly from "a relaxation of those maritime rights which our forefathers fought and bled to establish." In July a House of Commons committee produced a strident report, ascribed by Pinkney to George H. Rose, which urged strong measures against American commerce in order to save West Indian trade. Even the risk of war was justified, the report maintained, since the "one grand and primary evil [is] . . . the facility of intercourse between hostile colonies and Europe, under the American neutral flag." The outcries of West Indian interests were echoed by the East India Company, suffering from the double pressure of oversupply and a reduced European market, and by some manufacturers, merchants, and shipowners formerly engaged in European trade.[25] Commerce declined in the summer of 1807, particularly after Napoleon stepped up enforcement of the Berlin Decree in August. By the year's end all northern Europe was closed to trade except Sweden, soon for that reason to be attacked by Russia at Napoleon's behest. The nation of shopkeepers seemed in imminent danger of insolvency.

"The best way of protecting our own Commerce," Sir John Nicholl wrote in August, "is by pressing upon that of the Enemy.

[25] Henry Adams, *History of the United States during the Administrations of Jefferson and Madison* (9 vols.; New York, 1889–1891), IV, 80–81; Joseph Marryat, *Concessions to America the Bane of Britain; or the Cause of the Present Distressed Situation of the British Colonial and Shipping Interests Explained, and the Proper Remedy Suggested* (London, 1807); Pinkney to Madison, private, Dec. 31, 1807, Rives Collection; Wilson H. Elkins, "British Policy in Its Relation to the Commerce and Navigation of the United States of America from 1794 to 1807" (unpublished Ph.D. thesis, Oxford University, 1936), pp. 194–196; Alexander Baring, *An Inquiry into the Causes and Consequences of the Orders in Council; and an Examination of the Conduct of Great Britain towards the Neutral Commerce of America* (London, 1808), pp. 1–2.

. . . If they can have no Commerce but through our means, they will resort to us." In August neither Nicholl nor James Stephen, who offered the same advice to Perceval, could bring the Cabinet to break its usual summer vacation. Six weeks later the ministers began to reassemble. Castlereagh wrote to Perceval on October 1, urging retaliation against Napoleon's commercial assault. The next day the *Sun* announced that the government would retaliate in some fashion, and within a week the *Times* called for "the prohibition of all carrying trade whatsoever, except that of British manufactures and colonial produce; and . . . the seizure of all ships sailing in the European seas, except such as are bound to or from England." [26]

The Cabinet worked out the Orders in Council during a fortnight at the end of October. On the twelfth, Perceval circulated a long memorandum which argued that, since Napoleon had long since cast off the restraints of international law, England might act similarly. Neutrals, said Perceval, "if they complain justly, . . . will direct their complaint against those whose proceedings against us & our Trade, make it indispensable . . . to retaliate." Anyway, neutrals had abandoned their privileged status, since a state that failed to force Napoleon to observe its rights "ceases to be a Neutral, by ceasing to observe that impartiality which is the very life and soul of neutrality." [27] These arguments formed the core of the British defense of the Orders in Council for the next five years.

The American government never admitted that the priority of sin rested with Napoleon, usually pointing to Fox's Blockade instead. And even Lord Sidmouth, to say nothing of Jefferson and Madison, objected that it was unfair to assert that America had tolerated the Berlin Decree, thus forfeiting her claim to British leniency. At the time of the November orders, Perceval and his colleagues had no idea how the Americans would react to the first

---

[26] Nicholl to Canning, Aug. 15, 1807, FO 83/2205; Stephen to Perceval, Aug. 17, 1807, Perceval MSS, 33/1; Castlereagh to Perceval, Oct. 1, 1807, Charles W. Vane, Marquess of Londonderry, ed., *Correspondence, Despatches, and Other Papers, of Viscount Castlereagh, Second Marquess of Londonderry* (12 vols.; London, 1848–1853), VII, 87–88; *Sun*, Oct. 2, 1807; *Times*, Oct. 6, 1807.

[27] Perceval memorandum, Oct. 12, 1807, Perceval MSS, 36/2.

real enforcement of the decree. Of the ministers, only Bathurst questioned the right that Perceval postulated. Canning wrote, "I have never for a moment doubted the *justice* of retaliating to the full extent." He soon warned Monroe and Pinkney that since "the American Government has [not] taken any . . . effectual Steps, with respect to the decree of France," Britain reserved the right of retaliation.[28]

Details of the November orders proved more troublesome than the decision, in general terms, to act. Perceval had proposed to cut off trade only in colonial produce. In cabinet discussion his plan was considerably broadened, apparently largely at the suggestion of Westmorland, the Lord Privy Seal. Perceval's plan, to leave to neutrals—and all recognized that this meant chiefly the United States—direct trade with France in their own produce, was replaced by a clumsily stated but fairly complete ban on all trade with France and her satellites save that which passed through Great Britain, paying duties to the Crown.

Only two cabinet members, Bathurst and Canning, expressed serious misgivings. Portland entered a mild protest but was almost ignored. Bathurst criticized the new orders most strongly, both in Perceval's original form and in the final version. Canning recognized the dangers of the nakedly selfish form taken by the orders, with their almost open purpose of gaining for Britain a near monopoly of trade with the Continent. Rather cynically he suggested that he preferred to "keep out of sight" the most flagrant discrimination in favor of British trade. Like Portland, he favored a less extensive but even tighter blockade, one less offensive to neutrals: "I would

[28] Sidmouth to Bragge Bathurst [Dec. 1, 1807], George Pellew, *The Life and Correspondence of the Right Hon^ble Henry Addington, Viscount Sidmouth* (3 vols.; London, 1847), II, 487; Bathurst memoranda, n.d., Perceval MSS, 36/20; Canning memorandum, Oct. 14, 1807, *ibid.*; Canning to Monroe and Pinkney, Oct. 22, 1807, FO 5/54. All studies of this problem, the most detailed of which is Adams, *op. cit.*, rest primarily on the Perceval MSS, which contain numerous cabinet memoranda. Most historians have based their conclusions upon excerpts cited by Adams and by Perceval's biographer, Spencer Walpole, thus opening the way to possible error. Most of the memoranda are unsigned, or at best signed with only a scrawled initial. Walpole guessed at the authorship of most of them, but at least several of his guesses are open to criticism. The memorandum assigned by Adams to Hawkesbury is almost certainly by Westmorland, although Walpole marked it with Hawkesbury's name. The Perceval, Canning, Bathurst, Castlereagh and Portland memoranda are signed or titled.

rather confine the measures to a part of the Countries in the occupation of the Enemy (a large part to be sure; France & Holland for instance) and apply it in all its rigour to that part, than extend it to the whole, & relax it generally by complicated exceptions and regulations." [29] While the United States certainly would not have silently tolerated such a scheme, Canning was either somewhat more respectful of American rights or more aware of the possibilities of diplomatic controversy than his colleagues.

By the exchange of memoranda sketched above, the general line to be taken was decided by October 26, 1807. On November 10 the semiofficial *Courier* announced that stringent new regulations were in the offing, regulations that might require temporary sacrifices but would strike down the baneful American reëxport trade. On the eleventh William Pinkney rushed to the Foreign Office to try to prevent action, but only the Under-Secretary was there to meet him. It was too late. That same day the most important new Orders in Council were issued. The orders were extremely difficult to understand—committees of merchants visited the Foreign Office several times seeking enlightenment—but Perceval's summary was fairly accurate: "If you [France] will not have *our* trade, as far as we can help it you shall have *none*. And as to so much of any trade as you can carry on yourselves, or others carry on with you through us, if you admit it you shall pay [us] for it." [30]

The cabinet members agreed to certain relaxations to make the orders more palatable to the United States. They did so although this weakened their attempts to establish a commercial monopoly. Canning exaggerated when he described the concessions as proof that England "was actuated by the same Sentiments of Moderation by which His Majesty's conduct has been uniformly governed." [31] Britain might consider it a concession to permit American domestic

[29] Bathurst memoranda, n.d., Perceval MSS, 36/20; Bathurst to Perceval, Nov. 5, 1807, *ibid.*, 36/21–22; Canning memorandum, Oct. 14, 1807, *ibid.*, 36/5.

[30] *Courier*, Nov. 10, 1807; *Sun*, Nov. 11, 1807; Pinkney to Madison, Nov. 17, 1807, Despatches, Great Britain, Vol. XV; Perceval to Abbot, received Dec. 1, 1807, Abbot, *op. cit.*, II, 134.

[31] Canning #10 to Erskine, Dec. 1, 1807, Bernard Mayo, ed. *Instructions to the British Ministers to the United States, 1791–1812*, American Historical Association, *Annual Report, 1936*, III (Washington, 1941), 242–246.

produce, except cotton, to proceed to the Continent without paying a transit duty in England. The United States considered the direct trade unquestionably legal and knew that, except in cotton, there was little competition between British colonial and American produce in the European market. The obvious selfishness of the duty on American cotton embarrassed Canning and his colleagues; within a few months they placed American and West Indian cotton on an equal footing by forbidding all cotton shipments to the Continent. This negative gesture failed to satisfy Pinkney or his superiors.[32]

Two more important concessions appeared in the thicket of confusing regulations. Contrary to the Rule of the War of 1756, Britain did not interrupt direct trade between enemy islands and the United States. America had always eagerly sought this trade, and the Cabinet hoped that to permit it would show Britain's moderation. Second, the Cabinet agreed, over Castlereagh's objections and contrary to Perceval's original plan, to permit America to reëxport even the produce of enemy colonies through Britain to Europe upon payment of duties. These relaxations of the Orders in Council aimed, in Perceval's words, "to make it quite Clear . . . to America if she is wise to prefer the Neutral Trade, that will be left to her, to the total stoppage of her trade with the Enemy, & with ourselves too which war might occasion."[33]

The *Times* inveighed against "this system of concessions to Americans." Grenville, Grey, and company bitterly assailed the government for coöperating in Napoleon's project to destroy international trade. But most of the nation fell into line behind the government. All the important newspapers except the *Morning Chronicle*, even some that had advocated moderation during the *Chesapeake* crisis, supported the orders. The appearance of energy secured for them what Alexander Baring called "that ephemeral popularity which but too generally attends measures of novelty and violence." It would be months before their economic effect could be weighed. As one of Grey's lieutenants put it, "Nothing

[32] Canning to Erskine, separate, March 4, 1808, Mayo, *op. cit.*, p. 248 and n.; Pinkney to Madison, Feb. 23, 1808, Despatches, Great Britain, Vol. XV.

[33] Castlereagh to Portland, Oct. 26, 1807, Perceval MSS, 36/15-16; Perceval memorandum, Oct. 12, 1807, *ibid.*, 36/2.

can be worse than the present State of Trade and therefore every novelty, which holds out even a chance of improvement, is welcome." [34] In the spring of 1808 London and Liverpool merchants trading with America showed signs of restiveness, but the Orders in Council remained generally popular at least until the summer.

At the parliamentary session beginning in January, 1808, the Opposition attacked the new policy. Perceval blandly denied charges that he was jealous of American prosperity or would welcome a war with her. War would harm both (although America most), he said. "The prosperity of America was the prosperity of Great Britain, and he was as anxious to preserve peace with America, consistently with the rights and interests of this country, as any man." But international conditions required vigorous action, and the Orders in Council could not be further tempered. Perceval and his colleagues therefore sought legislative authority for charges upon goods in transit to Europe. With Lord Henry Petty, Baring, and Auckland's son in the van—and Howick, recently advanced to the Lords as Earl Grey by his father's death, sorely missed—the Opposition charged against the bill. They never rallied more than a third of the House of Commons to their side. After a session lasting until six in the morning, the House approved the Orders in Council Bill, and before the end of March the Lords added their approval. Although he admitted that Opposition members, particularly Petty, had often spoken ably, Perceval concluded with satisfaction that "the discussion . . . has set those orders so completely in their right light that there is no chance of their being able now to make any impressions upon the public against them." [35]

Although neither Monroe nor Rose received the new regulations before departing for America, Canning soon sent Erskine a lengthy justification of the orders, pointing out the lucrative channels still left open to American trade. After conversations in Washington, the British minister reported, "this Government does not

---

[34] *Times*, Nov. 17, 1807; Baring, *op. cit.*, pp. 10–11; Tierney to Howick, Nov. 12, 1807, Charles Grey, Second Earl Grey, MSS, The Prior's Kitchen, Durham University, from Tierney.

[35] *Hansard*, X, 329 and *passim*; Perceval to George III, March 12, 1808, Royal Archives; Perceval to George III, n.d., *ibid.*, fols. 14039–14040.

view those Modifications of the Principle of Retaliation in as favorable a light, as I was commanded by you to represent them." Nor did the United States accept the general principles asserted by Britain. The wilder Republicans considered the November orders "tantamount to a declaration of war." Actually, they were both less drastic and more humiliating. As Admiral Mahan later observed, taxation of goods bound for Europe was "literally, and in no metaphorical sense, the reimposition of colonial regulation." [36] The Cabinet hoped that Jeffersonian cowardice and national selfishness would lead the United States to accept the potentially profitable status left to it, and the government attempted to leave open just enough trade to seduce the Americans into this course. While the price offered for American neutrality was certainly low, until 1812 the policy of the United States seemed to vindicate the political judgment of Perceval and his colleagues.

America answered the increasing virulence of the Anglo-French war upon commerce with the Embargo. Most Englishmen agreed that this "most singular act, . . . little short of an absolute secession from the rest of the civilized world," was legitimized by international law, "however we may complain of the spirit which has produced it." [37] Some thought the Embargo would harm England almost as much as a war with the United States. But most Britons at first considered it a positive assistance, despite the loss of American supplies, or at least more harmful to France than to the British Empire. By restraining American shipping and exports the Embargo virtually ended the problem of neutral trade with France and conferred upon Great Britain a near monopoly of trade with the few remaining neutrals. The rising challenge to Jeffersonianism and the return of unemployed seamen to British service also served British interests. So George H. Rose reported, and Erskine, a man of very different political attitudes, agreed with him.

George Canning accepted this reasoning. When Pinkney brought him official notice of the Embargo, the Foreign Secretary received

[36] Erskine #12 to Canning, April 3, 1808, FO 5/57; *Reporter* (Lexington, Ky.), May 7, 1808; Alfred T. Mahan, *Sea Power in Its Relation to the War of 1812* (2 vols.; Boston, 1905), I, 178.
[37] *Times*, Jan. 27, 1808.

it with every sign of satisfaction. Throughout the spring of 1808 he was as courteous as ever to the American envoy. In March and April, with the backing of Castlereagh and Mulgrave, Canning opposed Perceval's proposal to seduce Embargo breakers by guaranteeing them unmolested passage to British ports.[38] That summer the Foreign Secretary evaded rather than embraced offers to repeal the Embargo. In fact, he considered these offers so unimportant that he twice forgot to mention them to the King. Only in September did he finally deign to transmit the formal note rejecting the American propositions in sarcastic and haughty fashion.

By the time the Pinkney-Canning exchanges were reported to Parliament, early in 1809, the commercial situation had somewhat deteriorated, thanks particularly to events in Europe and Latin America. After fifteen months of the Embargo, and just as its greater pressures at home were driving the Americans to abandon it, Britain at last began to feel the loss of American trade; at least, some argued, renewed trade with the United States would compensate for losses elsewhere. The Opposition therefore strongly attacked the government. But the assault failed to strike fire, perhaps in part because, as Lord Auckland wryly remarked, referring to the lively scandal involving Mrs. Clarke and the Duke of York, "it is like Whistling to the Winds to talk about great public businesses, whilst the whole attention of the Country is occupied in discussion with Prostitutes & with Swindlers." [39]

Nevertheless, a new departure was already under consideration. In January, 1809, Lord Auckland discerned "symptoms of a desire among the King's Ministers to give way." Only a wish to avoid the appearance of surrender restrained them; the United States must admit that the loss of trade harmed America more than Britain. Then, in March, news reached England that the Embargo would almost certainly be repealed. The embarrassment of seeming to be coerced by the Americans was removed. Canning, exulting that "the Yankees have been obliged to give way," immediately

[38] Canning memorandum, March 28, 1808, Perceval MSS, 36/27–28; Castlereagh memorandum, n.d., *ibid.*, 36/39; Mulgrave memorandum, April 3, 1808, *ibid.*, 36/30.

[39] Auckland to Grenville, Feb. 18, [1809], Boconnoc MSS, Lord Auckland.

requested Bathurst to meet with him to discuss future policy. Grenville eased the government's path by pledging the Opposition to refrain from recriminations if the government rescinded the Orders in Council. In mid-April Auckland, who planned to attack the orders in the House of Lords, wrote to Grenville: "It was hinted to me today that it was desirable to postpone this subject for a few days when it was probable that something w$^d$. be announced respecting it." [40]

The Opposition, the country, and America did not have long to wait. As early as July, 1808, Earl Bathurst suggested that the orders be replaced by a strict, geographically less extensive blockade of France and her immediate dominions, "a strong Order against France, which would not be liable to the present Objections & which America would certainly not feel as an advantage gained over us." Nothing came of this plan, which closely resembled Canning's suggestions of 1807, primarily because of the Cabinet's unwillingness to seem to surrender to the Embargo. Nor did the Earl secure cabinet approval when he put forward the same proposal in October.[41] In April, 1809, Bathurst and Canning tried again. The president of the Board of Trade and the Foreign Secretary agreed that the Embargo's impending repeal provided a good psychological setting, and Canning urged speedy action since a "fresh arrival from America might embarrass us." Bathurst circulated through the Cabinet a memorandum accompanied by a note of approval from Canning. Not a single minister objected to the general proposal, although Perceval apparently convinced them that the orders of 1807 should be gently replaced rather than directly repudiated. On April 27 and 28 the most important merchants trading with America, including Alexander Baring, met with Bathurst to discuss details of the new system.[42]

[40] Auckland to Grey, Jan. 27, 1809, Grey MSS, from 1st Ld. Auckland; Canning to Bathurst, March 24, 1809, Francis Bickley, ed., *Report on the Manuscripts of Earl Bathurst* (London: Historical Manuscripts Commission, 1923), pp. 86–87; Grenville to Grey, March 30, 1809, Grey MSS, from Ld. Grenville; Auckland to Grenville, April 19, [1809], Boconnoc MSS, Lord Auckland.

[41] Bathurst memorandum, July 29, 1808, FO 5/61; Bathurst to Perceval, received Oct. 21, 1808, Perceval MSS, 33/107–108.

[42] Canning to Bathurst, April 7, 1809, Bickley, *op. cit.*, p. 87; Bathurst memoran-

The new Order in Council closely followed the original Bathurst-Canning plan. It declared a general blockade against Napoleon, his immediate satellites, and French colonies,[43] but opened Germany and the Baltic to American commerce. The new decree strictly regulated the issue of licenses to trade with Europe, attempted to prevent discrimination against American ships, and reduced license charges, although all these rules later came to be violated. The government sharply lowered or entirely eliminated duties on goods in transit through the British Isles to Europe. These points went far to meet the American government's complaints against the British system in substance, if not in principle. The Orders in Council of November, 1807, passed quietly away. In reply to an Opposition taunt, Perceval explained that "they were not actually rescinded, but they were put in a state of modification which amounted to nearly the same effect." [44]

The ministry hoped the new order would lessen friction with America, although ministers denied making any concessions and insisted, in public, that the Republicans had acted first, baring their teeth at Britain's enemy by cutting off trade with France and closing American waters to French warships. While the United States did not recognize blockaded Holland as a Napoleonic satellite, nobody believed that an attempt to trade with that country would cause serious controversy. In any event, it was felt, America should be required to concede something.[45] The major question, whether the United States would consider the broad new blockade an effective and legal one, passed by default. The Cabinet assumed, or strongly hoped, that disappearance of the orders of 1807 would lead to good relations with the United States.

In Britain the ministry came under fire from two opposite directions, although the parliamentary Opposition generally fulfilled

---

dum, April 12, [1809], *ibid.*, pp. 87–88; Canning memorandum, March 30, 1809, *ibid.*, p. 89; Perceval memorandum, n.d., *ibid.*, p. 89; *Courier*, April 28, 29, 1809.

[43] This last provision rescinded a concession contained in the orders of 1807. Perceval suggested a limited opening of the British West Indies as an equivalent, but Liverpool and Eldon blocked this move. Perceval memorandum, n.d., Bickley, *op. cit.*, p. 89; Liverpool memorandum, n.d., *ibid.*; Eldon memorandum, n.d., *ibid.*

[44] *Times*, April 29, 1809.

[45] Canning to Bathurst, private, April 15, 1809, Bickley, *op. cit.*, p. 90.

Grenville's pledge to keep silent. Conservatives objected that the government had truckled to the United States. Journalistic enemies of the regime loudly proclaimed their satisfaction that the government had finally seen the misguidedness of a policy that wiser men had always opposed. The *Morning Chronicle* positively crowed over the corpse of the November orders, and added, "What has induced Ministers to make such concessions, so contrary to the boasted policy they have hitherto promulgated, we do not pretend to determine" Privately, Opposition leaders of course agreed. Lord Grenville wrote, "Ministers have at last given up their nonsensical orders in Council." [46]

Ministerial papers attempted to tread a narrow line between these two attitudes. Pointing out that the Embargo had been repealed, they denied that the new order was a surrender to America, although emphasizing that Pinkney had "been heard to express himself in the highest terms of satisfaction, of the liberality and candour of his Majesty's Ministers." While the old orders had been effective, government supporters argued, the Cabinet now desired to test American bona fides by a wise experiment. The *Morning Post* wrote that "after experiencing the most beneficial effects from . . . the Orders in Council . . . , our Ministers have fairly met, by a liberal regulation of those Orders, the amicable provision of the last Act of the American Legislature [the Nonintercourse Act], in respect to the terms upon which its commercial intercourse with this country should be renewed." The new blockade, it was claimed, would actually operate more effectively against French commerce, and the measure would bring greater unity in England, "as it concedes some points much dwelt upon by the Opposition, in both Houses of Parliament." [47] These arguments were expressed in a defensive manner; they were also obviously contradictory.

Less than eighteen months after issuing the Orders in Council of November, 1807, the Portland government had in effect aban-

[46] *Morning Chronicle* (London), April 28, 1809; Grenville to Grey, April 28, 1809, Grey MSS, from Ld. Grenville.
[47] *Edinburgh Evening Courant*, May 1, 1809; *Morning Post*, April 29, 1809; *Caledonian Mercury*, May 1, 1809. See also *Courier*, particularly April 28, 1809.

doned them. The Embargo was perhaps partially responsible for this, although Britain refused to act until the Americans had been driven from their ground and had provided a plausible opening through the Nonintercourse Act. The course of the war, and particularly the shift of the Spanish Empire to the British side, impelled England in this direction, since the November orders became partially obsolete. Doubtless Erskine's reports, which grossly exaggerated the new administration's desire for an accommodation with England, led the Cabinet to believe James Madison would modify Jefferson's policy. At any rate, the British government did shift its policy at a critical moment in the war, did seek at least a tacit understanding with the United States. All that seemed required was similar wisdom and good spirit on the part of the new American government. If the Foreign Secretary and his colleagues had been better informed about the situation in the United States, they would certainly not have embarked so hopefully upon this course. As one shrewd merchant engaged in American trade wrote, "a good has been done, but with an ill grace, and I fear more from necessity than choice. If however other concessions are made, almost equally essential, I think a foundation will be laid for the restoration of . . . friendly intercourse." [48] The ministry was fully satisfied that it had taken an important step, and it sat back to await American plaudits.

William Pinkney reacted ecstatically to the new policy. Officially he reported that "a great Step has been taken towards the complete accomplishment of our Wishes." In a private letter to the President, he wrote of his "hope that this Measure will open the Way to Reconcilement between this Country and America. . . . Our Honour is now safe, and by Management we may probably gain every thing we have in View." Such disparate personages as Sir Francis Baring, John Trumbull, and Napoleon shared Pinkney's opinion.[49] At almost exactly the same time, however, that the new

[48] Mullett to Whitbread, May 3, 1809, Samuel Whitbread MSS, Southill Park, Biggleswade, Bedfordshire.
[49] Pinkney to Smith, May 1, 1809, Despatches, Great Britain, Vol. XVI; Pinkney to Madison, private, May 3, 1809, Rives Collection; Sir Francis Baring to King, May 2, 1809, Rufus King MSS, New-York Historical Society, Vol. XII; Trumbull

order was issued, across the Atlantic the President and Secretary of State Robert Smith concluded negotiations with David M. Erskine which granted America even more favorable terms. The decree for which Earl Bathurst and George Canning had labored merely puzzled Madison, led newspaper editors to suspect that England planned to go back on concessions made through Erskine, and was only rarely recognized for what it was, a major shift in British policy.[50]

Late in 1808 David Montagu Erskine held important conversations with American leaders. At the first of these, with President Jefferson, Erskine clearly showed that he feared war would follow embargo. First Madison and then Gallatin and Robert Smith played upon this fear, but Canning's subsequent actions indicate that Erskine's government did not take it very seriously. The Foreign Secretary found far more interesting a second aspect of Erskine's reports. The President and the President-elect allowed Erskine to understand that the administration preferred peace to war, although, they said, it was under heavy pressure from Republican rank and file. In a private talk at Gallatin's home, the Secretary of the Treasury went even further (or so at least Erskine reported; Gallatin subsequently challenged his account). As did Madison in subsequent instructions to Pinkney, Gallatin pointed out that when nonintercourse passed it would place England and France on an equal footing. With it would end the discrimination of the Nonimportation Act and Jefferson's post-*Chesapeake* proclamation and thus the excuse for British complaints against American bias. The Secretary added that a law forbidding the employment of foreign seamen would soon come before Congress. Erskine claimed that Gallatin even stated that the United States might modify its opposition to the Rule of the War of 1756. The British

---

to King, April 30, 1809, *ibid.;* Champagny to Hauterive, May 13, 1809, Archives des Affaires Étrangères, Correspondance Politique, États-Unis (photostats, Library of Congress), Vol. LXII.

[50] Madison to Jefferson, June 10, 1809, Gaillard Hunt, ed., *The Writings of James Madison* (9 vols.; New York, 1900–1910), VIII, 62–63; *Enquirer* (Richmond), June 16, 1809; *Independent Chronicle* (Boston), June 15, 1809; *Annals,* 11th Cong., 1st and 2d sess., pp. 1452, 1645.

envoy believed that the incoming administration would embrace an opportunity to settle difficulties with Britain.[51]

The Foreign Secretary reacted optimistically to Erskine's already exaggerated accounts. He thought that, chastened by the Embargo and by French insults, the United States would accept almost any terms. In a private chat at a diplomatic dinner and subsequently during a long Sunday conference at his home, George Canning told William Pinkney what he planned. Pinkney had no powers to negotiate and therefore merely urged Canning to send new directions to Erskine.[52] By failing to criticize the proposals, Pinkney seemed to indicate that he did not find them upsetting. This unfortunate reserve encouraged the Foreign Secretary to send visionary instructions to his agent in America.

Canning's instructions—he signed a whole series on January 23, 1809—repeated the ideas put forward to Pinkney. The first provided for a *Chesapeake* settlement, but the commercial question was central. The Foreign Secretary offered to repeal the Orders in Council if America formally accepted three stipulations: British trade would be freely admitted to American ports while that of France remained excluded, opposition to the "made in Britain" Rule of the War of 1756 would cease, and Washington would permit the Royal Navy to seize American ships violating their own country's ban upon trade with France.[53] This last requirement, which really granted England the right to execute American law, showed how distorted was Canning's view of the situation in the United States. As Rufus King later commented, "should the U.S. [have] consent[ed], . . . in their own Eyes, as well as in the eyes of others, not excepting those of England, they would appear

[51] Memorandum of Nov. 9, 1808, Paul L. Ford, ed., *The Writings of Thomas Jefferson* (10 vols.; New York, 1892–1899), I, 335–338; Erskine #46, #47, #50 to Canning, Dec. 3, 7, 8, 1808, FO 5/58. For Gallatin's account see Gallatin to Erskine, Aug. 13, 1809, Henry Adams, ed., *The Writings of Albert Gallatin* (3 vols.; Philadelphia, 1879), I, 458–461.

[52] Pinkney to Madison, private, Jan. 23, 1809, Despatches, Great Britain, Vol. XVI.

[53] Canning #1–#4 to Erskine, Jan. 23, 1809, Mayo, *op. cit.*, pp. 264–267. Formal approval of these instructions and of the appointment of a special agent to carry them to America was not sought from the King until February 3, 1809, which suggests that cabinet discussions followed preparation of the instructions, but there is no written evidence that this is so. Canning to George III, Feb. 3, 1809, Royal Archives.

to have voluntarily submitted to Terms of Humiliation and Dishonor." [54]

Early in April, two and a half months after being framed, the instructions arrived at Washington by special messenger. Since Erskine had no desire to humiliate the United States, he abandoned some of the Foreign Secretary's requirements of his own volition, while Madison, working through the new Secretary of State, Robert Smith, induced him to drop others. In arranging reparation for the *Chesapeake,* the English negotiator failed to mention Canning's insistence upon formal revocation of the proclamation banning British warships. He did get the Americans to drop a demand that Berkeley be punished, but in return he accepted a note, nominally from Smith but actually written by the President, which insultingly declared that the United States believed punishment "would best comport with what is due from His Britannic majesty to his own Honor." [55]

The young Englishman knew Smith and Madison would never formally accept Canning's three stipulations, even to gain repeal of the orders. He did not reveal that they were *sine qua non*'s. Instead, knowing that he violated his instructions but insisting that he adhered to their spirit, the envoy accepted informal American explanations. The final settlement, the first important executive agreement in American history, took the form of an exchange of notes: Erskine promised that the Orders in Council "will have been withdrawn, as respects the United States on the 10th. day of June next," and Smith replied that trade with Britain would accordingly be reopened. As Canning had originally suggested, Erskine and Smith left the working out of details until a special envoy could come from England. "In the mean Time," Erskine wrote, "no injury can be derived, I conceive, from that *conditional Agreement*." [56]

News of the agreement reached London by semaphore from Portsmouth on May 21. The next day Canning drafted an angry

[54] King to Trumbull, July 31, 1809, King MSS, Vol. LXXX.
[55] Erskine #19 to Canning, April [18], 1809, and enclosures, FO 5/63.
[56] Erskine #20 to Canning, April 20, 1809, and enclosures, *ibid.*

rebuke to Erskine, stopping just short of formal disavowal of the arrangement. On the twenty-third the Cabinet discussed the situation for four hours, which suggests that no formal decision had yet been made; there were even rumors, highly improbable but possible, that a majority of the Cabinet desired to accept the agreement, but that George III blocked this because of the insulting passage on Berkeley's punishment.[57] If Canning wavered temporarily, he soon returned to his usual firmness. At a levee the next day, the Foreign Secretary drew Pinkney aside, "and, after observing that he was sure that I had anticipated what he was about to say, informed me that they must disavow M$^r$. Erskine." [58] Earl Bathurst informed merchants trading with America that the government would not ratify the agreement, and a short time later Canning told the House of Commons that Erskine had acted in complete disregard of his instructions. Formal disavowal soon followed.

Lord Grenville privately declared himself grieved that Britain had turned its back upon an opportunity to "cultivate . . . the only connection which promises us any real advantage." But Lord Grey was cautious, and the party newspaper did not exploit the issue at the time (although later it did so). Even the *Times*, then in a maverick stage, reversed itself within a week after initially praising the agreement as a step toward amity.[59] Not a single important public voice challenged the government.

As a matter of fact, both Opposition and ministerial papers criticized the ministry for its attempt to cushion the impact of repudiation in America. The government announced that American ships that sailed for Europe in a belief that the Orders in Council had been lifted would be permitted to complete their voyages. Annoyed at this concession to their rivals, 200 London merchants attended a protest meeting and sent a delegation bearing resolutions to wait

[57] Joy to Madison, May 24, 1809, James Madison MSS, Library of Congress; John Melish, *Travels in the United States of America, in the Years 1806 & 1807, and 1809, 1810, & 1811* (2 vols.; Philadelphia, 1812), I, 355.

[58] Pinkney to Smith, May 28, 1809, Despatches, Great Britain, Vol. XVI.

[59] Grenville to Grey, May 26, 1809, Grey MSS, from Ld. Grenville; Grey to Grenville, May 25, 1809, Boconnoc MSS, M$^r$. Grey L$^d$. Howick Earl Grey, 1808–1813; *Morning Chronicle*, Jan. 21, 1811; *Times*, May 23, 25, 26, 31, 1809.

upon the Board of Trade. Along the same line, the *Times* complained that, "as American warehouses are now full of goods, they will of course be emptied, and the Continental markets supplied, we may say for years, after the permission to trade with them directly has ceased: so that the injury is not limited to the duration of two months, but will be sensibly felt by the English merchant, so long as the hoard of merchandize poured into the Continental markets during those two months is in a state of consumption."[60] By its gesture to American sensibilities the government reaped far greater unpopularity than it did by rejecting the agreement itself.

The disavowal nevertheless deserves very serious consideration. Why did Canning and his colleagues reject this settlement? As a preliminary, it must be emphasized that the minister departed widely from his instructions. Samuel Whitbread rashly accused Canning of misleading the House of Commons on the content of the instructions, but later he had to withdraw this charge. Otherwise the Opposition, except Erskine's father, found it best to ignore this point. The British, if not yet the Americans, considered the violation of diplomatic instructions a serious matter, seldom to be condoned, particularly in a young neophyte.

Specifically, Erskine ignored orders by failing to insist upon any of Canning's three stipulations. In the Foreign Secretary's view, silence or mere oral agreement on these matters meant either that Britain abandoned an important position or that Madison had changed his attitude in an unfavorable way since Erskine's earlier reports. As Canning agreed, the Rule of the War of 1756 lay dormant in 1809, since France had lost not only all her own colonies except Guadeloupe, but also the trade of the Spanish Empire.[61] Still, the ministry wanted America on record, since the rule might again become important if Napoleon gained control of the Spanish dominions. It was far from acceptance to have the Secretary of State state orally that the rule would cause no trouble in the future, thus leaving him free to declare, as he did later, that

[60] *Leeds Intelligencer*, May 29, 1809; minutes of May 29, 1809, Board of Trade Records, Public Record Office, BT 5/19; *Times*, May 26, 1809. See also *Courier*, May 26, 1809; *Morning Chronicle*, May 25, 27, 1809.

[61] Pinkney to Smith, June 23, 1809, Despatches, Great Britain, Vol. XVI.

the United States continued to deny its validity. Similarly, Canning considered important Erskine's failure to win agreement that the Royal Navy might seize ships violating American law by trading with France. Pinkney had not protested when the Foreign Secretary put forward this idea. Canning did not consider it equivalent for Smith to state, as Erskine declared he did, that violators of American law could not expect assistance from their government if they fell into British hands, and Smith later denied he had even gone this far in the Washington conversations.[62]

Most important of all, Erskine did not secure a promise that the Americans would continue to prohibit trade with France. The Foreign Secretary later said "it was the *sine qua non* of the arrangement, that America should maintain her non-intercourse against France," and his conversations with Pinkney indicate that he considered this the critical point. Erskine's agreement left the way open for an American understanding with Napoleon. As a matter of fact, just after the Smith-Erskine exchange, the Secretary of State directed Armstrong to offer to reopen Franco-American trade if, in reply to repeal of the November orders, Napoleon would remove "the illegal parts of the French decrees," specifically not including those portions of the Berlin Decree that most seriously harmed Britain.[63] Had he known this, Canning doubtless would have felt even more certain of the wisdom of rejecting the Erskine agreement. He had no desire to hand the Americans a lever they might use to pry open French ports for their own purposes.

Lord Erskine may have been correct when he said, in defense of his son, that if a formal agreement had been signed and sent to a Senate "divided by contentious parties . . . not only the whole grace of the thing would have been lost, but so much ill blood stirred up . . . that the whole thing must have blown up."[64]

[62] Smith to Erskine, Aug. 9, 1809, enclosed in Erskine #34 to Canning, Aug. 31, 1809, FO 5/63.

[63] *Hansard*, XIV, 1025; Pinkney to Smith, May 28, June 23, 1809, Despatches, Great Britain, Vol. XVI; Smith to Armstrong, April 21, 19, 1809, Instructions, Vol. VII.

[64] Lord Erskine to Grey, Aug. 27, 1809, Grey MSS, from Ld. Erskine.

Canning perhaps paid too little attention to American constitutional practices and party politics. Possibly Smith and Madison would have shifted the orientation of American policy if Canning had endorsed the agreement. But the important point is that if the three conditions were only informally accepted, the United States was not bound. Canning's central purpose had been to tie America for the future.

Erskine completely misread Canning's intentions. On the basis of Erskine's reports, the Foreign Secretary believed it just possible that the new Republican administration would transform the policy of the old. Thus, although Canning spoke with cautious approval of the first "Symptom of a System of Impartiality," he really sought something more than an equally balanced America. As he put it, "the Sincerity of the good disposition professed by . . . the new American Administration, is the point the most important in the View of the British Government." Would America, while staying out of the war, join Britain in economic pressure upon France? This was the question. The restrained, lawyerlike attitude of Madison and Smith did not meet Canning's hopes; their casuistry over his stipulations destroyed hopes of finding a nonbelligerent ally. Canning did not share the obvious American desire to work toward eventual removal of all British and French restrictions on trade. He sought a system whereby Britain should "relax or modify His [Majesty's] Measures of Retaliation and self-Defence, in proportion as those of Neutral Nations should come in aid of them and take their Place." [65]

Then, of course, there was the important question of prestige. In Canning's view Erskine had acted "as if His Majesty had proposed to make Sacrifices to propitiate the . . . United States, in order to induce it to consent to the Renewal of Commercial Intercourse." [66] Doubtless the Foreign Secretary, who found the American habit of publishing diplomatic correspondence annoying, thought ahead to the inevitable day when President Madison would publish evi-

[65] Canning #2, #4 to Erskine, Jan. 23, 1809, Mayo, *op. cit.*, pp. 264, 267; Canning #3 to Jackson, July 1, 1809, *ibid.*, p. 284.
[66] *Ibid.*, p. 283.

dence of his triumph, evidence showing how skillfully he had forced Britain to abandon conditions she had set. The arrangement Erskine accepted did no more than meet an offer previously extended both diplomatically and, through the Nonintercourse Act, legislatively. England had steadily rejected suggestions of reciprocal repeal since the early days of the Embargo. Must she now confess her weakness by assenting? Most Englishmen saw only one possible answer to this question. As Canning said to Pinkney, in the existing state of the world, Britain not only could not concede, she must not even seem to concede.

Finally, and this is seldom noticed, the Erskine-Smith understanding undermined the Order in Council of 1809. Lord Erskine later declared the real issue was not whether his son had violated his instructions, "but whether Ministers after they had themselves revoked the orders in council by their order of the 26th of April last, which reduced the differences with America to literally nothing were justified in not giving a latitude to their minister there to settle the small remainder." [67] His lordship missed the point. The April order had the form of a spontaneous act, not a surrender. This concealed, carefully framed offer to the United States reopened much European trade; however, the Netherlands remained excluded so that the United States, which claimed a right to trade there, would also have to recede from its position. Whether Madison would have accepted this offer is problematical, but Erskine's broader concessions relieved him of the necessity of deciding. While George Canning would have preferred a tight agreement along the lines of his instructions, he must have been very angry that the less ambitious but still helpful plan embodied in the new Order in Council was never seriously tested.

Historians have often criticized Canning and the Cabinet for acting on such reasoning, arguing that rejection of the agreement helped to bring war three years later. Would the Erskine agreement really have ended discord? Later on Napoleon was shrewd enough to announce voluntarily the repeal of his decrees; in 1809 he might have tried the same gambit under pressure, and if he

[67] Lord Erskine to Grey, Sept. 28, 1809, Grey MSS, from Ld. Erskine.

had, we can only guess the consequences. Even without Napoleonic repeal, it is by no means certain that the Erskine agreement would have welded the United States to Britain for any length of time. The issue of impressment, for one thing, still remained, quiescent but potentially explosive. Actually, each side sought something quite different: America wanted neutral commerce (especially with France and her dependencies) restored to the seas; Britain wanted a nonbelligerent ally in the struggle against Napoleon.

The ministers, then, may have shown little imagination; they may be criticized for refusing to run risks in the search for a *rapprochement*. They certainly showed that they valued apparent advantages (actually largely illusory) for British commerce higher than American friendship. They did not act as they did simply because they detested Republicanism, James Madison, or the United States. If anyone deserves chief blame for the Erskine agreement, it is the man whose name it bears. He first misled Canning about the situation in America, then fumbled the Foreign Secretary's attempt to bind the United States to Britain's side, and also fatally undermined the gesture put forward in the Order in Council of April, 1809.

In American hearts David M. Erskine aroused false hopes, the blighting of which contributed to a general feeling of frustration, national dishonor, and dissatisfaction. Probably no other event from 1783 to 1815 was so generally celebrated as the Erskine agreement. Church bells rang, cannons boomed, candles illuminated windows, and, most important of all, the heavy flow of commerce to England was, albeit briefly, renewed. For the benefits of the agreement, some pious folk looked "with sentiments of fervent gratitude, beyond human agency, up to that awful Being, who guides and governs the affairs of men." Most Americans considered the Deity a passive spectator, and one of the attractive things about the Erskine agreement was that credit could be claimed by both parties. "One side rejoice because they think that the Embargo &cᵃ. has brought England to terms," wrote Rufus King, and "the other side rejoice because they believe that the opposition to the late Measures of Congress has obliged the administration to abandon their system, and to accept a Reconciliation with England." [68]

Then, three months later, came the news of Britain's disavowal. Ending the happy competition for credit, the parties now sought to apportion blame. Extreme Federalists blamed the administration for its trickiness with Erskine, Erskine for his simple-minded abandonment of his instructions; sometimes they pointed out that, under the new Order in Council, "our trade will have the same latitude, it was to enjoy by Mr. Erskine's arrangements and as qualified by our own laws, except Holland, and French Italy." Administration journals, and in private such Federalist leaders as King and Christopher Gore, declared that Canning's three conditions were entirely inadmissible. Republicans argued that the entire affair had probably been a trick to open a temporary channel of trade (two-thirds the normal amount of British exports went to the United States in 1809 as a result of the temporary relaxation of controls), and asserted that rejection of an agreement concluded in good faith "has capped the climax of atrocity towards this country." President Madison reluctantly broke his vacation at Montpelier to confer with the Cabinet at Washington. In some embarrassment, for his authority to act was uncertain, he issued on August 9 a proclamation again prohibiting trade with England. America had been humiliated once more. The Secretary of the Treasury gloomily commented that

we are not so well prepared for resistance as we were one year ago. All or almost all our mercantile wealth was safe at home, our resources entire, and our finances sufficient to carry us through the first year of the contest. Our property is now afloat; England relieved by our relaxations might stand two years of privations with ease; we have wasted our resources without any national utility; and, our treasury being exhausted, we must begin any plan of resistance with considerable and therefore unpopular loans.[69]

[68] Timothy Woodbridge, *An Oration, Delivered at Great Barrington . . . July 4, 1809* (Stockbridge, 1809), pp. 15–16; King to Trumbull, April 24, 1809, King MSS, Vol. LXXX.

[69] *Connecticut Courant* (Hartford), July 26, 1809; *National Intelligencer* (Washington), July 26, 1809; Gallatin to John Montgomery, July 27, 1809, Albert Gallatin MSS, New-York Historical Society.

The Erskine agreement, like the Embargo, had ended in total defeat. This time, save perhaps for a certain precipitancy in accepting Erskine's promises, the administration could not be blamed.

Canning knew that rejection of the agreement would seriously affront the United States. He attempted to repeat his post-*Chesapeake* delaying tactics, particularly by the dispatch of another special envoy. For the mission the Foreign Secretary very unwisely selected Francis James Jackson, an arrogant man whose appointmen to America Rufus King had blocked in 1801. Jackson it was who had transmitted the ultimatum that preceded the bombardment of Copenhagen, an ominous augury, although this time Jackson bore no ultimatum. Through him, the Foreign Secretary again offered to settle the *Chesapeake* affair, despite the offensive passage on this subject in Smith's note. Canning wisely instructed his emissary not to press the original British offer on commerce, but rather to offer to transmit to London any American suggestions, and he did recapitulate the advantages conferred upon American commerce by the order of 1809.[70] Although the instructions contained much argumentative and condescending language, Canning refrained from directing Jackson to read them to the Secretary of State. Their substance was about what might have been expected, for Canning believed that Madison, Smith, and Gallatin had inveigled Erskine into a one-sided agreement which they knew violated his instructions. The Foreign Secretary expected American anger to last for some time, but nothing in the Republican record suggested that the President or Congress would do much more than complain. Since British warehouses bulged with goods just received from America, Canning saw little reason to take the diplomatic initiative.

Secured from adversity by an exceptionally high salary, the promise of at least one year's service, an entourage of eighteen servants, and the company of the formidable Prussian baroness he had married, "Copenhagen" Jackson reached Washington in September. He took over the Erskines' double house. "A Scotchman with an American wife who would be a fine lady," the fastidious envoy commented after observing his quarters' uncleanly condi-

---

[70] Canning #1–#3 to Jackson, July 1, 1809, Mayo, *op. cit.*, pp. 277–287.

tion, "are not the best people to succeed on such an occasion." Socially, Jackson received great consideration from Robert Smith and the President; professionally, he suffered a real defeat at their hands. Instead of simply following Canning's instructions to preserve silence after repeating the *Chesapeake* offer, Jackson let himself become involved in the sort of disputation at which Madison excelled. Goaded by American notes, signed by Smith but written by the President, Jackson committed one indiscretion after another. In November the President quite justifiably declared that he would have nothing more to do with Jackson and would insist on his recall. The baroness angrily reported to her brother-in-law, "Francis being accustomed to treat with the civilized courts . . . of Europe and not with savage democrats, half of them sold to France, has not succeeded in his mission," and Jackson himself sent the Foreign Office a forty-five-page apologia which took the legation secretary fourteen hours to copy.[71] But Madison had had his triumph. "Copenhagen" Jackson spent the rest of his allotted year traveling about the United States. He accepted entertainment by Federalist bigwigs ready to welcome any enemy of Madison, and he prepared and subsidized propaganda in antiadministration journals.[72]

Shortly after Jackson's arrival in America, Canning's intrigues against Castlereagh blew the British government apart. Canning passed into the political wilderness. Until he returned to the Foreign Office in 1822, Canning had little influence upon policy toward America, although in 1812 he supported the Opposition call for a committee of inquiry into the Orders in Council. At that time he made it clear that, while he still favored commercial warfare against France, he strongly objected to the license system and particularly to its selfishness.[73]

When Canning left office in the fall of 1809, Anglo-American

---

[71] Jackson to Mrs. Jackson (mother), Oct. 7, 1809, Lady Jackson, ed., *The Bath Archives: a Further Selection from the Diaries and Letters of Sir George Jackson* (2 vols.; London, 1873), I, 17; Mrs. Francis J. Jackson to Sir George Jackson, Nov. 21, 1809, *ibid.*, I, 57; Jackson #19 to Canning, Nov. 16, 1809, FO 5/64.

[72] Josephine Fisher, "Francis James Jackson and Newspaper Propaganda in the United States, 1809–1810," *Maryland Historical Magazine*, XXX (1935), 93–113; Francis James Jackson MSS, Public Record Office, FO 353/58–61 *passim*.

[73] *Hansard*, XXI, 1139–1149.

relations were strained. They had deteriorated since the fall of the Ministry of All the Talents. However, by comparison with his successor, the pompous and inflexible Marquis Wellesley, Canning followed a liberal American policy. The chief charge against him is the appointment of Jackson, a bad choice for a mission of tranquilization, but even this failure had no immediate practical consequences. Despite defects of character which irritated Americans and later influenced historians, George Canning was not an Americanophobe. He favored policies more moderate than those advocated by his colleagues and far more intelligent than those for which the British press shrilly called. The Foreign Secretary prevented the *Chesapeake* affair from becoming even more serious than it was. He questioned the wisdom of the Orders in Council of November, 1807, and doubtless supported the almost unnoticed concessions they contained. He and Bathurst secured the virtual repeal of those orders through the new policy adopted in 1809. Perhaps Britain should not have rejected the Erskine agreement, but it was the minister himself, not Canning, who created the crisis, and even here the government attempted to lessen American resentment by conceding special privileges to ships that sailed after the agreement was signed. Thus, under Canning's leadership, Britain made several gestures to the United States. These concessions failed in their purpose, primarily because Canning and all England misunderstood Jeffersonianism and overestimated the amount of condescension America would tolerate. A lack of vision, a failure of understanding, rather than malevolence, may be charged against George Canning.

# CHAPTER

# VII

## AMERICA'S HUMILIATION

"The Lord the Mighty Lord must come to our Assistance, or I fear we are undone as a nation." [1] Thus wailed a Republican leader, not merely a carping Federalist, at the end of February, 1809. But Jehovah did not deign to aid his chosen people. Instead, He sent James Madison as his vice-gerent, and the new President was no Moses. Madison never pointed out any route to a promised land of peace and plenty, and for more than two years the United States wallowed in purposeless humiliation.

Although Federalism made a striking comeback in 1808, recapturing New England, Madison easily won election as Jefferson's successor. Vice-President George Clinton, an ambitious schismatic, could not even gain a majority of the electoral vote of his own state of New York. In Virginia, where James Monroe encouraged the use of his name against Madison, the administration ticket beat him by five to one. Federalism, bankrupt and divided, no

[1] Macon to Nicholson, Feb. 28, 1809, Joseph H. Nicholson MSS, Library of Congress.

longer had a truly national appeal. Madison won almost by default.

The new president took up his station on March 4, 1809. "I repair," he said, "to the post assigned me with no other discouragement than what springs from my own inadequacies to its high duties." This conventional self-depreciation seemed sincere on this occasion, for as Madison began his inaugural address he was pale and trembling. His audience strained to hear an oration that proved to contain nothing striking. In a dull, often platitudinous way, the President recited his principles in a series of clauses rather than individual sentences. Some Federalists, comparing the inaugural address with Jefferson's, concluded that the new administration would be more moderate. Actually the speeches simply reflected the different styles of thought of the two Republicans. The *National Intelligencer* described the speech as "chaste and nervous," meaning forceful, but actually "nervous" might better have been used in the more modern sense. The President apparently realized that his administration had not begun favorably. At the inaugural ball that evening he "seemed spiritless and exhausted," not triumphant. As soon as decency permitted, he hustled off to bed.[2]

Several years later an exceptionally scurrilous Federalist print unfairly described James Madison as the "political *pimp* to Thomas Jefferson, and Vice-Roy to the Grand Emperor of France." The President disliked Napoleon as much as he disliked Perceval, and he seldom sought Jefferson's advice. Madison's mistakes were his own. Enemies (and even Republicans like Senator Worthington) thought him weak and irresolute. "Something may be expected from his timidity," the London *Morning Post* predicted, "but nothing from his justice or his liberality." Friends (and General Turreau) agreed with Gallatin that "Mr. Madison . . . is slow in taking his ground, but firm when the storm arises."[3] Even his

[2] James D. Richardson, ed., *A Compilation of the Messages and Papers of the Presidents* (Washington, 1897), I, 466–468; Margaret B. Smith to Susan B. Smith, March ——, 1809, Gaillard Hunt, ed., *The First Forty Years of Washington Society . . . the Family Letters of Mrs. Samuel Harrison Smith* (London, 1906), pp. 58–64; *National Intelligencer* (Washington), March 6, 1809.

[3] *Federal Republican* (Baltimore), Jan. 27, 1812; Roy J. Honeywell, "President Jefferson and His Successor," *American Historical Review*, XLVI (1940–1941), 64–

most loyal supporters did not claim that the President was a natural leader.

The selection of a secretary of state revealed Madison at his worst. He planned to nominate Gallatin, but Senate opposition frightened him. Rather than fight, Madison at first thought of purchasing Senator Samuel Smith's support by offering the Treasury to the Senator's brother. When Gallatin, arguing that Robert Smith had scarcely distinguished himself as secretary of the navy, objected on the reasonable ground that Madison's plan would saddle him with the work of two departments, the President decided to leave his chief lieutenant at the Treasury. He named the utterly incompetent Robert Smith to the Department of State. This arrangement had no advantage save that it postponed quarrels with Samuel Smith and Senator Giles, who, eager to secure the State Department for himself, had spearheaded the opposition to Gallatin. Smith's appointment brought a disloyal subordinate into the administration's inner circle. It convinced ambitious congressmen that the new administration could be defied with impunity and forced the President to take onto his own shoulders most State Department business.

This episode merely marked the beginning of Madison's troubles. Gallatin aroused lesser men's jealousy, and his advancement to second position in the party hierarchy increased the number of his enemies. The Secretary fought constantly with the Smiths, and the two brothers sometimes found allies in their relative, Wilson C. Nicholas, and the erratic, ambitious Giles. Despite Giles's untrustworthiness, Madison let him continue as nominal administration leader in the upper house. In January, 1809, congressional votes, nominally on naval policy but actually challenges to Madison and Gallatin, showed how the President had lost control. More than half the Republican senators and one-third of the representatives deserted their leaders.[4]

---

75; *Morning Post* (London), April 17, 1809; Gallatin to Nicholson, Dec. 29, 1808, Henry Adams, *The Life of Albert Gallatin* (Philadelphia, 1879), p. 384.

[4] Gallatin memorandum, "The Navy Coalition of 1809," n.d., Albert Gallatin MSS, New-York Historical Society.

Seldom has Congress floundered more visibly than in the ten weeks from December, 1808, to Madison's inauguration. All agreed the nation must find some foreign policy upon which it could stand. But Jefferson had abdicated, Madison did not replace him, and rebellious congressional cliques found common ground only in attacks upon authority. "I do not believe," David M. Erskine reported, "that there are ten men who think alike upon any one important measure." Federalists opposed both war and commercial restrictions—in fact, everything. Some Republicans wanted to continue the Embargo system; nonintercourse was originally conceived as an adjunct to the Embargo, and in a last spasm the Enforcement Act of 1809 passed. Others, like Giles, George W. Campbell, and Attorney General Rodney, personally favored a declaration of war on one or both belligerents. Perhaps the largest group simply drifted, in Joseph Story's words, "without a guide or the wish for a guide." The net result was chaos. "You will see with regret," the President-elect wrote Pinkney in February, "the difficulty experienced in collecting the mind of Congress into some proper focus. On no occasion were the ideas so unstable and so scattered." [5]

Gallatin believed that above all the United States must not show the white feather by abandoning resistance. "If the Embargo is taken off," he wrote, "I do not perceive yet any median between absolute subjection and war," [6] and he and presumably Madison concocted a plan to slide the nation toward war. They and friends in the legislature decided to continue the Embargo until June, with an understanding that Congress, in a special session, would then declare war against those who continued to mistreat American commerce. If the announced intention to go to war frightened Britain or France, or if the American people became belligerent enough to support a declaration, or if European events made the com-

<hr />

[5] Erskine #10 to Canning, Feb. 6, 1809, Foreign Office Archives, Public Record Office, FO 5/62; Story to Fay, Jan. 9, 1809, William W. Story, *Life and Letters of Joseph Story*, I (Boston, 1851), 177–183; Madison to Pinkney, Feb. 11, 1809, *Letters and Other Writings of James Madison* (Congressional ed.; 4 vols.; Philadelphia, 1865), II, 429.

[6] Gallatin to Nicholson, Oct. 28, 1808, Nicholson MSS.

batants change their commercial policies, such a course might end in triumph or at least decision. All were unlikely. The proposed policy essentially only postponed the issue and sought to purchase acceptance of the Embargo for six more months by promising to lift it in the spring.

As secretary of state and president-elect, Madison might have been expected to launch the new policy. Instead the task fell to Gallatin, who prepared a long paper designed to prepare the way for action. On November 22, 1808, Congressman Campbell presented this manifesto to the House of Representatives. After reviewing the disputes with England and France, the report declared, "There is no alternative, but war with both nations, or a continuance of the present system." Selective war or reopened commerce, which Britain's sea dominion would enable her to monopolize, would have the effect of alliance with one of the offending powers against the other. Although Campbell's Report stopped short of calling for a declaration of war, it did suggest that war might soon be forced upon the United States. The Tennessee congressman asked his colleagues to approve resolutions asserting their intention to maintain American rights, closing American ports to the offending colossuses, and speeding military preparations.[7] The House completed action on Campbell's resolutions within a month and then resolved in favor of a special session at the end of May.

So far so good, but behind the façade lay rotten timbers. Fissures had already appeared, particularly in substantial Republican defections in balloting on Campbell's resolution against trade with Britain and France. New England Republicans pressed for an escape from the Embargo before June, and Southerners and administration supporters sought to keep them in line. The leader of the New England group, Ezekiel Bacon, pessimistically described the situation at the end of January in a letter to Joseph Story, who had returned to Boston:

Our Southern friends . . . now tell us that they are entirely willing to limit the Embargo, if we will at the same time unite in authorizing Letters

[7] *Annals*, 10th Cong., 2d sess., pp. 514–521.

of Marque to issue upon its repeal, that they are willing to support our commercial rights by the present System or by War as we shall think best, but that they will never consent to take non intercourse & non-importation as a substitute for the Embargo, that they will in Preference to this give up the whole ground of resistance to belligerent aggressions. . . . I am satisfied that N. England will not bear the Embargo . . . [or] War, the other parts of the union will support their commercial rights in no other Way, because they say the Nation can do nothing short of it honorably. The Result, in my opinion is that the rights of Commerce will be abandoned by the Nation.[8]

House action on resolutions presented by Wilson C. Nicholas confirmed the accuracy of Bacon's prediction. Nicholas' proposal, that at a date to be fixed, presumably in June, the United States repeal the Embargo and use force to reëstablish its rights, was the logical capstone to the structure that Gallatin and his friends desired. This added burden turned the fissures in the façade into ever-widening cracks which brought down the whole structure. The Virginian, in effect paraphrasing the argument of Campbell's Report, declared that he had always believed that "when the embargo failed, we must resort to the valor and patriotism of our citizens. Sir, we have too much reason to believe that the moment is at hand when nothing else can extricate us from our difficulties." The House refused to follow Nicholas either in his logic or his patriotism. In the debate only John W. Eppes supported his colleague without reserve; other members explored alternatives ranging all the way from immediate war to total submission. By an approximate two-to-one margin the House defeated a proposal to fix June 1 as the date for the decisive shift from Embargo to force, primarily because congressmen were unwilling, or believed New England unwilling, to tolerate the Embargo even that long. Then it voted approval of the section repealing the Embargo, to take effect within a month. On the evening of February 5 "a large & commanding Caucus of 50 or 60 was summoned," Bacon reported, "at which we *nerveless seceders* were pressed by all the force & all the weight of the Government machine to meet on the ground

[8] Bacon to Story, Jan. 22, 1809, Joseph Story MSS, Library of Congress.

of immediate or contingent War." Bacon and Orchard Cook answered harangues by Nicholas, Eppes, Giles, and other bellicose Republicans. The seceders kept their nerve.[9]

The Gallatin-Nicholas-Campbell plan collapsed in a shambles. "The only honorable course was from Embargo to war," Nicholas wrote to Madison. "I fear we cannot now obtain it, and I fear we must submit to the plan least disgraceful."[10] The next day confirmed Nicholas' fears, for the House defeated his proposal to vindicate American rights by force. Since, of Nicholas' scheme, only Embargo repeal remained, and that at an early date, the House had in effect voted in favor of submission to European arrogance only eight weeks after Campbell's nonsubmission resolution had been well-nigh unanimously approved. The Republicans desperately caucused again, ultimately agreed that they could not agree on any course to vindicate the nation's honor, and decided to shift responsibility to the Foreign Relations Committee. Many Republican rebels and Federalists opposed this step, fearing that the committee might attempt to reverse the decision rescinding the Embargo, and reference to the committee was secured by the narrow margin of sixty-five to fifty-five. Obviously no new bill, to stand a ghost of a chance of passage, could require very much in the way of national sacrifice.

The House committee and Senator Giles both produced plans designed to conceal American disgrace as far as possible. The House version, presented by Wilson C. Nicholas for a committee of which he, Campbell, and Bacon were the most prominent members, apparently owed much to the suggestion of the President-elect,[11] who belatedly made his wishes known. It proposed only to prohibit trade with Britain and France and to close American ports to their armed vessels. In the Senate the proposal which a Federalist called "the hopeful and lowly begotten Child of Farmer Giles" was somewhat bolder. In addition to provisions like those

[9] *Annals,* 10th Cong., 2d sess., p. 1172; Bacon to Story, Feb. 5, 1809, Story MSS.
[10] Nicholas to Madison, Feb. 9, 1809, William C. Rives Collection, Library of Congress.
[11] Irving Brant, *James Madison: Secretary of State* (Indianapolis, 1953), pp. 478–479.

put forward in the House Giles proposed to grant to the President
the power to reopen trade with either country, should it cease to
pillage American commerce, and to issue letters of marque against
the nation that continued its unlawful edicts. Giles admitted that
the plan did not meet his own wishes, which were for war. He
hoped that by spring the country would be ready for a declaration,
considered this the best stopgap that could be found, and warned
against adopting any lesser plan: "Strike only one key lower, sir,
and I fear it will end in national disgrace and dishonor." [12]

While the Senate accepted the lead of the Virginia musician, the
House preferred to play a lower note. In the upper chamber Federalists argued that, since Giles's plan virtually invited indirect
or illegal trade with the major belligerents, it could not really be
intended as a measure of coercion and must therefore be "nothing
more than a part of that miserable mosquito system, which is to
sting and irritate England into acts of hostility." [13] Although half
a dozen dissidents, including William H. Crawford and Nicholas
Gilman, joined with an equal number of Federalists to oppose it,
a bill was jammed through in one day, its supporters declining to
reply to their critics. The House of Representatives thereupon
dropped its own bill, which nobody defended with even a sem-
blance of enthusiasm. The low-noters, however, easily struck out
letters of marque, the chief attraction to the proponents of vigor.
On February 25, 1809, administration supporters, led by Madison's
brother-in-law, Congressman Jackson of western Virginia, tried
unsuccessfully to restore letters of marque or add other positive
provisions. Twice they sought adjournment to rally their dispirited
forces. Speaker Varnum's vote defeated this maneuver,[14] and the
resistance of Jackson and his friends collapsed. Two days later
the bill passed by a vote of eighty-one to forty. Both Federalists
and disappointed Republicans opposed it or, like Taggart on the

[12] Tallmadge to Tapping Reeve, Feb. 27, 1809, Charles S. Hall, *Benjamin Tallmadge* (New York, 1943), p. 201; *Annals*, 10th Cong., 2d sess., pp. 353–387.

[13] *Annals*, 10th Cong., 2d sess., p. 407 (Bayard).

[14] As an indication of the rot within Republicanism, it is interesting to note that
at the beginning of the session Varnum had been prepared to support continuation
of the Embargo or a declaration of war. Varnum to Eustis, Nov. 19, 1808, William
Eustis MSS, Library of Congress.

one hand and Jackson and Campbell on the other, declined to vote. The Senate accepted this lesser version of its own bill the next day, with reluctance and greater opposition.

The bill passed solely because it represented the lowest common denominator between those who would accept any substitute simply to confirm escape from the Embargo, and those who desired to make some sacrifices in defense of national interests and honor. Compromise is one of the strongest features of the American legislative system, but the Nonintercourse Act carried it to extremes. As a bitter Republican put it, just before the House vote, "the passage of this bill would be a novelty in legislation, for . . . it had not a friend in the House." Moreover, the final result was a defeat for congressional supporters of the incoming administration, a defeat for which James Madison was at least partially responsible. The administration undoubtedly desired a bill at least appearing to be the prelude to forceful measures, not simply a retreat from the Embargo. But after Gallatin's initial efforts executive leadership virtually collapsed. Although Madison perhaps provided at least the language of Wilson C. Nicholas' proposal, the President-elect made no strenuous efforts to get it passed, hastily accepted its defeat and suggested the futile measure of nonintercourse as a substitute, and failed to lift a finger in support of letters of marque. "The fact is," Ezekiel Bacon wrote to Joseph Story, "the administration have been completely beaten . . . by the Non Intercourse." [15] Bacon asked Story to keep the information secret. Why, it is difficult to determine, for nothing could conceal the executive's political poverty.

The Nonintercourse Act contained scraps of various plans. The act repealed the Embargo, closed trade, both export and import, with the British Empire and the areas controlled by Napoleon; prohibited armed British and French ships from entering American ports; and authorized the President to reopen trade with a power that ceased to violate American maritime rights. Nobody seriously believed that England and France, able to stand up

[15] *Annals*, 10th Cong., 2d sess., p. 1539 (William Milnor); Bacon to Story, Feb. 26, 1809, Story MSS.

against the Embargo, would be effectively coerced by this lesser pressure. "We have trusted our most precious interests in this leaky vessel," scoffed John Randolph in one of those colorful metaphors that studded his speeches, "and now, by way of amendment, we are going to bore additional holes in this machine, which, like a cask, derives all its value, if it have any, from being water-tight." Everyone knew that once American ships left their harbors they would go where they chose, for, as the Richmond *Enquirer* put it, the "calculation, that you can permit your vessels to go to sea, and whilst at sea, restrain them in their traffic, is void." In the first four months of the new administration seventy-nine ships sailed from New York in nominal search of a market in the Azores. There is no reason to believe that merchants elsewhere engaged in evasion on a lesser scale.[16] Here was commercial warfare clothed in provisions most troublesome to the United States itself, most burdensome to the honest American merchant.

Without extorting concessions from Downing Street in exchange, the new system actually favored Britain over France. The Embargo had hurt Britain more than France since she carried on larger commerce with the United States; the Nonimportation Act and the *Chesapeake* proclamation singled out Britain for special resentment. The new act, closing American harbors to both countries' armed vessels and prohibiting importations from either, put the rivals on an equal basis in law. In practice, these provisions actually worked against France, since the French had few overseas alternatives as export markets or points of shelter for their ships. "This decision," the French foreign minister complained, "is unfavorable to France against which the United States can have no complaint that she has attempted to invade their sovereignty nor to have committed acts of violence against their coasts and their vessels." [17]

---

[16] *Annals,* 10th Cong., 2d sess., p. 1466; *Enquirer* (Richmond), Feb. 10, 1809; Herbert Heaton, "Non-Importation, 1806–1812," *Journal of Economic History,* I (1941), 192. Per còntra, not a single ship sailed from New York for the Azores while American commerce with Britain was opened by the Erskine agreement. *Ibid.,* p. 193.

[17] Champagny to Hauterive, June 13, 1809, Archives des Affaires Étrangères, Correspondance Politique, États-Unis (photostats, Library of Congress), Vol. LXII.

Above all, the partial resumption of trade obviously favored England. The Royal Navy would make sure that relatively few American ships slipped into enemy ports, whereas the French could hope to intercept only a small proportion of those ships that chose to violate the law by sailing to England. Furthermore, within a short time a lively business developed in neutral ports, where British ships bearing English manufactures exchanged cargoes with American vessels carrying raw materials from the United States. Once again the Royal Navy saw to it that France did not similarly profit. Minister Turreau reported to Paris that "of every one hundred ships which leave the Ports of the Union for the high seas, the real object of ninety of them will be to satisfy the needs and the desires of England." [18]

These effects of the new law, with the disgraceful scenes that had accompanied its passage, led Englishmen to consider it a victory. Even before the act passed, David M. Erskine predicted that "it would be rather a nominal Prohibition than a rigorous Enforcement," and he never changed his opinion. Newspapers that supported the Portland ministry exulted over the American surrender. William Cobbett, who did not like the British Cabinet, grudgingly admitted that it had gained a victory. The Americans, wrote Cobbett, "*know* that their cargoes will come to England. . . . Aye, and they *intend* they shall come here, too; only their silly, their empty pride, will not let them acknowledge it. . . . No triumph can be more complete than that of ministers, in this case." [19] Not for years did the United States recover from the effect of the Nonintercourse Act.

With this feeble weapon the new administration faced the European titans. Ritualistically, Secretary Smith wrote Pinkney and Armstrong that, if one power lifted its decrees, the special session of Congress planned for the spring would "authorize acts of hostility on the part of the United States against the other." Neither

---

[18] Turreau #13 to Minister of Foreign Relations, April 15, 1809, *ibid*. Since Anglo-American trade was free for several months after the Erskine ageement, it is impossible to determine from annual statistics how much illegal trade was carried on.

[19] Erskine #12 to Canning, Feb. 10, 1809, FO 5/62; *Cobbett's Political Register* (London), XV (1809), 533.

Britain nor France, nor the American government itself, can have taken this very seriously. For the Americans, the conversations with David M. Erskine in the middle of April offered far more promise. They led to the temporary reopening of trade and apparent reconciliation with England. Seventy-two American vessels reached Liverpool in a five-day period in June, and Minister Turreau left Washington to avoid riotous celebrations. At its special session Congress promptly passed a law continuing nonintercourse with France. It did not even take up more stringent measures, as Smith had indicated it would, but David M. Erskine reported that, if France remained obdurate, these would probably follow soon. Then, in midsummer, there arrived news that Canning had rejected his subordinate's undertaking, primarily, Pinkney told Madison, because faltering at the last session of Congress had convinced Britain of America's "Inability to persevere in a System which was on the point of accomplishing all its Purposes." [20] Angry, weak, baffled, and uncertain, Madison's government returned to the grounds of the Nonintercourse Act.

The conversations with Francis James Jackson, which provided the administration with a technical diplomatic triumph, did not result in any substantive advantages. The special envoy declined scornfully to show any anger over the reclosing of British trade, observing sarcastically that "it was for America to determine whether it would be for her advantage to convey her Productions and receive those of other Countries through a circuitous Route, and by the expensive Intervention of a third Party." Nor did Jackson believe that the failure of his mission would be followed by hostilities: "That there is an Intention in this Government to go to War with Great Britain I do not believe; their Views do not assume that Magnitude; and if they did, support would not be given by the Country at large." New instructions sent to Pinkney

---

[20] Smith to Pinkney, March 15, 1809, Department of State Archives, National Archives, Instructions, All Countries, Vol. VII; Smith to Armstrong, March 15, 1809, *ibid.*; memorandum of June 15, 1809, enclosed in Joseph Bailey to Canning, June 17, 1809, FO 5/66; Turreau #22 to Minister of Foreign Relations, June 10, 1809, AAE, CP, E-U, Vol. LXII; Erskine #28 to Canning, July 3, 1809, FO 5/63; Pinkney to Madison, private, Aug. 19, 1809, Rives Collection.

in January, 1810, proved this accurate, for in them the American government took the initiative in seeking an accommodation despite the insults it had received.[21]

The only possible excuse for inviting a further rebuff was the hope that the reconstruction of the British ministry would lead to a policy more favorable to the United States. For months, with the tacit encouragement of colleagues who later abandoned him, Canning intrigued for Castlereagh's removal from the War Office, and failure of the Walcheren expedition brought these intrigues to a head. Tangled negotiations followed. The upshot was the departure from the Cabinet of both rivals (at a subsequent duel Castlereagh wounded Canning) and continuation of the government under Perceval's leadership. The Duke of Portland, whose incompetence had been accentuated by a mild stroke, was put out to grass. The new ministry seemed very weak. Grenville and Grey rejected overtures, Canning carried his followers (few in numbers, but effective workers) into opposition, and the Sidmouths remained outside the government. For some weeks offices went begging, and the *Morning Chronicle* sanctimoniously complained that "it is really disgraceful to a great Empire, that PERCEVAL and Co. should be allowed . . . to put up to a sort of Dutch auction, the Great Offices of Government." When the Cabinet was finally completed, the *Times* expostulated, "Surely this is not to be borne." [22] Political experts agreed that the government would have to tread warily if it wished to retain power for even a few months.

Since the Cabinet had divested itself of imaginativeness in ousting Canning and had shucked off at least the traditions of Whiggism by retiring Portland, only its weakness was encouraging to the United States. The State Department received word from its representative in London that, "though the Members of the late Cabinet, who have shewn themselves particularly hostile to our Rights and Interests, . . . are to be at the Head of the new Government, they will be less adventurous and more manageable than

[21] Jackson #7, #19, to Canning, Oct. 17, Nov. 16, 1809, FO 5/64; Smith to Pinkney, Jan. 20, 1810, Instructions, Vol. VII.

[22] *Morning Chronicle* (London), Oct. 31, 1809; *Times* (London), Nov. 1, 1809.

heretofore on all American Topicks." The President was not so optimistic. He believed the change "likely to make bad worse" unless the affairs of England were brought to an "extremity" by "the quackeries and corruptions of an administration headed by such a being as Perceval." [23]

Richard Colley Wellesley, Marquis Wellesley, the one important infusion of new blood, surprised Canning and the Opposition, both erstwhile political allies, by accepting the Foreign Office. The marquis liked office, he knew that the ministry would give determined support to his brother in the Peninsula, and Perceval needed whatever abilities and parliamentary accretions he could find. While not without capacity, as his service in India showed, Wellesley had most of Canning's failings and few of his strengths, although, primarily because his public papers had no fire, he never affronted American opinion as his predecessor had done. His personal attitude toward the United States is practically indiscernible, since he generally accepted the Cabinet's lead. As this suggests, Marquis Wellesley's most notable characteristic was sloth. In the winter of 1810–1811 no instructions, other than formal circulars, issued from the Foreign Office, and Francis James Jackson later commented that Wellesley "never goes to the Office, and is visible nowhere but in his harem." George III, who detested Wellesley, had urged that Bathurst continue in the office he had taken ad interim. By that time, however, florid letters were already en route from Seville, announcing that "I have obeyed the Summons of my Sovereign, & . . . I enter the King's Councils with a firm intention of devoting my exertions to His Majesty's cause." [24]

Wellesley's response to the demand for Jackson's recall illus-

---

[23] Pinkney to Smith, Oct. 5, 1809, Despatches, Great Britain, Vol. XVI; Madison to Jefferson, Nov. 6, 1809, Gaillard Hunt, ed., *The Writings of James Madison* (9 vols.; New York, 1900–1910), VIII, 78–79.

[24] Jackson to George Jackson, Feb. 22, 1811, Lady Jackson, ed., *The Bath Archives: a Further Selection from the Diaries and Letters of Sir George Jackson* (2 vols.; London, 1873), I, 216; George III to Perceval, Nov. 5, 1809, Royal Archives, Windsor Castle; Wellesley to Mulgrave, private, Oct. 30, 1809, Wellesley MSS, Series II, British Museum (Add. MSS 37274–37318), Add. MSS 37295. See also Wellesley to Perceval, private, Oct. 30, 1809, Royal Archives.

trates his laziness. Early in 1810, when William Pinkney handed him a note on this subject, Wellesley's comments led Pinkney to believe it would not cause trouble. Although prompt action might have lessened American anger, six weeks elapsed before the Foreign Secretary acted. In March he finally prepared a reply designed, as he told the King, "to avoid all topics of acrimonious discussion, to render justice to M^r Jackson's honest zeal for Your Majesty's service, & to conciliate the Government of America, without any compromise of the dignity of Your Majesty's Government." His note, intended to justify the envoy's motives without committing itself on the propriety of his actions, was so carelessly worded that Americans interpreted it as an outright attack upon the good faith of their government. A declaration that a chargé d'affaires would succeed Jackson, a comparatively mild reproof if the hiatus between envoys did not last too long, became an added insult when months passed without any evidence that Wellesley had even begun to search for a successor. Although the British note did not please William Pinkney, when he learned of the American reaction to it he hastened to assure the President that "it is not so bad in Intention as it is in Reality, nor quite so bad in Reality as it is commonly supposed to be. It is the production of an indolent Man." [25]

If repudiation of the Erskine agreement, the installation of a new Cabinet, and the Jackson affair showed Madison he could not count on English good will, so too Napoleon's action demonstrated that the new administration needed more vigorous support than the Nonintercourse Act to gain its ends with that enemy. In May,

[25] Pinkney to Smith, March 21, 1810, Despatches, Great Britain, Vol. XVI; Wellesley to George III, March 13, 1810, Royal Archives; Wellesley to Pinkney, March 14, 1810, enclosed in Pinkney to Smith, March 21, 1810, Despatches, Great Britain, Vol. XVI; Pinkney to Madison, private, Aug. 13, 1810, Rives Collection. Characteristically, Wellesley did not prepare instructions to Jackson until a month after Pinkney had been told that the minister would be recalled. Wellesley #1 to Jackson, April 14, 1810, Bernard Mayo, ed., *Instructions to the British Ministers to the United States, 1791–1812*, American Historical Association, *Annual Report, 1936*, III (Washington, 1941), 302. Long before this the delay was already bothering Wellesley's colleagues, as their minutes on and suggested changes in the note to Pinkney demonstrate. Wellesley to Pinkney, draft, n.d., Wellesley MSS, Add. MSS 37291, fols. 282–285; Perceval to Wellesley, n.d., *ibid.*, Add. MSS 37295, fol. 439.

1809, John Armstrong asked France, in response to the new American law, to modify or repeal her decrees, even clandestinely if necessary. Urged on by his foreign secretary, fearful of the new Order in Council's effect on American opinion, and briefly alarmed by Erskine's settlement, Napoleon considered concession. In the confused days after Aspern and Essling he found time to prepare a decree restoring American commerce to its status before the Milan Decree. Then word reached Schoenbrunn, where the Emperor had his headquarters, that the British government had repudiated Erskine. The threat of an Anglo-American reconciliation evaporated, and the Nonintercourse Act failed to chastise or tempt Napoleon. In June Champagny directed authorities left behind at Paris to temporize with Armstrong.[26]

That summer, his position bolstered by the victory at Wagram, Napoleon stepped up his assaults on American commerce. On August 22, in a note prepared under his master's eye, the Duke of Cadore (to which title Champagny had advanced) informed Armstrong that France would not relax her decrees until the British withdrew theirs.[27] For the rest of the year the French seized whatever American ships they could and forced their satellites to adopt a similar policy.

When Congress met in November, 1809, America faced dolorous prospects. William A. Burwell, who favored effective action against Britain, confessed that "the spirit of the nation is evaporated, and . . . I despair of taking any measure . . . which would not meet with such opposition as to make it useless." French seizures, more numerous than Britain's, offset Jackson's gaucheries; men of trade and some farmers desired free commerce above everything else; and internal rivalries and lack of leadership destroyed the Republican party as an instrument of legislation. The President's annual message, which criticized the European powers and con-

---

[26] Armstrong to Minister of Foreign Relations, May 2, 1809, AAE, CP, E-U, Vol. LXII; Champagny to Napoleon, May 26, 1809, *ibid.*; Napoleon to Champagny, June 10, 1809, *Correspondance de Napoléon I*[er] (32 vols.; Paris, 1858–1870), XIX, 110–111; Champagny to Hauterive, June 13, 1809, AAE, CP, E-U, Vol. LXII.

[27] Cadore to Armstrong, Aug. 22, 1809, AAE, CP, E-U, Vol. LXII; Napoleon to Cadore, Aug. 17, 21, 1809, *Correspondance de Napoléon*, XIX, 414, 438–439.

gratulated Americans on their good health and prosperity, refrained entirely from recommending any policy.[28] In the first months of the session little was done. The Senate voted to outfit American frigates, a cheap gesture attractive to many only because it promised to embarrass Gallatin and the Treasury. Both chambers condemned Jackson. The effect was largely nullified by vociferous opposition in the House, where debate often lasted until dawn and forty-one congressmen ultimately voted against a resolution supporting their own government.

Once again the Secretary of the Treasury attempted to give some direction to Congress. His annual report revealed the first deficit in years and pointed out that partial commercial restriction was unenforceable. Therefore, the Secretary declared, the United States must either return to complete embargo or abandon the attempts at restriction, "so far at least as they affect the commerce and navigation of the citizens of the United States." Nathaniel Macon introduced a bill drafted by Gallatin which adopted the second alternative. The bill freed American merchantmen to go wherever they chose and permitted importation of British and French goods brought in American vessels. At the same time Macon's Bill #1 closed American ports to merchantmen and warships of England and France, promising to remove this prohibition if either power rescinded its decrees. Since French ships could not and British merchantmen did not often come to the United States, this proposal could hardly be coercive. It would at least shift the burden of restriction from Americans to their oppressors, reopen trade, and assure increased receipts for the Treasury. The administration intended, as Bacon put it after talks with Gallatin, "to have a principal regard for our own Convenience, keeping up at the same time a sort of Protestation against the infringements of our rights." [29]

More subtle possibilities also existed. Britain might retaliate against the ban on her ships by excluding American merchantmen,

[28] *Annals*, 11th Cong., 1st and 2d sess., p. 1168; Richardson, *op. cit.*, I, 473–477.
[29] Adams, *op. cit.*, pp. 412–413; *Annals*, 11th Cong., 1st and 2d sess., pp. 754–755; Bacon to Story, Nov. 27, 1809, Story MSS.

as Jackson seems to have wished; if she did so, by her own actions England would make effective the ban on trade which supporters of the Embargo had long insisted would force her surrender. Or, as Jackson, Turreau, and Timothy Pickering believed, the freeing of American ships might be "for the Purpose of bringing on a War with Great Britain by the Collisions that will arise out of an Attempt in this Country to renew it's commerce with France." [30] (Some Republicans did find this a reason for swallowing the bill, but it probably played no part in the original plan.) Finally, a small number of bitter Federalists, particularly Barent Gardenier and Philip B. Key, favored Macon's Bill #1 because "in its operation it will be complete non-intercourse with France and free trade with England" since the Royal Navy could control the destination of American ships. [31]

Ranged against the bill, in addition to Republican factionalists who opposed everything from the other end of Pennsylvania Avenue, was a motley alliance of Federalists and war men. The Federalists desired completely free trade, and feared British retaliation if Macon's bill passed. Republican radicals wished to try convoys, letters of marque, war—anything to show more spirit. "If the conduct of the nation were not more energetic," one of them said, ". . . we should forfeit the little character we had acquired, and call down on us the contempt of every nation on earth; we should become contemptible even in our own eyes. . . . We had . . . tried this system for several years; it had done no good, and it was time to try some other." [32] This argument was two years premature in 1810. By the narrow margin of seventy-three to fifty-two, the moderates and the administration men gained passage of the bill after three weeks of debate.

Far more promptly, the Senate demonstrated its wishes. With Samuel Smith in the van it emasculated the bill on the very first day of debate, eliminating one provision after another until only the ban upon armed ships remained. Senator Smith later claimed

[30] Jackson #26 to Canning, Dec. 13, 1809, FO 5/64.
[31] ———— to Jackson, Jan. 22, 1810, Francis James Jackson MSS, Public Record Office (FO 353/58–61), FO 353/61.
[32] *Annals*, 11th Cong., 1st and 2d sess., p. 1161 (Sawyer).

that he opposed the House bill because it would provoke retaliation, and all the Federalist senators voted with him on this ground. But Smith also claimed that the House version undermined Senate efforts at stronger resistance,[33] and a majority subsequently joined him in calling for convoys. Thus it is apparent that in the Senate, as in the House, motives were mixed. Over the anguished protest of young Henry Clay, who preferred "the troubled ocean of war, demanded by the honor and independence of the country, with all its calamities and desolation, to the tranquil and putrescent pool of ignominious peace," [34] the Senate passed the gutted bill.

Deadlock ensued for five weeks. Conference committees failed to find a compromise. Both houses voted to stand firm, although by the margin of only two votes in the Senate (Federalist votes aiding) and seven in the House. On April 6, Nathaniel Macon wrote that he expected adjournment without any action having been taken.

In this letter the ex-Speaker minimized proposals made that morning by Congressman Taylor of South Carolina, and it is an indication of the feebleness of administration leadership that two weeks later Macon still did not know whether or not these proposals had the blessing of the White House.[35] Yet they led to a solution, although nobody liked them and Macon reluctantly introduced them to the House in his capacity as committee chairman. Taylor's scheme was the epitome of weakness: the removal of all restrictions on commerce plus a promise to restore total nonintercourse against the recalcitrant if one of the European powers ceased to violate American commerce. The bill, which to Macon's discomfiture became known as Macon's Bill #2, in effect combined surrender and bribery, "held up the honor and character of this nation to the highest bidder." [36]

Both House and Senate tried to strengthen Macon's Bill #2. The House voted to add discriminatory duties of 50 per cent on imports from Britain and France. The Senate, with Smith again

[33] *Ibid.*, pp. 604–609.
[34] *Ibid.*, pp. 579–582.
[35] Macon to Nicholson, April 6, 21, 1810, Nicholson MSS.
[36] *Annals*, 11th Cong., 1st and 2d sess., p. 1772 (Gholson).

in the van, amended the bill so that it permitted the President to use armed force in defense of commerce. Federalist senators voted for this amendment, doubtless as much to present Madison with an embarrassing choice as to further the interests of trade. Once again the two chambers deadlocked. Federalists gleefully observed the friction:

A more completely divided, bewildered disorganized set of men hardly exists. . . . The Cabinet is I believe equally bewildered with Congress; the Senate and the House of Representatives act in such entire harmony that when the one says I will the other says I wont. No majority in one House can calculate on a majority in the other, nor do I believe the President has really any majority that he can calculate upon in either.

Finally, in desperation, each house dropped its demands. "The result," said Josiah Quincy, who could always be counted upon to describe Republican shortcomings in harsh language, "was . . . a sort of bargain that, if the Senate would agree not to protect commerce, the House would agree not to burden the people with an additional tax." [37] In the form originally suggested by Taylor, the bill passed both houses and became law in May, 1810.

To most observers Macon's Bill #2 seemed to be surrender and in that sense a fitting successor to the Nonintercourse Act. From far away St. Petersburg, John Q. Adams expressed his approval of the new law on the ground that it was less irritating to the belligerents than its predecessor, and William Plumer endorsed it on the frankly pusillanimous ground that "we cannot snatch the trident from George, or the thunder bolt from Napoleon. We ought to stand still, wait events, & shape our course accordingly." Adams and Plumer were almost alone. Governor Tyler of Virginia complained, "We have lost our resentment for the severest injuries a nation ever suffered, because of their being so often repeated," and asked, "Is not this an undeniable proof of the bad state of morals in our country?" The *National Intelligencer*, which

[37] Taggart to Rev. John Taylor, April 27, 1810, George H. Haynes, ed., "Letters of Samuel Taggert, Representative in Congress, 1803–1814," American Antiquarian Society, *Proceedings*, n.s., XXXIII (1923), 347; *Annals*, 11th Cong., 1st and 2d sess., pp. 2051–2052.

avoided comment as far as possible, clearly showed that it expected no good to follow.[38]

The President, who played no visible part in framing the new bill, took a characteristically mixed view of it. In general he considered it feeble, noncoercive, and even disgusting. He also believed, or at least ascribed to the bill's supporters the belief, that the captures that would inevitably follow would "teach the advocates for open trade, . . . the folly, as well as the degradation of their policy" and perhaps prepare the nation for war at the next session of Congress. Madison, with an almost unique perceptiveness, also foresaw the possibility that the very imbalance of the bill, "which puts our trade on the worst possible footing for France," might inspire Napoleon to change his policy.[39] To take comfort from the losses facing American citizens and from the unevenness of the bill's effect was perhaps undignified, but these things were, indeed, the best that could be said for a law that marked the virtual abandonment of positive policy.

The President never expected Macon's Bill #2 to bring about repeal of the Orders in Council. The next instructions to Pinkney even admitted that the act benefited British commerce. Britain considered the bill as the best possible evidence that the United States was too weak to support her claims either by commercial pressure or by war. Throughout the winter British diplomats had reported with increasing assurance that, despite the Jackson affair, American opinion was turning in their favor, making war impossible. When Macon's Bill finally passed, the British consul at Norfolk commented that "after the Hurricane of Passion in which the Congress opened their Session, it is truly laughable to witness the miserable, feeble, Puff, in which they evaporated. It is indeed a very comfortable reflection that with every disposition to injure Great Britain, they have found themselves totally unable to do

[38] Adams to John Pope, Sept. 10, 1810, Worthington C. Ford, ed., *The Writings of John Quincy Adams* (7 vols.; New York, 1914–1917), III, 501–502; Plumer to Adams, May 18, 1810, William Plumer MSS, Library of Congress; John Tyler to Jefferson, May 12, 1810, Lyon G. Tyler, *The Letters and Times of the Tylers*, I (Richmond, 1884), 247; *National Intelligencer*, May 28, 1810.

[39] Madison to Pinkney, May 23, 1810, Rives Collection; Madison to Jefferson, May 25, 1810, James Madison MSS, Library of Congress.

so." London newspapers almost universally interpreted the act as a surrender to Britain brought about by the wise firmness of the ministry and the self-immolating effects of American commercial warfare. "Thus," declared the *Sun*, "after a long and obstinate perseverance, in measures which while they were in force destroyed the trade of America, reduced her revenue, and ruined her Merchants, the American Government has found it necessary to abandon her schemes of impotent resentment against Great Britain." [40]

America's political defeat opened pleasing commercial prospects. For the first time since 1807, aside from the brief Erskine interlude, British ships, goods, and imports were freed from American restriction and the added expense of clandestine or indirect trade. Exports to the United States almost regained the peak reached in 1807, the last previous year of untrammeled commerce. The clamor of manufacturers against the Orders in Council subsided to a whisper. At the same time American shippers embarked accumulated goods in such quantities that a shipping shortage developed in the United States. "Our great Staple Trade has seldom, if ever, been more brisk than it is at this moment," a Leeds newspaper exulted. [41] In the long run this influx meant oversupply in Britain so great that the President's own tobacco sold at only threepence a pound. In the early summer of 1810 a halcyon day seemed to be dawning; the position of Perceval's ministry and the Orders in Council approached impregnability.

French policy appeared to pose no danger to Britain. The Emperor's entourage, it is true, steadily urged him to relax his decrees, and for some weeks early in 1810 he toyed with the idea. Instead, his own greed and stubbornness, pique at the blatantly pro-British effect of the Nonintercourse Act, and Armstrong's irritating mixture of wheedling and obstinacy made him speed up his assault on American commerce. On March 23, 1810, by the Rambouillet Decree, the French monarch ordered all American ships that en-

[40] Smith to Pinkney, July 5, 1810, Instructions, Vol. VII; James Hamilton to Jackson, May 21, 1810, Jackson MSS, FO 353/59; *Sun* (London), June 9, 1810.
[41] *Leeds Intelligencer*, June 11, 1810.

tered his ports seized, whether or not they had touched at British ports or had been visited by the Royal Navy. "The late confiscations by Bonaparte," Madison wrote, "comprize robbery, theft, & breach of trust, and exceed in turpitude any of his enormities, not wasting human blood." [42] Anger perhaps caused some presidential exaggeration, but the truth was bad enough.

Within a few months the Emperor abruptly reversed his course. He may have been alarmed by reports of rising Francophobia in the United States, although his contempt for the young republic makes this unlikely. He certainly saw an opportunity to embroil the United States with Britain by relaxing his decrees. Equally certainly, he recognized that the European economy required goods only the Americans could provide. As early as June, with the commercial motive uppermost in his mind, the Emperor considered a plan to withdraw the decrees insofar as they affected American trade. With considerable cynicism he proposed to replace them with customs regulations that would effectively prohibit the importation of goods for which he had no need or which were primarily the produce of Britain's colonies. Repeal, in Napoleon's mind, thus would be purely nominal: "We will engage ourselves to nothing," he said, "but we can . . . let those goods which we need enter." John Armstrong informed the agent sent to consult him that only effective relaxation of the decrees for all American goods would satisfy. [43] As a result the Emperor dropped the idea for a short time.

In July the American minister presented to the Duke of Cadore a copy of the *National Intelligencer* containing Macon's Bill. Cadore offhandedly dismissed it on the ground that France could scarcely allow her policy to be influenced by newspaper reports. [44] At the end of the month the Foreign Minister's sense of punctilio was impatiently thrust aside by his master. The Emperor wrote to Cadore that Armstrong should be informed that, as a result of

[42] Madison to Jefferson, May 25, 1810, Madison MSS.
[43] Napoleon, "Notes for the Minister of the Interior," June 25, 1810, *Correspondance de Napoléon*, XX, 501–502; Armstrong to Smith, July 18, 1810, Despatches, France, Vol. XI.
[44] Armstrong to Smith, July 10, 1810, Despatches, Frances, Vol. XI.

Macon's Bill, "my decrees of Berlin and Milan will not have any effect after November first," if in the interim the Orders in Council of 1807 should be repealed or "the Congress of the United States shall fulfil the engagement it has made to reëstablish its prohibitions on English commerce." Two days later, still prodding his bewildered subordinate, Napoleon sent him the projet of a note to Armstrong, and on the morning of August 5, 1810, Cadore placed an official declaration of policy in the hands of the American minister. This note generally followed the tack of Napoleon's letter and projet, although the specific requirement that the United States prohibit trade with England was replaced by a vaguer demand that the Americans, "conformably with [Macon's Bill] . . . , shall cause their rights to be respected by the English." [45] Whether this phrase was preferred as an unusual concession to American sensibilities or as a veiled invitation to pile more vigorous measures on top of nonintercourse with Britain is not clear.

The Cadore letter, as the declaration came to be known, raised other and more serious questions. Was it really correct to say that the decrees were "revoked," when their effect was not to cease until November and then only if one of two conditions was fulfilled? Quite obviously not; as Cadore himself soon stated, the "decision of H.M. is . . . conditional. Its execution will depend on the measures which the United States shall take if England persists

[45] Napoleon to Cadore, July 31, 1810, *Correspondance de Napoléon*, XX, 644–645; Napoleon to Cadore, Aug. 2, 1810, and enclosure, *ibid.*, XXI, 1–2; Cadore to Armstrong, Aug. 5, 1810, enclosed in Armstrong to Smith, Aug. 5, 1810, Despatches, France, Vol. XI. Cadore stated in a report to the Emperor that at Napoleon's order he had made "kindly declarations" to Armstrong on July 25, but no record of this talk is preserved. Cadore also stated that he had prepared his letter to Armstrong on July 29; this was probably one of the very early drafts. Cadore to Napoleon, "Fragment de rapport," July 30, 1810, AAE, CP, E-U, Vol. LXIV. A draft of the Duke's letter, stating that France would repeal her decrees, "pourvu que" Britain withdrew her orders if the United States took measures against England, was changed by the Emperor, who inserted the phrase "bien entendu que," which became important in later discussions. Cadore to Armstrong, draft, Aug. 2 [?], 1810, AAE, CP, E-U, Vol. LXIV. This change, as well as the alteration mentioned in the text, raises baffling questions, and with some hesitation it may be suggested that the alterations possibly sprang from a desire on Napoleon's part to make the phraseology as loose as possible, both to increase the chances of Anglo-American disagreement and to preserve his own freedom of action. The possibility that both changes were designed to make the note sound somewhat less peremptory cannot, however, be dismissed.

in her orders of Council and in the principles of blockade which she has tried to establish." [46] This being so, did French action justify American action under Macon's Bill? Congress clearly failed to anticipate conditional action, and in the strictest legal sense the Cadore letter was inadequate. The law did not even authorize the President to call upon the recalcitrant belligerent to lift his decrees—an action only to be followed in ninety days by nonintercourse—until the other ceased to violate American commerce, and the Napoleonic declaration referred to a date months in the future. Still, the Cadore letter at least raised the hope that the end sought by Congress could be attained. America's harassed situation made inevitable a political rather than a purely legal decision. The risks of acceptance, however, were enormous, unless the Emperor clearly intended to follow the Cadore letter with more specific action favorable to American commerce.

Quite the contrary was true. On the very day of the Cadore letter, the Trianon tariff established customs regulations that effectively stopped most importations. This device, really the same scheme that Armstrong had refused to countenance a month earlier, showed that the commercial benefits of repeal would at best be minimal. The new tariff, which appeared in the *Moniteur*, reached America at the same time as the Cadore letter. Napoleon's second, even more important action was secret, although he could not conceal its implementation. By the so-called Trianon Decree (officially dated August 5 but actually made a few weeks later), he ordered the sale of sequestered American ships and cargoes. The decree applied only to arrivals since the spring of 1809 and did not specifically order their condemnation, although transfer of the proceeds to the treasury certainly implied that a final decision had been taken. When at last Albert Gallatin procured a copy in 1821, he declared that publication in 1810 would have altered the entire direction of American policy. "It is unnecessary," he added, "to comment on such a glaring act of combined injustice, bad faith, and meanness as the enacting and concealment of the decree exhibits." Even in 1810 the tenor of French policy was clear enough.

[46] Cadore to Turreau, Aug. 23, 1810, AAE, CP, E-U, Vol. LXIV.

The Duke of Cadore admitted to Armstrong that arrivals, though no longer subject to automatic seizure under the Rambouillet Decree, would be subject to the Berlin and Milan decrees at least until November. Armstrong also learned that release of ships already in French hands was extremely unlikely, and he immediately perceived that the Trianon tariff virtually obliterated the commercial advantages to be drawn from the Cadore letter. All these things he reported to Washington, albeit in his usual imprecise way, before leaving for the United States on September 12.[47]

Accounts by way of England, which preceded Armstrong's dispatches, reached America late in September. Federalist newspapers denounced the Cadore letter as a trick to bring about increased friction with England. They pointed out that the alleged repeal was so framed that Britain could have no motive to reciprocate and America, in commercial terms, scarcely a greater one: "After all, the bait does not half cover the hook." The *Aurora* hailed Napoleon's action and urged the use of force to prevent British interference with Franco-American trade, and the Lexington *Reporter* reached absurd (and ungrammatical) heights when it declared: "France has performed the penance which we demanded. . . . Thank God, the removal of the French decrees have placed us exactly again in the clean straight forward path." Reasonable Americans took a more moderate view. A Washington correspondent reported, "It is admitted on all hands, by candid men, that the *manner* in which French has accepted our proposition, is ungracious. The question, however, is, whether it is not better, all circumstances considered, to close with the offer, than reject it." As late as October 24 the *National Intelligencer* declined to take a stand on the French offer or to predict the administration's decision.[48]

With the confidence that, we may presume, has characterized

[47] Gallatin #186 to Adams, Sept. 15, 1821, and enclosure, Henry Adams, ed., *The Writings of Albert Gallatin* (3 vols.; Philadelphia, 1879), II, 196–199; Cadore to Armstrong (dictated by Napoleon), Sept. 7, 1810, AAE, CP, E-U, Vol. LXIV; Armstrong to Madison, private, Aug. 5, 1810, Madison MSS; Armstrong to Smith, Sept. 10, 1810, Despatches, France, Vol. XI.

[48] *Connecticut Courant* (Hartford), Oct. 10, 1810; *Aurora* (Philadelphia), Oct. 2, 1810; *Reporter* (Lexington, Ky.), Oct. 20, 1810; *Columbian* (New York), Oct. 6, 1810; *National Intelligencer*, Oct. 24, 1810.

fish from time immemorial, President Madison believed it possible to feed on the bait without swallowing the visible hook. Delay would encourage Napoleon to pull his line from the stream, whereas immediate acceptance might cause Britain to cast even more appetizing food upon the water. At Madison's direction the Secretary of State sent word to London on October 19. If the eagerly awaited dispatches from Armstrong confirmed the authenticity of Cadore's letter (still known to the American government only through newspaper reports), and if Britain failed to withdraw her regulations, "on the first day of November the President will issue his proclamation conformably to the act of Congress, and . . . the non-intercourse law will consequently be revived against Great Britain." At the same time Robert Smith warned the young British chargé, John P. Morier, that English obduracy would threaten "the future Harmony between the two Countries." [49]

On November 2 the President officially proclaimed that the "edicts of France have been so revoked as that they ceased on the first day of the present month to violate the neutral commerce of the United States." Instructions sent to Paris on the same day showed that the President actually took no such simple view of the matter. The instructions avoided as far as possible any specific declarations which would require French response and were, in effect, a rather tortuous attempt to turn Napoleon's "bien entendu" back upon himself. They declared that the United States was acting upon the assumption that "the reservations under the expression 'it being understood' are not condition precedent affecting the operation of the repeal." Although necessary to justify action under Macon's Bill, the language of Cadore's letter made this dubious— French correspondence unknown to Madison made it positively fallacious—and the President wisely did not insist that France accept this interpretation before the United States acted. Similarly, the instructions declared that the American government presumed that France had agreed to restore sequestered American property or would soon do so, an action made a necessary preliminary to any

[49] Smith to Pinkney, Oct. 19, 1810, Instructions, Vol. VII; Morier #15 to Wellesley, Oct. 26, 1810, FO 5/72.

settlement in instructions sent to Armstrong as recently as July but actually extremely unlikely after the secret Trianon Decree. The President, however, again did not make American action against Britain dependent upon the accuracy of his anticipation. Finally, the instructions declared that America assumed that, in addition to the decrees of Berlin and Milan, all other maritime edicts violating her rights had been withdrawn.[50] James Madison well understood the equivocal nature of Cadore's letter but had determined nevertheless to seize the opportunity it presented.

Since this decision led ultimately to war, the President's reasoning must be analyzed, his justifications examined. To him the moment seemed fleeting. Napoleon's notorious combination of volatility and stubbornness made it likely that, if the United States delayed or haggled, the French autocrat would immediately swing back to the decrees he had so tenaciously defended. It could be argued that the prohibitory French duties and even the licenses which Napoleon, to Madison's great anger, made a condition of trade with his dominions were really "domestic regulations," for surely a state had a right to impose conditions upon trade with itself. The issue of sequestered property was embarrassing, but only because the President had chosen, in the July instructions, to make restoration a condition of settlement. Macon's Bill #2 required the belligerents to cease their violations, not to make amends for past robberies. Finally, simply because Cadore's letter was so equivocal, the President could adopt whatever interpretation seemed most desirable, perhaps even lead France to accept his view.

Commercially, these arguments made little sense. "Municipal regulations" and licenses stifled trade with Europe nearly as effectively as the decrees. The approved trade did not compare in value with the American ships, nearly 200 in all, for which compensation had been sought. Yet if America did not secure pay-

[50] Smith to Armstrong, Nov. 2, 1810, Instructions, Vol. VII. These instructions declared that the United States would demand repeal of Fox's Blockade as well as of later Orders in Council, but they also warned that America did not consider herself pledged to make the abandonment of other blockades a condition of any agreement with Britain. While seeking to make England respect her rights, America did not accept the French definition of what those rights were.

ment as a condition of anti-British action one could hardly expect so rapacious a man as Napoleon to grant it later on. Politically, Madison accepted great risks. Napoleon's entire career demonstrated his trickiness and bad faith. The Cadore letter left the door open for him to exercise these qualities and gave Britain a plausible excuse for refusing to relax the Orders in Council. Should it be demonstrated—and only one day after the French promise allegedly went into effect Madison could have no proof one way or the other—that the Berlin and Milan decrees had not really been lifted, even for American commerce alone, the President would face serious criticism at home and abroad.

Madison's decision rested primarily on one conviction which he felt compelled him to take the risk of accepting the French declaration. Recent history demonstrated that the United States could expect only humiliation if it tried to exert pressure upon both major belligerents at the same time. "The new scene opened by the revocation of the Fr. Decrees," Madison wrote in recalling his attorney general to discuss it, "will I hope terminate in a removal of the embarrassments which have been as afflicting as they have been unexampled. It promises us, at least an extrication from the dilemma, of a mortifying peace, or a war with both the great belligerents." As the Erskine agreement had already shown, the President was prepared to use agreement with one great power as a lever in negotiations with the other. In 1810 he was not sanguine about the prospects of British repeal. He took consolation in the thought that, even if this desirable end could not be attained without war, the nation would unite when the time came to assert its rights by force. "We hope from the step," he wrote to Jefferson, "the advantage at least of having but one contest on our hands at a time." [51]

Like so many Republican calculations, this one assumed that logic always governed men's decisions. Ignoring American partisanship and Anglophilia, Madison expected the people to rally behind the government's demand for justice from England. "I do

[51] Madison to Rodney, Sept. 30, 1810, Rodney Family MSS, Library of Congress; Madison to Jefferson, Oct. 19, 1810, Hunt, ed., *Writings of Madison*, VIII, 109.

not believe," he said, "that Cong°. will be disposed, or permitted by the Nation, to a tame submission; the less so as it would be not only perfidious to the other belligerent, but irreconcilable with an honorable neutrality." [52] Minimizing England's emotional commitment to the Orders in Council, the President hoped Britain would seek material advantage through concession; if she did not, he expected Perceval to be too vulnerable to domestic criticism to press an armed conflict with the United States. These miscalculations grew out of Madison's central mistake, a belief that Napoleon could be trusted to execute the bargain he offered. The President was not so foolish as to expect generosity, and the instructions of November 2 showed him at least fearful that Napoleon would narrowly construe the Cadore letter. But surely the Emperor would see the advantage of uniting America against England, and the even greater potential disadvantages of insulting a people already restive under continued aggravation. Such seem to have been the presidential calculations. Hindsight shows us that most of them were wrong, but the initial decision is understandable. The President is most to be condemned for failing to revise his analysis when new facts became available. "The revocation of the Decrees of Milan and Berlin has become a personal affair with Mr. Madisson," the French minister reported nine months later. "He announced it by his proclamation and has consistently maintained it since." [53] Perhaps in part because he had suffered such deep humiliation through the Erskine agreement, James Madison refused to admit that he had erred.

Napoleon considered the United States a harlot whose embraces could be cheaply purchased, and throughout the winter of 1810–11 Armstrong's successor, Jonathan Russell, struggled vainly to convince the Emperor that American charms deserved a higher price. Russell, a lawyer, merchant, and politician from Rhode Island, previously distinguished chiefly for his devotion to Republican orthodoxy, considered himself a Francophile and later warmly

[52] Madison to Jefferson, Oct. 19, 1810, Hunt, ed., *Writings of Madison*, VIII, 110.
[53] Sérurier #22 to Minister of Foreign Relations, July 24, 1811, AAE, CP, E-U, Vol. LXV.

252

advocated a war against Britain. At Paris, however, he found it impossible to accept Napoleon's policy without protest. At first, it is true, the new chargé proposed for tactical reasons to suffer disappointment in silence:

Having a right from the tenor of the verbal & written communications of this Government to consider the revocation of the Berlin & Milan decrees to be absolute, I have thought it unwise, whatever doubts the British Cabinet may affect to entertain on the subject, to ask for an explanation here which might at once be construed into a justification of these doubts by indicating a participation in them—and leave this government at liberty to give to those communications whatever meaning the views of the moment might decide.[54]

Increasing French hostility to American commerce, Britain's insistence upon clearer proof of revocation of the decrees, and finally the instructions of November 2 caused Russell to alter his tactics. To London he sent optimistic accounts of French policy and what meager evidence he could obtain showing that the decrees had been repealed, but he did so only to assist American efforts to bring the Orders in Council to an end. His reports to Washington and his talks with French officials show that his real views were quite different. From November onward, more and more firmly, even irritably, the American chargé pressed the imperial government for explanations. "The Emperor was only asked," he repeated three times in one conversation, "to provide the opportunity for an honorable and vigorous war against England." [55] Russell became increasingly pessimistic as Napoleon's intentions unfolded.

Imperial policy operated in three distinct spheres united by a common theme of disdain. Although he avoided directly saying so, Napoleon declined to release or make compensation for American ships seized under his various decrees before November. The United States affected to consider him pledged to do so, but Jonathan Russell did not force this issue to a crisis. Second, the French monarch in effect withdrew most of the advantages he had presum-

---

[54] Russell to Smith, Sept. 26, 1810, Despatches, France, Vol. XII.
[55] Sérurier to Minister of Foreign Relations, Nov. 7, [1810], AAE, CP, E-U, Vol. LXIII.

ably granted to American ships coming to European ports. Vessels that arrived between November and the news of American prohibitions on English commerce in February were not permitted to depart or to sell their cargoes until the latter date. Napoleon's repeal, in other words, was shown to be conditional on effective American action toward British trade. Although Cadore's successor, the Duke of Bassano, finally informed Russell in May that post-November arrivals could proceed with their business,[56] France still insisted upon licenses and ciphered letters of permission from her consuls in America, thus stopping all but a trickle of trade between the two countries. The Continental System had been altered in form far more than in substance.

The third phase of Napoleon's policy clearly showed that the decrees had not been rescinded for American ships bound to and from enemy ports. A few ships visited at sea by the Royal Navy escaped condemnation when they came within the reach of French power, but the decrees, particularly that of Milan, were otherwise rigorously enforced. Ships touching at British ports continued to be seized, on the basis of Napoleonic reasoning very similar to that Canning used in demanding permission for the Royal Navy to enforce American prohibitions against trade with France. "One should say," the Emperor declared in a session with his subordinates, "the Decrees of Berlin and Milan are repealed as to the United States; but, as all ships touching at English ports or destined there are ships without character, which American laws punish and confiscate, they may be confiscated by France." One year after the Cadore letter, Jonathan Russell ruefully observed that the French had not released one ship bound to or from an English port.[57] All protests had been vain.

Because an economic crisis gripped Britain by the end of 1810, Napoleon refused to relax his commercial warfare, even at the risk of American displeasure. Politically, he saw the advantage of refusing clarifying, liberalizing declarations. Russell believed that

[56] Bassano to Russell, May 9, 1811, *ibid.*, Vol. LXVII.

[57] Note dictated in the councils of Administration and of Commerce, April 29, 1811, *Correspondance de Napoléon*, XXII, 144–146; Russell to John S. Smith, private and confidential, Aug. 2, 1811, Samuel Smith MSS, Library of Congress.

"the great object . . . is to entangle us in a war with England. They abstain therefore from doing any act which would furnish clear & unequivocal testimony of the revocation of their decrees least it should induce the extinction of the British orders & thereby appease our irritation against their enemy." The French carefully arranged releases and condemnations to muddy rather than clarify the waters.[58]

The French attitude disheartened President Madison. His annual message, presented in December, disappointed Turreau, who considered it a "cold and methodical exposé" rather than a rallying cry against England. It would have been much worse had not Gallatin urged his chief to adopt a more confident tone. Early in February, in one of those malicious or stupid indiscretions that soon cost him his post, Secretary Smith "declared . . . confidentially [to the British chargé] his Opinion that those Decrees were not repealed, and that before the rising of the present Congress the whole of their restrictive commercial System would be entirely done away with." A partisan Federalist declared three weeks later that scarcely five members of Congress believed the decrees "efficiently repealed." [59]

Passage of a new nonintercourse bill directed at Britain advertised Republican doubts. Macon's Bill provided that trade should end ninety days after the President proclaimed that only one belligerent, the other having rescinded its decrees, continued to violate American commerce; this action did not require legislative sanction. Thus the nonintercourse bill introduced by John W. Eppes exposed doubts that the actions of Napoleon or Madison truly met the requirements of Macon's Bill, and bad news from France soon led Eppes himself to propose postponing the bill "until the doubts hanging over our foreign relations were dissipated." In debate, Republicans declared American faith pledged by the proclamation even if it were based on a Napoleonic lie. Randolph

[58] Russell to Monroe, private and confidential, July 13, 1811, Despatches, France, Vol. XII.

[59] Richardson, op. cit., I, 483; Gallatin to Madison, n.d., Rives Collection; Morier #12 to Wellesley, Feb. 4, 1811, FO 5/74; Taggart to Rev. John Taylor, Feb. 25, 1811, Haynes, op. cit., p. 358

harried them with lashing metaphor, Gardenier with ponderously impressive logic. Randolph's motion for outright repeal of Macon's Bill failed only by a margin of forty-five to sixty-seven. Congress then laid Eppes's bill aside for three weeks to await arrival of the new French minister, Louis Sérurier. Sérurier disappointed Republicans, for, as Quincy observed, "the Minister is as parsimonious as his master is voracious. He has not condescended to extend one particle, not one pinch of comfort to the Administration." [60] However, news from France that post-November arrivals would be admitted when the United States cut off British trade decided the Republicans to go ahead. After scenes of turbulence and animosity exceeding even those of Embargo days, the Eppes bill was rammed through the House at sunrise on February 28, 1811. The Senate and Madison quickly added their assent.

This commercial legislation, the last of a series running back to the Nonimportation Act five years before, contained interesting new provisions. The bill required American courts to accept Madison's proclamation as conclusive evidence of French repeal. In the absence of such a precaution, some of the many Federalists still on the bench might rule that the decrees had not really been rescinded, thus destroying the legal grounds for condemnation of ships trading with England. No government could permit hostile judges to overthrow its policy in such a fashion; on the other hand, this provision strengthened the Federalist claim that the government itself knew the decrees were still in force. Second, although the Eppes bill authorized the President to continue prohibitions on British commerce until the Orders in Council were removed,[61] the act did not cut off all Anglo-American trade, chiefly because Americans wanted commercial warfare to be as little painful as possible. The new act, which turned away British ships and goods,

---

[60] *Annals*, 11th Cong., 3d sess., pp. 863, 1017.

[61] Irving Brant, *James Madison: the President* (Indianapolis, 1956), p. 250, suggests that the administration, through Eppes's original bill, aimed to correct an oversight in Macon's Bill, which failed to authorize a restoration of free trade if a belligerent revoked its decrees after nonintercourse against it had gone into effect. Doubtless this aspect was involved, but it was scarcely emphasized in debate or correspondence. Had Madison been confronted by British repeal, there seems no reason why he could not have proclaimed at least provisional repeal of nonintercourse until a special session met.

did not prohibit the departure of American vessels or produce to England. Furthermore, virtually admitting that until passage of the act shippers might justifiably have expected nonintercourse never to go into effect, the law permitted the entry of cargoes embarked from Britain before February. The last legal cargo of English goods arrived at New York toward the end of April, bringing to a close spring importations of approximately normal size. Thereafter, although in the fall *Niles' Register* suggested that the act be better enforced or else retitled "An Act for the Better Encouragement of Roguery and Other Purposes," nonimportation seems to have been effective. With return cargoes forbidden by American law, exports to Britain also fell off sharply, although those of cotton and tobacco remained fairly stable.[62]

After Eppes's bill there could be no turning back if even the shreds of America's reputation were to be preserved. Still, to persevere was not easy in the face of increasing evidence of French perfidy. The *National Intelligencer* professed to believe steadfastness more important than adjustment to the facts: "Shall we, like chaff before the wind, be driven by every breeze that wafts a rumor across the Atlantic?" But in the same article the *Intelligencer* virtually admitted that not breezes but a gale blew from the Tuileries, for it declared: "If both [nations] continue their aggressions, we must eventually set them both at defiance." The administration's mouthpiece argued that no amount of sin on Napoleon's part excused Britain, for "our rights are absolute, not contingent."[63]

Self-evident to Americans, this last assertion naturally received little endorsement in Great Britain. The Orders in Council had long been defended—sometimes honestly, often insincerely—as acts of retaliation to last only as long as the Continental System. Britons therefore considered the meaning of imperial action critically important, and London newspapers joined battle over the Cadore letter. Opposition sheets urged repeal of the Orders in

[62] C. Northcote Parkinson, ed., *The Trade Winds: a Study of British Overseas Trade during the French Wars* (London, 1948), p. 222; *Niles' Weekly Register* (Baltimore), Oct. 26, 1811; Heaton, *op. cit.*, p. 194; François Crouzet, *L'Economie Britannique et le Blocus Continental* (2 vols.; Paris, 1958), II, 703–704.

[63] May 18, 1811.

Council, primarily because they wished Britain to take advantage of Cadore's statement that the decrees would be lifted, even for English trade, if Britain abandoned the orders. The *Times* shilly-shallied, ultimately favoring British repeal despite suspicions of French fraud. Ministerial prints declared that no reasonable person, not even the creatures at Washington, could possibly consider the Cadore letter the sort of repeal that called for British reciprocity. The *Courier,* as always the most strident British paper, declared: "There is but one Navy in the World, the British Navy. . . . As long as BONAPARTE persists in his present system, we warn all Powers that the Continent is in a state of blockade, and they must not presume to trade with it without our leave." [64]

Merchants engaged in American trade steadily pressed the government to revoke the orders and thus prevent action under Macon's Bill. They were turned from one official to another—from Rose to Bathurst to Wellesley to Under-Secretary Hamilton—until at last they ceased their importunities. The government even refused to sanction the dispatch of one American vessel to French ports as a test case, to prove whether or not the decrees still stood. [65] Wellesley was equally obdurate with William Pinkney. He wrote that the Cadore letter could not be considered sufficient evidence of repeal, adding that "whenever the repeal of the French Decrees shall have actually taken effect, . . . His Majesty will feel the highest satisfaction in relinquishing a system, which the conduct of the Enemy compelled him to adopt." Subsequent notes repeated the same theme. [66]

[64] *Morning Chronicle,* Aug. 20, 1810; *Times,* Aug. 20, Dec. 20, 1810; *Star* (London), Aug. 18, 1810; *Sun,* Aug. 18, 1810; *Courier* (London), Jan. 21, 1811.

[65] *Times,* July 1, 1811, printing an account by a participant.

[66] Wellesley to Pinkney, Aug. 31, 1810, enclosed in Pinkney to Smith, Sept. 3, 1810, Despatches, Great Britain, unnumbered volume; Wellesley to Pinkney, Dec. 29, 1810, FO 5/72; Wellesley #1 to Foster, April 10, 1811, Mayo, *op. cit.,* pp. 310–318; John S. Smith to Monroe, May 25, 1811, Despatches, Great Britain, Vol. XVII. Wellesley also made it clear that the Cabinet would insist upon repeal of substitute regulations which restored the decrees in another guise and, for its own part, would not consent to withdraw regulations anterior to those of November, 1807, nor to relax its claimed right of blockade.

This British reaction ended the last hope of a bloodless American triumph. Madison had risked much in accepting Cadore's assurances at more than their face value, and by the spring of 1811 all the world could see he had failed. France had briefly roused American hopes, then quickly fallen back to a policy of tantalizing hints and crude menaces. Far from uniting American opinion against Britain as Madison had hoped, the President's policy, by reinforcing the plausibility of Federalist claims that he was a minion of France, led to disunity of the most dangerous kind. Wellesley's declarations, challenging on all too supportable grounds the fundamental premise of American policy, diverted attention from permanent issues. As the *National Intelligencer* had observed, America's claims against Britain were absolute, not conditional. Madison's great folly was to emphasize the one claim that did involve conditions, rather than to recoil in search of new avenues. The President had placed American policy in an untenable position. Aside from another humbling surrender by the United States, only an uncharacteristic act of Napoleonic charity or abject British capitulation could provide a peaceful exit. The ultimate alternative was war, a war the administration sometimes considered likely and even desirable, but a war for which it had neither psychologically nor militarily nor even financially armed the nation.

In March, 1811, the Eleventh Congress dispersed, leaving behind a record that reflected no credit on itself or the President. In the two years since Jefferson had ridden off to Monticello, the United States had continued its modest progress in manufactures. It had obtained a small portion of the Floridas and was on the brink of a campaign, equally lacking in nicety, to despoil the Spanish Empire of more of that province. The critical issues had not been solved. With a majority of two to one over the Federalists, Republicans had proved unable to develop any consistent legislative policy. Factionalism and administration reservations defeated a bill to recharter the Bank of the United States, depriving the nation of an instrument sorely needed in any effective marshaling of financial strength. Just before Madison's inauguration, Republican factionalism spawned the Nonintercourse Act, and the

Eleventh Congress put Macon's Bill #2 on the statute book. Each bill represented a relaxation of will; each also provided a brief moment of triumph, triumph that only made the ensuing humiliation more bitter. The nation's capacity to absorb insult had been found generous. Whether or not it was inexhaustible remained to be seen.

As chief executive during these years, James Madison was given much of the blame. This criticism often overshot the mark. The President knew what he wanted as a sequel to the Embargo, he acted decisively with Francis James Jackson, he showed boldness in accepting the Cadore letter, he even reached the reluctant conclusion to support the Bank of the United States, which he had so firmly opposed twenty years before. Not decisiveness was lacking, but the quality of leadership. The effect of democratic theory upon Republican practice, the difficulties of succeeding a man who had long overshadowed him, the disciplinary decay that had set in before his inauguration—all these created challenges that Madison had not the strength to overcome.

"Jefferson by a system of intrigue and low cunning managed the party," wrote Samuel Taggart, but "M[adiso]n is a mere puppet or a cypher managed by some chiefs of the faction who are behind the curtain." Taggart's partisan language aside, this fairly accurately described the role once played by Jefferson. It woefully missed the mark with Madison. No one "managed" the President. On the other hand he himself did very little managing, of Congress or of public opinion. "Little better than a man of straw," not "half the independence of an old clucking hen"—so too wrote the Federalist congressman.[67] That Taggart, Randolph, the opposition press, and even disgusted Republicans could make such claims is far more important than the truth or falsehood of what they said. The appearance of weakness was as fatal to an effective exercise of presidential leadership as weakness itself. American self-respect required more than had been tendered the nation in the recent past.

[67] Taggart to Rev. John Taylor, April 27, 1810, Feb. 4, 1811, Haynes, *op. cit.*, pp. 347, 354.

# CHAPTER

# VIII

## WAR HAWKS ARE FLEDGED

Even before the Eleventh Congress gathered for its last session, selection of a successor had begun. By the time Speaker Varnum closed the session and headed home to Dracut, most states, including all the large ones except Virginia, had held their elections. The next winter Congressman Wright declared that defeat of half of his former colleagues showed that the country repudiated their craven policies.[1] This Republican veteran, already sixty years old, did not claim that the new members represented a rising generation more vigorous than his own. Nevertheless, the Twelfth Congress, led as it so frequently was by very young men—ex-Senator Clay, the bridegroom Calhoun, bitter Felix Grundy—later acquired an aura of youthful vigor. The facts do not demonstrate that the American people consciously sought such a Congress in the elections of 1810–11, nor is it clear that the Twelfth Congress deserved its reputation.

An able historian summarized the usual view when he wrote, "Everywhere but in New England, men who temporized or fa-

[1] *Annals*, 12th Cong., 1st sess., p. 472.

vored negotiation were turned out of office and their places given
to those . . . who frankly stood for war; young, energetic, active
men, preponderantly from the West and the frontiers of the older
sections." Thomas Jefferson, writing to James Monroe shortly
after the Virginia election, took a sharply different view. The ex-
President, then in a pacific mood which he assumed Monroe shared,
stated:

the last two Congresses have been the theme of the most licencious reproba-
tion for printers thirsting after war, some against France, & some against
England. but the people wish for peace. they feel no incumbency on them
to become the reformers of the other hemisphere, and, to inculcate, with
fire & sword, a return to moral order. when indeed peace shall become
more losing than war, they may owe to their interests, what these Quixots
are clamouring for on false estimates of honor. the public are unmoved by
these clamours, as the re-elections of their legislators show, and they are
firm to their Executive on the subject of the more recent clamours [for
decisive action].[2]

Isolated on his hilltop, Jefferson had cut back his newspaper sub-
scriptions, and he was not privy to the views of Madison and the
government. Was he therefore an inaccurate observer?

The Twelfth Congress did not have markedly more new members than either of its two immediate predecessors. If those of the
dozen replacements who entered the Eleventh Congress and later
secured election to the Twelfth are considered as carry-overs,
eighty-three veteran members returned to the new Congress along
with fifty-nine new representatives. The Tenth Congress contained
ninety-six veterans, the Eleventh eighty-six. The Congress elected
in 1812–13, after expansion made necessary by the census of 1810,
had eighty-five old members and just under a hundred newcomers.
The Twelfth Congress merely conformed to the pattern of the
times. Some states, notably New York and South Carolina, returned far fewer new members than after the last preceding election. In other states there was a substantial turnover. This often

---

2 Charles M. Wiltse, *John C. Calhoun, Nationalist, 1782–1828* (Indianapolis,
1944), p. 53; Jefferson to Monroe, May 5, 1811, Thomas Jefferson MSS, Library
of Congress.

reflected either a small shift in closely balanced constituencies or the habit of rotation in office. New Hampshire, for example, did not reëlect one congressman from 1806 through 1812, and about one-third of the Pennsylvania and Virginia delegations were regularly new members. Many congressmen not reëlected, perhaps half, declined to stand. John Taylor of South Carolina, the real author of Macon's Bill, did not run only because he was being promoted to the Senate.[3]

Although the Republicans gained about a dozen seats,[4] including some held by Clintonians and other dissidents, they did not quite recover the majority held during Jefferson's second term. The Republicans gained most in states north of the Potomac, particularly in Massachusetts and Pennsylvania. A few Republican veterans, among them John Rea of Pennsylvania and Matthew Lyon of Kentucky, each of whom had served four terms, lost contests with other Republicans. In general, no clear pattern emerges. It is not demonstrable that a great upsurge of public feeling flung aside Federalists and cautious Republicans in favor of avowed War Hawks, although in seven or eight states the election took place just after news of the Cadore letter arrived.[5] This news, unaccompanied by information revealing the equivocal nature of French repeal, should have provided those who favored strong action against Britain with an effective talking point.

Equally doubtful is the contention that the new Congress con-

---

[3] James L. Harrison, ed., *Biographical Directory of the American Congress*, 69th Cong., 2d sess., H. Doc. 783 (1928) provides the membership of all Congresses as well as brief sketches of the members. The sketches are not always entirely accurate, and they are often silent and sometimes incorrect on party affiliation. For membership and dates of birth the volume is very useful, and it provides most of the information in this and succeeding paragraphs.

[4] *Niles' Weekly Register* (Baltimore), Dec. 5, 1812, breaking down the party affiliations by states, concludes that the House contained 106 Republicans and 36 Federalists.

[5] Connecticut, Delaware, Georgia, Ohio, Pennsylvania, Massachusetts, North Carolina, and South Carolina all voted between October 1 and the end of 1810. For dates of election and the issue of credentials, see Credentials, 12th Congress, Legislative Section, National Archives. In Kentucky, on the other hand, the election took place in August, just after news of the Rambouillet Decree, which Henry Clay described as "an act of infamous treachery, if not of open robbery." This news apparently did not help the Federalist cause. Clay to Rodney, Aug. 6, 1810, James F. Hopkins, ed., *The Papers of Henry Clay*, I (Lexington, Ky., 1959), 481.

tained an unusual proportion of young men. Of course Clay and Grundy were only thirty-five, Richard M. Johnson (a two-term veteran, incidentally) was thirty, Calhoun a youth of twenty-nine. On the other hand, two Republicans, William Findley and John Smilie, had been born in Ireland eighty years before, and Robert Whitehill boasted eighty-three years, at least eight more than the oldest Federalist. The Federalist file leader, Josiah Quincy, was only thirty-nine, and two of his lieutenants, Harmanus Bleecker and Henry M. Ridgely, were thirty-two. As a matter of fact, the average age of the members of the Eleventh and Twelfth Congresses was almost exactly the same. When Congress finally voted on war in June, 1812, those voting for it had an average age of forty-seven; the opponents, just under forty-six. New members on both sides were of almost exactly the same age.[6]

Of course, Congress bore the stamp of its leadership, but leaders had been young before. Robert Goodloe Harper had not reached thirty-five when he led the Federalists during the undeclared war with France, and Randolph, Bacon, Eppes, and Campbell stepped forward to the front rank before reaching forty. In the new Congress, if such leaders as Richard M. Johnson, Langdon Cheves, and Peter B. Porter were youthful, they were also veterans of previous service. Essentially not youth but effectiveness, vigor, and tenacity distinguished the new leadership.

Another generalization may be made about the new Congress: there is little evidence that individual contests were mandates against past diplomacy. In strongly Federalist Delaware, it is true, Henry M. Ridgely squeaked through by the infinitesimal margin

[6] The following table is compiled from Harrison, *op. cit.*, omitting from the age calculations eight members whose birth date is unknown.

|  | For war | | Against war | |
|---|---|---|---|---|
|  | Number | Age | Number | Age |
| Members of 12th, preceding, and succeeding Congresses | 29 | 50.5 | 16 | 48.9 |
| Members of 12th and succeeding Congresses | 24 | 40.3 | 6 | 44.0 |
| Members of 12th Congress only | 15 | 47.6 | 15 | 42.1 |
| Members of 12th and preceding Congresses | 11 | 51.8 | 12 | 47.5 |
| Total and average | 79 | 47.0 | 49 | 45.9 |

The average age of members of the House, including those not voting in June, was 46.2 years when the Congress convened.

of seven votes,[7] which may suggest growing restiveness in that state. In Pennsylvania and Massachusetts, where the Republicans did particularly well, the foreign policy issue did not stand alone. In the Bay State the Republican victory was so surprising that, according to Christopher Gore, it "entirely destroyed the spirit of the Federalists"; feebly fighting the legislative election six months later,[8] they permitted the selection of a General Court that named Joseph B. Varnum to replace Timothy Pickering in the Senate. But in November, 1810, Bay State Republicans for the most part only regained congressional seats they had lost in the great reaction against the Embargo two years before. In Pennsylvania, voting took place just after Cadore's letter became known. The Republicans gained a near sweep, losing only one of the three Philadelphia seats and capturing the rest of the state. James Milnor, the Federalist who succeeded in Philadelphia, ran nearly 2,000 votes behind the Republicans elected with him under the state's system of plural representation.[9] Frequently, in these states and others, personality rather than principle as usual proved decisive. John G. Jackson, who had been crippled in a duel with a North Carolina Federalist congressman, observed disgustedly after the defeat of his anointed successor that "here the People vote for men more than principles." [10]

The danger in considering the election a barometer of public opinion is very apparent. The New York canvass, inconclusive in any event, took place in May, 1810, far too early to make it expressive of sentiment at the time the War Hawk Congress met. In state elections held in 1811, Republicanism of the Clintonian variety defeated the orthodox. Felix Grundy of Tennessee won in a contest in which the principal issues were not questions of international relations but rather land policy, his recent arrival in

[7] John A. Munroe, *Federalist Delaware, 1775–1815* (New Brunswick, 1954), p. 235n.

[8] Gore to King, May 5, 1811, Rufus King MSS, New-York Historical Society, Vol. XIII.

[9] Credentials, 12th Congress; Dice R. Anderson, "The Insurgents of 1811," American Historical Association, *Annual Report, 1911*, I (Washington, 1913), 173.

[10] John G. Jackson to Madison, April 19, 1811, James Madison MSS, Library of Congress.

the state, and his training as a lawyer, a profession mistrusted by rude frontiersmen.[11] In Maryland the election of three men who later voted for war proved but little, for they succeeded three retiring members who had advocated strong measures. In Virginia, where voting did not take place until April, 1811, the success of six Federalists, as well as Randolph and one of his followers, largely offset the election of fourteen administration supporters. The question of war does not appear to have been an issue, and the new congressman from Jefferson's district, Hugh Nelson, proved to be a peace man. John G. Jackson's seat fell into Federalist hands for the first time since 1793. Randolph's reëlection, in a contest with John W. Eppes, perhaps showed a mild trend in favor of the government. Although Eppes did not actively campaign, he won a few more votes than the candidate who opposed Randolph in 1809; on the other hand, he was far better known than Randolph's earlier rival.[12]

Two states most often considered hotbeds of the war spirit, Kentucky and South Carolina, contributed to the haphazard overall pattern. In the Blue Grass State, Anthony New, a War Hawk, trounced Matthew Lyon, a veteran Republican who had long since abandoned the radicalism that marked his views in the 1790's. The other selections proved little. Three incumbent Republicans were returned unopposed, as was Henry Clay, who succeeded a man appointed to federal office. Clay, who had previously served briefly in the Senate, announced that he preferred "the station of an immediate representative of the people." This commendably democratic sentiment was reinforced by an awareness that his particular talents would find a more fertile field in the lower house. Replying to Monroe's congratulations on his election, Clay wrote, "Accustomed to the popular branch of a Legislature, and preferring the turbulence . . . of a numbrous body to the solemn stillness of the

[11] Joseph H. Parks, *Felix Grundy: Champion of Democracy* (University, La., 1940), pp. 33–37.
[12] Charles H. Ambler, *Sectionalism in Virginia from 1776 to 1861* (Chicago, 1910), pp. 91–92; Charles H. Ambler, *Thomas Ritchie* (Richmond, 1913), p. 56; William C. Bruce, *John Randolph of Roanoke* (2 vols.; New York, 1922), I, 591–592. For Randolph's explanation of his slightly reduced margin, see his letters to Joseph M. Garnett, March 19, April 16, 20, 1811, *ibid.*, pp. 754, 750.

Senate Chamber, it was a mere matter of taste that lead me . . . to change my station." The Congressman-elect said nothing about any mandate to press affairs with Britain to a climax.[13] In South Carolina, where the Republicans already held all the seats, four incumbents (including Cheves, who served briefly in the Eleventh Congress) were returned. Lemuel J. Alston, a very wealthy lawyer often accused of Federalism, suffered defeat at the hands of a War Hawk. Calhoun ran for a seat given up by a rather elderly cousin. His speeches showed that he favored war, but the Republican tradition of the district and the half-hearted campaign of his opponent made success by an overwhelming margin inevitable. In most other districts, retiring members left the field to successors approved without a contest.[14]

The election of 1810–11 presented a fuzzy picture, at best. Certainly some candidates, especially those striving to oust incumbents, promised that they would fight for a forthright national policy. Certainly a few results reflected growing discontent with the cowardice shown by Congress since 1808. Still, few newspapers claimed at the time that the new House of Representatives differed much from its predecessor. Most congressmen came to Washington in the fall of 1811 unpledged, probably undecided. Events between the elections and the congressional vote for war, an interval sometimes as long as two years, tipped the balance in favor of armed resistance.

In the spring of 1811, not the last congressional elections but the purging of a cabinet member most effectively served the nation. As a diplomat, Robert Smith was incompetent. Furthermore, he constantly betrayed administration secrets and criticized government policy. He never subordinated the interests of his brother's

[13] Credentials, 12th Congress; Ellery L. Hall, "Canadian Annexation Sentiment in Kentucky Prior to the War of 1812," Kentucky State Historical Society, *Register*, XXVIII (1930), 377; Bernard Mayo, *Henry Clay, Spokesman of the New West* (Boston, 1937), p. 360; *Reporter* (Lexington, Ky.), May 19, 1810; Clay to Monroe, Nov. 13, 1810, James Monroe MSS, Library of Congress.

[14] John H. Wolfe, *Jeffersonian Democracy in South Carolina*, James Sprunt Studies in History and Political Science, Vol. XXIV, no. 1 (Chapel Hill, 1940), p. 241; Wiltse, *op. cit.*, p. 51.

faction to those of the administration, he brawled constantly with Gallatin (even their wives quarreled), and he was a party to rising journalistic attacks upon the Secretary of the Treasury which aimed to discredit the entire administration. At last, in March, 1811, Gallatin offered his resignation, actually a politely worded demand that the President choose between his two secretaries, the loyal and the disloyal. Madison, who may have known of the resignation offer in advance, declined to accept it. Instead, he called in the Secretary of State and demanded his resignation, offering at the same time to appoint Smith minister to Russia. When the Secretary asked to succeed Pinkney at London, the President made it plain—cruelly plain—that he sought only to shelve Smith, replying that the London appointment was impossible since "it was a place of discussions & negotiations, calling for appropriate talents & habits of business." [15]

Although Robert Smith briefly considered the appointment to honorable exile at St. Petersburg—what would John Quincy Adams, the incumbent, have thought had he known that the President so considered it?—he soon decided on an open break with the administration. Writing to his brother, Smith declared that Madison's "overthrow is my object and most assuredly will I effect it." The chosen vehicle was a pamphlet published in June despite the Senator's warnings. In his *Address to the People of the United States*, the ex-Secretary ascribed to the President the two Macon bills, "as unwise as humiliating," and in general sought to show that Madison's policy had been pro-French. Some of Smith's details were accurate: abandonment of the demand that France make compensation for seizures as a condition precedent to action against Britain, Madison's refusal to permit Smith to grill the new French minister on the exact state of imperial policy. There were also obvious falsehoods; who could but laugh when Smith claimed that during the Jefferson administration Madison relied upon him

[15] Memorandum on Smith's resignation, April ——, 1811, Gaillard Hunt, ed., *The Writings of James Madison* (9 vols.; New York, 1900–1910), VIII, 137–149. Macon commented that Madison's offer of the St. Petersburg legation was characteristic of the President, who "cannot yet say no quite easy enough." Macon to Nicholson, Sept. 21, 1811, Joseph H. Nicholson MSS, Library of Congress.

for stylistic improvement of diplomatic correspondence? And the address breathed such malignance and pomposity that few could take it seriously, even Federalists ordinarily delighted to have evidence of Madison's Francophilia. William Lee and Joel Barlow answered the *Address*, but in general the administration let the ex-Secretary hang himself with his own rope. It was, said Randolph's friend, James M. Garnett, "one of the rare instances of a man's giving the finishing stroke to his own character, in his eagerness to ruin his enemy." [16]

Before Madison challenged Smith, he had already decided that James Monroe should be the new secretary of state. The President's choice was possible only because Monroe's feelings had undergone a steady change since he returned home in December, 1807, and let his name be put forth against Madison in the presidential election. Early in 1809 Monroe offered his services as a special envoy to London and Paris. Such a mission, he said, might result in a settlement with one power which would let America concentrate her fire against the other. (Monroe clearly showed that he preferred arrangement with Britain, since he believed Napoleon aimed ultimately at the conquest of America.) The outgoing president, who declined Monroe's offer, correctly interpreted it as evidence his old protégé was drifting back into the fold. Toward the end of the year, when Monroe declined appointment as governor of Upper Louisiana, he made it clear he would accept higher office if the new president offered it. [17]

In January, 1811, Monroe became governor of Virginia. Before the election he declared that he intended to coöperate with the national administration, and Madisonian votes elected him. Jeffer-

[16] Smith to Samuel Smith, March 26, 1811, Samuel Smith MSS, Library of Congress; *Robert Smith's Address to the People of the United States* (Baltimore, 1811); Lee to Sarah P. Lee, Sept. 9, 1811, Mary L. Mann, ed., *A Yankee Jeffersonian: Selections from the Diary and Letters of William Lee* (Cambridge, 1958), p. 140; Garnett to Randolph, July 23, 1811, John Randolph MSS, Library of Congress.

[17] Monroe to Jefferson, Jan. 18, 1809, Monroe MSS; Jefferson to Monroe, Jan. 29, 1809, *ibid.*; Monroe to Jefferson, Feb. 2, 1809, Stanislaus M. Hamilton, ed., *The Writings of James Monroe* (7 vols.; New York, 1898–1903), V, 93–101; Jefferson to Madison, March 30, 1809, Jefferson MSS; Jefferson to Madison, Nov. 30, 1809, Andrew A. Lipscomb and Albert E. Bergh, eds., *The Writings of Thomas Jefferson* (Memorial ed.; 20 vols.; Washington, 1903–1904), XII, 330–332.

son congratulated the new governor, "altho' it is not a field on which much genius can be displayed," because the election restored Monroe to prominence and demonstrated Republican faith in him. John Randolph, on the other hand, wrote in his diary, "Richmond, Monroe, Traitor." From this point on, the already weakening tie between them was broken, although Monroe attempted for a time to preserve it.[18]

Reassured by the available evidence but still unwilling to risk rebuff, President Madison asked Senator Richard Brent to write to Monroe shortly after Congress adjourned. Would Monroe, the Senator's letter inquired, accept appointment as secretary of state? Brief but intense negotiations followed. Monroe obviously eagerly sought office, partly because he hoped to turn policy in an anti-French direction, and his Quid friends, Taylor of Caroline and Littleton Tazewell, urged him to join the Cabinet. On the other hand, Monroe disliked the weakness he thought he saw in administration policy and clearly feared that connection with it would harm his own political fortunes. To Monroe's queries Madison replied with a letter that was in large part a masterpiece of obfuscation. He did state that "in favor of a cordial accommodation with G. Britain, there has certainly never ceased to be a prevailing disposition in the Executive Councils, since I became connected with them." Reassured as to the neutrality of government policy, perhaps confident that he himself could provide the needed vigor, Monroe accepted office at the end of March.[19] On April 4, 1811, he left Richmond by stagecoach, and on the morning of the sixth he took up his duties at the Department of State.

Monroe's appointment caused a good deal of speculation. Some Federalists thought it showed that Madison, recognizing his errors, had decided to adopt a policy more favorable to England. Others, more cynical, explained the appointment as a political bribe to

---

[18] Jefferson to Monroe, Jan. 25, 1811, Monroe MSS; diary entry of Jan. 12, 1811, Bruce, *op. cit.*, I, 348.

[19] Monroe to Tazewell, March 14, 1811, Monroe MSS; Monroe to Brent, March 18, 1811, *ibid.*; Monroe to Madison, March 23, 1811, *ibid.*; Madison to Monroe, private, March 26, 1811, Madison MSS; Monroe to Madison, March 29, 1811, Monroe MSS.

eliminate Monroe as a presidential candidate in 1812, and the British chargé, Morier, went even further when he combined with this a suggestion that sheer economic necessity had influenced Monroe.[20] A number of considerations actually caused the governor to accept national office. Despite the deep wound suffered at the hands of Jefferson and Madison, Monroe remained basically a loyal Republican, at least to the extent of believing that the success of Federalism or of factionalism would be fatal to the nation. His own appointment, he hoped, would contribute to party unity. Personal ambition, of course, also played a part in his decision; in no other way could he so effectively restore himself to the front rank of presidential contenders, even if he would have to await the completion of Madison's second term. Finally, Monroe obviously expected to alter the direction of American policy. As always, he considered peace with Britain the object of highest priority. He wanted to work for it; he assumed, like so many contemporaries, that he could thrust his will upon Madison; and he was confident the British Cabinet would provide no insuperable obstacle. Within a short time Monroe would learn that British demands went far beyond any that he was prepared to accept.

The first step toward conversion resulted from a naval clash in May, 1811, brought on by a spate of impressments near the American coast. "We are all in a Bustle," Samuel Smith wrote to his son, "in Consequence of the Cruel Conduct of Four British Cruisers who have been off the Coast for these few weeks. they press the Young Men from our Coasters & in one Instance a Young Man who never had been at sea before." Early in May Commodore Rodgers sailed from Norfolk in U.S.S. *President*, and the American people leaped to the conclusion that he had been ordered to demand the release of impressed Americans. "Indeed the impressments can no longer be tolerated," Senator Smith continued. "Pusyllanimity has been Charged on the President," and the nation hoped that he had changed his course. Few desired that war

[20] *Columbia Centinel* (Boston), April 10, 1811; Gore to King, May 5, 1811, King MSS, Vol. XIII; *Federal Republican* (Baltimore), April 4, 1811; Morier #23 to Wellesley, May 9, 1811, Foreign Office Archives, Public Record Office, FO 5/74.

should follow, "but if it should, the Nation will meet it on this Ground with Alacrity. all parties are outraged, federal & Democrat are all . . . united on this point." [21] When even Samuel Smith declared himself ready to rally behind the President, the national temper was certainly aroused.

Actually, Rodgers apparently carried only general orders nearly a year old. Neither these orders nor any others that have come to light directed Rodgers to use force to recover seamen recently impressed, and Monroe subsequently denied that any such orders had been issued. The nation believed they had, and the *National Intelligencer*'s equivocal language strengthened this impression.[22]

Just after sundown on May 16, 1811, after a long chase, Rodgers overhauled H.M.S. *Little Belt*, a Danish-built sloop taken at Copenhagen. A brief cannonade followed, and the *Little Belt* struck her colors. Each commander subsequently claimed the other had fired first. For the Englishman this would have been foolhardy, considering the disparity of force, unless he was convinced that the *President* was French. On the other hand, a slight preponderance of the evidence supports Rodgers' claim that the *Little Belt* did fire first. In any event, the evidence was conflicting enough to permit both governments to support their respective commanders. Whatever Madison and his Cabinet desired, the public reaction made it prudent to do so. Even the *Columbian Centinel*, Boston's Federalist bellwether, supported the recovery of impressed seamen by force. This, it said, "would not be *War*, but *Reprisal*, justified by the Law of Nations." The *National Intelligencer* soon announced that commanders who forcibly vindicated national rights would get administration support.[23]

The conflict naturally produced an equivalent reaction in England. A few newspapers emphasized the difficulty of establishing which commander had fired first, and the *Morning Chronicle*

[21] Samuel Smith to John S. Smith, May 23, 1811, Samuel Smith MSS.

[22] Charles O. Paullin, *Commodore John Rodgers* (Cleveland, 1910), pp. 211–212, 220 ff.; *National Intelligencer* (Washington), May 23, 1811.

[23] *Columbian Centinel*, May 29, 1811; *National Intelligencer*, June 6, 1811. The *Centinel* combined its defense of the forcible recovery of deserters with the usual personal assaults upon Madison.

charged that the clash, for the precipitation of which, however, it blamed Rodgers, sprang ultimately from the Cabinet's "folly in not confirming the arrangement that Mr. Erskine so sensibly made." Most papers threw the entire responsibility on the Americans. The *Courier* even called for war: "The blood of our murdered countrymen must be revenged, and war must ensue.—The conduct of America leaves us no alternative." [24] The government contented itself with a well-publicized dispatch of naval reinforcements to the American theater.

At Washington, Secretary Monroe's initial moderation pleased the new British minister, Jackson's long-delayed successor. Monroe's mildness did not last long. The administration accepted Rodgers' story, fixing blame on the *Little Belt*, and realized that America had been exhilarated by this retaliation for the insult offered to Barron four years before. In the middle of July and again in September, the United States government categorically declined to consider a British request for reparation, at least until the earlier *Chesapeake* affair had been settled. Even then, the British minister predicted, admission of guilt was highly unlikely.[25]

The *Little Belt–President* clash helped breed the psychological setting for war. Englishmen considered it an unprovoked attack made successful only by the bully's size. They feared that, unless forced to apologize, America would lose all respect for the mistress of the seas. Most British newspapers reprinted a gleeful American statement that *"She Stoops to Conquer, or the Mistakes of a Night, a new play with an old title,* was performed with *loud* applause . . . off the Capes of Virginia, by the frigate *President,* and a British picaroon, to the gratification of all America." [26] This attitude, so offensive to Britons, was indeed widespread in the United States. The shrill cheers for Rodgers showed that the American people, while not yet ready for full-scale war, were ashamed of the debilitating, sterile policies of the recent past.

Six weeks after the sea fight, a British minister at last arrived

---

[24] *Morning Chronicle* (London), July 17, 1811; *Courier* (London), July 17, 1811.
[25] Foster #2, #7, #11 to Wellesley, July 2, 18, Sept. 17, 1811, FO 5/76.
[26] *Sun* (London), July 1, 1811.

in America. Since August, 1810, a chargé, John Philip Morier, had headed the legation. Morier told Jackson, "I had rather get into a soupe, by a conduct spirited & spurning at their infamous proceedings toward us, than by one of the milk and water kind," but he actually followed a moderate course. He became comparatively popular in Washington and, years later, looked back upon his stay with complacent pleasure.[27] Although young, Morier had had diplomatic experience in Eastern Europe, and in other times his sem ible pedigree would have been considered a compliment to the U ed States. As it was, his junior diplomatic rank outweighed ev rthing else. As a matter of prestige, the United States could not continue Pinkney as minister to London while a mere chargé headed the British mission to America. In 1811 Pinkney returned home.

Too late to prevent Pinkney's departure, the slothful marquis settled upon Augustus John Foster as the new minister. Foster's parents, unless one accepts the romantic stories that the Prince Regent actually sired him, were a member of Parliament and an earl's daughter who, upon being widowed, had become first the mistress and then the wife of the Duke of Devonshire. His aunt was married to the Earl of Liverpool, a cabinet member. After an Oxford education Foster toured Europe in the grand style, then served in the United States under Merry. Recently he had been chargé d'affaires at Stockholm.[28] With his mother's assistance, Foster actively sought the Washington post, hoping it would lead to rapid advances in the diplomatic corps. His availability further condemns Wellesley for letting the post remain vacant so long.

In 1811 Foster was thirty-three. He was handsome, self-assured, and so confident of his superior breeding that he felt able to ignore American crudities and insults. Foster's diary and letters are full

[27] Morier to Jackson, Jan. 24, 1811, Francis James Jackson MSS, Public Record Office (FO 353/58–61), FO 353/61; Morier to Bagot, Sept. 17, 1817, Sir Charles Bagot MSS, Levens Hall, Westmorland, Letters Received 1817.

[28] Foster's background is sketched in the introduction to Richard B. Davis, ed., *Jeffersonian America: Notes on the United States of America . . . by Sir Augustus John Foster, Bart.* (San Marino, 1954), and this volume of course contains his account of the winter in Washington. More information about the young man and his mother will be found in Vere Foster, ed., *The Two Duchesses* (London, 1898).

of contemptuous comments—he was particularly amused when an uncouth congressman urinated in his fireplace and when other legislators, confusing caviar for jam, had to spit out their overly large mouthfuls—but he successfully concealed his contempt beneath a bland exterior. At Washington Foster cut a wide social swath and spent, he later claimed, £9,000 on entertainment. "Mr. Foster is a pretty young gentleman," a Federalist commented. "But his appearance is too much that of a boy for a Minister Plenipotentiary. He looks as if he was better calculated for a ballroom or drawing room, than for a foreign minister." Foster's diffident manner did not project British sternness to congressmen, and his inner antirepublicanism prevented him from accurately weighing events. "Foster is a very gentlemanlike young man, quite equal to do nothing at his post," Francis Jackson observed. Jackson incorrectly thought this "now the best possible policy to follow." [29] The days of Rose and of Jackson himself had passed.

The Cabinet failed to see this. The ministers believed the United States would soon realize what seemed so obvious, that France had not really repealed her edicts. Then the Americans would either reverse their policy or insist upon effective French repeal, and then Britain might withdraw the Orders in Council. There seemed to be no hurry. Presidents had talked angrily, Congress had stirred before. Elections known to the Cabinet by April, 1811, gave no clear hint of a new departure. Consequently the most important instructions handed to Foster merely rehearsed the arguments justifying the Orders in Council. Other instructions directed Foster to protest against the threat to Spanish West Florida without using "any hostile or menacing language." England did not intend to "vindicate the Rights of Spain by force of Arms." Thus these foolish instructions ordered Foster to irritate the Americans by criticizing their policy without authorizing him to make protests powerful enough to serve any useful purpose. On the other

[29] Taggart to Rev. John Taylor, Dec. 30, 1811, George H. Haynes, ed., "Letters of Samuel Taggart, Representative in Congress, 1803–1814," American Antiquarian Society, *Proceedings*, n.s., XXXIII (1923), 374; Jackson to George Jackson, Feb. 19, 1811, Lady Jackson, ed., *The Bath Archives: a Further Selection from the Diaries and Letters of Sir George Jackson* (2 vols.; London, 1873), I, 213.

hand, instructions on the *Chesapeake* affair were tailored to fit Pinkney's view, as Wellesley understood it, of what the United States required.[30]

In preparing Foster's main instructions, on the Orders in Council, the Foreign Office drew heavily upon a memorandum prepared by Spencer Perceval.[31] Since Perceval was the most forthright defender of the orders in the Cabinet, the memorandum and the instructions, though loosely organized, are a comprehensive defense of the British position. The Orders in Council, Perceval maintained, retaliated against the Berlin Decree, which released Britain from the restraints of international law. When the French abandoned the principles of the Continental System, Britain would gladly withdraw her edicts. She could not consider the Cadore letter adequate, and its acceptance by the United States was an unfriendly act. The letter proclaimed not absolute but conditional repeal, as subsequent French action made clear. Even more important, the repeal promised by Cadore was meaningless, since other French regulations had virtually the same effect as the Berlin and Milan decrees. These so-called municipal regulations, Perceval said, by "prohibiting all Commerce in British articles all over the Continent, would leave the most pernicious & injurious parts of the Berlin & Milan decrees in full force & operation." The Perceval ministry clearly intended to make America suffer the loss of a continental market as long as Britain did. Selfishness so naked could be clothed only in terms of economic necessity, not right; the British usually tried to keep this unattractive garb out of sight.

The British government refused to consider Fox's Blockade of 1806 part of the same system as the Orders in Council, but maintained that it met the requirements of international law because

---

[30] Wellesley to Prince Regent, May 15, 1811, Royal Archives, Windsor Castle. For the instructions see Bernard Mayo, ed., *Instructions to the British Ministers to the United States, 1791–1812*, American Historical Association, *Annual Report, 1936*, III (Washington, 1941), 310 ff.

[31] Perceval memorandum, n.d., Spencer Perceval MSS (examined while temporarily on deposit at the Register of National Archives, London), A/15; Wellesley #1 to Foster, April 10, 1811, Mayo, ed., *Instructions*, pp. 310–318. The following paragraphs rest on these two sources.

Fox had proclaimed it only after receiving assurances that the Royal Navy could make it an effective and not a mere paper blockade. If Britain consented to lump this regulation with the Orders in Council, admittedly illegal except as retaliation, France could claim that Britain was confessing her own priority of guilt against the law of nations. At the same time, apparent acceptance of the extremely restrictive French definition of blockade would compromise England's right to restore blockades like Fox's if conditions later made them advisable. The last paragraph of the instructions, doubtless prepared with an eye to future publication in navy-proud Britain, put the argument in high-flown language: "No Extremity can induce His Royal Highness to relinquish the ancient and established Rules of Maritime War, the maintenance of which is indispensable, not only to the Commercial Interests, but to the Naval Strength, and to the National Honor of Great Britain, as well as to the rights of all Maritime States, and to the general prosperity of Navigation and Commerce throughout the Civilized World."

Two practical alterations, one soon withdrawn, somewhat softened the instructions. The British government made it clear that, while insisting upon the legitimacy of blockades, it considered Fox's Blockade submerged in the Orders in Council. "That Blockade," read the instructions, "would not be continued after the repeal of the Orders in Council, unless it should be maintained by an adequate force . . . according to the acknowledged Law of Nations." Perceval's memorandum reveals his fear that the United States would adopt the French view that blockades, to be legal, must include investment by land and sea. If America did not, however, this particular issue would disappear. The other, short-lived concession involved ships that had been captured after sailing from American ports in an honest conviction that the Cadore letter would bring about repeal of the Orders in Council. Condemnation proceedings against these ships, both Perceval's memorandum and the instructions stated, would be stayed "as long as any hope can be entertained of prevailing on America to correct that error [accepting Cadore's letter], and to render justice to Great Britain."

Unfortunately, later in the month the Cabinet abandoned hope of changing America's mind and told Foster that condemnation would no longer be stayed.[32]

Some of Perceval's arguments had force. As he charged, French repeal had been conditional and incomplete. Napoleon's definition of blockade did not accord with traditional practice, nor could England possibly accept it. Fox's Blockade had perhaps conformed with the requirements of international law. It might even be that "the rights of all Maritime States, and . . . the general prosperity of Navigation and Commerce throughout the Civilized World" depended upon successful British resistance to Napoleon. Except with that messianic argument Britain could in no way defend her insistence that America tolerate the Orders in Council until Europe admitted English goods. Uncandidly, the instructions claimed that British policy had been "calculated for the purpose of encouraging the Trade of Neutrals through Great Britain," whereas actually the license system, revivified after temporary suspension following the Order in Council of 1809, notoriously discriminated against neutrals. The ministry, which announced tenderness for innocent American merchants deluded by their government and stayed condemnation of their ships, did not release these vessels and, quickly abandoning hope for a major shift in American policy, soon vindictively condemned the innocents. Whether reasonable or not, the instructions of April, 1811, were undeniably obdurate. Canning's flashing phrases and Wellesley's ponderous sentences added up to about the same thing. Unlike Canning, the marquis had the misfortune to act when America was at last raising itself from the mire.

Supplementary instructions prepared on the eve of Foster's departure showed that Britain, if she shifted her policy at all, intended to move toward greater firmness. Not only did Wellesley announce that court proceedings on the *Fox* would proceed, he also ordered Foster to protest the new nonintercourse legislation

[32] Wellesley #6 to Foster, April 29, 1811, Mayo, ed., *Instructions*, p. 323. Wellesley to Prince Regent, May 15, 1811, Royal Archives, indicates that two weeks later these instructions had still not been dispatched.

and to warn America, although discreetly, that Britain was not unarmed for a commercial contest. "A perseverance in the . . . hostile measures already commenced towards our Maritime and Commercial Rights and Interests," Wellesley huffed, "will compel us to resort to adequate means of [economic] retaliation." [33]

Augustus Foster sailed in H.M.S. *Minerva* early in May, 1811. He left behind a broken romance with the girl who later married Lord Byron, but he carried with him a staff of seven servants and a new secretary of legation, Anthony St. John Baker. On June 29, when the *Minerva* arrived off Annapolis, a deserter leaped overboard to risk the three- or four-mile swim to shore. The same day William Pinkney sailed into the bay in U.S.S. *Essex.* Ignoring the possible symbolism of these events, Foster entered upon his duties with a good spirit. After a brief stay in Georgetown he established a new legation in the Seven Buildings, at Pennsylvania Avenue and Nineteenth Street, rejecting the old legation selected by Merry as too small and too distant for his purposes. On July 2 Monroe introduced Foster to the President. Four days later, after an Independence Day celebration from which Foster prudently absented himself, Madison entertained him pleasantly at the White House, and the secretaries soon followed suit. Already the new minister had begun talks with Monroe. "I found in the American Secretary, a tone & manner of the most mild & conciliatory nature," he reported.[34]

This tone did not last long. Foster's instructions precluded any real mutuality, as the Secretary of State learned when the British minister revealed the contents at one of their first meetings. State Department files, not available to Monroe while he sulked at Albemarle, showed how much Britain had changed since the days of the Ministry of All the Talents. This information aided Madison, most effective and stubborn in private discussion, in bringing the new secretary to his own position. Even before Foster arrived, the administration newspaper declared that if his negotiations

---

[33] Wellesley #6, #7 to Foster, April 29, 1811, Mayo, ed., *Instructions*, pp. 323–324; Wellesley #8 to Foster, secret, April ——, 1811, *ibid.*, pp. 324–325.

[34] Foster #1, #2 to Wellesley, June 29, July 2, 1811, FO 5/76.

failed, as they were almost certain to do, the United States must rigorously enforce nonimportation or "substitute for it some measure more consonant to the feelings of the nation." [35] This characteristically opaque language at least showed a determination not to abandon the ground to Britain. Apparently with little protest, James Monroe fell in with this line. To have done otherwise would have been politically ruinous, for Monroe had burned his bridges with Federalists and Republican dissidents.

Although Foster believed Monroe's attitude milder than Madison's, their conversations do not bear him out. Monroe made suggestions which he said were his own, but on no occasion did these compromise basic American positions. Bait dangled by the Secretary on his own responsibility left the United States free to try a more attractive fly or even a naked hook later on. On most subjects the Secretary was certainly firm enough. He rejected the British protest against threats to West Florida, observing casually that the province must sooner or later fall into American hands. He adopted an increasingly rigid line on the *Little Belt* affair. He insisted that his government would never admit that Cadore's letter had not resulted in repeal of the decrees. "I know of no arguments, no mode of reasoning, which can avail in a discussion with such tempers," Foster complained with some asperity. Only increased French action against commerce, the minister believed, would shake Madison and Monroe from their position.[36]

Two items indicated that the administration still hoped for settlement with Britain, even if it meant offending France. Monroe told Foster that the President considered the British position on Fox's Blockade satisfactory. America welcomed the assurance that future blockades would be effectively maintained, and would not join France in demanding formal revocation of the blockade of 1806.[37] Monroe put forward an important hint concerning the Orders in Council. "He assured me," Foster reported, "that if Great Britain would issue such a conditional and ambiguous prom-

[35] *National Intelligencer*, April 16, 1811.
[36] Foster #3, #5, #6, #7, #8 to Wellesley, July 5, 7, 12, 18, 18, 1811, FO 5/76.
[37] Foster #5, #6 to Wellesley, July 7, 12, 1811, *ibid*.

280

ise of a revocation of Her Orders as France did of the decrees last August, that it will be considered enough to authorize the cessation of the operation of the Non-importation act against her Commerce." [38] Two fake repeals would be considered to cancel each other out. Foster felt unable to meet this tremendous leap toward common ground with even a genteel step forward. When the British Cabinet finally tiptoed in this direction months later, America had clambered back to higher terrain.

Far from urging his government to pick up Monroe's hint, which might have cut the ground from under future War Hawks, Foster advised firmness and adopted it himself.[39] In formal notes, he demanded America's proof of French repeal and threatened retaliation if nonimportation continued. After reading one of these notes Madison wrote: "Foster seems more disposed to play the diplomatist, than the conciliatory negotiator. His letter though not very skillfully made up, is evidently calculated for the public here, as well as for his own Govt. In this view his evasion & sophistical efforts may deserve attention." Attention they got, in two assaults upon the British position prepared jointly by Madison and Monroe. These notes, somewhat defensive in discussing French repeal and the American interpretation of "municipal regulations," were devastating when they ripped into Foster's statement that the orders would be maintained until Napoleon permitted British goods to enter the Continent.[40] When the notes became public through transmission to Congress in the autumn, England's audacity astounded even the Federalists. This demand apparently made the administration, or at least Monroe, realize the barrenness of all hopes for an immediate accommodation. "A demand so entirely inconsistent with the rights of the U States, and degrading to them as an independent nation," Monroe wrote an English correspondent, "has been viewed in no other light than that of evidence of a determined hostility in your government against this country."

---

[38] Foster #8 to Wellesley, July 18, 1811, *ibid.*
[39] Foster #6 to Wellesley, July 12, 1811, *ibid.*
[40] Irving Brant, *James Madison: the President* (Indianapolis, 1956), pp. 340-343; Madison to Monroe, July 2, 1811, Monroe MSS. Madison's letter, certainly misdated, should probably read August 2, 1811.

Threateningly, perhaps with emphasis for political effect in Britain, the Secretary added: "War, dreadful as the alternative is, could not do us more injury than the present state of things, and it would certainly be more honorable to the nation, and gratifying to the publick feelings." [41]

By the end of July, 1811, deadlock clearly had been reached. The President and the Secretary withdrew to Virginia, carrying on correspondence by courier. Monroe suffered a painful injury when brushed from his horse, but he was able to take whatever action was required by notes that flowed southward from the departmental clerk left in charge at Washington. Meanwhile, Foster wended his way northward to Philadelphia, a favorite summer mecca of diplomats. In Chester he dined at a tavern owned by a member of Congress. Neither there nor anywhere else did he pick up information that caused him to warn his government that the American temper might be changing. The country's alarm over reports that Britain would declare war as retaliation for nonimportation or the attack on the *Little Belt*, Foster reported, "proves pretty forcibly how very little is to be dreaded that this Country will originate measures of hostility against us." [42]

While Foster, Madison, and Monroe vacationed, news of an impending Indian war flowed through the Appalachians. In October, 1809, Governor William Henry Harrison of the Indiana Territory inveigled Indians assembled at Fort Wayne into a cession of nearly 3 million acres. The Madison administration, while ratifying this treaty, directed Harrison not to occupy the ceded territory immediately. The weak warnings of Secretary of War Eustis, however, deterred the governor far less than threats delivered to him in the summer of 1810 and again in 1811 by Tecumseh, speaking for a new Indian league organized by Tecumseh himself and his brother, the Prophet. Harrison's provocative statements to the legislature, accounts of increased subsidies to tribes

---

[41] Monroe to [Holland?], n.d., Monroe MSS, fol. 3145. This letter, written in reply to one of July 15, was probably sent in late September or early October. Hamilton, *op. cit.*, V, 191, suggests that it was addressed to Auckland, but references to Fox, Holland's relative, make Holland the more likely addressee.

[42] Foster #16 to Wellesley, Sept. 17, 1811, FO 5/76.

that visited Canada, and, in 1811, news that Tecumseh had gone southward to attempt to add other tribes to his confederacy ignited a real fear of Indian hostilities all along the Western frontier. Foster, who made passing reference to propaganda connecting Britain with the Indians, did not consider it particularly important.

The crisis did not come until after Foster's return to Washington. In July, 1811, responding to Harrison's reports of approaching war, Secretary Eustis ordered a detachment of regulars to the governor's aid. Three days later the Secretary wrote that Madison still hoped for peace and trusted that Harrison would follow a pacific policy. As Madison and Eustis should have known, peremptory orders alone could restrain the aggressive governor. Harrison gathered together an expedition of regulars and volunteers, construed in his own fashion directives from Eustis, and plunged northward to break up the Indian forces and establish white possession of the Fort Wayne cession. At dawn on November 7, 1811, Indians from the Prophet's Town attacked Harrison's army. At the cost of about 200 men, Harrison narrowly held his position, then burned the Indian settlement and retired precipitately to the Ohio. News of this encounter, called the battle of Tippecanoe, ran swiftly across the nation.[43]

Americans blamed the British for the Indian troubles. During the crisis preceding the Jay treaty and again after the *Chesapeake* affair, friction with the Western tribes had accompanied difficulties with England. Few Americans accepted as coincidental a recurrence of this friction in 1810 and 1811. As early as 1810, calling for the conquest of Canada, Henry Clay demanded: "Is it nothing to us to extinguish the torch that lights up savage warfare?" Newspapers in Clay's part of the country took up the cry. One called for decisive action to wipe out the threat of "the tomahawk and scalping knife, which for many years past, and at this very moment the inhuman blood-thirsty cabinet of St. James had incessantly endeavored to bring on the *women* and *children* of our west-

---

[43] For the chain of events leading to the battle of Tippecanoe, see Freeman Cleaves, *Old Tippecanoe: William Henry Harrison and His Time* (New York, 1939), pp. 63 ff.; Dorothy B. Goebel, *William Henry Harrison, A Political Biography*, Indiana Historical Collections, Vol. XIV (Indianapolis, 1926), pp. 115 ff.

ern frontiers." Another sanctimoniously bewailed the fact that "British intrigue and British gold . . . has greater influence with them [the Indians] of late than American justice and benevolence." [44]

After Tippecanoe such complaints multiplied. Andrew Jackson denounced "Secrete agents of Great Britain" as catalysts of the attack. The Lexington *Reporter* asked if Congress intended to "treat the citizens of the *Western country* as they have treated the [impressed] seamen" for eighteen years, then added, "The *whole* body of Western citizens call for the probing of this British villiny to the bottom." Back East, Duane's *Aurora* proclaimed that "war has been begun with British arms and by the Indians instigated by British emissaries. The blood of American citizens have already been shed in actual war, begun undeclared." [45] Denunciations continued throughout the winter, until even Foster recognized their importance.

The easiest way to end the Indian threat, many agreed, was to drive the British from Canada. Jefferson considered the conquest of Canada, at least as far as the walls of Quebec, an almost costless corollary of war with England. During the war scare of 1807 one of his young supporters even argued for enlistment for the duration rather than for a twelve-month period, on the ground the former would actually be shorter. Five years later Andrew Jackson appealed to the youth of Tennessee to seize the opportunity of "performing a military *promenade*" by joining him in a visit to Niagara Falls and Quebec. "That which pleases me most in these people, Monseigneur," the French minister reported to his chief, "is the tranquil confidence they have in their means of aggression and of resistance." [46] Sérurier intended no sarcasm.

[44] *Annals*, 11th Cong., 1st and 2d sess., p. 580; *Reporter*, Nov. 24, 1810; *Kentucky Gazette*, Aug. 27, 1811, quoted in Julius W. Pratt, *Expansionists of 1812* (New York, 1925), p. 45.

[45] Jackson to Harrison, Nov. 30, 1811, John S. Bassett, ed., *Correspondence of Andrew Jackson* (7 vols.; Washington, 1926–1933), I, 210; *Reporter*, Dec. 7, 1811; *Aurora* (Philadelphia), Dec. 10, 1811.

[46] Wirt to Dabney Carr, Aug. 12, 1807, John P. Kennedy, *Memoirs of the Life of William Wirt* (2 vols.; Philadelphia, 1850), I, 202; Jackson, divisional orders, March 7, 1812, Bassett, *op. cit.*, I, 222; Sérurier #26 to Minister of Foreign Relations, Aug. 31, 1811, Archives des Affaires Étrangères, Correspondance Politique, États-Unis (photostats, Library of Congress), Vol. LXVI.

In 1811 and 1812 few Americans stopped to ask for a real "probing of . . . British villiny to the bottom." After all, the *Independent Chronicle* argued, "it is not rational to conclude that the Indians would have taken up arms against us, had they not been instigated by British mercenaries." Time did not provide evidence to back up this logic. In his war message the President merely stated that it would be difficult to account for Indian hostilities unless they had been inspired by the British. A House committee report on the message, presented by John C. Calhoun, admitted the evidence was uncertain but added, "your committee are not disposed to occupy much time in investigating." [47]

British policy was not what most Americans assumed it to be. Canadian agents maintained close connections with Indians living in American territory and sometimes encouraged the Indians to think Britain would support an offensive war against the United States. At the top level, however, British policy was essentially precautionary, based, as Castlereagh put it, on the principle that "we are to consider not so much their Use as Allies, as their Destructiveness if Enemies." Indian neutrality in an Anglo-American war, although desired by Bathurst even after hostilities began in 1812, was felt to be unattainably utopian. [48] Britain therefore tried to make sure that if war came the Indians would side with her. Both to husband Indian strength and to avoid a flare-up against Britain precisely like that which arose in 1811, the Cabinet tried to prevent war between Indians and frontiersmen.

Sir James Craig and Isaac Brock, the principal Canadian executors of this policy, loyally attempted to implement it. Craig once even informed Washington of Indian plans he was attempting to check, and in 1811 Brock specifically stated to the Indians that British supplies would cease if they fought the United States. Brock warned his superiors that the distinction between encouraging Indians and simply preserving their friendship was a difficult one, and after Tippecanoe he added that the existing policy would

[47] *Independent Chronicle* (Boston), Dec. 5, 1811; James D. Richardson, ed., *A Compilation of the Messages and Papers of the Presidents* (Washington, 1897), I, 503–504; *Annals*, 12th Cong., 2d sess., p. 1551.

[48] Castlereagh #19 to Craig, April 8, 1809, Colonial Office Records, Public Record Office, CO 43/22; Bathurst #6 to Prevost, Aug. 10, 1812, CO 43/23.

eventually destroy British influence among the tribes. However, only a month before the American declaration of war he wrote, "The utmost attention is continued to be paid that no just cause of umbrage is given, in our intercourse with the western tribes, to the United States Government." [49] Policy was one thing, execution another; from time to time subordinate officials and Brock himself stepped over the line sketched by London. But no responsible Englishman desired the clash of arms which began along Harrison's perimeter, knowing full well that this could only strengthen America's sense of grievance.

History is often influenced as much by erroneous conviction as by truth. Believing that the tendrils of Indian war wound back to Canada, many Westerners desired to apply their axes to the root. In addition, some Americans doubtless wanted to conquer Canada to gain for their country a monopoly of the fur trade. John Randolph, who ascribed every conceivable evil motive to the War Hawks, alleged that the Western farmer and his spokesmen wanted to plunder the British Empire of fertile agricultural land in Upper Canada. But millions of acres of desirable land were still available south of the border, and on the other hand British possession of Canada did not prevent frontiersmen from settling there. Four of every five settlers in Upper Canada were American by either birth or descent, only a small proportion of them Loyalist refugees. Any Westerner troubled by a land shortage could follow a well-worn path to Canada. National loyalties did not yet have binding force, at least among impoverished or marginal farmers.[50]

[49] Brock to Craig, Feb. 27, 1811, Ferdinand B. Tupper, *The Life and Correspondence of Major-General Sir Isaac Brock* (2d ed.; London, 1847), p. 95; Craig #37 to Liverpool, March 29, 1811, FO 5/92 (filed at Feb. 7, 1812); Brock to ———, Dec. 2, 1811, Michigan Pioneer and Historical Society, *Historical Collections*, XV (1889), 57; Brock to Liverpool, May 25, 1812, Francis Bickley, ed., *Report on the Manuscripts of Earl Bathurst* (London: Historical Manuscripts Commission, 1923), p. 175.

[50] *Annals*, 12th Cong., 1st sess., p. 533. The land hunger argument was put forward in Louis M. Hacker, "Western Land Hunger and the War of 1812: a Conjecture," *Mississippi Valley Historical Review*, X (1923–1924), 365–395. Almost immediately, this theory was demolished, primarily on agriculturo-economic grounds, in Julius W. Pratt, "Western Aims in the War of 1812," *Mississippi Valley Historical Review*,

A more convincing economic explanation of rising Western discontent emphasizes fluctuations in the price level. The West, particularly the southerly cotton and tobacco areas, overexpanded production after 1805. For a short period farmers got extraordinary profits, but low quality, high costs, and feeble marketing and credit structures made the West really "a sort of marginal area in relation to world markets." When prices collapsed in 1808, Westerners blamed foreign restrictions on trade, ultimately concentrating on the Orders in Council. The West supported commercial warfare until it was proved ineffective, then demanded more vigorous measures. In the summer of 1811, when the price level of goods exported from New Orleans stood 30 per cent below the peak of 1807, many thought war might reopen foreign markets and restore prosperity.[51]

Such reasoning owed more to emotion than to rational thought, for a war with the mistress of the seas was certainly unlikely to bring an immediate increase in foreign commerce. Nevertheless, perhaps from frustration, many Westerners adopted it. Andrew Jackson asked volunteers to join him in a fight to secure, among other things, "a market for the productions of our soil, now perishing on our hands because the mistress of the ocean has forbid us to carry them to any foreign nation." Some Westerners found such naked self-interest embarrassing or perhaps doubted that war would open blocked channels of trade. Although strongly for war, the Lexington *Reporter* at first regretted that it was to be fought for a market rather than to free impressed seamen. Later, attacking Congress for delay, the *Reporter* combined the Indian and economic arguments for war: "The SCALPING KNIFE and

---

XII (1925–1926), 36–50, and no scholar has seriously endorsed Hacker's thesis since that time. However, neither Pratt nor those who think like him have, it would seem, sufficiently emphasized the feebleness of international boundaries as a barrier to settlement. In this connection see Marcus L. Hansen and John B. Brebner, *The Mingling of the Canadian and American Peoples* (New Haven, 1940), pp. 66–114, esp. p. 90.

[51] This argument has been very convincingly brought forward by George R. Taylor in two articles, "Agrarian Discontent in the Mississippi Valley Preceding the War of 1812," *Journal of Political Economy*, XXXIX (1931), 471–505, and "Prices in the Mississippi Valley Preceding the War of 1812," *Journal of Economic and Business History*, III (1930–1931), 148–163. Taylor is particularly careful to emphasize that these factors are only one cause, although an important one, of the War of 1812.

TOMAHAWK of *British savages, is now again devastating our frontiers. Hemp* at three dolars. *Cotton* at twelve dollars. *Tobacco* at nine shillings. Thus will our farmers, and wives and children, continue to be *ruined* and *murdered,* whilst those half-way, *quid,* execrable measures and delays preponderate." [52] The *Reporter*'s columns probably fairly accurately reflected Western feelings, placing on an almost equal level of importance the rights of seamen (and through them the nation), Indian warfare, and economic depression.

An emphasis on Western war spirit can distort the national picture. The frontiersman certainly was more volatile, more directly subject to pressure, and perhaps also more sensitive to the imperatives of honor. However, at least during the summer and fall of 1811, well after the congressional elections, feelings of frustration and even bellicosity temporarily influenced the entire nation, not merely the sparsely populated West. The *Little Belt* affair aroused all sections. Economic pressure fell upon the nation fairly generally, although not so heavily on food growers in the Middle States. South Carolina, for example, suffered seriously when the price of cotton fell by two-thirds from 1808 to 1811. During the war session her congressmen served in the front ranks of the war men, often frankly admitting that commercial motives placed them there.[53] At Boston prices fell substantially, although not so sharply as at New Orleans, and, according to Senator Smith, Baltimore's commerce was in "a deplorable situation." [54] Port towns, even in New England, became increasingly bellicose. Huge segments of Northern opinion steadily resisted the ultimate remedy, partly because they saw that war with England would not cure commercial ills, but the greatest opposition to war developed only after hostilities proved to be neither a certain nor a quick solution. In 1811–

[52] Jackson, divisional orders, March 7, 1812, Bassett, *op. cit.,* I, 222; *Reporter,* Dec. 10, 1811; March 14, 1812.
[53] Margaret K. Latimer, "South Carolina—a Protagonist of the War of 1812," *American Historical Review,* LXI (1955–1956), 914–929.
[54] Taylor, "Prices in the Mississippi Valley," p. 155; Samuel Smith to John S. Smith, June 13, 1811, Samuel Smith MSS.

1812, unlike 1808–1809, most New England Republicans stayed loyal. Finally, while the outbreak of hostilities on the Wabash most directly threatened transappalachia, virtually the entire country believed that the conflict had revealed Britain as an inveterate, jealous, intriguing enemy. The anti-British trend did not unite the East or even the South, nor was it long-lived. Temporarily, it affected the entire nation.

Thus the cry for Canada. Doubtless there were sectional reasons for urging its conquest: Westerners sought to end the Indian menace, Southerners conceivably hoped to purchase support for their Florida aims by backing war against Canada, some Northerners believed annexation would shift the center of power within the Union to the free states.[55] The central, universal theme was far simpler: strike at Canada, the most vulnerable British target, the easiest way to inflict punishment and extort concession. "The great advantage to be derived from the acquisition of these possessions," a Richmond paper declared, "will not accrue so much from the tenure of them as a conquest, . . . but from the very important consequences which their loss will occasion to the British." In Cincinnati the *Liberty Hall* warned Britain that unless she rescinded the Orders in Council and abandoned impressment (Indian intrigues were not mentioned), "the most valuable of all her colonies, will be torn from her grasp, & thus she will accelerate her own destruction." This view found steady expression in newspapers and in the halls of Congress. "What," asked a leading War Hawk in January, 1812, ". . . is the object of all our military preparations? The object has been repeatedly avowed to be to retaliate on Great Britain the injuries which she has inflicted upon

[55] On the alliance of South and West see Pratt, *Expansionists of 1812*. Pratt states but hardly emphasizes his view that the Indian menace and the South-West alliance were only a part of the entire picture, but even so the latter argument does not seem convincing, although an informal logrolling understanding may have existed. The nearest expression of a real understanding is to be found in the speech by Felix Grundy, *Annals*, 12th Cong., 1st sess., pp. 426–427. For Northern desires for Canada, see *Connecticut Courant* (Hartford), which opposed war, Jan. 15, 1812; John A. Harper (a War Hawk) to Plumer, May 13, 1812, quoted in Pratt, *Expansionists of 1812*, p. 149.

our maritime rights, by an invasion of her provinces, as the only quarter in which she is vulnerable." [56] On such a program alone could supporters of war from all parts of the nation unite.

During these months Canada and the Orders in Council received far more emphasis than impressment. Every day of the year, two or three men fell into the clutches of press gangs,[57] and yet America showed little concern. In February, 1811, Congressman Wright proposed that the United States make an end to impressment as well as to the Orders in Council a prerequisite to renewed commercial intercourse with England. Only twenty representatives supported the proposal. The Madison administration virtually ignored impressment in negotiations with Foster. The President's annual message in November, 1811, wherein there appeared a catalogue of British crimes, remained silent on the kidnaping of seamen. *Niles' Register,* one of the few to place impressment at the head of the list of American grievances, complained in the autumn of 1811 that the practice had gone on so long "the acuteness of feeling so natural on account of it, has become blunted, and our sailors have begun to make a kind of *calculation* upon it. How base and degrading! How inconsistent with our pretensions to sovereignty and independence!" Even John Quincy Adams, who believed America ultimately must fight on this issue, advised a cabinet member that "it seems clearly better to wait the effect of our increasing strength and of our adversary's more mature decay, before we undertake to abolish it by War." [58] Not until later did war men emphasize impressment.

British insults and ship seizures, even in coastal waters of the

[56] *Virginia Argus* (Richmond), Nov. 11, 1811; *Liberty Hall* (Cincinnati), Jan. 1, 1812; *Annals,* 12th Cong., 1st sess., p. 793 (Porter).

[57] The rate of impressment is very difficult to establish. James F. Zimmerman, *Impressment of American Seamen,* Columbia University Studies in History, Economics and Public Law, Vol. CXVIII, no. 1 (New York, 1925), p. 256, estimates that from 750 to 1,000 seamen a year were impressed in this period. Rufus King, however, believed that "perhaps at no former period have the impressments been less numerous." King to ———, private, Dec. 10, 1811, King MSS, Vol. XIII. For a contrary view, claiming that "the barbarous *Thefts of American Citizens* . . . have of late increased to an astonishing degree," see *Independent Chronicle,* May 27, 1811.

[58] *Niles' Register,* Nov. 2, 1811; Adams to Eustis, Oct. 26, 1811, Adams Family MSS (microfilm), Massachusetts Historical Society, Vol. CXXXV.

United States, roused far more feeling. In August, 1811, H.M.S. *Tartarus* seized two merchantmen off Norfolk. When she boldly followed this action by a visit to the American port, the British consul warned the captain, "For God-sake if you are not already gone—get to sea as fast as you can." The *Tartarus* cut her cable and scuttled out of the harbor just ahead of mob action. Later in 1811 British squadrons established virtual blockades of Chesapeake Bay and New York harbor. Rumor suggested that Admiral Yorke's squadron, reportedly dispatched to America after the *Little Belt* affair, would enforce by arms a demand for satisfaction. The few available American naval vessels put to sea to show the flag and perhaps resist British aggressions by force.[59] Although in 1811 the British seized fewer ships than in other years, captures aroused strenuous American criticism.

All these things—war on the Wabash, Foster's demands, naval arrogance, and even the temporarily overlooked continuation of impressment—seemed to show mounting British scorn for the United States. Thomas Jefferson might argue, as he did in September, that America's reputation would rise if she showed her wisdom by remaining immune from Europe's madness.[60] But more and more of his countrymen felt that only direct action could vindicate the nation's character. Of course, to disentangle honor and self-interest is often difficult, and editors and congressmen frequently cloaked material appeals in the rhetoric of honor, sovereignty, and independence. Still, materially the United States was little if any worse off than in previous years. It seems reasonable to believe that the psychological consequences of British assaults, and the accumulating embarrassment over the cowardly policy followed since 1806, were the chief influences stirring the American people in 1811.

References to national honor foreshadowed later congressional emphasis upon this valuable but intangible feeling. To a British

[59] Hamilton to Capt. John Pasco, Aug. 29, 1811, and Pasco to Admiral Sawyer, Jan. 19, 1812, both enclosed in Sawyer to Croker, Feb. 29, 1812, Admiralty Papers, Public Record Office, Adm 1/502; Graham to Monroe, Sept. 6, 1811, Monroe MSS; Paul Hamilton to Madison, Sept. 9, 17, 1811, Madison MSS.

[60] Jefferson to Eppes, Sept. 6, 1811, Jefferson MSS.

correspondent Monroe wrote, "Instead of the insults & injuries which are so constantly offered to the U States, & to their government, . . . treat us as a nation having rights, possessing passions, and much sensibility to national honor, & the result would not fail to be satisfactory." Newspapers echoed the cry. The *New-Hampshire Patriot*, for example, argued: "Things have now arrived at that crisis, that something spirited must be done, or the United States will become proverbial for servility and debasement. . . . At present we feel all the evils, without reaping any of the advantages of a war. . . . Let us at once . . . declare to the world, in the language of our fathers, that 'the States are, and of right ought to be, FREE, SOVEREIGN, and INDEPENDENT.'" At least philosophically, many Federalists agreed that independence and honor must be defended. "The Honor of a Nation is the only legitimate cause of war," declared Rufus King, but he and many other Federalists insisted that Napoleon had challenged American honor as much as Britain had.[61]

Certainly the great Corsican continued to show little respect for the United States. His policy was confusing, complex, and contradictory, partly because he wished to sow discord between Britain and America. Napoleon no longer subjected to automatic condemnation ships visited at sea by the Royal Navy. He did seize those that touched at British ports, although formal condemnation was delayed. Furthermore, as the Czar drifted toward ultimate war with Napoleon, American trade with Russia suffered as a symbol of the break between the two emperors. As soon as the ice broke up in 1811, American ships entered the Baltic to take advantage of Russia's break with the Continental System. Napoleon replied by ordering the confiscation of all American ships bound for Russia.[62] Although his Danish satellites often executed Napoleon's policy, Americans knew who deserved the blame.

Napoleon treated American trade with France almost equally

[61] Monroe to [Holland?], n.d., Monroe MSS, fol. 3145; *New-Hampshire Patriot* (Concord), Oct. 29, 1811; King to ———, private, Dec. 10, 1811, King MSS, Vol. XIII.

[62] Napoleon, Note dictated in the councils of Administration and of Commerce, April 29, 1811, AAE, CP, E-U, Vol. LXVII; Cadore #8 to Sérurier, May 16, 1811, *ibid.*, Vol. LXIV; Napoleon to Duke of Massa, Sept. 6, 1811, Léon Lecestre, ed., *Lettres Inédites de Napoléon $1^{er}$* (2 vols.; Paris, 1897), II, 159.

harshly, and his announcement that ships arriving after November, 1810, might sell their cargoes had little practical effect. The Trianon tariff and the requirement of certificates of origin signed by French consuls impaired trade. Fearing clandestine importations of British goods, Napoleon prohibited the introduction of sugar, coffee, and tobacco, with or without certificates of origin. He insisted that the Americans carry away only goods of which he had a surplus, notably silks and wines. Like the British, Napoleon issued licenses authorizing departures from his regulations. American merchants did not snap them up as he had anticipated, and the United States government complained that the licenses were an unfair condition of trade. All told, only forty-nine cargoes were admitted to French ports in the year after repeal allegedly went into effect. "It is hardly worthwhile to go to war with England for such an object," wrote Jonathan Russell.[63]

Louis Sérurier, the bland, experienced diplomat who arrived at Washington in February, 1811, to replace the vesuvian amateur, Turreau, found it impossible to soothe American sensibilities. Sérurier believed that Madison was basically pro-French, and unlike most observers he considered the President strong enough to dominate American policy. Nevertheless, first in the spring, again before Madison and Monroe left on vacation, and once more in the fall, the Frenchman received strenuous complaints from them. Without compensation for seizures prior to November, 1810, and increased freedom for trade, they told Sérurier, they could not lead the American people into more vigorous anti-British action. So strong was feeling against France that when Congress opened Augustus Foster thought his own country had a golden opportunity, by only minor concessions, to "render the whole Country cordially united with Us."[64]

[63] Napoleon, Note dictated in the councils of Administration and of Commerce, April 29, 1811, AAE, CP, E-U, Vol. LXVII; Cadore #8 to Sérurier, May 16, 1811, *ibid.*, Vol. LXIV; Montalivet, Report to the Council of Commerce, Nov. 25, 1811, quoted in Frank E. Melvin, *Napoleon's Navigation System* (Menasha, Wisc., 1919), p. 290; memorandum enclosed in Bassano #17 to Sérurier, Dec. 30, 1811, AAE, CP, E-U, Vol. LXIV; Russell to Samuel Smith, private and confidential, June 29, 1811, Samuel Smith MSS.

[64] Foster #20 to Wellesley, Nov. 5, 1811, FO 5/77. For Sérurier's opinions see his dispatches #9, #11, #14, #18-#23, #31 to Bassano, April 10-Oct. 23, 1811, AAE, CP, E-U, Vols. LXV-LXVI.

To seek amelioration of French policy and also to demonstrate to the American people his hopes for warmer relations, Madison dispatched a new minister to Paris in July, 1811. Russell had already been in charge of the legation nearly a year, and further delay in sending a minister would be harmful both with Napoleon and the American public. As early as February, 1811, Madison had chosen Joel Barlow for the post at Paris. The barrenness of Sérurier's communications delayed the envoy's departure and made Barlow himself wonder if the trip would be worthwhile. When mildly favorable news arrived from Paris, however, the President ordered Barlow to sail. His instructions recapitulated American complaints against France and warned that "much is yet to be done by her, to satisfy the just claims of this Country. To revoke blockades of boundless extent, in the present state of her marine, was making no sacrifice. She must indemnify us for past injuries and open her ports to our commerce on a fair and liberal scale." Madison and Monroe had no illusions about Napoleon's basic attitude. The man whom Barlow replaced had at least as few. He declared that ships touching at British ports continued to be excluded from the Napoleonic empire and stated also that he had no good proof the French decrees had been repealed.[65]

Gallic policy embarrassed newspapers supporting the administration. The *National Intelligencer* admitted that Napoleon continued to mistreat American commerce "in a most vexatious and unprincipled manner," but went on to argue, "still he has complied with *the letter of our law*." His municipal regulations, said editor Gales, did not affect the justice of America's claims against Britain or the propriety of nonintercourse. The *Independent Chronicle*, New England Republicanism's most effective voice, took the same position. Its editor, Benjamin Russell, admitted that Napoleon had treated the United States badly but added, pointing particularly to impressment, "the question is not which nation alone is culpable, as they are both so: The only question is, which is the

[65] Barlow to Jefferson, May 2, 1811, Jefferson MSS; Monroe to Barlow, July 26, 1811, Department of State Archives, National Archives, Instructions, All Countries, Vol. VII; Russell to John S. Smith, private and confidential, Aug. 2, 1811, Samuel Smith MSS.

*greatest* and most *iniquitous* aggressor?" [66] To Republicans, there could be but one answer.

The quarrel with France partially offset growing anger against England. On the other hand, for a people increasingly conscious of their honor, the very fact of Britain's insistence that President Madison had been duped provided a reason for not letting Franco-American relations deteriorate to the breaking point. Total paralysis and complete humiliation must be avoided. Paradoxically, the very incompleteness of Napoleonic repeal made some Americans even more insistent that the country resist British demands.

Americans of all parties shared the feeling of malaise. Was it not time, Benjamin Rush asked one of the two ex-presidents with whom he corresponded, for a third declaration of independence, to complete those of 1776 and 1800? "Lighthorse Harry" Lee, a Revolutionary hero of undoubted Federalism, wrote to Madison in August that, while he still hoped for peace between the "only two nations . . . in the world who understand the meaning of liberty," he believed that a "continuance in the present state of half war, is of all others the most debasing to the national character & nearly as injurious as war itself to individual prosperity. Take us out of the odious condition," the general pleaded, "by restoration of amity, or by drawing the sword." From London Senator Smith's son wrote that, if the United States hoped to have its rights respected, it must show a willingness to fight for them. "If we have no respect for ourselves, others will have none for us," said John Spear Smith. "We shall never write ourselves into the character and reputation our temporizing & cringing policy has lost us." [67] The chargé shared the anti-Madison bias of his father, but his comments on the policies of the President reflected a spirit that was national and even stirred James Madison himself.

Before leaving for Montpelier in July, Madison had issued a

---

[66] *National Intelligencer*, June 15, 1811; *Independent Chronicle*, May 27, 1811. Later news, showing that Napoleon had decided to admit ships arriving after November, affected the attitude of administration newspapers remarkably little.

[67] Rush to Jefferson, Aug. 26, 1811, Jefferson MSS; Lee to Madison, Aug. 19, 1811, Madison MSS; John S. Smith to Samuel Smith, Oct. 20, 1811, Samuel Smith MSS.

proclamation calling Congress into session a month before the usual date. Foster expected the new Congress to have a more respectful view of British power than its predecessors, and Sérurier had recently reported with disgust that America's spirit had evaporated when London news made it clear that Admiral Yorke had not been directed to attack the United States.[68] The last autumn of peace was a golden one, and dry roads and eager anticipation carried the new congressmen to Washington more rapidly than usual. Even John Randolph, whose attendance was as erratic as his personality, was present when Congress opened on November 4, and of all the major leaders only John C. Calhoun, whose bride expected a child, arrived after the session got under way. Of 144 members, 120, an unusually large proportion, sat in the representatives' chamber on November 5, 1811, to hear the President's third annual message. All wondered if James Madison would make his wishes known. Far to the west the Lexington *Reporter* waited with unconcealed suspicion for the message: "If a president stands as a mere stock, or block, or statue, and barely . . . refers to the documents with which he furnishes congress . . . , it is perfectly indifferent whether we have a *British agent*, a *monarchist*, or *federalist* for president. But we are *assured* . . . that the president's message will be *decisive* this year. If so, we will be decisive also." [69]

Although Madison's message satisfied the *Reporter* and was generally interpreted as a call to action, the national climate really made it so. In Britain, where the text preceded accounts of its reception, newspapers almost unanimously agreed that the President's message, while unfriendly, did not differ substantially from earlier ones. As a matter of fact, Madison himself seems to have planned to send in a more vigorous statement. His secretary of the treasury, called upon as always to comment on the draft, this time urged moderation. Gallatin's arguments mingled Republican constitutional theory, a pessimistic assessment of America's economic resources, and fear that a clear warning of war might tempt

---

[68] Foster #22 to Wellesley, Nov. 9, 1811, FO 5/77; Sérurier #28 to Minister of Foreign Relations, Sept. 18, 1811, AAE, CP, E-U, Vol. LXVI.

[69] Nov. 2, 1811.

Britain to strike first.[70] Since Madison still hoped Britain would come to her senses and offer honorable terms, and probably also because he did not want or expect war before spring, he adopted many of Gallatin's suggestions without accepting his subordinate's central thesis, that nonimportation was preferable to war.

The first half of the message [71] recounted the events of the past year: Foster's demand that "commerce should be restored to a footing that would admit the productions and manufactures of Great Britain, when owned by neutrals, into markets shut against them by her enemy"; his threats of retaliation for nonimportation; the British protest on Florida; the *Little Belt* affair. The President passed over impressment in silence, a course perfectly natural if he still hoped for a negotiated settlement but inconsistent with a determination to lead the people to high moral ground. Nor did Madison even suggest British responsibility for the Indian difficulties soon to blaze into conflict at Tippecanoe; these he blamed only on "a fanatic of the Shawanese tribe." Finally, adapting a paragraph provided by Gallatin, Madison sharply criticized French policy. This he had to do to anticipate and blunt charges of partiality, but again the effect was to dampen American ardor. Over all, the roster of insults differed very little from those provided for Congress every fall since 1805.

Nevertheless, the President recommended military preparations. England, he said, persevered in her unjust course. "With this evidence of hostile inflexibility in trampling on rights which no independent nation can relinquish, Congress will feel the duty of putting the United States into an armor and an attitude demanded by the crisis, and corresponding with the national spirit and expectations." Madison spoke equivocally of naval increases, and his suggested strengthening of commercial restriction left the way open for a lengthy dependence upon it before putting the new military machine into motion. Since military improvements had been proposed before, and since Madison carefully avoided any clear indication that he would subsequently ask for a declaration of war,

[70] Gallatin memorandum, n.d., William C. Rives Collection, Library of Congress.
[71] Richardson, *op. cit.*, I, 491–496.

the annual message of 1811 can only be considered a modest step forward. Still, the message did mark an advance. Without abandoning the opaque prose, the multifarious conditional clauses, or the wearisome commas of his earlier presidential papers, Madison had sidled in the direction of greater vigor.

Copies of the address sped to all parts of the nation—within ten hours to Philadelphia, two and a half days to Boston—and citizens set to work to parse it. Federalists and some extreme War Hawks criticized it. In perhaps the most vicious attack, the *Virginia Patriot* pronounced it an "imbecile prelude to an imbecile course . . . inadequate to bring us back to that honourable station . . . from which the head of the democratic party . . . has precipitated the nation." The *Columbian Centinel* found the message both "threatening" and "not unlike many of its predecessors," but even the *Centinel* had to admit that "if the facts respecting Mr. Foster's mission are as stated, there can hardly exist a chance for an accommodation." [72]

Although Josiah Quincy said the message disappointed congressional War Hawks, most Americans believed that it presaged a forceful, honorable policy. Even William Duane, whose *Aurora* spearheaded the anti-Madison cabal in Pennsylvania, praised it. In Boston even the Federalist prints were said to "fall four tones below their usual sound," and at Quincy old John Adams laboriously scratched out a letter to James Monroe thanking him for sending a copy of the message. Sometimes, as in the *Virginia Argus*, plaudits appeared in company with embarrassed explanations of past weakness or suggestions that a mere show of determination would cause Britain to back down. Others announced willingness to go the whole way. "In '76," declared editor Ritchie of the always bellicose Richmond *Enquirer*, "we strove for our *existence*, as a nation; and now we must strive for our *rights*, as one." The *National Intelligencer* also considered Madison's message a call for a new American jehad. No earlier message, it said, had "kindled

[72] *Virginia Patriot* (Richmond), Nov. 12, 1811; *Columbian Centinel*, Nov. 9, 1811.

a holier and brighter flame." The President had done his duty; the rest lay with Congress and the nation.[73]

Metaphorically, it would be far more apt to say that Madison's message fell upon the surface of a rising tide and was borne with it. Since the spring of 1811, after the selection of the Twelfth Congress, the American people had increasingly begun to grope for some means of redemption. It remained to be seen whether the desire for vindication would last any longer or receive more presidential encouragement than that which followed the assault upon U.S.S. *Chesapeake* four years earlier. Cynics believed not, believed that the cries of the War Hawks were insincere, that the presidential message would not lead (and was not designed to lead) to effective action. The message, one Connecticut congressman wrote a fortnight after its delivery, "sleeps quietly in the Arms of the Committees to whom it has been sent." [74]

---

[73] Quincy to Otis, Nov. 8, 1811, Harrison Gray Otis MSS, Massachusetts Historical Society; *Aurora*, Nov. 7, 1811; Levi Bartlett to Josiah Bartlett, Dec. 16, 1811, Josiah Bartlett MSS, Library of Congress; John Adams to Monroe, Dec. 19, 1811, Monroe MSS; *Virginia Argus*, Nov. 11, 1811; *Enquirer* (Richmond), Nov. 8, 1811; *National Intelligencer*, Nov. 7, 1811.

[74] Tallmadge to Frederick Wolcott, Nov. 18, 1811, Charles S. Hall, *Benjamin Tallmadge* (New York, 1943), p. 207.

# CHAPTER

# IX

## REPEAL OF THE ORDERS

In a more leisurely fashion than the War Hawk Congress two months before, Parliament convened at Westminster after the Christmas holidays of 1811. Almost immediately the Orders in Council came under heavy attack. Had this attack succeeded quickly, the fillip to America's commerce and particularly to her self-respect would have prevented a declaration of war. Ironically, Britain surrendered just a few weeks too late to preserve peace, while America, so accustomed to English obduracy that she ignored omens of concession, embarked upon war just too soon to enjoy the fruits of Britain's surrender.[1]

---

[1] The repeal of the orders is a very neglected subject. Henry Adams, *History of the United States during the Administrations of Jefferson and Madison* (9 vols.; New York, 1889–1891), VI, 267–288, discusses it, but his account is somewhat colored and he did not and could not examine a number of important sources. Very helpful recent studies, based on a wider sampling of British materials, are Reginald Horsman, "British Opinion and the United States of America, 1806–1812" (unpublished M.A. thesis, University of Birmingham, 1955), and François Crouzet, *L'Economie Britannique et le Blocus Continental* (2 vols.; Paris, 1958), II, 809–829 and *passim*. Few other students have made a real attempt to understand English developments culminating in repeal of the Orders in Council.

The movement for repeal contains other ironies. For one thing, the assassination of Spencer Perceval delayed rather than speeded repeal. For another, defense of the orders collapsed after two years during which, having ridden out heavy criticism, they seemed beyond successful attack. The depression which felled them began, not while British trade was under pressure from American restrictions, but when that trade was freest. Contemptuous scorn for American threats encouraged Englishmen to believe the danger of war fading, and a leisurely course consequently possible, at the precise moment when a last-ditch War Hawk drive carried America into war.

In 1808 and again in 1809, the Opposition had attacked the Orders in Council. In 1808 they forced Parliament to hear witnesses, and Henry Brougham and Samuel Whitbread effectively examined them. Most independent members either accepted James Stephen's argument that the trade recession had preceded rather than followed the orders, or felt that the new system should be given a more lengthy trial. In some embarrassment the Opposition dropped the issue rather than force it to a division.[2]

The next year the Opposition coupled the general issue with complaints against Canning's cavalier rejection of the American offer to suspend the Embargo. In the Lords one session lasted until three in the morning, primarily because Grenville spoke at great length about the importance of the American market and the danger of provoking the United States to war. The comments of Melville and, to an even greater degree, of Sidmouth showed that doubts about the orders had spread to uncommitted peers. When the Lords voted (proxies being counted, as they so often were in that chamber), 70 ballots were cast in favor of Grenville's motion, only 115 against. In a report to the King, Lord Liverpool professed to be satisfied. Actually, considering the ministry's usual strength, the size of the opposition vote was an astonishing shock. Lord Auckland half expected it to be followed by repeal, and

---

[2] *Journals of the House of Commons,* LXIII, 163–417 *passim; Journals of the House of Lords,* XLVI, 493–524 *passim; Morning Chronicle* (London), Feb. 22, 1808; *Hansard,* X, 1182–1183, 1304–1305; Horsman, *op. cit.,* pp. 140–145.

William Pinkney stayed away from the House of Commons' subsequent debate so that he would not seem to be gloating over ministers' discomfiture. But it was not to be. Whitbread's vitriolic opening speech, in which he accused Perceval and company of ruining British trade and seeking a war with America, probably alienated more men than it convinced. Baring, Grattan, and Lord Henry Petty spoke more moderately, and Stephen and Canning, for the government, said almost nothing that had not been said a score of times, but again the independent members hung back. After a debate lasting until breakfast time, the government won by a vote of 83 to 145.[3]

In two successive sessions the Opposition had made the Orders in Council a major item of complaint. They came close to success in 1809; Stephen even told Brougham he thought the end near for the system over which they had fought.[4] Yet final success eluded Grenville, Whitbread, and Brougham. Many M.P.'s who might otherwise have been tempted to join the Opposition felt that surrender either to Napoleon's decrees or Jefferson's Embargo would probably simply encourage further demands. Time and again ministerial speakers accused their enemies of truckling to France or to America. At a time of national crisis this was an effective debating tactic.

Primarily, parliamentary attacks failed because they did not strike fire in the country. No major London newspaper except the *Morning Chronicle*, and few outside the capital, had criticized Perceval's system. Few of Brougham's witnesses before the House of Commons in 1808 were leading businessmen, many could be accused of self-interest, and they obviously represented only a fraction of the commercial world. In London the Committee of American Merchants defeated a proposal to petition for repeal of the orders, forcing Alexander Baring to circulate one on his own. A

[3] *Hansard*, XII, 771–803; Liverpool to George III, Feb. 17 [18], 1809, Royal Archives, Windsor Castle; Auckland to Grey, March 6, 1809, Charles Grey, Second Earl Grey, MSS, The Prior's Kitchen, Durham University; Pinkney to Richard Sharp, March 5, 1809, Samuel Whitbread MSS, Southill Park, Biggleswade, Bedfordshire; *Hansard*, XII, 1159–1210.

[4] Smith to John Allen, Feb. 21, 1809, Nowell C. Smith, ed., *The Letters of Sidney Smith* (2 vols.; Oxford, 1953), I, 155.

Liverpool meeting—chaired by a government M.P. and unfairly packed, the *Morning Chronicle* charged—endorsed the orders. Colonial interests and shipowners supported the government, as the pamphleteering efforts of Nathaniel Atcheson (secretary of the Society of Shipowners), Joseph Marryat, and Lord Sheffield demonstrated. Most important of all, the great bulk of the commercial world hung back, refusing to support either side. Three years later, when businessmen at last spoke up against the orders, an early critic wrote: "I have never ceased to regret that they did not afford us their aid when we would have arrested the Evil in its Origin! Their Efforts now I fear will be too late!" [5] The comment was apt.

To stir the public both Brougham and Baring composed pamphlets attacking the Orders in Council. Baring argued that mistaken jealousy of America's prosperity, which really rewarded Britain by swelling her export market, lay behind the orders. He predicted that they would lead to a declaration of war or to commercial retaliation almost as harmful. Baring's *Inquiry into the Orders in Council* came under attack, most strenuously from Cobbett, who argued that it was not only "long and most soporific" but also a reflection of Baring's personal interest in American trade. Brougham's study, less open to these charges, was also far broader than Baring's pamphlet, for, as the subtitle declared, it was *An Examination of the Justice, Legality, and Policy of the New System of Commercial Regulations*. Both essays alarmed James Stephen,[6] and Baring's work provided the minutiae while

[5] *Times* (London), March 9, 10, 18, 1808; *Morning Chronicle*, March 18, 1808; Crouzet, *op. cit.*, I, 345–348; Nathaniel Atcheson, *American Encroachments on British Rights* (London, 1808); Joseph Marryat, *Hints to Both Parties; or Observations on the Proceedings in Parliament upon the Petitions against the Orders in Council* (London, 1808); John B. Holroyd, Earl of Sheffield, *The Orders in Council and the American Embargo Beneficial to the Political and Commercial Interests of Great Britain* (London, 1809); Mullett to Whitbread, May 4, 1812, Whitbread MSS.

[6] Alexander Baring, *An Inquiry into the Causes and Consequences of the Orders in Council; and an Examination of the Conduct of Great Britain towards the Neutral Commerce of America* (London, 1808), *passim*; *Cobbett's Political Register* (London), XIII (1808), 273–274; Henry Brougham, *Orders in Council; Or, An Examination of the Justice, Legality, and Policy of the New System of Commercial Regulations* (2d ed.; London, 1808); Stephen to Perceval, n.d., Spencer Perceval

Brougham suggested the outline for future efforts, but neither seems to have convinced many people at the time.

For the next two years the Orders in Council encountered no challenge so serious as that of 1809. The Opposition became convinced that the country could not be aroused, and, encouraged by the Embargo's collapse, the British government adopted a more flexible line toward the United States. As James Stephen put it, after repeal of the Embargo it could no longer be said that "we had a threat hanging over our heads to frighten us into the concession; the experiment had been tried, it was put in force against us, and completely failed." [7] The government felt free to issue, at the behest of Bathurst and Canning, the Order in Council of April, 1809, which most Englishmen considered a more than fair offer to the United States. Canning also opened negotiations through Erskine which resulted in an exposure of Madisonian demands so sweeping that even the Opposition did not defend them. The Orders in Council pretty much disappeared from the political scene, to be replaced by such items as the Walcheren expedition, scandal at the Horse Guards, war in the Peninsula, and, later on, the political consequences of George III's new attack of insanity.

Had the general blockade proclaimed by the order of 1809 been fully enforced, the Percevellian system would probably have escaped serious attack even longer than it did. The order professed to be "a blockade, peculiar, indeed, in its nature, but strict and rigorous in its operation, and unparalleled in its extent." [8] In its original form the new regulation met the demands of those who hoped to cripple Napoleon by cutting off vital imports. It also ended the complaints of men who argued that the complicated system, established by the orders of 1807, of licenses and fees designed to introduce British goods into the Continent was bad policy, unfair to neutrals, and illegal to boot.

The difficulty was that Perceval, Stephen, and Rose did not

MSS (examined while temporarily on deposit at the Register of National Archives, London), 33/44; Stephen to Perceval, May 23, 1808, *ibid.*, 33/16.

[7] *Hansard*, XII, 1183.

[8] Joseph Phillimore, *Reflections on the Nature and Extent of the Licence Trade* (2d ed.; London, 1811), p. 46.

wish to deprive Napoleon of all sources of supply. They merely wished to make sure that those sources should be British, or at least that the English should profit from all European importations. After learning that the new order had not mollified the United States, the British government began once again to issue special licenses. Upon application to the Board of Trade, ships and cargoes received exemption from the blockade of Europe. Theoretically, American ships were not discriminated against in the issue of licenses. In actual practice the Board of Trade found European flags far more useful and more amenable to control. Since no trade to the French Empire could be safely carried on without them, licenses were extremely valuable, worth sometimes as much as £15,000 on the open market, where they were freely traded. Disappointed merchants accused members of the Board of Trade of corruption, and in 1810 the board sought prosecution of the *Morning Chronicle* for allegedly slanderous hints that George Rose had profited from the sale of licenses.[9] The entire system combined, or seemed to combine, selfishness, discrimination, fraud, corruption, and even collusion with France.

Although others had issued licenses, the Perceval ministry was the first to make exemption from the law the rule rather than the exception. In 1808, doubling the number issued the preceding year, it authorized nearly 5,000. In 1809, despite the pause to await America's reaction to the new order, more than 15,000 licenses were issued. For the next three years, the number ranged between 15,000 and 20,000.[10] Far from being a general blockade, the new Order in Council became a screen behind which the ministry attempted to manipulate trade for its own mercantilist ends. Joseph Phillimore, a bitter enemy of the practice, summed it up when he wrote that scarcely had the orders of 1807 and 1809 been issued,

when, to their ostensible object was super-added another, utterly irreconcilable with the idea of blockade, namely, that of forcing British manufac-

[9] Board of Trade minutes, Public Record Office, Feb. 16, 1810, BT 5/21.
[10] Adam Seybert, *Statistical Annals . . . of the United States of America* (Philadelphia, 1818), p. 70n; Frank E. Melvin, *Napoleon's Navigation System* (Menasha, Wisc., 1919), pp. 330–331, 331n.

tures and British colonial produce into the ports of the Continent. . . . Thus, while, with one hand, we hermetically sealed the ports of France and Holland, against neutral commerce—with the other, we opened the same ports, by means of Licenses, to the shipping and mariners of our enemies —while we closed one door upon America, we opened another, and a wider, to Denmark, Prussia, Holland, and, even France herself.[11]

Friends of the Orders in Council joined Phillimore in criticism of the license system. As early as 1808, in a pamphlet written to defend the November orders, Joseph Marryat attacked licenses on the twin grounds that they relaxed pressure upon Napoleon and exposed merchants to "the arbitrary and variable will" of members of the Board of Trade. The *Quarterly Review* objected that licenses were dishonorable, since they granted to British traders privileges denied to Americans and other neutrals. In 1811 Phillimore devoted an entire pamphlet to the evils of this traffic,[12] and Lord Sidmouth and George Canning, opponents on virtually every other issue, both objected to it in 1812.

The license trade also strengthened American complaints against the entire British system. Because the Emperor's policy was fully as selfish and discriminatory as that of England, he too at first roused the anger of the United States. "The collusive scheme which has been hatched on the banks of the Seine and reared to maturity in the purlieus of the British Exchange . . . ," the *National Intelligencer* declared, "is a coalition for the prostration of neutral commerce." After France announced repeal of her decrees, American complaints concentrated against British licenses. In April, 1812, in an effort to stave off war, the ministry offered to abandon them. It was too late. The President's war message accused Britain of seeking "a monopoly . . . for her own commerce and navigation. She carries on a war against the lawful commerce of a friend that she may the better carry on a commerce

---

[11] Joseph Phillimore, *A Letter Addressed to a Member of the House of Commons, on the Subject of the Notice Given by Mr. Brougham, for a Motion Respecting the Orders in Council and the Licence Trade* (2d ed.; London, 1812), pp. 22–23.

[12] Marryat, *op. cit.*, pp. 38 ff.; *Quarterly Review* (London), V (1811), 461–462; Phillimore, *Reflections on the Licence Trade.*

with an enemy." [13] In effect, the license trade revived the hated Orders in Council of November, 1807, under another name.

Until the summer of 1810 the United States found it difficult to protest effectively. Napoleon's brutal treatment of American commerce, the Nonintercourse Act and Macon's Bill #2, the dreadful impression of lack of will produced by flight from the Embargo—all these virtually precluded a vigorous campaign. With a dilatoriness that irritated William Pinkney, Lord Wellesley vaguely turned aside American complaints. In August, 1810, Pinkney concluded that argument was useless in the face of "the obvious Unwillingness of this Government to touch . . . on any thing connected with . . . the System of the Orders in Council." [14]

One week later Pinkney received news of the Cadore letter from John Armstrong. On August 25, 1810, the American minister requested His Majesty's government to execute its pledge to withdraw the orders when French regulations were repealed. Hastening back from Dorking, where he had been idling on the plea of illness, Wellesley immediately entertained Pinkney at dinner. Apparently fearing that America would join the French camp, he promised prompt cabinet discussion of French repeal, nomination of a new minister within a fortnight, and settlement of the *Chesapeake* affair. Wellesley's panic—if that is what it was —failed to affect his colleagues, for none of the promises was executed. Wellesley even coolly informed Pinkney that England could not act until "the repeal of the French Decrees shall have actually taken place," or, in other words, until November 1, at which date Cadore's pledge came into operation. Although Wellesley's shift angered Pinkney, he recognized the plausibility of this argument and decided to permit the summer to pass without further protest.[15]

[13] *National Intelligencer* (Washington), Sept. 24, 1810; Castlereagh #9 to Foster, April 10, 1812, Bernard Mayo, ed., *Instructions to the British Ministers to the United States, 1791–1812,* American Historical Association, *Annual Report, 1936,* III (Washington, 1941), 364–367; James D. Richardson, ed., *A Compilation of the Messages and Papers of the Presidents* (Washington, 1897), I, 502.

[14] Pinkney to Smith, Aug. 14, 1810, Department of State Archives, National Archives, Despatches, Great Britain, unnumbered volume.

[15] Pinkney to Wellesley, Aug. 25, 1810, Foreign Office Archives, Public Record

On November 3, as soon as he received a *Moniteur* announcing the restoration of American commerce, Pinkney again demanded British repeal. A month of inconclusive jousting followed until, early in December, the Foreign Secretary asked Pinkney to present his full arguments in writing. Pinkney's long note, dated December 10, summarized the American position. Arguing that the French decision was not conditional but "absolute, precise and unequivocal," he called upon Britain to execute her promise of reciprocal repeal. Pinkney's elaborate exegesis on the Cadore letter, designed to show that French repeal did not depend on American or British action, was more ingenious than convincing; it justified Perceval's endorsement, "Surely this is sophistical or rather trifling." More forcefully, Pinkney argued that in any event the Orders in Council monstrously violated American rights, particularly since they rewarded British trade at the expense of neutrals.[16] As Wellesley no doubt intended, the note of December 10 forced the British Cabinet to make a decision. The delay since August, partly the fruit of the Foreign Secretary's own sloth, also reflected honest doubt in the Cabinet; now, the Cabinet had to make up its mind.

In the discussions, Spencer Perceval argued that French repeal was not bona fide—a contention that became the heart of Britain's position—but merely "a Notification of a Conditional Decree *at a future date*" which Napoleon might well refuse to implement. Several of Perceval's colleagues nevertheless felt that Britain should at least lessen her pressure upon neutral commerce. "How can the question of interpretation be decided," asked the Earl of

---

Office, FO 5/72; Pinkney to Smith, Aug. 29, 1810, Despatches, Great Britain, unnumbered volume; Wellesley to Pinkney, Aug. 31, 1810, enclosed in Pinkney to Smith, Sept. 3, 1810, *ibid.*; Pinkney to Smith, Sept. 24, 1810, *ibid.* In accordance with instructions from Smith, however, Pinkney presented a long note assailing Fox's Blockade and coupling it with the Orders in Council as a violation of American rights. Pinkney to Wellesley, Sept. 21, 1810, FO 5/72. Tactically, this may have been unwise, for it discouraged repeal of the orders; on the other hand, it put the American position on the record and made clear that any British repeal that omitted this blockade would leave an important issue between the two countries.

[16] Pinkney to Wellesley, Nov. 3, 1810, FO 5/72; Wellesley to Pinkney, Dec. 4, 1810, enclosed in Pinkney to Smith, Dec. 14, 1810, Despatches, Great Britain, unnumbered volume; Pinkney to Smith, Dec. 14, 1810, *ibid.*; Pinkney to Wellesley, Dec. 10, 1810, FO 5/72.

Harrowby, "but by allowing the trial to be made: i.e. by suspend-ing the execution of our orders? . . . I am . . . at a loss to find stateable grounds on which we can refuse to repeal at least our orders of Nov 1807 & April 1809. They profess'd to be retaliatory. That which oblig'd us to retaliate is done away." Lord Bathurst, too, felt that good faith as well as wise tactics required England to rescind the orders issued since November, 1807.[17]

Several ministers raised the specter of war with America. The First Lord of the Admiralty warned, "We have full employment at present for all our *money, Ships, & Troops.*" He wished to sus-pend the blockade of Europe long enough for France's real pur-pose to become clear to the Americans. Another colleague won-dered "how far we could carry the opinion of ye People . . . with us to support an American difference upon the nice reasoning whether France has repealed her decrees or not, when to a com-mon observer she seems to have done so & to have satisfied the American Government." Earl Bathurst warned that a "war with America will not readily be supported upon so cold & disputable a point." He added that "our orders, as at present executed, are . . . difficult to defend, and their effect [is] not thought to be very advantageous." Both those who wished more trade with France and those who desired none, the Earl stated, would op-pose the government if it stood on the existing system.[18]

The premier warned his compromise-minded colleagues that appeasement would probably only increase American demands. Perceval said that, while he would reluctantly consent to rescind all the orders if the Berlin and Milan decrees had really been repealed, he would not support half measures: "If we do not re-peal them in toto, we do not keep our word—and I think we may depend upon it, we shall not gain our object, if that object be to avoid the Consequences from America, which we may apprehend from not respecting them. . . . America would be much less

---

[17] Perceval memorandum, Dec. 19, 1810, Wellesley MSS, Series II (Add. MSS 37274–37318), Add. MSS 37292; Harrowby-Bathurst memorandum, [Dec. 15, 1810?], *ibid.*

[18] Yorke memorandum, Dec. 22, 1810, *ibid.*; "W" [Westmorland?] memoran-dum, n.d., *ibid.*, fol. 236; Harrowby-Bathurst memorandum, [Dec. 15, 1810?], *ibid.*

likely to go to war with us, if we appeared fearlessly & decidedly to uphold our System, than if we seemed to shrink from it in part, keeping it alive as to the remainder." Specifically, Perceval warned that Fox's Blockade and the order of January, 1807, which Bathurst hoped to use to break up intra-European trade, were integral parts of the American demands upon Britain.[19]

The Chancellor of the Exchequer had his way, and it can be argued that his success set in train the events culminating in war a year and a half later. At least four members of the Cabinet, however, supported concessions, and even Perceval admitted that it might be necessary, later on, to alter Britain's course. A full year before the Opposition's last, successful attack upon the Orders in Council and before American nonimportation began, the Cabinet's determination had weakened. Unfortunately, no hints of ministerial doubts reached the Americans. Just after Christmas Wellesley wrote Pinkney that Britain demanded less equivocal proof of French repeal. In Pinkney's opinion, the firm British note proved "what scarcely requires proof, that, if the present Government continues, *we cannot be friends with England.*" [20]

The American therefore decided to return home, leaving the legation in the hands of a chargé. Although first conceived of and nominally explained as retaliation for Britain's failure to send a replacement for Francis J. Jackson, Pinkney's withdrawal reflected his conviction that he could serve no further useful purpose at London. Nagged by illness and prodded by anger, he sent a sputtering reply to Wellesley's declaration and requested an audience of leave. The Foreign Secretary attempted to prevent Pinkney's departure by belatedly appointing Foster, but Pinkney merely replied sarcastically, "I presume that, for the Restoration of Harmony between the two Countries, the Orders in Council will be relinquished without Delay, that the Blockade of May 1806 will be annulled, that the Case of the Chesapeake will be arranged . . . , and, in general, that all such just and reasonable acts will be done

---

[19] Perceval memorandum, Dec. 19, 1810, *ibid.*
[20] Wellesley to Pinkney, Dec. 29, 1810, FO 5/72; Pinkney to Smith, Jan. 17, 1811, Despatches, Great Britain, unnumbered volume.

as are necessary to make us Friends." When Wellesley coldly replied that Foster's appointment was "not in consequence of any Change of System," Pinkney went ahead with his plans.[21] On the last day of February, 1811, he took his leave of the Prince Regent and ended his mission.

The government attempted to minimize Pinkney's withdrawal. Friendly newspapers, which ascribed it to American petulance over the vacancy in Britain's legation at Washington, argued that the appointment of Foster showed that negotiations would continue. On the day of Pinkney's audience with the Regent, Spencer Perceval told the House of Commons that "nothing in the manner in which the American minister, now about leaving this country, took his departure, . . . could give reason to any one to suppose that . . . an interruption [in negotiations] had occurred."[22] Insofar as Foster's later disputations with Monroe could be described as negotiations, this was true, but no serious discussions took place at London after Pinkney's departure.

For nearly five years, since he had first arrived to join Monroe, Pinkney had served at London. Representing feeble administrations, confronted by the granite stubbornness of a ministry that considered this quality a virtue, he could hardly be expected to argue Perceval, Canning, or Wellesley into submission. He more than held his own in disputes with them, and his notes and dispatches, when later published, helped to mobilize opinion in the United States. He seldom made a misstep, his reports were far more accurate than those of his American contemporaries at other capitals or of the British representatives at Washington, and his close association with Opposition leaders helped to inspire their campaign against the Orders in Council. During most of his stay Anglophobes attacked Pinkney for his alleged subserviency to England; at the end of his mission Federalists attacked him—one

[21] Pinkney to Wellesley, Jan. 14, 1811, FO 5/79; Wellesley to Pinkney, Feb. 15, 1811, *ibid.*; Wellesley to Pinkney, private, Feb. 15, 1811, *ibid.*; Pinkney to Wellesley, Feb. 17, 1811, *ibid.*; Wellesley to Pinkney, private, Feb. 23, 1811, *ibid.*; Pinkney to Wellesley, Feb. 23, 1811, *ibid.*

[22] *Morning Post* (London), March 1, 1811; *Sun* (London), March 1, 1811; *Hansard*, XIX, 113.

called him "our metaphysical mechanic . . . at St. James"—as a crafty intriguer, malevolently determined to bring about war with Great Britain. In actual fact, to quote a tribute by Samuel Whitbread, he was "a man of sound sense and strict integrity, and had uniformly appeared to be actuated by a sincere desire to conciliate the government of this country." [23] His conversion into a War Hawk, the product of his conviction that ordinary diplomacy could no longer hope to succeed, illuminated the ominous drift in Anglo-American relations.

Pinkney's departure failed to shock the Cabinet into any action except Foster's appointment. Those ministers who had favored compromise at the end of 1810 made no further efforts during most of 1811. The Cabinet saw that the French decrees had not really been repealed. They believed neither that Britain was obligated to repeal the Orders in Council nor that her trade with the Continent would benefit if she did so. They expected the Americans to become disgusted with Napoleon, and in any event the angry American disunity so evident to all convinced them that the United States would not act forcefully against Great Britain. Finally, Britain did not feel the impact of America's commercial restrictions until late in the spring, after Parliament adjourned, and then the ministers hoped that economic warfare would boomerang, as they thought it had done in the days of the Embargo and Nonintercourse acts.

The government therefore brushed aside parliamentary complaints. The exchange of notes between Wellesley and Pinkney, and the American's departure, failed to bring on an important debate in either chamber. In June an attack by Samuel Whitbread misfired, Perceval arguing that debate would prejudice Foster's negotiations. When the Commons discussed distresses in the manufacturing towns, only Baring stressed the importance of the lost American market. The ministry fairly easily convinced the House to let the economic cycle run its natural course.[24]

The Cabinet also permitted the condemnation of the *Fox* and

---

[23] *Annals*, 11th Cong., 3d sess., p. 1017 (Quincy); *Hansard*, XXI, 765.
[24] *Hansard*, XIX, 111–113; XX, 339–343, 431–437, 609–610.

other American vessels that had sailed for France in the autumn of 1810, expecting the Cadore letter to bring withdrawal of the Orders in Council. In May, upon learning that Congress had voted nonintercourse with England, Wellesley withdrew the objection to court proceedings which he had expressed in January. Sir William Scott, who heard the case, granted the *Fox*'s advocate a delay to produce further evidence rumored to have arrived from Paris. The justice's final decision, shot through with distrust of France and criticism of Madison, at the same time showed great reluctance to strike at American commerce. Scott declared that, while the Orders in Council could not outlive the decrees, in the absence of official notification that these had been repealed, "I think I am bound to pronounce that no such revocation has taken place, and therefore that the Orders in Council subsist in perfect justice as well as in complete authority." [25] Wellesley's original intervention, Scott's delay and then his cautious language can now be seen to indicate official misgivings. At the time, particularly when coupled with Foster's demands, the *Fox* decision appeared to close the door on American hopes opened by the Cadore letter.

Opponents of the Orders in Council refused to admit that they "subsist[ed] in perfect justice." Joseph Phillimore argued that the "Orders in Council proclaim a blockade by notification; that it is a fundamental principle of the Law of Nations that a blockade by notification alone, is irregular and null." Only the stationing of ships off blockaded ports legalized a blockade, but under the orders Britain prosecuted one not so much offshore as upon the open seas.[26] Defenders of the orders answered, as had Scott, that France had first violated the law of nations; Britain simply exercised the right of retaliation which was universally admitted to govern such situations. This right, Perceval's supporters never tired of repeating, had been most eloquently stated in the preamble to the order of January, 1807, issued by the Ministry of All the Talents.

---

[25] Christopher Robinson to Wellesley, Jan. 29, 1811, FO 83/2205; Wellesley to Robinson, May 18, 1811, *ibid.*; Thomas Edwards, ed., *Reports of Cases Argued and Determined in the High Court of Admiralty* (London, 1812), pp. 311–326.

[26] *A Letter to a Member of the House*, p. 13.

To this the Opposition had ready replies. They insisted that the doctrine of retaliation no longer applied, since Napoleon had repealed his Continental System. At the very least a decent respect for international law required Britain to test his good faith. To maintain that he had in effect reimposed his system by domestic regulations, rather than international acts, was no answer, since this was outside the law of nations.[27] It was dangerous to push too far the assertion that French repeal made obligatory the rescinding of the orders, for by the end of 1811 the incompleteness of Napoleon's repeal was fairly obvious. Thus Alexander Baring, who had previously put the issue in its simplest form, argued at the end only that "at the time America declared that France had revoked her decrees, she had fair ground for saying so, and therefore just reasons for expecting us to follow up the commencement of conciliation on the part of France."[28]

More effectively, legal critics pointed out that the orders aimed at "profit and monopoly, and not retaliation or self-defence." The Orders in Council and the ancillary license trade really closed the Continent only to Britain's commercial rivals. As William Cobbett put it, referring to two famous prize fighters whose battles titillated England, "If Belcher were to beat Mr. Perceval and Lord Liverpool in the street, Crib would not, for that reason, be justified in beating them too." America, not France, suffered most from the British system. Surely, then it was absurd to assert that the Orders in Council were justified by the right of retaliation.[29]

[27] The same argument occurred to one member of the Cabinet in the discussions of December, 1810: "I must confess, I do not see, what right, we have to complain of these severe Custom House regulations—What right America has to complain of these Custom House Regulations as any Invasion of Neutral Rights—much less that we have any reason to complain of America trading to France under these regulations, or not quarreling with France on account of this Municipal Code." "W" [Westmorland?] memorandum, n.d., Wellesley MSS, Add. MSS 37292, fol. 233.

[28] *Hansard*, XXII, 1106.

[29] *Edinburgh Review*, XIX (1812), 307; *Cobbett's Register*, XX (1811), 262. The licensing system made it even more difficult to sustain the retaliation argument. The ministry and its supporters usually evaded discussion of this flagrantly unfair and discriminatory device, but, toward the end, perhaps out of desperation, they became more frank. On March 5, 1812, the London *Courier* defiantly declared that the license trade "is an attempt, under the pressure of a war carried on by the enemy upon new, extraordinary, and extravagant principles, to prevent trade from passing out

Perceval's enemies relied most heavily upon the argument that the orders had undermined Britain's economy. Down to the summer of 1810, because England enjoyed comparative prosperity, this argument was ineffective. The best the Opposition could do was to suggest that this prosperity sprang, not from the Orders in Council, but from "the extended commercial genius of the country, from the benignant influence of our happy constitution, and the unexampled industry of our population." [30] In 1810, by sheer coincidence, at the same time that the Cadore letter opened the orders to a different sort of attack, the most painful depression since 1797 struck England. The strains of rapid industrialization and a series of bad harvests no doubt played a part in the crash, but wartime developments were more immediate causes: overspeculation in Latin American trade, the multiplication of paper money to finance the war, a great glut in warehouses and factories brought on by reduced trade with Europe. The license trade failed to relieve the pressure of oversupply, particularly after the Trianon tariff made it far less profitable, and the American consul at Liverpool accurately stated that the "distresses are more to be attributed to the difficulty of introducing goods from this Country into the ports of the Continent than to any other Cause." [31] In the precipitation of this depression, Madison's policy played no part. The crash followed the ineffective restraints of the Nonintercourse Act and coincided with the entire removal of restrictions under Macon's Bill.[32]

---

of our hands into those of other powers—to prevent America from engrossing the whole trade of Europe, while we are excluded from it. This may be called sordid and pitiful and pedlar-like. . . . But we trust we shall always have Ministers sufficiently sordid and pedlar-like to think the commerce of this country worth preserving at any rate and at any risk."

[30] *Hansard*, XV, 345–348. The quoted phrase is Grenville's.

[31] Maury to Madison, April 11, 1811, James Madison MSS, Library of Congress.

[32] This statement differs somewhat from the general theme of Frank O. Darvall, *Popular Disturbances and Public Order in Regency England* (London, 1934), which gives greatest emphasis to the lost American trade as a cause of depression and distress. As far as the initiation of the crash is concerned, timing alone seems to demonstrate that this is not so, although it is incontrovertible that American commercial pressure deepened and lengthened the depression and above all that, as in 1808 and 1809, many people considered renewed American intercourse a panacea for economic ills. For a general discussion of the factors causing depression see Crouzet, *op. cit.*, II, 615–640.

Depression gripped England for two years. Trade fell off approximately one-fourth, although the government attempted to demonstrate, by juggling already questionable customs figures, that the drop was inconsequential. To see the fallacy of this assertion, Brougham replied, "we have only to turn our eyes towards our gaols filled with debtors, our poor houses crowded with the objects of mendicity, and our midland counties, where so great is the distress, that the people are driven even to insurrection." Although food prices rose, the general price level declined sharply, as did wages. Seven thousand business firms failed, Lancashire production dropped more than 40 per cent, and at the height of the crisis more than 15,000 paupers received relief in Liverpool alone. In March and November, 1811, there were scattered popular disturbances. Then, after a brief period of calm, a whole series of riots swept the Midlands in the spring of 1812. The riots formed an effective backdrop to the more respectable protests of factory owners, who blamed the Orders in Council for the depression.[33]

American policy, which did not precipitate the depression, certainly worsened it. Since return cargoes were illegal and Britain in any event faced oversupply rather than shortage, imports from the United States declined sharply in 1811. Far more serious was the end of American purchases. In 1810 more than one-sixth of all British exports went to the United States; in 1811 America took less than 5 per cent of England's exports, all of them illegally after February. The loss represented one-half of the total decline.[34] William Cobbett declared, "The system of the Emperor Napoleon has completely succeeded. . . . [We are] *completely cut off from the continent of Europe and the United States of America.*" [35]

Amazingly, the government escaped serious attack during most of 1811. The *Caledonian Mercury* argued that, "if it appears that our trade and our maritime rights cannot exist together, a doubt must actually strike every person of reflection as to the utility of

---

[33] *Hansard*, XXI, 1101; Thomas Tooke, *A History of Prices, and of the State of the Circulation, from 1793 to 1837* (2 vols.; London, 1838), I, 330n, 357; William Smart, *Economic Annals of the Nineteenth Century* (London, 1910), I, 265.

[34] *Commons Journals*, LXVIII, 763.

[35] *Cobbett's Register*, XIX (1811), 458–459.

these maritime rights, an adherence to which necessarily leads to the ruin of our trade." No politician went that far, although in June Samuel Whitbread ascribed the depression exclusively to the Orders in Council, declaring that "all this distress was the effect of the ruinous commercial policy which had been pursued by ministers." [36] Neither the *Mercury* nor Whitbread created a stir at the time.

Until the end of the year the British position remained essentially unchanged. Jonathan Russell, who arrived from Paris in November to replace the temporary chargé left by Pinkney, recognized that any new demand for repeal would simply invite a rebuff, so he confined himself to routine business. The American consul at London reported that only a few manufacturers and the merchants trading to the United States opposed the orders, and a visiting Yankee wrote home that "little or no interest is taken in our affairs, & even the suspension of exports to our country excites very little conversation." The government, hoping for improved trade, particularly in the Baltic, and immunized to the danger of controversy with America by events of the past, preferred to wait for developments. In January, 1812, Jonathan Russell hazarded the opinion that there would be no "relaxation in the present system until some great national disaster shall drive the present ministry from power." [37]

Russell underestimated the effect of the depression, which showed no signs of abating. In the fall of 1811 and the first months of 1812, claims multiplied that the orders had caused the depression or prevented recovery through exploitation of the American market. The *Times* printed a long letter from "Philo-Pacificus" on the distresses caused by the orders, although editor Walter did not yet accept his correspondent's reasoning. A fortnight later Lord Lansdowne opened an attack in the House of Lords by asserting

[36] *Caledonian Mercury* (Edinburgh), March 2, 1811; *Hansard*, XX, 716.

[37] Russell to Monroe, private, Nov. 22, 1811, Despatches, Great Britain, Vol. XVIII; Reuben G. Beasley to Monroe, private, Sept. 27, 1811, Consular Letters, London, Vol. IX; Henry Lee to Peter Remsen, Nov. 24, 1811, Kenneth W. Porter, ed., *The Jacksons and the Lees*, Harvard Studies in Business History, Vol. II (Cambridge, 1937), p. 1000; Russell to Barlow, Jan. 14, 1812, Jonathan Russell MSS, Brown University Library.

that the Orders in Council had ruined the export trade, sacrificed an annual market of £12 million to cut off a paltry trade between America and France, and stimulated the permanently harmful growth of American manufacturing. The first of Brougham's massive assaults upon the ministry, ably backed by Baring, soon developed the same points in the House of Commons. Manufacturers' petitions, far more numerous than those presented in 1808, descended upon Parliament. A young American visitor, writing home to unconvinced, stanchly anti-Madisonian parents, reported that "it is the opinion of some of the best politicians in this country that, should the United States either persist in the Non-Intercourse Law or declare war, this country would be reduced to the lowest extremity." [38]

To meet their critics, government supporters put forward several arguments. There was the familiar assertion that repeal of the orders would cripple the already depressed shipping interest.[39] There was the announced belief that America was utterly dependent upon British manufactures. One member of Parliament scornfully proclaimed: "As for America, she could not do without Birmingham—she could not even shave herself, or catch her mice without their aid." The Board of Trade officially reported that stories of increasing American manufactures were probably propaganda to frighten England into concession.[40]

Taking full advantage of incomplete and often contradictory statistics, governmentalists also argued that the recession was at worst a very mild one, that it had no connection with the American market, or that commercial famine hurt America far more than Britain. "If the measures which she had thought proper to adopt

[38] *Times*, Feb. 13, 1812; *Hansard*, XXI, 1043–1045, 1092–1116, 1126–1131; Morse to Jedediah Morse, March 25, 1812, Edward L. Morse, ed., *Samuel F. B. Morse, His Letters and Journals* (2 vols.; Cambridge, 1914), I, 67.

[39] John W. Croker, *A Key to the Orders in Council* (London, 1812), p. 17: "The British shipping interest would be annihilated, and that of America would rise up in its stead."

[40] *Hansard*, XXII, 431; Board of Trade minutes, Jan. 16, 1812, BT 5/21. To the taunt a Boston paper replied: "If America cannot shave *herself*, she can *shave old England*, as the battles of Bunker-Hill, Saratoga, &c. plainly evince:—And as to *mousing*, we ask, who manufactured the *mouse-traps* in which BURGOYNE and CORNWALLIS were 'taken?'" *Independent Chronicle* (Boston), May 25, 1812.

were injurious to us," declaimed George Rose, "what were they less than ruinous to her? . . . America . . . must be suffering in her resources in every direction." As late as April, 1812, Lord Liverpool asserted, "The Distress in the Commercial Districts of this Country . . . arises from temporary and incidental Causes." [41] Mounting attacks and continued depression ultimately made a mockery of these defenses of government policy.

Early in 1812 news of the War Hawk Congress began to arrive in England. Since as early as 1808 the Opposition had warned against "add[ing] America to the long and formidable catalogue of our enemies." Few took this danger seriously until 1812. American news, particularly the Foreign Affairs Committee's report, allowed the Opposition to emphasize this fear. In the Lords Auckland declared that, even if his other arguments could be ignored, the danger of war made repeal imperative, for "as to the horrible idea of going to war . . . , he could not for one moment entertain it, or suppose that their lordships would consent to continue the Orders in Council, if they should be proved to lead to that unfortunate consequence." In the other house Whitbread raised the question in even more forceful language:

War with America . . . would be a great evil: and war once commenced, no man could tell what might follow. It was an easy thing to talk and write of putting down America, of inflicting chastisement, &c. as if it was in the power of England to annihilate her: we might talk this well, but we could not put America down. She was there where we had placed her; it was not in the power of England to annihilate her, and it was therefore the interest of England to be her friend.[42]

In January, 1812, the *Morning Chronicle* warned that, by diverting the Royal Navy, an American war would give Napoleon a chance to rebuild his naval power, while the dispatch of British troops to Canada would weaken efforts in Spain and elsewhere. The *Times*, whose shift from support of the orders to a middle

[41] *Hansard*, XXII, 1102; Liverpool to Wellington, private, April 28, 1812, MSS of the first and second Earls of Liverpool, British Museum (Add. MSS 38190–38489, 38564–38581), Add. MSS 38236.
[42] *Hansard*, X, 312; XXI, 1066, 770.

position hinted at a drift among political independents, declared at the same time: "The aspect is, in truth, most threatening; as every measure tending to war has been carried by a large majority." The paper went on to report Congressman Porter's call for an invasion of Canada, commenting, "We are far from making mockery of these efforts." [43]

James Stephen declared that if war came it would be the fault of America and not of Britain. One backbencher argued that the only honorable way to meet the war threat was to issue a declaration in advance of an American one. More effectively, defenders of the orders asserted that the United States was, as usual, merely bluffing. The American consul at London, looking back some months later, observed that "there existed among the people two opinions . . . , the one, that we never intended to go to war, and the other, that our Government, if so inclined, would not hazard it on account of the opposition it would meet with from the Eastern States." Many maintained this position until the very end. Even as Congress debated Madison's war message, a die-hard newspaper scoffed, "We have so often been threatened and then forgiven . . . by the American democratics, that we have our doubts whether they are really in earnest even on the present occasion." Wiser heads shared the feelings of William Wilberforce, a wavering supporter of the government, who pointed out the dangers of acting on this hypothesis: "It may be so; but nine times out of ten it is a game of brag, wherein each party depends upon the giving way of the other, or would not himself push on so warmly." [44]

The fear of war fluctuated rather than accumulated. It was very pronounced in January and early February, and this perhaps explains the comparative moderation of the speech from the throne as well as the strong Opposition emphasis at that time. On the other hand, some members of Parliament felt obligated to support the government at a moment of crisis. When Samuel Whit-

[43] *Morning Chronicle*, Jan. 27, 1812; *Times*, Jan. 28, 1812.

[44] *Hansard*, XXI, 773, 782; Beasley to Monroe, June 15, 1812, Consular Letters, London, Vol. IX; *Star* (London), June 5, 1812; Robert I. Wilberforce and Samuel Wilberforce, *The Life of William Wilberforce*, IV (2d ed.; London, 1839), 5.

bread sought a full-dress debate on British policy on February 13, the government replied that this would only encourage American bellicosity. Spencer Perceval declared that the government, while "alive to all the advantages of reconciliation with America," could not allow Britain's essential maritime rights to be called into question. Whitbread secured only twenty-three votes.[45]

From February until May, war fears diminished as a result of contradictory news from America. Success of the call for a committee to examine the effect of the Orders in Council owed very little to a war scare, being based almost solely on the hardships of depression. As a matter of prudence the government ordered three regiments to Canada, but the War Office directed its Canadian commander to return two of them for more urgent service elsewhere if, as expected, the war threat evaporated. Late in February an American representative at London wrote that "the general opinion [is] that we do not mean to go to war, notwithstanding all our preparation; and the idea of our taking Canada is laughed at." Another reported, "I cannot perceive the slightest indication of an apprehension of a rupture." [46]

Toward the end, after the fate of the orders had really been settled, reports of renewed American activity stirred England once again. On May 9 the Foreign Office sent a tentative war warning to the Admiralty. In June ominous reports from Foster helped to precipitate a hasty notification of repeal. Still, the danger of permanent loss of the American market, far more than any fear of the military and naval consequences of a war, brought this about. Although Henry Adams declared that "the danger . . . of an American war caused the sudden . . . surrender," [47] it is as certain as such things can be that the British feared war only insofar as it threatened to extend and perhaps make stronger the commercial pressure that had already deepened the depression. In a direct sense, the antics of the War Hawk Congress did little more

[45] *Hansard*, XXI, 762–801.

[46] Liverpool #10 to Prevost, April 2, 1812, Colonial Office Records, Public Record Office, CO 43/23; Beasley to Monroe, Feb. 28, 1812, Consular Letters, London, Vol. IX; Russell to Monroe, private, March 20, 1812, Russell MSS.

[47] *Op. cit.*, VI, 286.

than help to inspire the beginning, in January, of the final attack upon the orders.

The new Parliament opened with political developments that first threatened and then seemed to strengthen the position of the orders. In January Lord Wellesley, who really hoped either to be given a stronger position by Perceval or to form a new ministry around his own person, offered his resignation. The Prince of Wales, regent since 1811 but only just invested with full powers, opened negotiations with Grenville and Grey, and it appeared that the entire Percevellian structure would collapse. The Opposition leaders declined the Regent's offers, however, and no parliamentary combination emerged. After a good deal of vacillation the Prince came to the aid of ministers with whom he had quarreled for years. "The Prince Regent," he sanctimoniously declared, "is the last person in the Kingdom to whom it can be permitted to dispair of his Royal father's recovery," and it ill behooved a loyal son to create a situation in which, upon regaining health, George III would discover the government in the hands of men he detested.[48] The Prince Regent's declaration astounded political observers, since his filial piety had been far less notable than his hatred of Perceval. It nevertheless encouraged the ministry to attempt to carry on with the aid of royal support.

In the shuffling of offices that ensued, Viscount Castlereagh received the Foreign Office. Although a notable failure at the War Office from 1807 to 1809, Castlereagh wanted to return to it. But for Liverpool's unwillingness to change offices, the opening of the greatest foreign-secretaryship in British history would at least have been delayed. In 1812 Castlereagh seemed at best an assiduous, unemotional, loyal politician; he had shown no signs of imagination, and the *Times* noted that "his name, above all others, is noted for mischance: he has been the very darling of misfortune." Castlereagh's appointment was soon followed by greater attention to American affairs, more mildness in language and even in policy, but no evidence that he had a liberal concept of Anglo-American

---

[48] Prince Regent to Ministers, [Feb. 13, 1812], Arthur Aspinall, ed., *The Letters of King George IV*, I (Cambridge, Eng., 1938), 5–6.

relations. Castlereagh's colorless mien and Perceval's continuation in power led Jonathan Russell to conclude: "The successor of Lord Wellesley will follow whithersoever Mr. Perceval may lead. . . . Whatever uncertainty might have hitherto enveloped the designs of this government . . . no longer exists—its course is now distinctly marked out—nor," added Russell, now as angry as Pinkney had been, "can ours well remain doubtful." [49]

The state of the Opposition also discouraged hope. Except for Henry Brougham, the attacking forces were almost an army without generals. Lord Grenville, pessimistic about the prospects of success, enjoyed retirement at Boconnoc too much to stir from Cornwall. Illness often prevented Lord Auckland, probably the best informed on Anglo-American trade, from contributing more than his proxy in the House of Lords. Grey and Erskine gave scarcely more help. In the Commons, although Stephen Ponsonby nominally led the Opposition, Brougham depended chiefly upon the support of Alexander Baring and Samuel Whitbread, one a young banker married to an American and the other a parvenu brewer. Neither was the sort of person likely to influence the House of that day, and even members of the Opposition distrusted Whitbread. When, in February, 1812, he moved for papers on American relations, the Speaker privately noted with satisfaction that "neither Ponsonby, Tierney, nor any of the Grenvilles attended to support Whitbread." [50] Opposition rivalries forced Brougham to carry the parliamentary load almost alone. [51]

[49] *Ibid.*, I, 19n; Charles K. Webster, *The Foreign Policy of Castlereagh, 1815–1822* (London, 1925), Introduction *passim; Times,* May 19, 1812; Russell to Monroe, private, Feb. 19, 1812, Despatches, Great Britain, Vol. XVIII.

[50] Charles Abbot, Lord Colchester, ed., *The Diary and Correspondence of Charles Abbot, Lord Colchester* (3 vols.; London, 1861), II, 369. Ponsonby warned Whitbread in advance that he would not be present. Ponsonby to Whitbread, Feb. 13, 1812, Whitbread MSS. Wellesley, on the other hand, believed that Foster's correspondence should be presented to Parliament in order to unite the country and thus discourage an American declaration of war. Perceval defied the recommendation of his outgoing foreign secretary. Wellesley to Perceval, private, Feb. 6, 1812, Perceval MSS, 1/58.

[51] Had he so desired, the Prince Regent could have made Brougham's task much easier. There is some reason to believe that the Regent favored a conciliatory policy toward America. At an unusual private reception of the newly arrived chargé, the Prince listened carefully to an explanation of American policy and commented to Wellesley, who was present, in a fashion that implied at least partial acceptance of

Fortunately, Brougham received great support outside the House, particularly from businessmen whose voices commanded the respect of independent members. Earlier, Baring had correctly observed that "the great interest in American intercourse is with manufacturers scattered over the whole country, . . . who are never able to act as a body with a weight corresponding to their importance." [52] In 1812 the intensity of the depression and the alluring nostrum of an American market for once united businessmen. They swamped Parliament with petitions signed by thousands although some of them, including Josiah Wedgwood, insisted that laborers not be allowed to join the protests. From the Midlands, the North, from ports trading with America, petitions descended upon London, overwhelming less broadly supported counterpetitions from rival groups at Glasgow and Liverpool. When the House of Commons held hearings on these representations, 150 witnesses appeared, almost all of them businessmen. Twenty-two Birmingham men testified, principally metal goods manufacturers. Three Sheffield steel and cutlery makers, leading potters (including Wedgwood), cotton and woolen magnates, and commission merchants all appeared before the House. Of the major business areas only London was sparsely represented (by two merchants, an insurance man, and three silkmakers); neither Baring nor Thomas Mullett, a regular correspondent of Whitbread's and a steady advocate of repeal, testified. They were scarcely missed. The witnesses that did appear made an impressive case. The testimony is full of such passages as, "Has had nine ships . . . at one time. Now has not one; but is satisfied, that if the Orders in Council were repealed, he should have a great many," or, "Has Orders from America for the whole of his goods, provided the Orders in Council were rescinded." [53]

Russell's argument that the French had really repealed the Berlin and Milan decrees. In March a close friend of the Prince reportedly told Lord Grey that His Royal Highness favored concession. But there is no evidence, in his own papers or those of his ministers, that the Regent ever intervened to support the movement for repeal. Russell to Monroe, private, Jan. 25, March 20, 1812, Despatches, Great Britain, Vol. XVIII.

[52] *Op. cit.*, pp. 4–5.
[53] *Hansard*, XXII, 1, 245–246, 424–427, 500–501, 1059–1062; XXIII, 164–165,

From the press, too, Brougham gathered support. In 1812 only one pamphlet (and that by an Admiralty official) appeared in defense of the orders. Opponents published at least six. One, by Phillimore, argued that Britain should encourage American trade with the Continent as a means of introducing her own manufactures. Two lengthy efforts by George Joy, the son of a Tory *émigré* from Boston, endorsed American claims unreservedly, vindicated Jefferson and Madison from charges of sympathy for France, and warned Britons against a vain hope that the Federalists would gain power and alter major outlines of American policy. A fourth pamphlet closed with the eloquent plea, "Sirs ye are brethren: why do ye wrong one to another?" [54]

Magazines and newspapers added their voices. The *Edinburgh Review* of course remained a sturdy opponent of the orders. The *Monthly Review*, albeit not until May, came to support repeal. The *Annual Register*, in a volume appearing early in 1812, warned that the United States "already exert a powerful influence upon our commercial prosperity" and argued that fair treatment of America by one belligerent would focus hostility upon the other. Newspapers in port towns trading with America, notably the *Caledonian Mercury* and the Liverpool *Mercury*, urged repeal. The London *Globe* steadily attacked Perceval's "ruinous policy," but as early as January it gloomed, "The best friends of both countries consider the die as cast, and that sufficient time would not be allowed to avert the blow." Almost every issue of the *Morning*

---

220–221, 232–236; *Journals of the House of Commons*, LXVII, 348–349, 372, 390, 412, 427; *Minutes of Evidence Taken before the Committee of the Whole House, to Whom It Was Referred to Consider of the Several Petitions Which Have Been Presented to the House, in this Session of Parliament, Relating to the Orders in Council* (London, 1812), *passim*; *An Abstract of the Evidence Lately Taken in the House of Commons, Against the Orders in Council* (London, 1812), *passim*. Quotations are from the *Abstract*, pp. 43, 15.

[54] Croker, *op. cit.*; Phillimore, *A Letter to a Member of the House*; George Joy, *The American Question* (London, 1812); George Joy, *Dispute with America; War without Disguise; Or, Brief Considerations on the Political and Commercial Relations of Great Britain and Ireland, with the United States of America* (Liverpool, 1812). See also reviews of *The Crisis of the Dispute with America* and *Conciliation with America the True Policy of Great Britain* in *Edinburgh Review*, XIX, 290–317, and *Monthly Review; or Literary Journal* (London), LVIII (1812), 59–74.

*Chronicle,* the most influential newspaper urging abandonment of the orders, carried an article upon relations with America, and the *Chronicle* had a large circulation, much of it outside London.

So too did *Cobbett's Political Register,* and unlike the *Chronicle* Cobbett could not be accused of merely accepting the Opposition's lead. Until the end of 1810 Cobbett vehemently attacked the United States. He then reversed himself and began an equally violent attack upon the British government and its commercial system. In February, 1812, he demanded not only repeal of the orders but also an end to impressment. When the orders were withdrawn, Cobbett concentrated his fire on impressment, and after war began he wrote, "The grievance . . . is certainly very great, and cannot be expected to be borne by any nation capable of resistance." [55] Cobbett was almost always long-winded and sometimes viciously unfair. However, his wide circulation, like that of the *Chronicle,* ensured diffusion of the arguments against the orders throughout the British Isles.

An overwhelming majority of businessmen, a representative portion of the press, and a solid Opposition bloc thus opposed the Orders in Council. This did not reflect any particular love of America, although Russell exaggerated when he wrote, "We are really unpopular in this country & in case of a rupture shall have much fewer friends than in '75." Cobbett came nearer to the truth when he declared, "Nothing, I am convinced, will ever make an American war popular in England." [56] While a feeling of kinship and memory of the costs of the American Revolution doubtless impressed many Britons, the central concern of all those who took America's part was the loss of the export trade.

Perceval's enemies faced formidable obstacles. Conciliation could be pictured as abject surrender to an upstart republic and the betrayal of cherished maritime principles, and defenders of the orders made the most of these arguments. The London *Courier*

[55] *Annual Register, 1811* (London, 1812), p. 49; *Globe* (London), Jan. 27, 1812; *Cobbett's Register,* XXI (1812), 65–77.

[56] Russell to Barlow, Feb. 26, 1812, War of 1812 Papers, William L. Clements Library, Ann Arbor; *Cobbett's Register,* XXII (1812), 107.

regularly scoffed at the chances of an American war—"we hardly think she will be mad enough to risk it"—and defended the orders even after the government had given them up, deprecating this "sacrifice of a great national right" on the ground that a "yielding policy is never wise, no, not even, with a mere view to commercial gain, a profitable policy." [57] The *Sun,* another leading metropolitan paper, the *Quarterly Review,* and the *Gentleman's Magazine* spoke much the same language. Two other important organs, usually on the side of the government, were somewhat less bellicose. The *Star* exhibited doubts from the beginning, and, when the Americans presented new evidence in May, 1812, that Napoleon had given up his decrees, the paper became an advocate of appeasement. The *Times,* which generally backed the ministry, increasingly criticized the license trade and particularly the government's claim that the orders could not be lifted, even for American commerce alone, until Napoleon freely admitted British commerce. Thus there were serious differences of opinion even among those who usually supported the administration. As early as January, 1812, Cobbett thought he saw evidence that the *Courier* and the *Times* were preparing the way for flight from the Orders in Council. [58]

The ministry received firmer support from the shipping and West India interests, inveterate enemies of a liberal policy toward America, and from traders with the Peninsula and some other parts of Europe. Four large groups of shipowners, one from London, petitioned Parliament, and four owners appeared as witnesses in favor of the orders. Among them was John Gladstone (father of William), soon Canning's sponsor in a successful challenge for Brougham's seat in Liverpool. Another witness was Joseph Marryat, the pamphleteering defender of the orders, who spoke at this time for the West India traders. For the parliamentary hearings, however, the ministry could find, aside from a small group of Londoners, only four Liverpudlians and one Glaswegian to sup-

[57] March 5, June 17, 1812.
[58] *Cobbett's Register,* XXII, 107.

port its cause. Not a single manufacturer testified in favor of the orders.[59] Although Parliament had a habitual sympathy for colonialists and especially the merchant marine, successful defense of the orders required far broader support among the nation's business leaders.

If the parliamentary Opposition suffered from internal weaknesses, so too did the government. Bathurst, like some of his colleagues, had secret doubts about the wisdom of maintaining the orders. In the House of Commons Perceval's chief support came from James Stephen, George Rose, and, after Wellesley resigned, Lord Castlereagh. Stephen, spiritual father of the orders he defended "with a firmness that amounted to obstinacy," [60] was a choleric, rambling, ineffective debater. Rose aroused mistrust as one of the most notorious place- and profit-hunters in England, and Castlereagh as yet had no important parliamentary following. In addition, two important figures, Wilberforce and Canning, veered toward the Opposition camp in the early months of 1812. Although outright defeat was unlikely, Perceval occupied an unhappy position.

The session's only pitched battle on the Orders in Council (and the first on this subject since 1809) took place on March 3, 1812. Henry Brougham had given notice that he intended to move, that day, for an investigation of the Orders in Council and the license trade. The whole parliamentary world recognized the importance of the occasion, and absent members flocked to Westminster; Coke of Norfolk traveled up from Holkham and another M.P. abandoned the pleasures of Shropshire hunting for the combat at St. Stephen's. Actually, aside from "a long declamatory speech of very loud tone" by Brougham and another by Canning, eagerly awaited since he had helped frame the orders, the speeches were not particularly interesting, although more than 350 M.P.'s sat through the night to hear them.

Brougham alluded briefly to a war with America, "the last of

---

[59] *Hansard*, XXIII, 202–205, 238–239; *Minutes of Evidence, passim.*
[60] Henry Brougham, *The Life and Times of Henry Lord Brougham* (2 vols.; Edinburgh, 1871), II, 5.

disasters," toward which the Cabinet's "mean and profligate policy" was propelling the country. In general, he and Baring, his principal supporter, preferred to emphasize the depressed state of trade. They blamed this on the Orders in Council and the license trade, and they attacked the shift from commercial retaliation against France to an attempt to secure European trade at the expense of America as unwise, economically harmful, and unjust. Perceval, Stephen, and Rose replied that the depression could not be blamed on the orders, since these had first been followed by three years of economic improvement. They also defended their system as a legitimate and proper effective exercise of the right of retaliation, but at the same time they were drawn into a perhaps too-frank exposition of their attempts to favor British commerce at America's expense. Both sides quoted freely from customs reports and tonnage figures, which hardly enlivened the debate. Attempting to revitalize the Opposition, Samuel Whitbread closed the debate with an emotional harangue, but his jaw ached and the speech lacked his usual force.

Midway through the night George Canning gave the debate its moment of drama. He assailed the government for transforming the Orders in Council from a blockade into "a measure of commercial rivalry." The former Foreign Secretary declared "he was for giving the Orders in Council a full, unlimited, unmitigated vigor of operation, restoring them to their first spirit. . . . They were most perfect as they approached towards a belligerent measure, and receded from a commercial one." Supporters of the ministry considered this a disingenuous excuse for opposition actually inspired by pique at Castlereagh's advance. Still, the speech was in character, for in 1809 Canning had urged a rigorous general blockade and had played no part in its later relaxation through licenses. Some ministerial backbenchers growled "hear! hear!" at Canning's calls for vigor and directness, but few joined their former colleague in supporting Brougham's motion.[61]

<hr />

[61] *Hansard,* XXI, 1092–1164; diary entry, March 3, 1812, Edmund Phipps, *Memoirs of the Political and Literary Life of Robert Plumer Ward, Esq.* (2 vols.; London, 1850), I, 445–450. Brougham considered American military strength so

At half past four in the morning the legislators wearily filed past the Speaker's chair into the division lobbies. One hundred and forty-four members supported Brougham, 216 opposed him. Although some considered the result a government victory, Brougham himself was encouraged by his showing. He urged businessmen to redouble their pressure upon Parliament, confident a majority could be brought to demand repeal and prevent "a rupture with our best customers and most natural, the free and English people of America." Brougham's vision was sure. The ministry won this battle primarily by mobilizing country members who would not stay throughout the session. Many supporters, particularly merchants sitting in the House, could not be counted upon to remain loyal much longer. Canning's defection cost the Cabinet only about a dozen votes, and the Prince Regent's friends (except Sheridan, who ostentatiously absented himself) backed the administration. But the Melville and Sidmouth factions joined with the Opposition, and Wilberforce and his coterie deserted their fellow Saints, Perceval and Stephen. A small group headed by General Gascoyne, Brougham's colleague from Liverpool, formerly an earnest defender of the orders, showed the effect of commercial pressure by voting for the motion.[62] For the first time the Orders in Council aroused deep concern among floating members of the House of Commons.

To strengthen his parliamentary defenses Perceval brought Viscount Sidmouth into his Cabinet. Sidmouth, who made agreement on maritime policy a condition of union with the government, insisted upon termination of the license trade. Perceval agreed, both to silence parliamentary enemies and to conciliate America.

---

unimportant that he even argued that a Franco-American war would not serve British interests. He believed that the opportunities for evasion of the Continental System through use of American ships were far more important than any military contribution the United States could make.

[62] George Eden to Auckland, March 4, 1812, William Eden, Baron Auckland, MSS, British Museum (Add. MSS 34412–34471, 45728–45730), Add. MSS 34458; Russell to Monroe, private, March 4, 1812, Despatches, Great Britain, Vol. XVIII; diary entries, March 3, 4, 1812, Phipps, *op. cit.*, I, 449–451; Brougham to J. Walker, March 6, 1812, Brougham, *Life and Times of Henry Brougham*, II, 8–11; Brougham to ——— Thorneley, March 4, 1812, *ibid.*, II, 12–13; Hansard, XXI, 1163–1164.

If we "offer to America the renunciation of our Licenses," he wrote, "undoubtedly we shall appear to be making, as we shall undoubtedly be making a greater sacrifice for accommodation, than if these Licenses had never been granted." Sidmouth did not reply to the suggestion that the more violent the crime, the more credit one would get when ceasing it, but he and his friend Vansittart agreed to join the government. On April 10 Castlereagh sent new instructions to Foster. After lamely defending the use of licenses in the past, these instructions offered to abandon them if the United States would reopen trade with Great Britain.[63] Considering the strength of Perceval's desire to monopolize European trade, he had made a significant surrender, although far too late to assuage the Americans.

A week later the Cabinet made another gesture that misfired. On April 21 the ministers issued a formal statement of policy. This declaration reviewed events since the Cadore letter, argued that France sought simply to trick the United States, and stated that the orders would continue until Britain received an unambiguous statement of French repeal. In London and in America people assumed the ministry had decided to stand on the Orders in Council, and this declaration played a decisive part in the American decision for war. Perceval's reputation for inflexibility had served his country ill. The declaration really sought to convince domestic opponents and Americans, if they remained reasonable, that refusal to repeal the orders had been forced upon Britain by French policy. The whole paper was shot through with virtual pleas to France to provide a plausible excuse for withdrawal of the orders.[64]

The camouflage soon fell away from the government's retreat.

[63] Perceval to Sidmouth, March 15, 1812, First Viscount Sidmouth MSS, County Record Office, Exeter, Devon; Sidmouth to Perceval, March 15, 1812, *ibid.*; Castlereagh #9 to Foster, April 10, 1812, Mayo, *op. cit.*, pp. 363–367. Perceval had little hope that this step would conciliate the Americans, although he considered it worth trying and, from a domestic point of view, necessary. Perceval memorandum, n.d., Perceval MSS, A/13. Sidmouth, on the other hand, expected the United States to be assuaged, and he was one of the few prominent politicians in England (Willberforce was sometimes another) who took the war threat seriously.

[64] Enclosure in Castlereagh to Foster, April 21, 1812, Mayo, *op. cit.*, p. 372n. *Hansard*, XXII, 853–856, prints the wrong proclamation at this point.

The Cabinet postponed a debate on the orders in the House of Lords, and Grenville heard rumors of angry disputes among ministers and between the Cabinet and the Regent.[65] Then, on April 28, the government, which had so ferociously resisted the same suggestion in March, declined to oppose a new call for a committee. George Rose, who announced the decision, and James Stephen declared that they expected the committee to find no evidence against the orders. Stephen caustically stated that "if the yellow fever raged in the country, and it was the belief of many persons that it proceeded from the Orders in Council, he would consent that the subject should be examined, merely for the sake of removing the false impression." Perceval half admitted that there might be substance in his opponents' arguments: "Supposing . . . that it were proved that the distresses complained of were in some degree, or altogether, occasioned by the Orders in Council, it would still remain a question for parliament to decide, whether, weighing the disadvantages against the benefits, they should be abandoned." The premier added, in a show of strength, that acceptance of a committee by no means meant he was committed to repeal. Nevertheless, the government could not conceal that it had been forced to give way, and it had no answer to the taunts with which Tierney greeted the announcement.[66]

In both houses of Parliament witnesses appeared before committees of the whole. In the Commons, working in relays for as many as eight hours at a time, Brougham and Baring examined friendly witnesses; James Stephen cross-examined them and presented a few shipowners and colonialists in rebuttal. Although it lasted for weeks, the testimony added little that was new, serving chiefly to emphasize the business community's conviction that only repeal of the orders and recovery of the American market would end the depression. For the first time, as a result of the impression the hearings conveyed, Jonathan Russell allowed himself to be hopeful. "In my intercourse with men both in & out of power since

[65] Grenville to Thomas Grenville, April 22, 1812, Thomas Grenville MSS, British Museum (Add. MSS 41851–41859), Add. MSS 41853.
[66] *Hansard*, XXII, 1092–1112.

my arrival here," he wrote, "I think I have witnessed a gradual softening of temper towards us and a less & less disposition to proceed to extremities. It is the increasing want of our intercourse, however, more than an apprehension of our aims, that leads to this conciliatory spirit." Russell did not yet risk a direct prediction that the orders would be repealed, at least so long as Perceval remained in power.[67]

On May 11 administrative business kept Spencer Perceval away from Commons until late in the day. Shortly after five, hurrying to hearings already well under way, he entered the lobby of the House alone. James Bellingham, who conceived himself to have been mistreated by the ministry, stepped forward and fired a pistol at point-blank range. Perceval died instantly. Chaos ensued as lords and commoners, in scenes reminiscent of the Gunpowder Plot, raced through corridors, examined closets, and seized arms to defend themselves against further attack. Not for some time did it become apparent that Perceval's murder was the solitary act of a man with a deranged mind.

The drama of Perceval's death and his extreme "Englishness" provoked lachrymose sentiments among his peers, although in some cities the lower classes cheered his demise. Parliament voted pensions to his widow and his covey of children, and even Samuel Whitbread stepped out of character to deliver a graceful eulogy. "I confess," Lord Grenville dourly wrote, "I am a little sick of the Apotheosis of a man whom I believe to have been a very good, moral, & charitable man in private life, but as factious a partisan in opposition, & as bad a Minister in Government as the Country ever saw."[68] Strongly partisan Perceval certainly was, an able, determined, indefatigable, dedicated politician of narrow views. He had held the Cabinet together through the war's gloomiest years despite failures, the opposition of distinguished men, and internecine quarrels which would have led a more pessimistic, less tenacious man (like Grenville himself) to despair. Perceval died

[67] Russell to Monroe, private and confidential, May 9, 1812, Despatches, Great Britain, Vol. XVIII.
[68] Grenville to Thomas Grenville, May 15, 1812, Thomas Grenville MSS, Add. MSS 41852.

just as the success of Wellington and the prospect of Franco-Russian conflict lightened the English skies. Unfortunately, confirmed in his prejudices by his friend Stephen, he followed a disdainful policy toward America for too long, and war quickly followed his death.

Bellingham's pistol shot caused a ministerial crisis that lasted for a month. Offices, Catholic policy, and military strategy formed far more important items of discussion than the Orders in Council and American affairs only because all apparently recognized the inevitability of repeal. Intensive negotiations between Perceval's survivors on the one hand and Wellesley and Canning on the other revealed no disagreements on American policy. Grenville and Grey, who virtually threw away a chance to return to power because of their own lassitude, pessimism, and desire for revenge on their former friend, the Regent, had long planned to make repeal one of their first acts. Lord Moira, a personal friend of the Prince who received a commission to form a government, counted withdrawal of the Orders in Council among the chief items in his proposed program. Neither Wellesley, the Opposition, nor Moira found it possible to patch together a parliamentary majority, and on June 8 the Prince Regent formally reinstalled the remnants of Perceval's ministry under the leadership of the Earl of Liverpool. This result, the least expected of all (except by Lord Grey, who steadily forecast it), aroused derision. Even Liverpool had scant hope that the Cabinet would be able to maintain itself. Actually, he was beginning the longest uninterrupted premiership in British history since Walpole. Although Canning rejected extremely generous offers made him in the summer of 1812, the government's parliamentary position steadily improved. Even before a successful election in the fall, it had a majority in the House of Commons of approximately seventy.

The new government groped toward repeal of the Orders in Council. Quite obviously the threat of an American war did not trouble the ministers, and neither they nor the Opposition understood the importance of rapid action. (In the interregnum following Perceval's death, Brougham insisted that the hearings continue, but nobody suggested that repeal must be settled immediately.) The Cabinet sought some arrangement that would permit them to abandon an untenable position without admitting defeat at the hands of parliamentary enemies and mercantile opinion. In the days immediately following their confirmation in power, Liverpool and Castlereagh received delegations of merchant complainants. Liverpool urged them to tolerate the system just a little longer on the grounds that the Americans would soon give way, permitting a graceful withdrawal which would not encourage them to raise their demands.[69] As it turned out, it was already too late to prevent an American declaration of war, but the activities of these last weeks show clearly that domestic political and economic considerations, not American maneuverings, brought about repeal.

On May 20, while the ministers still held office ad interim, Jonathan Russell presented to Castlereagh a French decree he had just received from Joel Barlow. This decree, dated April, 1811, unequivocally repealed the pronouncements of Berlin and Milan for the Americans, and the American chargé professed to believe it the formal instrument Britain demanded. The new paper was rightly suspected to be a French forgery, predated for effect but actually recently concocted in reply to the English declaration of policy, to bring about repeal of the orders or further embroil Britain and the United States. Russell found it embarrassingly transparent, Castlereagh told the House of Commons it was "so palpable a juggle" the government intended to ignore it, and the *Morning Chronicle* joined ministerial prints in challenging its authenticity.[70] The false decree did not give formal approval to

[69] *Star*, June 13, 15, 1812.

[70] Russell to Castlereagh, May 20, 1812, and enclosure, FO 5/90; Russell to Monroe, private, June 30, 1812, Despatches, Great Britain, Vol. XVIII; *Hansard*, XXIII, 287–288; *Morning Chronicle*, May 23, 1812. Irving Brant, "Joel Barlow, Madison's Stubborn Minister," *William and Mary Quarterly*, 3d Series, XV (1958), 442–443, clearly shows that Barlow considered the decree a forgery but potentially useful to the interests of the United States. See especially Barlow to Madison, May 12, 1812, William C. Rives Collection, Library of Congress, where the American minister expresses a strong suspicion that the decree "was created last week . . . & in consequence of my note of the 1st of May" asking proof of French repeal. "I know not in State-ethics by what name such management is called," Barlow wrote. Three days after denouncing the decree Castlereagh sent it to the law officers for comment. Crouzet, *op. cit.*, II, 824n.

trade in British goods, a requirement Foster had been instructed to insist upon. Nevertheless, after some delay the Liverpool ministry made this obviously fraudulent document the sole excuse for withdrawal of the orders, primarily as a device, none too successful, to conceal its own weakness.

Brougham finally got around to a formal motion against the Orders in Council on June 16. Save for the absence of James Stephen, who usually intervened in any debate upon them, there was no indication that the government intended to give way. Brougham opened the proceedings with an extremely lengthy speech, chiefly a summary of the testimony taken during the preceding six weeks. As in March, Rose and Baring followed him, repeating the usual arguments. Rose's speech in favor of the orders supports the hypothesis, put forward at the time, that the Cabinet intended to hold firm yet a little longer if the temper of the House permitted. Apparently it did not, for when Baring sat down Castlereagh rose from the front bench and, after denying that the French decree recently received really met the requirements laid down by Britain, declared:

Nevertheless, it might not be unwise to put the country in a situation to receive explanations upon it. If the American government should be found disposed to make representations to France, to induce her to satisfy the just expectations contained in his royal highness the Prince Regent's declaration [of April 21], Great Britain would be disposed to consent to the suspension, for a limited period, of the restrictive system of both countries; or, in other words, she would consent to suspend the Orders in Council, if America would consent to suspend her Non-Importation act.

A brief baffled silence, then a confused hubbub followed these opaque words. Whitbread bobbed to his feet to say that he was, "as on most occasions, completely unable to understand the meaning of the noble lord. He begged the noble lord would say what it was he meant." Clarity was undoubtedly not exactly what Castlereagh desired. Under harassment he ultimately agreed that the government intended to suspend the orders without even waiting to see if the United States would at the same time renew intercourse with Britain. Ponsonby, titular leader of the Opposition, pronounced the whole proceeding "a confession both to France and America, that the English government had resorted to measures which bore so hard on herself, that she could not persevere in them." Brougham, who exulted almost childishly at a victory for which he could claim chief credit, agreed to withdraw his motion until the government announced its full intentions.[71]

The Cabinet debated its next move for just a week, a delay strengthening the feeling that Castlereagh's announcement had been a tactical step, not the result of a fixed decision. Some ministers desired to stop at a temporary suspension of the British system. If the United States raised its price, the orders could easily be restored; if, on the other hand, America reacted favorably, the disgrace of surrender would be lessened by a parallel relaxation across the Atlantic. Other cabinet members, perhaps a narrow majority, argued for going the whole way. They pointed out that American law provided for the abandonment of nonimportation after the cessation, not merely the suspension, of English edicts. The Opposition, its blood up, now insisted on outright repeal, and in the long run there was little practical difference between the two courses, since the orders could be reproclaimed if the United States refused to open trade with Britain.[72]

On June 23, prodded by Brougham's call for a new debate, Castlereagh made it known that the government had revoked the Orders in Council. Significantly, he met with a group of "Members from the Manufacturing Counties" before the House convened. The revocation, which actually took the form of a new Order in Council, was then communicated to Parliament. The government insisted that the repeal was voluntary, a gesture of

[71] *Hansard*, XXIII, 486–548; Crouzet, *op. cit.*, II, 826. Instructions sent to Foster the next day outlined the government's intentions at this point. Britain planned to suspend the orders as of August 1, with suspension to last until May, 1813, unless French conduct permitted an extension beyond that date. Suspension was conditional upon the removal of American restraints on British trade and the use of her ports by the Royal Navy. Castlereagh #20 to Foster, June 17, 1812, and enclosure, Mayo, *op. cit.*, pp. 381–385.

[72] Russell to Monroe, private, June 30, 1812, Despatches, Great Britain, Vol. XVIII; Joy to Madison, June 20, 1812, Rives Collection; *Hansard*, XXIII, 587–592, 719.

conciliation inspired but not required by the French decree. It insisted that new measures against American trade would follow if nonimportation continued. These qualifications were largely bravado; the Percevellian system followed its creator into the grave.[73]

Revocation provoked general celebration, particularly in the Midlands, and Brougham and the other heroes of the battle were tendered testimonial dinners. Workers found employment once again, and factories put on extra shifts to produce goods for the American market. Fifty ships sailed from Liverpool for the United States within two weeks, bearing, it was reported, more than 2 million yards of calico cloth as well as a supply of good English cheese for the White House.

The resumption of trade, coinciding with news of the outbreak of war between France and Russia, created unusual optimism in England. Cobbett, it is true, warned his countrymen that America would not be satisfied until impressment ceased, and the *Courier* gloomily predicted that America, "seeing us yield one point, will press the others." The great majority of the press congratulated the country on its good fortune. In Parliament, the happy climax of an arduous campaign intoxicated the Opposition. Brougham praised the ministry's "frank and manly conduct," and he and Lord Lansdowne pledged their supporters to rally around the government if America challenged any of Britain's undoubted maritime rights. Grenville and Grey agreed with Auckland that the tardy repeal of the orders should "have been follow'd rather by an impeachment than by a compliment," and Sydney Smith wrote, "I am very much affronted with Brougham's panegyric upon the Ministry. It was injudicious and savoring of pomp. Their late measures were surely not conceded, but extorted. Their jaws were forcibly distended, and an emetic thrust down their throats. Are they to be praised for rendering what they could not retain, and to be told that their compulsory sickness does them the highest honor?" The flood of congratulation buried these complaints.

[73] Castlereagh to Prince Regent, June 23, 1812, Royal Archives; *Hansard*, XXIII, 715–721, 716n–718n.

338

Repeal of the Orders in Council gave popularity to a ministry whose hold had been tenuous and established the government in a position vis-à-vis America which the nation was prepared to endorse.[74]

Henry Brougham later declared, "The repeal of the Orders in Council was my greatest achievement." [75] As leader of a campaign in which too many prominent Opposition figures had lost hope, Brougham could legitimately claim great credit. He deserved testimonial dinners, although he might have accepted more modestly the plaudits that came his way. For Brougham could not have succeeded without the well-nigh unanimous support of the business community. Abandonment of the orders is one of the first examples in British history of a government's surrender to outside, nonpolitical opinion. The defection of men like Gascoyne and Wilberforce, who sat for commercial areas in the Midlands, warned the government that it could not count upon its followers. The cessation of licenses, though it might rekindle the enthusiasm of those who favored commercial war *à outrance,* could not assuage the business community. Long before Perceval's death, after the March debate or at least by early April, swelling industrial protest doomed the orders. When Midland representatives met with Lord Castlereagh on the day repeal was announced, some objected to the casuistry of basing it upon the new French revelation. "Aye," said the Foreign Secretary, "but one does not like to own that we are forced to give way to our manufacturers." [76]

The depression of 1810, totally unconnected with events in America, secured for the United States what Jefferson's Embargo had been unable to obtain. The British business community reacted hesitantly to the depression at first, for many of its members nor-

---

[74] *Cobbett's Register,* XXII, 1027; *Courier,* June 17, 1812; *Hansard,* XXIII, 715–719; Auckland to Grey, June 29, 1812, Grey MSS, from 1st Ld. Auckland; Smith to Lady Holland, June 7, 1812 [?], Smith, *op. cit.,* I, 222. Cobbett later declared that the Opposition's fatuous pledges on this occasion encouraged the ministers to refuse further compromise and thus became responsible for the continuation of the War of 1812. *Cobbett's Register,* XXIII (1813), 687.

[75] *Life and Times of Henry Brougham,* II, 1.

[76] Diary, June 24, 1812, Robert I. Wilberforce and Samuel Wilberforce, *The Life of William Wilberforce* (2d ed.; 5 vols.; London, 1839), IV, 35.

mally counted themselves supporters of Perceval and anyway disliked the very idea of outside pressure upon Parliament. America's resumption of nonimportation in 1811, the result of Napoleonic caprice rather than of acute Madisonian analysis, deepened the depression in England. Manufacturers and merchants became convinced that only reopened sales to America could restore prosperity, and they undertook the campaign of protest which finally forced the government to give way. The final result did not vindicate the Jefferson-Madison theory of the invincibility of American commercial pressure. The Republican leaders had always assumed that this pressure alone would cripple European nations, whereas success actually depended upon the coincidence of American pressure with depression in Europe. In prosperous times, as in 1807 and 1808, Great Britain could have ridden out the storm.

Nor did revocation show that Britain took very seriously the threat of an American war. Hostilities were feared, if at all, not for themselves, but because they threatened to close still more firmly the door to the American customer. The embargo of March, 1812, passed largely as a prelude to war, troubled England chiefly for economic reasons. Even Henry Brougham argued that the United States was too weak to pose an important military threat or to arouse jealousy:

Jealousy of America! I should as soon think of being jealous of the tradesmen who supply me with necessaries, or the clients who entrust their suits to my patronage. Jealousy of America! whose armies are yet at the low . . . —whose assembled navies could not lay siege to an English sloop of war:— jealousy of a power which is necessarily peaceful as well as weak . . . [and] is placed at so vast a distance as to be perfectly harmless! [77]

Great Britain clung to this view even after the United States declared war. The Cabinet believed American strength and will so contemptible that it expected Madison to revoke the declaration after learning that the Orders in Council had disappeared.

While news of repeal was still on its way to him by ship through the Baltic, John Quincy Adams expressed a hope that, "with

[77] *Hansard*, XXIII, 504–505.

a little more Patience and Forbearance, we shall see the downfall
of that infamous compound of Robbery, Perjury, and Fraud by
the weight of its mischief recoiling upon its authors, without being
obliged on our part to resort to force for its destruction." Adams'
hope was fulfilled; so too was his gloomy expectation that Perceval's death would delay the denouement too long to prevent an
American declaration of war. When news of repeal reached the
United States, the *Aurora* crowed that "the *Leviathan* of the sea
has floundered and crouched to the *terrapin!*—The sovereign
pedlar of the seas has lowered topsails to the Yankee *cockboat*."
In the same article, however, William Duane called for a vigorous
campaign to take Montreal before winter. Like many of his countrymen, Duane considered the Cabinet's tardy concession too little
to stop a war that it might have prevented. The *Raleigh Star* declared: "Their wit has come too late." [78]

[78] Adams to John Adams, June 29, 1812, Adams Family MSS (microfilm), Massachusetts Historical Society, Vol. CXXXIX; *Aurora* (Philadelphia), July 30, 1812;
*Raleigh Star*, Aug. 7, 1812.

# "THE ASSEMBLED WISDOM
# OF THE COUNTRY"

John Spear Smith, the young chargé d'affaires selected by William Pinkney, had previously visited St. Petersburg and Paris. At neither capital did the youth show more than a passive interest in politics. Six months' exposure to British frigidity (and particularly to Lord Wellesley) changed all that. Like Pinkney before him and Jonathan Russell afterwards, young Smith concluded that the traditional policy of protests, pinpricks, and commercial warfare imperiled America's interests and reputation. Two weeks before Congress gathered, Smith wrote to his father, the Senator from Maryland:

This will no doubt find you at Washington, where the assembled wisdom of the Country is to decide upon its fate. It is my sincere prayer that all may come armed with the courage & energy so necessary in these times, and determined to set out on a new system for obtaining redress. Without this, we may rest ad infinitum in the mean and degrading position we have so long had. If we have no respect for ourselves, others will have none for

us, resistance is the only means of meeting oppression, for tyrants are rarely
merciful, and Power in the hands of Nations is used only for their own interest. We shall never write ourselves into the character and reputation our
temporizing & cringing policy has lost us.[1]

As John Spear Smith argued, America could regain European
consideration—and self-respect as well—only by breaking loose
from past policy. "Courage & energy," so long lacking, were now
required in even greater measure. The session saw a struggle between Republicans possessed of these qualities and others who, for
one reason or another, wished to temporize. Since the Federalists
avoided alliance with any Republican group, while the administration did not throw its full weight into the struggle, the battle lasted
for more than seven months. In June, 1812, a burst of desperate
energy carried the declaration of war against England.

At the outset, vigor triumphed in Henry Clay's selection as
speaker of the House. James Varnum now sat in the Senate as the
replacement for Pickering. Ex-Speaker Macon was tinged with
Quiddism. William Bibb of Georgia, another front-runner, was
an administration hack. On the Sunday before Congress met, a
group of Republicans caucused to seek a more satisfactory nominee.
They settled upon Henry Clay. Having greater determination
and numbers than other factions, this group fixed its choice upon
the party, and Clay easily secured election. So unknown was he
that Augustus Foster almost ignored his selection, while the Columbian Centinel confused him with his cousin, Matthew Clay
of Virginia.[2]

Although backed by both young and old men, the Kentucky
gamecock epitomized the new generation of Republicans. An unrestrained nationalist, a supporter of manufacturing as well as of
agriculture, a rip-roaring orator, a debonair favorite of the ladies,
a bold gambler at cards and politics—how different from the
generation of Jefferson, Madison, and Macon!—Clay did not have

[1] John S. Smith to Samuel Smith, Oct. 20, 1811, Samuel Smith MSS, Library of
Congress.
[2] Bernard Mayo, ed., *Henry Clay, Spokesman of the New West* (Boston, 1937),
p. 403 and n.; Foster #24 to Wellesley, Nov. 12, 1811, Foreign Office Archives,
Public Record Office, FO 5/77; *Columbian Centinel* (Boston), Nov. 9, 1811.

the intellectual powers of the two presidents (a friendly critic, William Plumer, observed, "He declaims more than he reasons"), but he had more force. During two part terms in the Senate he had opposed half measures, and in the summer of 1811 he wrote ahead to Washington that if Britain "persists in them [the Orders in Council], and France is honest and sincere in her recent measures, I look upon a War with G. Britain [as] inevitable." [3] Clay desired to embrace, not to evade the inevitable.

The new speaker quickly showed that he did not intend to be a mere figurehead. Down to his time the speakership had been primarily an honorific office, with the holder expected to respond to the directions of more powerful leaders. As internal feuds and presidential caution weakened administration control, a great vacuum opened. Henry Clay stepped in to fill it, making policy decisions himself, treating the other leaders of the House as his lieutenants, often descending from the rostrum to speak in important debates, and effectively wielding hitherto almost unused powers to check the obstructiveness of the Federalists and their passing ally, John Randolph. The expulsion of Randolph's favorite bitch, a massive hound who had accompanied her master to the House in the days of other speakers, symbolized the new regime.

In appointing standing committees, Clay made no pretense of seeking balance. He packed them, almost ignoring the Federalists and making sure that War Hawks outnumbered moderate Republicans. All the chairmen had had some previous experience in the House, and the Speaker did not push them forward more rapidly than was then normal. Ezekiel Bacon, who headed the Ways and Means Committee, had already served four years; David R. Williams of North Carolina, chairman of the Military Affairs Committee, was returning for a third term after a two-year absence; and Peter B. Porter, who received the most important assignment of all, chairman of the Foreign Affairs Committee, had been a

[3] Entry of Feb. 13, 1807, Everett S. Brown, ed., *William Plumer's Memorandum of Proceedings in the United States Senate, 1803–1807* (New York, 1923), p. 608; Clay to Rodney, Aug. 17, 1811, Rodney Family MSS, Library of Congress. This and subsequent paragraphs draw heavily upon Mayo, *op. cit.*, pp. 401 ff.

member of the Eleventh Congress. Only the Naval Affairs Committee's Langdon Cheves could be considered a newcomer, and even he had served during one previous session. The chairmen, except for Cheves, disappointed Clay and perhaps made him wish that he had totally ignored the qualification of prior service. Williams proved eccentric, opposing several important measures of preparedness; Bacon was a loyal party man rather than a War Hawk, and he deserted in the battle over naval building; Porter wavered during the winter and resigned before the job had been finished. Fortunately for Clay, other committee members served his purpose better than the chairmen. On the Foreign Affairs Committee he placed three War Hawks cut from the classic pattern—youthful, newly elected, vigorous—Calhoun, Grundy, and John Adams Harper, a thirty-two-year-old from New Hampshire subsequently denied reëlection by more pacific constituents. Joseph Desha shared all the attributes of these men except inexperience, and the two moderate Republican members usually went along with the majority. John Randolph, whose membership was almost traditional, and the sole Federalist member, Philip Barton Key, who fought for the British during the Revolution, found themselves swamped. So did minority members on other committees.

Whether the Congress contained, as John Spear Smith thought, "the assembled wisdom of the Country," is a moot point. The British minister, whose praise came hard, reported that the "present Congress has certainly brought with it a considerable accession to both Houses of men of talents and respectability, although there still continue in it too many low and uneducated Individuals who are too ignorant to have any opinion of their own." [4] Others preferred to emphasize the debilitating effect of Republican factionalism. With a presidential election in the offing, many Clintonians opposed anything that might benefit Madison. Reapportionment made necessary by the census of 1810 became the first order of business, emphasizing the conflicting interests of North and South and opening differences never completely forgotten in debates over national issues.

[4] Foster #35 to Wellesley, Dec. 21, 1811, FO 5/77.

On foreign policy, congressmen divided into a kaleidoscope of shifting factions so intricate and febrile that classification baffled even the members. Nathaniel Macon discerned at least six factions in the House, none large enough to work its will unaided. Samuel Taggart, a rancidly bitter Federalist but also an indefatigable analyst, divided the Republicans into four groups. The first of these, the War Hawks, was largely counterbalanced by a second clique composed of Republicans determined to preserve peace even if it meant continuing economic warfare. In the middle lay what Taggart called the "scarecrow" party, "those who vote for war without any sincere intention to go to war, but in hopes that Great Britain may be intimidated by the din of our preparations to relax her system so that they will eventually come off with flying colors." A fourth group, usually voting for measures of preparedness, did so to embarrass Madison rather than to bring on hostilities or run a bluff against Britain.[5] Taggart admitted that many representatives did not fall neatly into any group, and he perhaps overemphasized the importance, if not the intensity, of anti-Madisonian feeling. Otherwise the Massachusetts congressman's description suggests the divisions that actually existed.

The true War Hawks, the *Montagnards* of the Twelfth Congress, had the cohesive vigor that had bestowed success upon Maximilien Robespierre and an earlier minority. Clay, Cheves, and Lowndes shared with an equally bellicose senator, George Bibb of Kentucky, a boardinghouse proudly described by Lowndes as "certainly the strongest war mess in Congress." A Massachusetts Federalist considered these men and a tardy arrival, John C. Calhoun, the strongest men in the Republican party, and added that they, "although deluded by the false glare of Democracy, are gentlemanly & apparently at least candid men."[6] This foursome shared the lead with Felix Grundy, who was perhaps even more

[5] Macon to Nicholson, Nov. 21, 1811, Joseph H. Nicholson MSS, Library of Congress; Taggart to Rev. John Taylor, Jan. 20, 1812, George H. Haynes, ed., "Letters of Samuel Taggart, Representative in Congress, 1803–1814," American Antiquarian Society, *Proceedings*, n.s., XXXIII (1923), 376–377.

[6] Lowndes to Elizabeth Lowndes, Feb. 9, 1812, Harriott H. Ravenel, *Life and Times of William Lowndes* (Cambridge, 1901), p. 100; William Reed to Pickering, Feb. 18, 1812, Timothy Pickering MSS, Massachusetts Historical Society, Vol. XXX.

eager for war than his coadjutors but sometimes harmed the cause by his lack of discretion. Some War Hawks questioned the purity and even the legality of the reëxport trade and detested the men who carried it on; they repeatedly declared they did not wish the United States to fight for it. Others were prepared to expand the navy to defend all commerce and, equally important, to increase the weight of the nation in international affairs. All had in common a deep belief that "we have suffered national degradation too long, and endured insult and injury with too much patience." The senator who wrote these words added, toward the end of February, that the government "must vindicate the rights & honor of the nation. There appears at present no honorable ground upon which, war can be avoided—a change in the measures of G. Britain . . . could alone preserve peace—and there is not any . . . reason to calculate on such an event." [7] National honor was the War Hawks' central concern.

Like Senator Campbell, almost all the War Hawks would have considered American honor satisfied by repeal of the Orders in Council, and all would have been satisfied if impressment also ceased. If, as they expected, Britain made no concessions, Campbell, Clay, and Calhoun, as well as followers like William R. King and John A. Harper, were lightheartedly prepared to go to war. After all, war did not seem so serious in those days. The easy conquest of Canada and the speedy starvation of the British West Indies were articles of faith among Americans. David Rogerson Williams, speaking for the entire faction, said that it "appeared to him much easier to settle the terms of a new peace, than to patch up the old quarrel. When he considered the limited extent of our demands, and the nature of the pressure on the enemy, he could not but believe our objects would be attained." [8]

[7] Campbell to Blount, Nov. 29, 1811, Weymouth T. Jordan, *George Washington Campbell of Tennessee: Western Statesman,* Florida State University Studies, Vol. XVII (Tallahassee, 1955), pp. 95–96; Campbell to Blount, Feb. 24, 1812, George W. Campbell MSS, Library of Congress. To warnings of the cost of war, another War Hawk, William Widgery, replied: "What is all our property, compared with our honor and our liberty. It is not commerce only for which we are about to fight, but for our freedom also." *Annals,* 12th Cong., 1st sess., p. 658.

[8] *Annals,* 12th Cong., 1st sess., pp. 689–690.

Some Republicans who took war more seriously nevertheless voted with the War Hawks. They favored what Taggart called the "scarecrow" policy, arms bills and noisy oratory to frighten England into surrender. Within this group could be found Clintonians, who seized the preparedness issue as a stick to belabor the administration, but also many old-line Republicans, who were not yet ready for war but recognized that self-immolating policies would no longer serve. For some the policy was sheer bluff; for others it was a temporary expedient, with no future course charted out; still a third group recognized that war might possibly follow but considered the risk worth taking. Naturally, the success of this policy depended upon the impression of sincerity conveyed by Congress, and scarecrow men often spoke almost like War Hawks in public. William Findley, an exhausted radical, declared in December that "the time was fast approaching when we must repel national insults or surrender our independence," but in almost the next sentence he made the elliptic statement that preparation was the best way to avoid war. Toward the end, in an obvious effort at escape, some thirty of these men joined with Federalists to support a proposal for adjournment which would probably have prevented a declaration of war.[9]

Until Christmas time the administration's position fell short of the War Hawks but still beyond the bluffers. The President and the Secretary of State considered it possible that Britain could be frightened into surrender. On the other hand, the government (or at least Monroe) saw that, as the Secretary put it, "we have been so long dealing in the small way, of embargoes, non-intercourse, and non-importation, with menaces of War &c that the British Government has not believed us." If Britain remained firm, the administration was prepared to fight in the spring. Meanwhile, they would try to inveigle Foster and his superiors by a judicious combination of threats and enticements. The President repeatedly told Foster that the United States asked no sacrifice of principle on Britain's part, that America would not insist on England's admitting that she had wrongly questioned the Cadore

[9] *Ibid.*, pp. 501, 1315–1316.

letter, and even that he personally "would be satisfied provided their [the orders'] practical effect was to cease without any public abandonment of them." On the other hand, in comments too often minimized by Foster, the President and the Secretary repeatedly refused to bring into question the validity of French repeal, warned that the use of force would eventually come, and delayed publication of correspondence that might lessen anti-British feeling. As time passed the administration's line gradually tautened, but on the whole it clung to the hope, as described by Sérurier, that declarations and military preparations would "suffice to convince the English Ministry of the strong intention here to resist, and to determine it not to add another powerful enemy to the terrible enemy it confronts." [10] With far less enthusiasm than the War Hawks, the President faced a war he still hoped to avoid.

The administration kept its own counsel, except for one meeting between Monroe and the Foreign Affairs Committee. Many congressmen thought the executive shared the opinions of scarecrow men or possibly even of the peace faction. Hugh Nelson, a neighbor of Madison's, believed he expressed the President's feelings when he challenged War Hawk declarations that the United States was pledged to war,[11] and many War Hawks harbored doubts of the administration. Those determined to avoid war hoped for presidential support when the crisis came.

This last Republican group, described by Henry Adams as "honest and perhaps shrewd men . . . , who saw more clearly the evils that war must bring than the good it might cause," considered war a quixotic exercise. Many, like former Attorney-General Rodney, still thought that commercial pressure alone would bring England to her knees. Others, sharing the feelings of a Republican newspaper in Trenton, believed that the true policy of the United States was *"peace, while peace is either practicable or tolerable.*

[10] Monroe to Taylor, June 13, 1812, James Monroe MSS, Library of Congress; Foster #29 to Wellesley, Nov. 29, 1811, FO 5/77; Foster #7 to Wellesley, secret, Jan. 31, 1812, FO 5/84; Sérurier #42 to Minister of Foreign Relations, Jan. 12, 1812, Archives des Affaires Étrangères, Correspondance Politique, États-Unis (photostats, Library of Congress), Vol. LXVII.

[11] Nelson to Charles Everett, Dec. 16, 1811, Hugh Nelson MSS, Library of Congress.

Notwithstanding the embarrassments of our trade . . . , the nation was probably never so prosperous as at the present moment. . . . And shall we jeopardize or sacrifice this prosperity by war, if war is avoidable?" The Trenton *True American* endorsed preparedness but added, "Peace is a gem which ought not to be rashly flung away—it may cost much toil, and blood and treasure to recover it." Many New England Republicans, Adam Boyd of New Jersey, Nathaniel Macon, and others took this position until Federalist taunts and the logic of the situation created by War Hawks and their disingenuous allies caused them, like the *True American,* to support the war declaration, although with great reluctance. Others, most notably Senator Worthington of Ohio, opposed war on the issue of timing until the very end.[12]

At the extremity of the Republican party, so far from the War Hawks that they entered into virtual alliance with the Federalists, stood John Randolph and a handful of Quids. Weakened as usual by illness and hypochondria, Randolph nevertheless delivered more major orations than any other opponent of war, and as always his lashing tongue raised the hackles of his enemies. The North Carolina schoolteacher, Richard Stanford, used more restrained language. He opposed the conquest of Canada on the ground, borne out by later history, that in British hands it served as a "pledge for her better behaviour." Stanford scoffed at the easy way congressmen compared individual and national duels for honor. "The truth is," he said, "we cannot liken, nor will the similitude hold good between an individual's honor, or his sensibility to it, and that of a nation." [13] At least until the spring, few Federalists

[12] Henry Adams, *History of the United States during the Administrations of Jefferson and Madison* (9 vols.; New York, 1889–1891), VI, 170–171; Rodney to Gallatin, Oct. 20, 1811, Albert Gallatin MSS, New-York Historical Society; *True American* (Trenton), Nov. 18, 1811; May 18, 1812; journal entry, June 14, 1812, Thomas Worthington MSS, Library of Congress.

[13] *Annals,* 12th Cong., 1st sess., pp. 673, 511–513. A similar complaint, made to Monroe by an outside observer, declared that congressmen "never touch the subject, but . . . blare out in Emotions. . . . among these Gentlemen, eternal changes are rung upon *public feelings,* national *sensibilities,* national *Honor,* & even the peculiarly royal & military phrase of *National Glory.* The small voice of reason . . . is seldom heard." Walter Jones to Monroe, Dec. 8, 1811, Monroe MSS.

spoke as frankly as Stanford and Randolph in opposing the establishment of national honor as a mainspring of policy.

Even this description makes Republican factions seem more tidy, more cohesive than they were. Actually, members floated from camp to camp or concealed their true views behind the glare of oratorical fireworks. Many simply drifted with the wind, confounding all attempts to place them. The Quids never numbered more than six or eight, but the other three groups probably divided fairly evenly the Republican membership of the House. The War Hawks and the scarecrow men, if aided by their share of the drifters, usually found it possible to get their way, although in several instances success came by a very narrow margin.

In the Senate an even more complicated situation prevailed. The Republican membership spread from George Washington Campbell, still the advocate of positive action as he had been earlier as a congressman, to Richard Brent, an alcoholic Virginian still clinging to the essentially Anglophile position that he had shared with his friend, James Monroe, a year earlier. Brent opposed measures looking to war, although at the last moment he tottered into the chamber to vote for the declaration. Somewhere between the extremes represented by Campbell and Brent lay Samuel Smith, William B. Giles, Michael Leib of Pennsylvania, and New Hampshire's Nicholas Gilman, all primarily individualists moved chiefly by a desire to crimp James Madison's political future. Although the major debates took place in the lower house, on two occasions—passage of the army bill and the declaration of war—the Senate played an important part.

The thirty-seven Federalist congressmen (there were also seven senators) were too few to be able to afford factionalism. Nine lived together at Birch's, 70 rods south of the Capitol, and five more at Coyle's boardinghouse, a traditional Federalist hostelry, arrangements that also facilitated a united front. Aided by Harmanus Bleecker of Albany, an energetic and personable young man, Josiah Quincy commanded the Federalists. Their ranks included able men, as strong in debate as the War Hawk leaders, but the tactical design adopted after vigorous dispute required them to curb their appetites for opposition.

The plan was Quincy's. Rufus King, who feared the scheme would misfire, and Timothy Pickering, always the advocate of blunt attack, warned against it, and unsophisticated constituents often complained, but the congressional delegation accepted it. Quincy's scheme was based upon a conviction that "Federalists, in abandoning the doctrines of Washington, of efficient protection, have lost their discriminative character, and, in their fears about the event of the European contests, *their national character*. Instead of a patriotic opposition to an oppressive government, they are in great danger of degenerating into a mere faction" without political appeal. He proposed to support military legislation, to avoid being provoked into defense of England, and to keep generally silent in debate, letting the Republicans expose their own internal disagreements. Quincy, who of course did not want war, argued, perhaps not entirely sincerely, that the "present situation of the commercial parts of the country *is worse than any war, even a British one*." [14] Destruction of Republican rule by exposing the incapacity of that party seemed the only way to restore prosperity.

Almost all Federalists believed the Republicans did not mean what they said when they talked of war. "It has been," wrote Quincy, "the burden of their successive songs, every session, for six years past." Two Federalists visited Foster to urge England to maintain the Orders in Council so that the Republicans would be forced to the wall. Another wrote to Francis J. Jackson in the same sense:

The only way to dislodge the prevailing party from the post of power, is by saddling them with a war which they have neither the means [nor] the ability to conduct, or by allowing them to place themselves in a situation . . . which would expose their weakness and pusillanimity, and render them contemptible . . . in the eyes of all mankind. The first situation, I believe, . . . they could not be kicked into, while we enjoy the delightful

[14] Quincy to Eliza S. Quincy, n.d. [Dec., 1811], Edmund Quincy, *Life of Josiah Quincy* (Boston, 1867), p. 241; Quincy to Otis, Nov. 8, 1811, Harrison Gray Otis MSS, Massachusetts Historical Society.

spectacle of seeing them decoyed or turned into the other, like a flock of geese into a pen. We have them snug enough, and if they make their escape the British government will have to answer for the crime of rescuing them.

The *Alexandria Gazette* reminded fellow Federalists of the fable of the boy who cried "Wolf," but Federalist congressmen preferred their own legends, among them a belief that the Republicans were too weak to go to war.[15]

The state of the nation made Federalist blindness understandable. As Henry Adams put it, "A passion that needed to be nursed for five years before it acquired strength to break into act, could not seem genuine to men who did not share it." Of course, fourteen of the seventeen state legislatures passed resolutions favoring an end of pacifism; this was but a normal and indeed habitual occupation of legislators. Of course, War Hawks talked as though war was inevitable; Federalists knew they were not so confident as they seemed. The public seemed resigned rather than bellicose. The anger roused by the *Little Belt* affair, Foster's demands, and even Indian warfare (although climaxed by news of Tippecanoe shortly after Congress met) soon subsided into sullen dislike of Britain. Early in 1812 Sérurier reported that the people, although ready to face war, did so unenthusiastically. Two months later Taylor of Carolina warned Monroe that the country wanted war no more than it had wanted to fight France in 1798.[16] Federalists concluded that the danger of war did not exist, for at times of equal or even (in 1807) greater public excitement members of Congress had shown no inclination to abandon peace.

For the first months of the session Augustus Foster viewed the situation almost as complacently as the Federalists. Foster lived at the center of town, whereas his rival, Sérurier, had rented Barlow's house three miles away. The Britisher met everybody, at

[15] Quincy to Otis, Nov. 25, 1811, Otis MSS; Hanson to Jackson, March 7, 1812, Francis James Jackson MSS, Public Record Office (FO 353/58–61), FO 353/61; *Alexandria Gazette*, Jan. 22, 1812.

[16] Adams, *op. cit.*, VI, 113; Sérurier #42 to Minister of Foreign Relations, Jan. 12, 1812, AAE, CP, E-U, Vol. LXVII; Taylor to Monroe, Jan. 2, 1812, Monroe MSS.

official occasions, on visits to Federalist and even War Hawk hostelries, and particularly at his own entertainments. Foster kept what Sérurier described as "une forte bonne maison," and he sometimes dined as many as 200 guests at a time, a practice which exhausted his expense account by mid-December. Federalists and all sorts of Republicans attended his parties. Amidst all these sources of information, the British minister failed to see any clear indication that war impended. In his November reports he surrounded very qualified hints of possible war with contrary evidence. Thereafter, even in describing difficult conversations with the President, Foster emphasized the ease with which American resentment could be turned aside. Almost any offer would draw the final sting, he reported in the last dispatch of the year, "provided an appearance of conciliation is exhibited." [17]

The young envoy might have learned something from the reception of his offer to settle the *Chesapeake* issue. As early as June, 1810, Lord Wellesley told William Pinkney that England would drop the demand, made through Rose, Erskine, and Jackson, that America rescind the proclamation banning British ships from American waters. The éclat of making a settlement was reserved for the new minister to America, and formal instructions were not issued until April, 1811. Even then Foster dawdled. At last, just before Congress met, he presented the British offer. Madison ignored it in the message that greeted the legislature and, after accepting it, passed the correspondence on to Congress without a single sign of gratification. The *National Intelligencer* commented in the coldest possible fashion, and less official Republican journals suggested that the British action was "merely an attempt to paralize the proceedings of Congress." Foster fatuously reported that the settlement was "regarded by M^r. Monroe and myself as a kind of stepping stone to a general arrangement." [18] He failed to discern

[17] Sérurier #43 to Minister of Foreign Relations, Jan. 21, 1812, AAE, CP, E-U, Vol. LXVII; Foster to Wellesley, most secret, Dec. 28, 1811, FO 5/77. See also Foster #20–#35 to Wellesley, Nov. 5–Dec. 21, 1811, *ibid.*

[18] Pinkney to Smith, private, June 13, 1810, Department of State Archives, National Archives, Despatches, Great Britain, unnumbered volume; Wellesley #2 to Foster, April 10, 1811, Bernard Mayo, ed., *Instructions to the British Ministers to the*

that, while the administration had to accept an offer that met American demands, Madison and Monroe had no desire to use it to dampen what they considered a useful spirit of antagonism toward Britain.

Although failure of the *Chesapeake* settlement demonstrated that American love could not be purchased with tardy tinsel, during the first three weeks of the session Foster and the Federalists seemed correct in minimizing the chances of war. Congress did absolutely nothing, the administration failed to stir, and war men and bellicose editors became restive. After all, Congress had come together with a great bustle in 1807, and the next year the House whooped through the noble resolutions presented by George W. Campbell. "Strike but the chord that sounds of war," a correspondent wrote to William Duane's *Aurora* in 1810, "and we fly as regularly to proclamations as Quixotte to arms." [19] Republican factionalism, Madison's reputation for hesitation, failure to credit the sincerity of men who said they would vote for war when the time came—all these gave plausibility to the thesis that war was very unlikely.

Nor did the Foreign Affairs Committee's report on Madison's message provide clear evidence that Congress desired war. Joseph Desha urged the committee to recommend convoys to protect American trade with Europe, [20] a step that would certainly have

United States, *1791–1812*, American Historical Association, *Annual Report, 1936,* III (Washington, 1941), 318–319; James D. Richardson, ed., *A Compilation of the Messages and Papers of the Presidents* (Washington, 1897), I, 496; *National Intelligencer* (Washington), Nov. 14, 1811; *Enquirer* (Richmond), Nov. 19, 1811; Foster #23 to Wellesley, Nov., 12, 1811, FO 5/77. The United States declined to accept reparation for the lives lost in the attack, on the theory that no payment could compensate for them. The two surviving men from the *Chesapeake*—two had died—were returned to the deck of the ship from which they had been taken. The Admiralty moved very slowly, however, and the seamen were not delivered to the *Chesapeake*, then in Boston harbor, until July 11, 1812, a month after the American declaration of war. Anthony St. J. Baker #11 to Castlereagh, July 23, 1812, FO 5/87.

[19] *Aurora* (Philadelphia), Feb. 5, 1810.

[20] *Annals*, 12th Cong., 1st sess., pp. 483–484. Augustus Foster reported that in a preliminary vote the committee had determined upon convoys, only to be forced by John Randolph to reverse this decison. The make-up of the committee, however, makes War Hawk defections the critical factor. Foster #31 to Wellesley, Dec. 18, 1811, FO 5/77.

led to an early clash with the Royal Navy, but a majority, including several War Hawks, was unready to go that far. They had no desire to open themselves to ridicule by bringing in bellicose resolutions and then finding themselves deserted by their own party leaders. Finally, at a long committee meeting that lasted well into the night, the Secretary of State pledged the administration to support a declaration of war in the spring, if measures of preparedness did not bring about a British surrender in the meantime. Only after this promise did the committee decide to recommend military legislation to the House. The news soon spread, but many emphasized that the redemption of Monroe's pledge was not only conditional but also months away. That the war men feared the government would renege is obvious from Grundy's account of the meeting with Monroe, in which he said: "Rely, on one thing, we have War or Honorable peace before we adjourn or certain great personages have produced a state of things which will bring them down from their high places, If there be honest men enough to tell the truth loudly." [21] Suspicions did not evaporate until Madison finally presented a war message to Congress six months later.

The committee report, which bore the name of chairman Peter B. Porter, reached the House on November 29. Emphasizing the threat posed by the Orders in Council, but also dilating on impressment, the report declared that "the period has arrived, when, in the opinion of your committee, it is the sacred duty of Congress to call forth the patriotism and resources of the country." The committee recommended legislation to bring the regular army up to statutory strength, the enlistment of three-year men and other volunteers, the approval of drafts of state militia, outfitting of the navy, and authorization for merchant ships to arm.[22] Porter's Report encouraged congressional neophytes like Jonathan Roberts and prowar journals like the Richmond *Enquirer*, frightened

[21] Grundy to Jackson, Nov. 28, 1811, Andrew Jackson MSS, Library of Congress. See also Lowndes to Elizabeth L. Lowndes, Dec. 7, 1811, Ravenel, *op. cit.*, pp. 89–90; Richard M. Johnson to Barbour, Dec. 9, 1811, James Barbour MSS, New York Public Library.

[22] *Annals*, 12th Cong., 1st sess., pp. 373–377.

various commercial houses and some Federalist congressmen like Samuel Taggart. The *National Intelligencer*, however, declined to throw the administration's weight behind it, and Federalist journals, noting that the report committed America to nothing for months to come, considered it a bluff. Some bellicose newspapermen criticized it as too mild, among them Hezekiah Niles, who declared that Porter's Report fell far short of the people's demands.[23]

Congress, in its characteristically leisurely fashion, waited a week before beginning the debate. Chairman Porter led off with a call for war if Britain did not repeal the orders and make some "arrangements" on impressment, but at the close he weakened the effect of his speech by warning his colleagues not to proceed to war too rapidly.[24] Felix Grundy, attempting to regain the lost ground with a violent oration, fell into indiscreet admissions. He acknowledged what Federalists had long charged, that economic warfare was very painful to the nation that prosecuted it. "This, and our plighted faith to the French government," he said, "have tied the gordian knot; we cannot untie it; we can cut it with the sword."[25] The other War Hawk speeches contained strong appeals to honor as well as repeated assurances that the Canadian plum lay waiting to fall into the lap of American invaders. Some speakers, notably Desha and Calhoun, spoke without reserve. Others, including Porter himself, Roberts, and William R. King, admitted that they did not want to go to war for the reëxport trade. These War Hawks apparently considered American honor a graduated

---

[23] Roberts to Matthew Roberts, Nov. 30, 1811, Jonathan Roberts MSS, Historical Society of Pennsylvania; *Enquirer*, Dec. 3, 1811; Gordon, Trokes, Leitch and Co. to Ellis and Allan, Dec. 4, 1811, Ellis-Allan MSS, Library of Congress; Taggart to Rev. John Taylor, Nov. 30, 1811, Haynes, *op. cit.*, p. 364; *National Intelligencer*, Nov. 30, 1811; *New-York Evening Post*, Dec. 2, 1811; *Niles' Weekly Register* (Baltimore), Dec. 7, 1812.

[24] In London the *Courier* (Jan. 24, 1812) commented harshly on Porter's speech: "A more noisy, silly, blustering speech—a speech more unstatesman-like we never read. But perhaps the American Committee meant little more than to bully. Mr. PORTER is against entering the war prematurely. Aye, take Counsel again; second thoughts may be best. If America spread the cloth, we may furnish some dishes to the feast which her guests may not relish."

[25] *Annals*, 12th Cong., 1st sess., p. 426. For the entire debate see pp. 414–547.

commodity, far more seriously challenged by impressment and a check on exports than by other British measures.

Scarecrow men and moderates destroyed any chance that Congress would appear determined to vindicate American rights. Not one true Republican opposed the resolutions—it took a bold man to confess he considered the United States too weak to resist aggression—but several declared that a vote for Porter's resolutions did not commit them to support specific legislation recommended by the committee, to say nothing of a declaration of war later on. Macon talked this way, and Adam Boyd and Hugh Nelson. Speaking, as he thought, for the administration against enemies who desired to maneuver it into early war, Nelson descanted at length on the dangers of armed conflict, the questionable wisdom of permitting America to become an adjunct of Napoleon, and the necessity of preserving freedom of action. According to Samuel Taggart, Nelson's speech "carried terror and dismay into the ranks of the war party." [26] By expressing doubts shared by many silent Republicans, the Virginian threatened the War Hawk program of steady preparation culminating in war, and at the same time gravely reduced the possibility that the strategy of bluff would succeed. His was the most important speech of the debate.

In oratorical fireworks John Randolph's two major orations carried the palm. Since Quincy's Federalists left the debate to their opponents, Randolph bore almost the entire burden of challenging the report. The master of Bizarre was ill and tired. His speeches suffered through disorganization, but individual passages had his trade-mark. He accused Republicans of apostasy to their own creed, referring to the conflict between Macon and Grundy by saying, "If we must have an exposition of the doctrines of Republicanism, he should receive it from the fathers of the church, and not from junior apprentices of the law." He twitted Grundy for his "gordian knot" statement and emphasized the folly of tilting the balance of power in favor of Napoleon, "him who had effaced the title of Attila to the 'Scourge of God!'" In his most

[26] Nelson to Charles Everett, Dec. 16, 1811, Nelson MSS; Taggart to Rev. John Taylor, Dec. 14, 1811, Haynes, *op. cit.*, p. 369.

famous passage Randolph declared, "Agrarian cupidity, not maritime right, urges the war. Ever since the report . . . came into the House, we have heard but one word—like the whip-poor-will, but one eternal monotonous tone—Canada!—Canada!—Canada!" If war came, he said, it would not be "a war for our homes and fire-sides—a war that might generate . . . manly sentiments —but, a war of rapine, of privateering, a scuffle and scramble for plunder." [27] This accusation, later taken up by historians, overlooked the fact that most references to Canada simply pointed to it as the easiest target for American military power.

In the most reasonable War Hawk speech, his maiden effort, Calhoun replied to two of Randolph's central arguments. While admitting that the European blockade kept agricultural prices down, he denied that a desire to force open the transatlantic market was more than a subsidiary motive for war; patriotism and honor were the chief factors, he said. Calhoun also rebutted Randolph's argument that Napoleon posed a greater threat than England. Since America could not fight both at once, prudence required her to select the more vulnerable. "It is absurd," said Calhoun, "for us to talk of the balance of power, while they by their conduct smile with contempt at our simple, good-natured policy." [28] Calhoun's speech was the sole reply to Randolph. Other Republicans passed their time affirming that cause for war existed, while disagreeing whether it should be declared, even at some distant date in the future.

Nearly three weeks after Porter's Report the House concluded debate. The resolutions sailed through easily, not more than twenty-two votes being cast against any of them, although Quincy failed to prevent a handful of Federalists from breaking away to join Randolph, Stanford, and other Quids in opposition. Louis Sérurier thought the President's message and the report had "placed Congress, like the administration, in one of those positions from which it is no longer possible to retreat." On the other hand, Federalists scoffed at the slow pace. In two days, said the Baltimore

[27] *Annals*, 12th Cong., 1st sess., pp. 441–455, 525–546.
[28] *Ibid.*, pp. 482–483.

*Federal Republican,* the huge Republican majority could pass legislation to implement the sentiments in Porter's resolutions. "They do not choose, they prefer to bluster and bully, and talk big, and take the chance of frightening the Prince Regent into a repeal of edicts, to which they have submitted for four years." Congress passed no legislation before the Christmas recess, and Senator Campbell feared none would be passed.[29]

After the holidays, action on army and navy bills demonstrated Congress' weakness. A new law authorized short-term volunteers without settling their purpose, and the conditions of enlistment made it practically useless. Congress also emasculated the administration's plan for an additional army of 10,000 men to serve for three years. This army, although theoretically tailored to the requirements of a campaign against Canada, was actually planned to be just large enough to impress Britain and just small enough to require no impossibly burdensome additional taxation. In the Senate, to embarrass Madison, Giles presented an amendment expanding the army to 25,000 men. This forced the administration, as well as those who favored a sedate pace toward a war they still hoped to avoid, either to oppose a larger and presumably more effective army or to accept a measure that cast doubt on their own original purpose and would require extensive new taxes. Faced with this dilemma, the Madison men and the moderates first stood firm behind the original plan. War Hawks, on the other hand, were perfectly willing to move more rapidly if they could find the votes. Led by Henry Clay, who intervened in debate for the first time, they abandoned the plan arranged at the Foreign Affairs Committee's session with Monroe and accepted Giles's proposal. Eventually, faced by Senate firmness and the difficulty of seeming to support half measures, opposition collapsed. With only minor changes, Giles's bill became law.[30]

The additional army bill could not be taken seriously. It established a target figure beyond America's reach although no more

[29] *Ibid.,* pp. 546–548, 564–566; Sérurier #39 to Minister of Foreign Relations, Dec. 9, 1811, AAE, CP, E-U, Vol. LXVI; *Federal Republican* (Baltimore), Jan. 2, 1812; Campbell to Jackson, Dec. 24, 1811, Andrew Jackson MSS.

[30] *Annals,* 12th Cong., 1st sess., pp. 35–97, 596–691, *passim.*

than adequate to the requirements of effective war.[31] Frequent congressional references to the psychological effect upon Britain lessened the law's effectiveness as an instrument of bluff. A realistic program, instantaneously executed, would have served this end far better. Foster declared the bill "more an electioneering than a war measure," [32] and he was right. Giles aimed to hurt Madison. The small group of Federalists who joined Quincy to support the larger force acted with Machiavellian motives. Moderates gave in to avoid ridicule and to mask the nakedness of the strategy of bluff far more than because they were convinced by arguments for 25,000 as opposed to 10,000 men. The administration detested the end product, which reflected upon its own original plans and saddled it with a politically harmful burden.

In a different fashion, the fate of a bill to expand the navy showed Congress' divided mind. As soon as the army legislation passed, Langdon Cheves brought in his committee's recommendation for the construction of a dozen ships of the line and twenty frigates. This proposal quickly ran into determined opposition. Many Republicans, even sincere War Hawks, opposed expansion of a service they considered a heritage from Federalism. Others objected to the expense or argued that a building program could not be completed in time to frighten England. Defeatists repeatedly declared that the United States could never hope to challenge the Royal Navy with success. In vain did Cheves argue that national unity required action to defend commerce, "the second great interest of the country." In vain did Henry Clay, descending again to the floor, attempt to rally inland votes by pointing out the need for sea defense of the great outlet of Western produce at New Orleans. Despite almost unanimous Federalist support, despite paring down of the original plan, the House rejected naval building on January 27 by a vote of sixty-two to fifty-nine. Calhoun, Cheves, Lowndes, and two dozen other Republi-

---

[31] In an account written some time later, Lowndes declared that Secretary of War Eustis, who drafted the bill, sabotaged the 25,000 figure. William L. Lowndes, Historical Anecdotes, and Observations, MSS, Library of Congress. In any event, few more than 1,000 men were enlisted in the army between January and May.

[32] Foster #3 to Wellesley, Jan. 16, 1812, FO 5/84.

cans, mostly from states north of the Delaware, voted for the proposal. Fifty congressmen who later voted for war, the entire Pennsylvania delegation as well as Westerners and Southerners including David R. Williams and Felix Grundy, killed the frigate bill.[33] With it died the chance of strengthening the war spirit in coastal areas.

Having ensured unpreparedness on land and sea, "the assembled wisdom of the Country" turned to financial requirements. Only a few carefree congressmen, like William Widgery of Maine, considered taxation an easy problem: "We are told, a war will be very expensive. Granted. What is money? What is all our property, compared with our honor and our liberty?" For most congressmen the cost cast a shadow over the army and navy bills. On January 10 Albert Gallatin sent fiscal proposals to Ezekiel Bacon, chairman of the Committee on Ways and Means. Scarcely one remunerative area escaped the eye of the Secretary of the Treasury, who proposed to double import duties, tax salt, levy excises, and institute a stamp tax like that which had aroused a furor against Britain in 1765. Unlike most Yankee Republicans, Bacon opposed naval building. When he released Gallatin's letter at the height of the battle over frigates, suspicious War Hawks thought he did so to kill the naval program.[34]

Bacon's revelations cast a cold douche upon the war spirit. The National Intelligencer came to Gallatin's support; the Richmond Enquirer, although critical of details, suggested that determined Virginians would not let a few taxes cool their ardor; and some reasonable Republicans observed that the unpleasant dose must be swallowed to ensure national strength.[35] Otherwise, at least until Henry Clay accepted the inevitability of taxation and exerted his influence, Republicans almost unanimously denounced Gal-

[33] Annals, 12th Cong., 1st sess., pp. 803–1005 passim.
[34] Ibid., p. 658; Gallatin to Bacon, Jan. 10, 1812, Henry Adams, ed., The Writings of Albert Gallatin (3 vols.; Philadelphia, 1879), I, 501–517; Grundy to Jackson, Feb. 12, 1812, Andrew Jackson MSS; Harper to Plumer, Feb. 17, 1812, William Plumer MSS, Library of Congress.
[35] National Intelligencer, Jan. 28, 1812; Enquirer, Jan. 25, Feb. 8, 14, 1812; Troup to Governor D. B. Mitchell, March 17, 1812, Edmund J. Harden, The Life of George M. Troup (Savanah, 1859), p. 107.

latin. William Plumer, Jonathan Roberts, and Felix Grundy wanted to postpone taxes until the declaration of war, which alone could make them necessary. The Secretary of the Treasury received a letter from a former colleague, Henry Dearborn, reporting that New Englanders ask "why is it necessary to check the ardour of the people at so critical a moment, why not postpone . . . [most of the] taxes . . . until war shall have actually commenced, then the people will expect to bear such taxes as circumstances shall require." Less restrained critics added charges of "*Apostacy* and TREACHERY" to attacks upon Gallatin's wisdom; indeed, many believed the recommendations showed that he and his administration desired to avoid war. Young John A. Harper swallowed reports that the letter to Bacon had been prepared in arrangement with Foster, adding, "If reports are true, Foster's carriage is frequently seen at Gallatin's house at such hours of the night as honest men are asleep." Even a Republican who believed that Congress would ultimately vote taxes and then war admitted that this "does not seem as palpably true now as a few weeks ago. To say that the retrograde step is commenced . . . would be saying too much; but that the war mercury has sunk a little, nobody here can doubt. The letter of the Secretary of the Treasury has done this." [36]

The panic owed more to congressmen than to the man upon whom they wished to shift the blame. A war movement cast into such despond by a statement of costs necessarily appeared a feeble thing, and the war men's desire for delay showed that they had no faith in the people's firmness or else still hoped to escape without proceeding to open war. Gallatin's letter to Bacon was a private one, not intended for immediate publication, as he later convinced reasonable men like Clay. Although neither the Secretary nor Madison left any record of their intentions, as prudent administrators they must have felt that Congress should consider the costs of war when gaily legislating preparation for it. The tax proposals

[36] Plumer to Harper, Jan. 28, 1812, Plumer MSS; Roberts to Matthew Roberts, Feb. 3, 1812, Roberts MSS; Grundy to Jackson, Feb. 12, 1812, Andrew Jackson MSS; Dearborn to Gallatin, March 29, 1812, Gallatin MSS; *National Intelligencer*, Jan. 28, 1812; *Aurora*, Jan. 25, 1812; Harper to Plumer, Feb. 17, 1812, Plumer MSS.

were too detailed to be communicated orally, like Monroe's promise to the Foreign Affairs Committee. Sometime the question of money had to be faced, however, and Gallatin asked for no more revenue than seemed absolutely necessary. It was not his fault that congressmen found the bill of particulars an unpleasant sight.

For four weeks gloomy Republicans tried to screw their courage to the sticking point. In an air of forced humor, the members considered a proposal to tax marriage licenses in the District of Columbia, Clay observing that "marriage ought not to be taxed, but promoted," while Smilie facetiously proposed a bounty instead of a tax. Finally, on February 17, Bacon reported for the committee. In addition to loans to carry the main burden, he proposed doubled import duties; a direct tax of $3 million levied on the states; an impost of 20 cents a bushel on salt; a stamp act; taxes on distillers, tavernkeepers, wine sellers, and vendors of foreign merchandise; and excises on sugar and carriages.[37] The outline generally followed Gallatin's suggestions. The most interesting thing about Bacon's report was that it proposed to impose the new taxes only when war actually began. While this gesture might somewhat lessen voter resentment, it confessed that many members still hoped to avoid war, created a good reason for opposing a declaration, and destroyed the opportunity for financial preparedness, all without materially easing the path of the tax program.

The House accepted increased import charges after only one day of debate. Internal taxes encountered serious difficulty. James Fisk, a Vermonter usually allied with the war men, proposed to set these taxes aside, saying that "as all were agreed these taxes were war taxes, he thought it time enough to agree upon them when war became certain; . . . there was no doubt the resources of the country were amply sufficient whenever Congress determined to call them forth, but he saw no necessity for alarming the people with odious taxes beforehand." Peter B. Porter seconded Fisk's motion. Although easily beaten, this proposal drew the ominous support of Fisk, Porter, and other Republicans.[38]

[37] *Annals*, 12th Cong., 1st sess., pp. 1041–1042, 1050–1056. For the entire debate, incompletely reported, see pp. 1092–1155.
[38] *Ibid.*, pp. 1109–1110.

The next day a far more serious blow fell. The salt tax, a major source of revenue and linchpin of the entire group of internal taxes, suffered defeat by a vote of fifty-seven to sixty. In general the vote followed sectional rather than factional lines, although the leading War Hawks and sternest Federalists supported the levy for quite opposite reasons. Congressmen from the West, where free salt licks abounded, voted for it. Agrarians from the coastal states, which purchased large amounts of salt, opposed it. In alliance with those who opposed any new taxes, in principle or to slow war preparations, they had their way. The *National Intelligencer* complained that Congress had moved hastily without considering the implications of its action. After having decided "the greater question" by authorizing military increases, the paper argued, it was silly to balk at "the comparatively unimportant question of taxation," particularly since the main costs of war would be met through loans.[39] Still, ruin once again threatened the war movement.

After a week end of troubled thought and conversation, Thomas Gholson of Virginia came to the rescue. He announced that he had changed his mind, now supported the salt tax, and moved reconsideration. Gholson did not pretend to be enthusiastic, but, said he, "I . . . would vote two dollars a bushel on salt, rather than see the present course of policy frustrated. Mr. Speaker, we who form the majority have all the same end in view: the maintenance of the rights, honor, and independence of the country against the lawless aggressions of our enemy." Ten Republicans, all but two from coastal states south of the Hudson, rallied to this call and changed their votes. The salt tax was restored by a vote of sixty-six to fifty-four.[40] Bitter personal attacks on Gallatin and a vengeful proposal to place heavy taxes on Western distillers failed to shake the newly constructed majority.

On March 4, exactly four months after the opening of Congress, the tax bill passed the House of Representatives. Almost no Republicans opposed it on the final roll call, although forty, including Peter B. Porter and David R. Williams, absented themselves.

[39] *Ibid.*, pp. 1114–1115; *National Intelligencer*, Feb. 29, 1812.
[40] *Annals*, 12th Cong., 1st sess., pp. 1118–1127.

Federalists voted in the negative to concentrate the blame for higher taxes upon their opponents.

When this long battle opened, Senator Bayard wrote, "I shall consider the taxes as the test, and when a majority agree to the proposed taxes, I shall believe them in earnest and determined upon war." At the end of the fight James Madison wrote to Monticello that, having "got down the dose of taxes," Congress could be expected to proceed to war in the spring.[41] Without doubt the war men had achieved an important victory; had they lost the fight for tax resolutions, the game would have been up. But it was essentially a defensive victory. Scarecrow men still had an avenue of escape, and Federalists would certainly abandon their passive tactics when the final crisis came. Furthermore, Bacon's resolutions were only resolutions, not law. Final action did not come until after the declaration of war, and even then the oppressive internal taxes were left for consideration the next fall. Apparently the War Hawks dared not risk failure by pressing for legislation, while moderate Republicans, who feared their constituents or still hoped for peace, preferred silence to action.

Throughout the debates the specter of Franco-American relations continually appeared. Honest men found it difficult to support an active policy toward Britain while ignoring Napoleonic insults. They knew that the country's unity would be incomplete while France's crimes counterbalanced England's. Men determined upon peace, whatever the price, exploited the obvious argument that both European powers treated American commerce so badly that a contest with one alone was unjustifiable. "Shall we confine our indignation to injuries received from one quarter," the *Alexandria Gazette* asked, "and be totally insensible to the deadly blows received from another?" By the beginning of 1812 few could maintain that the Berlin and Milan decrees had been repealed in more than the most technical sense, and most Americans believed they had not been repealed at all. In July, 1811,

[41] Bayard to Andrew Bayard, Jan. 25, 1812, Elizabeth Donnan, ed., *Papers of James A. Bayard, 1796–1815*, American Historical Association, *Annual Report, 1913*, II (Washington, 1915), 190; Madison to Jefferson, March 6, 1812, Gaillard Hunt, ed., *The Writings of James Madison* (9 vols.; New York, 1900–1910), VIII, 182.

watching events from St. Petersburg, John Quincy Adams wrote that "France had already violated her own engagements in a manner which absolved us from all obligation." [42] For tactical reasons most War Hawks denied that French repeal fell short of America's legitimate demands. In their hearts they had to agree with Adams.

President Madison also concealed his misgivings. Naturally, the President had reasons of pride for refusing to confess that he had been tricked by the Duke of Cadore's imperial master; even the admission that he had taken an unsuccessful long-shot gamble would be uncomfortable. Moreover, the United States government had made the alleged French repeal the most important basis for its demand that Britain withdraw the Orders in Council, and it could not abandon one without abandoning the other. Not realizing that the policies of Jefferson and himself had convinced England that she need not fear war, Madison hoped that visible American determination would drive Great Britain into surrender. A retrograde step in French relations would lessen this already feeble hope. At Paris and Washington American diplomacy therefore combined private complaints with an absolute unwillingness to admit, either in public or in conversations with British representatives, that French repeal was questionable. Secretary Monroe had to argue, in successive interviews with Foster and Sérurier, first that the decrees were and then that they were not repealed. Still, this ludicrous policy was almost the only one open to Madison, caged in as he was.

Joel Barlow, who arrived at Paris in September, 1811, utterly failed in his mission. Not for two months did Napoleon condescend to receive him. Even then the Emperor replied to Barlow's felicitations with remarks that contained, as the American put it, "some symptoms of the same obliquity which has been so long continued." This, as well as the very belated negative reply to his protest against past and current treatment of American commerce, should have shown Barlow that the situation called for direct action. Instead,

---

[42] *Alexandria Gazette*, Nov. 7, 1811; Adams to Thomas B. Adams, July 31, 1811, Adams Family MSS (microfilm), Massachusetts Historical Society, Vol. CXXXV.

the poet-diplomat allowed himself to be diverted when the French, seizing upon an isolated passage in his communication, offered to negotiate a new commercial treaty. Barlow failed to see that, at best, this injected new, confusing issues into Franco-American discussions, and that, at worst, the French offer was a smoke screen (as it actually was) to hide unwillingness to settle larger problems. From December onward the American talked of little but a commercial treaty. Madison warned him that, until France made compensation for past seizures, "there can be neither cordiality nor confidence here; nor any restraint from self redress in any justifiable mode of effecting it; nor any formal Treaty on the subject." In the search for his will-o'-the-wisp, however, Joel Barlow continued to turn away from America's deepest concerns.[43]

At home, Madison and Monroe had no more success. Both officials warned Sérurier time and again that effective action against England depended upon satisfactory relations with the French Empire. The climax of these conversations came on New Year's Day, when Napoleon's envoy paid a formal call at the White House. Bitterly criticizing continued French seizures, the President angrily declared that "such proceedings were in his eyes just as definite acts of hostility as were those of England, against which the Republic was taking up arms." Fortunately for Sérurier, the swirling crowd separated them before he had to absorb any more presidential ire. In an equally spirited conversation at the State Department, Monroe threatened to call off the campaign against England. On French repeal, he said, "all the present system of the administration is based, and . . . if it were not really unconditional, . . . war . . . with England [would become] very imprudent, and without purpose."[44] Sérurier advised his superiors to make some gesture to inspirit the Americans, and Bassano so urged Napoleon, but the Emperor valued the United

---

[43] Barlow #3 to Monroe, Nov. 21, 1811, Despatches, France, Vol. XIII; Barlow to Bassano, Nov. 10, 1811 AAE, CP, E-U, Vol. LXIV; Bassano to Barlow, Dec. 27, 1811, *ibid.*; Madison to Barlow, Feb. 24, 1812, Hunt, *op. cit.*, VIII, 177–182.

[44] Sérurier #41 to Minister of Foreign Relations, Jan. 2, 1812, AAE, CP, E-U, Vol. LXVII.

CHARLES JAMES FOX
*Portrait by Karl A. Hickel*

ALEXANDER BARING
*Portrait by Thomas Lawrence*

SAMUEL WHITBREAD
*Portrait by John Hoppner*

HENRY BROUGHAM
*Portrait by James Lonsdale*

JAMES MADISON
*Portrait by John Vanderlyn*

JOHN C. CALHOUN
*Portrait by*
*Charles B. King*

HENRY CLAY
*Portrait by an unknown artist*

JOHN RANDOLPH
*Portrait by John W. Jarvis*

JOSIAH QUINCY
*Portrait by Gilbert Stuart*

States as lightly as ever. French corsairs and *douaniers* the length of the Empire continued to harass American commerce.

Publication of the Henry letters, produced by the administration to reveal an intrigue between Federalists and British agents, promised at first to provide a psychological equivalent for the settlement with France which eluded Madison and Monroe. John Henry, an Irishman who became a secret agent for Canadian authorities after living for some time in the United States and even serving in the United States Army, journeyed to Boston during the Embargo to investigate the extent of disaffection there and perhaps open regular communication with dissidents. Henry, accompanied by his wife and two young children, was received in friendly fashion by leaders of the town, for he had obtained impressive letters of introduction, had married into a prominent Philadelphia family, and was known to some from the days of his army service in Boston. The British agent learned that New England detested Jefferson and the Embargo—information that he could have found in the newspapers—but he heard so little reliable secessionist talk that he never dared open himself to any Americans. Paid only £200 by Governor-General Craig, rebuffed when he sought appointment as spy-cum-consul in Vermont, refused additional payment when he traveled to London, John Henry set out for America to gain revenge upon an ungrateful ministry. He planned to sell to the United States government his old reports to his British employers. This scheme appears to have been suggested by a personable young Frenchman who called himself Count Edouard de Crillon (but was actually an experienced rogue named Soubiron), with whom Henry became friendly during his trip to London. Crillon offered to manage negotiations with the American authorities.

Stopping in Boston only long enough to procure letters of introduction from Governor Gerry, Henry and Crillon proceeded to Washington. Crillon introduced himself to the French minister and offered to serve his country by securing publication of the incriminating documents. Sérurier was too fastidious to enjoy intrigue, and he was intelligent enough to doubt Crillon's identity. (The count later sought money from Foster to keep the documents secret. Foster, recognizing him as an impostor, exposed inaccuracies in Crillon's story at a dinner to which prominent War Hawks were invited.) Still, the French envoy felt he could not cast aside an opportunity to forward the war movement. He gave his blessing to the conversations Crillon opened with the Secretary of State. Sérurier's recommendations, Gerry's letters, and reiterated assurances from the sottish Senator Brent, who became an intimate of Crillon's, caused Monroe and Madison to accept the man doubted by almost everyone else in town. Early in February Monroe agreed to pay $50,000 for copies of reports to Craig which supposedly incriminated Great Britain and the Federalists. This sum, subsequently transferred to Crillon by Henry for a nonexistent château in France, represented the entire available secret service fund, and it was paid for letters Monroe had never once been allowed to see. When Monroe received the copies, he discovered that they were filled with emendations, omissions, and rows of asterisks designed to hint that incriminating passages had been removed. The Secretary asked Henry to name Federalists who had engaged in treasonable conversations with him. The traitor demurred, self-righteously declaring that while he sought revenge upon ingrates in London he would not compromise American friends who had confided in him. Presumably Madison and Monroe realized that their eagerness had betrayed them; there was no proof of a conspiracy. Perhaps they might better have given up the game at this point. But at least the letters showed that a British spy had visited America. Therefore, on March 9, just after the House endorsed Bacon's tax proposals, the President sent the Henry papers to Congress, accompanied by a letter solicited from Henry to suggest that no money had been paid for them.[45]

[45] A masterpiece of narrative history, untangling this complicated affair, is Samuel E. Morison, "The Henry-Crillon Affair of 1812," *By Land and By Sea* (New York, 1953), pp. 265–286. Ernest A. Cruikshank, *The Political Adventures of John Henry* (Toronto, 1936), deals with the careers of Henry and Crillon in exhaustive detail. Manuscript references to the adventurers are too numerous to cite. Richard B. Davis, ed., *Jeffersonian America: Notes on the United States of America . . . by Sir Augustus John Foster, Bart.* (San Marino, 1954), pp. 70 ff., and Georges de Caraman, "Les

At first Federalists suffered while their opponents exulted. Young Harper saw, or thought that he saw, Pitkin begin "to kick and *squirm.* . . . Quincy looked pale . . . and was much agitated as was Tallmadge, Champion and finally there was little difference between them, except in Deacon Davenport, on whose face I actually saw, not only great drops of sweat, but it really ran down copiously on his face." The *National Intelligencer* burst forth with an exultant editorial. Foster flew into a panic, listened glumly to Federalist complaints that England had compromised them on the eve of success, and endorsed Sérurier's reported comment that "if this event does not produce a war nothing will do so." [46]

The tide quickly turned. Even in the debate that followed the President's message, Thomas Gholson and William R. Troup congratulated the Federalists on Henry's inability to produce evidence that any of them were disloyal. Led by Quincy, Federalists forced Monroe to admit that the Department of State could not tie individual Americans to Henry's disclosures. They soon tracked down the payments to Henry, and some Republicans joined them in protesting the expenditure of $50,000 for his empty reports. [47] Recovering his *sang-froid*, Foster visited the White House, where he was the center of attention but received no insults from the crowd and only courtesy from the President. Ezekiel Bacon urged the government to abandon an affair that threatened to backfire. Federalist newspapers took the offensive, alleging a trick to influence the impending Massachusetts election, charging that nothing Henry had revealed compared with the activities of Madison's agents in Spanish Florida, and particularly emphasizing that Henry's failure to find Federalists whom he dared trust vindi-

États-Unis Il Y a Quarante Ans," *Révue Contemporaine*, 1st Series, III (1852), 229 ff., give the accounts of the British minister and a French attaché.

[46] Harper to Plumer, March 11, 1812, Plumer MSS; *National Intelligencer*, March 10, 1812; Foster #14 to Wellesley, secret, March 12, 1812, FO 5/84.

[47] *Annals*, 12th Cong., 1st sess., pp. 1162–1196; Quincy to Otis, March 19, 1812, and enclosure, Otis MSS; *Niles' Register*, March 21, 1812; *Sentinel of Freedom* (Newark, N.J.), March 24, 1812. The second volume of the *Annals* for this session bears the misleading subtitle, "12th Congress, 2nd Session," but this obvious error has been corrected here and below.

cated the party from the stale charge of treason.[48] Aside from causing a Federalist boycott of the White House which reduced grocery and liquor bills, the President benefited in no way from the disclosures. He had made the most stupid if not the most important misstep of his presidential career.

As a result of the Henry fiasco, Foster returned with renewed confidence to his original diagnosis, that the Republicans were bluffing and had no intention of going to war. Firmness on Britain's part, he reported, "appears likely to be attended with the very best effects." The war threat did not trouble the commercial world. Long past the turn of the year, ships regularly departed for Europe and insurance rates remained steady. This, said Foster, showed "how little in earnest the Government are supposed to be by the mercantile part of the Community." Over and over again, Federalists congratulated themselves on the perspicuity of their initial analysis. From the first, Federalists had argued that war talk was "rather manufactured for exportation than home consumption being destined to go to Europe . . . to flatter France and terrify Britain." Now they asked, "What reason have we to conclude that they are more serious now than they were several years ago? . . . We have heard the same sort of gasconade in Congress more than three thousand times." [49]

In Congress, War Hawks angrily denied the bluff charge. Outside it, their allies' comments showed that they really feared it might be true. "You went to the house-tops, and proclaimed resistance," a bellicose editor, Thomas Ritchie, reminded congressmen. "You talked big; you deprecated submission and threatened war." Ritchie warned that those who deserted now would be held responsible by their constituents for the destruction of the country's reputation. Jonathan Russell, who knew he would have to endure

[48] Journal entry, March 11, 1812, Foster journal, Augustus J. Foster MSS, Library of Congress; Bacon to Gallatin, March 15, 1812, Gallatin MSS; *Columbian Centinel*, March 18, 21, 1812; *Alexandria Gazette*, March 13, 1812; *Federal Republican*, March 11, 12, 1812; *Rhode Island American and General Advertiser* (Providence), March 17, 1812; *Connecticut Courant* (Hartford), April 1, 1812; Foster to Wellesley, separate and secret, March 24, 1812, FO 5/85.

[49] Foster #7 to Wellesley, secret, Jan. 31, 1812, FO 5/84; Taggart to Rev. John Taylor, Dec. 2, 1811, Haynes, *op. cit.*, p. 365; *Alexandria Gazette*, April 14, 1812.

the taunts of all London if America backed down, wrote, "I hope it will not prove to be merely a show. I should indeed hang my head if there were any retrog[r]ade movement after so much blustering." [50] The War Hawks were not certain of their fair-weather friends.

The aura of insincerity sapped the effectiveness of the threat to England. Senator Giles had less attractive reasons for insisting that the new army be expanded from 10,000 to 25,000 men, but a good one was his assertion that the impression of weakness, "the necessary result of our former measures, has become so general, both at home and abroad, that we have much to do to retrieve our lost reputation." Dr. Stevenson Archer, a young War Hawk from Maryland, warned members of the House that Britain was unlikely to be impressed by anything short of force. "She knows too well," he said, "your conduct heretofore, to believe you are in earnest." [51] The campaign of intimidation failed in 1807; there was no reason to believe it would succeed in 1812.

Nevertheless, in ways that few foresaw, the events from November to March contributed to the coming of war. They convinced Britain that the United States was merely repeating a stale and rather ineffective drama, and discussion of the orders proceeded under the assumption that neither a new nor a speedy denouement need be anticipated. On the other hand, the legislation passed by Congress created a sort of momentum which eventually imprisoned many who believed that they had preserved their freedom of action. In March a Federalist, Abijah Bigelow, exulted that "the poor souls have got themselves into a sad dilemma, they know not how to go forward, or how to retreat, and what is still more disgraceful they have no settled plan which they mean to pursue, they depend upon the chapter of accidents." Unfortunately for Bigelow and his friends, "the chapter of accidents" pushed moderate Republicans and bluffers toward the War Hawks. When congressional posturing failed to bring about British concessions, when

[50] *Enquirer*, March 27, 1812; Russell to John S. Smith, Feb. 11, 1812, Samuel Smith MSS.
[51] *Annals*, 12th Cong., 1st sess., pp. 41, 561.

the country rang with charges that Congress had never intended to go to war, when humiliating surrender stared the scarecrow men in the face, a reluctant vote for war became the only palatable alternative. After all the oratory, Jonathan Russell observed, Congress must go on or "the notoriety we shall have given to our cowardice by our blustering will expose us to the injustice & contumely & the contempt of every nation which will condescend to take the trouble to spurn or plunder us." [52] Preparedness agitation worked in a way certainly not anticipated by Federalists and moderate Republicans who abetted it. Probably not even the War Hawks understood the long-range implications of the campaign they spearheaded.

In the first months of 1812 the odds on war baffled everyone, both because of evidences of bluffing and because, as Taggart noted, "the war fever . . . has its hot and cold fits." "The *War Chariot* drags on heavily," the *Columbian Centinel* noted toward the end of January, and George Poindexter, the delegate from the Mississippi Territory, was almost alone in predicting eventual war. Felix Grundy feared betrayal. So did George M. Troup of Georgia, although he noted that "nothing short of war or free commerce . . . can satisfy the expectations of the Southern people, who have been bearing the brunt of the restrictive system from the beginning." At the beginning of February Federalists Taggart and Reed became blindly enthusiastic and estimated that not more than half a dozen representatives were ready to vote for war. Randolph was more doubtful. James A. Bayard, a cautious Federalist who feared that the doldrums might merely presage a new storm, nevertheless concluded: "One can discover very little war spirit in either House of Congress. And yet the members will tell you very coldly, that war is inevitable. But I have found no one willing to declare war and very few to adopt any measure of hostile character." [53] War prospects appeared very slim.

[52] Bigelow to Hannah G. Bigelow, March 22, 1812, Clarence S. Brigham, ed., "Letters of Abijah Bigelow, Member of Congress, to His Wife, 1810–1815," American Antiquarian Society, *Proceedings*, n.s., XL (1931), 332; Russell to Adams, March 9, 1812, Jonathan Russell MSS, Brown University Library.
[53] Taggart to Rev. John Taylor, Jan. 20, 1812, Haynes, *op. cit.*, p. 377; *Colum-*

The next few weeks brought some indications of renewed progress. Peter B. Porter, whose own legislative record was spotted with hesitation, delivered a fiery philippic on the necessity for speed. "And if we continued to go on preparing for war in the good-natured, desultory way we had hitherto pursued," Porter warned, Britain might undertake an anticipatory attack, "for which, if justly imputable to our tardiness and indecision, we could never be forgiven." Congress must set in motion the attack upon Canada. Except for the occupation of Halifax and the siege of Quebec, to which the army might "proceed at their leisure," this could be completed "in a few weeks." This vision of easy conquest inspirited many congressmen, and two days later Foster reported home that, barring British concessions, war might follow within a fortnight.[54] On March 10, after Congress "got down the dose of taxes," Gallatin informed his political mentor at Monticello that a declaration of war was inevitable, and Jefferson believed Virginia awaited it with calm expectancy.[55]

As March wore on, other observers thought the *National Intelligencer* was whistling in the dark when it announced that Congress proceeded toward war with "a deliberate but firm step." Pouncing upon another metaphor much in vogue among War Hawks, the *Aurora* scoffed, "As to the *fever heat* created at Washington, it must be a species of intermittent, what is vulgarly called the *shaking ague.*" War journals challenged the sincerity of those who professed to be ready to make war but argued that a declaration must await hardening of the roads to Canada or the return of U.S.S. *Hornet,* sent in December to carry accounts of Porter's Report to Europe and to bring home news of European

*bian Centinel,* Jan. 22, 1812; Grundy to Jackson, Feb. 12, 1812, Andrew Jackson MSS; Troup to Mitchell, Feb. 12, 1812, Harden, *op. cit.,* p. 107; Taggart to Rev. John Taylor, Feb. 6, 1812, Haynes, *op. cit.,* p. 382; Reed to Pickering, Feb. 6, 1812, Pickering MSS, Vol. XXX; Randolph to James M. Garnett, Feb. 5, 1812, John Randolph MSS, Library of Congress; Bayard to Andrew Bayard, Feb. 13, 1812, Donnan, *op. cit.,* p. 193.

[54] *Annals,* 12th Cong., 1st sess., pp. 1059–1063; Foster #10 to Wellesley, secret, Feb. 26, 1812, FO 5/84. But see Foster's quite contrary recollection in Davis, *op. cit.,* pp. 90–91.

[55] Monroe to Jefferson, March 10, 1812, Thomas Jefferson MSS, Library of Congress; Jefferson to Madison, March 26, 1812, *ibid.*

politics. One paper pointed out that the spring sun had already dried the roads, and it asked why troops had not been raised and directed northward to take advantage of the perfect campaigning weather. Steadfast as ever for war, the Lexington *Reporter* noted with disapproval, "Ever since her sailing the cant word has been, the *Hornet,* the *Hornet*—what a sting she will bring on her return!!" The *Reporter* wryly repeated a Federalist jibe that the *Hornet* would never return, giving the Republicans an excuse for permanent inactivity.[56]

When Washington's most beautiful season arrived, the only storms to be seen lay on the brows of troubled congressmen. The autumn had been pleasant, with good pheasant shooting enjoyed by James A. Bayard and Augustus Foster, who exchanged political information as they hunted; the winter had been brief but cold, permitting sleighing in the usually snow-free District. By the middle of March frogs were piping in the little creek that crossed Pennsylvania Avenue below the Capitol, and with the change of seasons Foster expanded his entertainments, which no longer needed to be entirely indoors. Now he reported dinners of up to 500 persons, and it seemed that he meant to feed the entire population of Washington if that would lessen the chances of war. Four months had passed since Congress met, and yet no one could argue that the nation was prepared for war, psychologically or materially. Impractical army legislation, a refusal to expand the navy, grudging approval of the principle of new taxes—these were almost as useless as no preparation at all. In March the nation was as far from war as it had been at the beginning of November. Or so at least it seemed.

[56] *National Intelligencer,* March 19, 1812; *Aurora,* March 11, 1812; *Sentinel of Freedom,* March 10, 1812; *Reporter* (Lexington, Ky.), March 21, 1812.

CHAPTER

# XI

## WAR AT LAST

"What a Ridiculous Farce has been played off in the Face of the Nation," a former congressman expostulated as March ended. ". . . why Sir, Congress have made themselves so Ridiculous and insignificant that all their War Measures are regarded . . . just as men would Regard Boys cracking Nuts at [a] Distance."[1] March saw the nadir. From then on, prodded by the threat of disgrace, Congress moved slowly and sometimes erratically toward war. The declaration passed by a narrow margin, and many of the majority went along with deep misgivings. The people obviously did not want war, and if further delay had been permitted their voice would have prevented it. Still, war came, bringing the trials and the glory (here, infrequent glory) which follow in the train of Mars. America embarked upon a second war for independence, a war to recover the nation's honor and affirm her claim to act as an independent power.

In midafternoon on March 20, 1812, Lieutenant Green, borne

[1] James Kelly to Pickering, March 30, 1812, Timothy Pickering MSS, Massachusetts Historical Society, Vol. XXX.

across the Atlantic by the *Gleaner*, chartered at a cost of £5,000, arrived at Washington with instructions from Wellesley to Foster. Unless Wellesley, who had already offered his resignation, desired to embarrass his successor, expensive haste had no purpose. The instructions repeated the old, old declaration that, French repeal being fraudulent, Britain would continue the Orders in Council. They rebuked Foster for entertaining ideas of compromise.[2] The strategy of bluff appeared to have failed. War talk recommenced. "There is," Hezekiah Niles declared, "no middle course left for the United States to pursue. The embargo system, at once the safest and best, has been disgraced by the time-serving conduct of its friends—war or submission present themselves; and all that sophistry can devise, the fear of [un]popularity invent, or personal pusillanimity dictate, cannot offer another alternative." William Duane, visiting Washington to sell a house to his rival editor, Joseph Gales, thought the future far less clear. And, although Madison recommended and Congress passed a general embargo within a fortnight of the *Hornet*'s arrival, Louis Sérurier doubted the Republicans' sticking power. With some relief but not complete conviction, he soon reported that Madison's journal, the *National Intelligencer*, had adopted a bellicose line.[3]

The President's embargo message, as the full story will show, gave an illusory appearance of decisive leadership. Still, after a winter during which the White House had most closely resembled the oracle at Delphi, any appearance of forthrightness took on significance. Since his November message the President had pretty much kept his own counsel. In January, to expose England's rigidity, he submitted to Congress correspondence between Monroe and

---

[2] Journal entry, March 20, 1812, Foster journal, Augustus J. Foster MSS, Library of Congress; Wellesley #1 to Foster, Jan. 28, 1812, Bernard Mayo, ed., *Instructions to the British Ministers to the United States, 1791–1812*, American Historical Association, *Annual Report, 1936*, III (Washington, 1941), 340–344; Wellesley #2 to Foster, secret, Jan. 28, 1812, *ibid.*, pp. 344–346.

[3] Harper to Bartlett, March 22, 1812, Josiah Bartlett MSS, Library of Congress; *Niles' Weekly Register* (Baltimore), April 4, 1812; Duane to Jefferson, July 17, 1812, Worthington C. Ford, ed., "Letters of William Duane," Massachusetts Historical Society, *Proceedings*, 2d Series, XX (1907), 350; Sérurier #52, #53 to Minister of Foreign Relations, April 9, 19, 1812, Archives des Affaires Étrangères, Correspondance Politique, États-Unis (photostats, Library of Congress), Vol. LXVII.

Foster; in March he made public the Henry letters, with consequences that reflected upon his good sense and harmed the war movement. Otherwise the President acted more like William McKinley in 1898 than James Knox Polk in 1846, and War Hawks and peace men both claimed him. Republicans pleaded for a clear lead, and late in March several imploring letters reached the White House within a few days.[4] The embargo message, an apparent answer to this prayer, did not convince suspicious men. In March John C. Calhoun temporarily abandoned his doubts of the administration, writing, "Their Zeal and intelligence can not now be doubted." Shortly after the message his doubts returned, and he commented, "Our President tho a man of amiable manners and great talents, has not I fear those commanding talents, which are necessary to controul those about him. . . . He reluctantly gives up the system of peace. It is to be hoped, that as war is now seriously determined on, the Executive department will move with much more vigour. Without it it is impossible for Congress to proceed."[5] A single message extorted by demanding legislators could not destroy Madison's reputation for weakness.

Party doctrine and personal preference caused President Madison to follow a silent course. Republican constitutional theory glorified the legislature at the expense of the executive, providing an excuse for presidential silence on the question of war. This silence angered, among others, Speaker Clay, who bluntly told the administration: "Altho' the power of declaring War belongs to the Congress, I do not see that it falls less within the scope of the President's constitutional duty to recommend . . . measures . . . than any other which, being suggested by him, they alone can adopt." In dealing with legislative problems Madison showed none of the boldness, even rashness, that led him to accept the assurances of Erskine and Cadore. In the war session he did nothing to prevent preparedness legislation, but he also did far less than

[4] William Crawford to Madison, March 28, 1812, James Madison MSS, Library of Congress; Thomas Lehre to Madison, March 30, 1812, *ibid.*; James Barbour to Madison, March 30, 1812, *ibid.*

[5] Calhoun to Macbride, March 22, April 18, 1812, Robert L. Meriwether, ed., *The Papers of John C. Calhoun*, I (Columbia, S.C., 1959), 95, 99–100.

he might have done to encourage it. In pacific times this intelligent man might have been a successful president. But he was not cut in the heroic mold. "*Madison* may be *good*," an editorialist commented, "but in a *national view*, there is a great distinction between *Good*, and GOOD ENOUGH." [6] Left to himself, with a Congress like the Tenth, James Madison would have been a complete failure in 1812.

This is not to say that because he lacked determination when dealing with his Cabinet, his party, and the legislature the President took a cowardly, indecisive view of America's position. His enemies accused him of attempting to preserve the support of both War Hawks and peace men for the election of 1812 or, later, suggested that he supported war only after War Hawks threatened to prevent his reëlection.[7] This was nonsense. Since the very beginning of the session Madison's analysis had been based upon more honorable grounds. It combined simplicity and complexity, optimism and pessimism in baffling degrees, but it was consistently maintained.

Toward the end of November Madison told Foster that for America "anything was better than remaining in such a state" as the existing one. (Madison naturally failed to add that the state of the nation owed much to his own activities as secretary of state and president.) If war became the only alternative, the President would face it. Summarizing his position, although characteristically bestowing the power of choice upon Congress and directing his musings to an American safely distant at St. Petersburg, the President wrote that the question "simply is, whether all the trade to which the orders [in Council] are . . . applied, is to be abandoned, or the hostile operation of them, be hostilely resisted. The apparent disposition is certainly not in favor of the first

[6] Clay endorsement on Clay to Monroe, March 15, 1812, James F. Hopkins, ed., *The Papers of Henry Clay*, I (Lexington, Ky., 1959), 637; *Virginia Patriot* (Richmond), May 12, 1812. For this and the subsequent paragraphs I am indebted to Theodore C. Smith, "War Guilt in 1812," Massachusetts Historical Society, *Proceedings*, LXIV (1932), 319–345, and Irving Brant, *James Madison: the President* (Indianapolis, 1956), *passim*, though my interpretation of Madison's position differs sharply from their interpretations.

[7] Brant, *op. cit.*, pp. 452 ff., convincingly demolishes this old canard.

alternative, though it is more than probable, that if the second should be adopted, the execution of it will be put off till the close of the Session approaches." Not a single piece of reputable evidence suggests that the President abandoned this conviction at any time, although he reserved the right to decide later whether hostility should be shown with a fly whisk, a club, or a sword. When Foster described Monroe as "a mild moderate man, . . . with whom I am happy to say it has been my good fortune to be on the best terms," he really was indirectly comparing the Secretary and the less complaisant President. On April 1, just at the time here being discussed, Foster scribbled in his diary, "go to the President's— He very warlike, calls our orders tantamount to Letters of marque." [8] But if he spoke freely to Foster, Madison never made his position clear enough to give direction to Congress, and throughout the winter, while resignedly prepared to go to war, the President hoped for some acceptable solution to the nation's problems which would make war unnecessary.

As Bernard Mayo has observed, the President "seemed less intent upon harnessing the chariot of war than upon driving the old coach of diplomacy." He combined warnings and invitations in his conversations with Foster. So frequent were his suggestions that Britain, without doing serious damage to herself, might modify her restrictions upon commerce in a way palatable to the United States, that Foster finally reported: "The name of the Orders in Council has become more objectionable to him than the substance." Undoubtedly the British envoy misunderstood Madison, who surely required benefits of substance as well as of form. On the other hand the Chief Executive would almost certainly have accepted an accommodation that did not concede all that some Americans desired. Even when he recommended an embargo to Congress, a step the political world interpreted as a harbinger of war, the President went out of his way to inform Foster that timely

<hr />

[8] Foster #25 to Wellesley, Nov. 21, 1811, Foreign Office Archives, Public Record Office, FO 5/77; Madison to Adams, private, Nov. 15, 1811, Gaillard Hunt, ed., *The Writings of James Madison* (9 vols.; New York, 1900–1910), VIII, 167; Foster #14 to Wellesley, secret, March 12, 1812, FO 5/84; journal entry, April 1, 1812, Foster MSS.

British concessions could prevent a declaration.[9] Down to the very end, albeit with increasing pessimism, James Madison clung to a hope that commercial pressure and American war preparations would bring England to terms.

The President overlooked one obvious opportunity to demonstrate American determination and simultaneously to strike at the Achilles' heel of Britain. From 1809 onward, the English Achilles, Viscount Wellington, engaged in a desperate struggle with Napoleonic marshals in Spain. To supply his army and the people in his rear, Wellington depended largely upon American grain. Shipments to the Peninsula, which totaled less than 80,000 bushels in 1807, leaped to more than 230,000 in 1810, 835,000 in 1811, and more than 900,000 bushels in 1812. In April, 1812, a British observer at Lisbon wrote that "provisions [are] plenty, but principally from America . . . ; and if it was not for the supplies from America, the army here could not be maintained." [10] Here was a perfect opportunity to apply the cherished Republican policy of economic warfare, particularly after the European harvest of 1811 proved disappointing.

Many Americans saw the opportunity. In January, 1812, Jonathan Russell urged Monroe to end Peninsular shipments, and on the same day he wrote Joel Barlow that "this very war which preserves the existence of the present ministry—so hostile to us— is fed & pampered by our supplies and without us must be abandoned." Monroe's son-in-law told him that this was "the most effectual weapon that can be wielded against G Britain." Madison himself felt that Peninsular starvation would be the most important consequence of a general embargo. Incredibly, Madison and Congress permitted this opportunity to escape, fatuously pre-

---

[9] Bernard Mayo, ed., *Henry Clay, Spokesman of the New West* (Boston, 1937), p. 439; Foster #23 to Wellesley, April 3, 1812, FO 5/85; Richard B. Davis, ed., *Jeffersonian America: Notes on the United States of America.... by Sir Augustus John Foster, Bart.* (San Marino, 1954), pp. 91–92; journal entry, April 2, 1812, Foster MSS.

[10] Robert G. Albion and Jennie B. Pope, *Sea Lanes in Wartime* (New York, 1942), p. 108; Milne to George Hume, April 9, 1812, Edgar E. Hume, ed., "Letters Written during the War of 1812 by the British Naval Commander in American Waters (Admiral Sir David Milne)," *William and Mary Quarterly*, 2d Series, X (1930), 286.

ferring nonimportation to a ban on exports until the spring of 1812. Perhaps the President feared an outcry from grain producers in the Middle States; perhaps, like Jefferson, he considered a "vent for our produce" [11] necessary. In any event the chance was missed.

Instead, the administration tardily and reluctantly accepted a congressional proposal for a general embargo on American ships and exports. In the middle of March, first in conversation with Monroe and then formally in writing, Speaker Clay suggested a thirty-day embargo, to be followed by war. No other measure, he thought, could so clearly show that Congress and the administration were in earnest. The administration hesitated. Ten days later, speaking for the Foreign Affairs Committee, Peter B. Porter, John Smilie, and John C. Calhoun prodded the executive. Still a week later Chairman Porter virtually demanded that Monroe inform the committee when the administration would be ready to proceed to "ulterior measures." [12]

The Secretary of State journeyed to Capitol Hill for a conference with the committee on the afternoon of March 30. The administration, he said, believed that Congress ought to declare war before adjourning if Britain did not abandon her hostile policy, a course that Foster's recent declarations made unlikely. The Secretary indirectly suggested an embargo of sixty days to allow time for the *Hornet* to return with news from Europe. Monroe reported that the nation was inadequately prepared for war; he admitted that he considered preparedness legislation valuable largely as "an appeal to the feelings of the foreign Govt."; and he did not pledge the administration to ask for a declaration of war when the *Hornet* returned. This negativism communicated

[11] Russell to Monroe, private, Jan. 14, 1812, Department of State Archives, National Archives, Despatches, Great Britain, Vol. XVIII; Russell to Barlow, Jan. 14, 1812, Jonathan Russell MSS, Brown University Library; Hay to Monroe, Jan. 23, 1812, James Monroe MSS, New York Public Library; Madison to Jefferson, April 3, 1812, Hunt, *op. cit.*, VIII, 186; Jefferson to ——— Gibson, April 12, 1812, Thomas Jefferson MSS, Library of Congress. On this entire subject see W. Freeman Galpin, "The American Grain Trade to the Spanish Peninsula, 1800–1814," *American Historical Review*, XXVIII (1922–1923), 24–44.

[12] Clay to Monroe, March 15, 1812, Hopkins, *op. cit.*, I, 637; Porter, Smilie, and Calhoun to Monroe, March 24, 1812, Monroe MSS, NYPL; Porter to Monroe, March 30, 1812, *ibid.*

itself to Chairman Porter, who suggested that Congress postpone an embargo until after a short recess and even push back a declaration of war until September. Calhoun brusquely replied, "Some decisive measure is required that would give a tone to our legislation which has not been hitherto perceived," and John A. Harper bluntly asked the Secretary if the administration would recommend an embargo. Monroe answered, "If you give me the necessary assurance that it will be acceptable to the House the Executive will recommend it." He declined to promise a manifesto rallying the country for war, saying, "The Executive will not take upon itself the responsibility for declaring that we are prepared for war." [13] This qualified courage, this caution, this desire to thrust responsibility upon Congress was the best that the committee could extort from Monroe or from the President, whose reaction Monroe reported to the congressmen the next day.

On April 1 the President recommended a general embargo in a cryptic one-sentence message submitted to a secret session. Porter quickly presented a bill for a sixty-day embargo, but his remarks showed that he had no enthusiasm either for an embargo or for war. Nathaniel Macon attempted to postpone a decision, and with support from Quincy and the Federalists he came within three votes of attaining his objective. Randolph denounced the project as a fake, since the nation could not be ready for war in two months' time, and he objected that it was "too high a price to pay for the consistency of gentlemen who think they have gone too far to recede." Grundy, Clay, Smilie, and Adam Seybert, on the other hand, declared that this was a real step toward war and that the President so considered it. The war men drove the House forward, and at an early hour in the evening the House of Representatives passed the bill reluctantly fathered by Porter by a vote of seventy to forty-one. Only a handful of congressmen who later voted for war opposed the embargo, but ten failed to vote at all, and the seventy favorable votes fell short of a majority of the whole

<hr />

[13] Unsigned [Randolph?] memorandum, March 30–31, 1812, Samuel Smith MSS, Library of Congress.

House.[14] This vote, like the even more discouraging one on the tax resolutions, left it very uncertain that a majority for war could be attained.

The House bill sought, belatedly, to cut off the flow of American supplies to Spain and Portugal, as several legislators stated in the debates. The bill also aimed to clear American ships from the ocean where they would be easy prey for British cruisers when war came, and this purpose too was openly avowed. Finally, the embargo aimed to convince the American and perhaps the British people that Congress was in earnest. Not one of these purposes was completely achieved. The Senate weakened the embargo; it was almost everywhere evaded; and, at least in the days just after Madison signed the bill, the administration weakened its impact by playing a mixed game.

The Senate passed the embargo by a vote of twenty to thirteen, with Giles and Samuel Smith, two leading Republican dissidents, joining Federalists in opposition. A Federalist senator privately claimed that many more Republicans who disliked it submitted to the demands of party solidarity. Even this grudging approval came only after the Senate had completely transformed the meaning of the bill. On the motion of Michael Leib, another vindictively anti-Madisonian Republican, the embargo was extended from sixty to ninety days.[15] Everyone understood that the Senate wished to give time for further negotiations and at worst to put off the evil day of war as long as possible. From a vigorous measure, the embargo bill had been transformed into a temporizing one. When the revised version was returned to the House of Representatives, Josiah Quincy taunted the Republicans for insincerity, declaring that the embargo was not a step forward, as the war men claimed, but rather "a substitute for the question of war." The Federalist's taunts decided War Hawks to accept the Senate bill rather than risk another quarrel with the Senate like that which had paralyzed the government before the passage of Macon's Bill

14 *Annals*, 12th Cong., 1st sess., pp. 1587–1598.
15 *Ibid.*, pp. 187–189.

in 1810. On April 4 Madison's signature made the ninety-day embargo bill a law.[16]

Just as senatorial action robbed the bill of its appearance of vigor, so the flight of ships from American ports deprived it of its coercive and precautionary effect. Even before the President sent his message to Congress, rumors of an impending embargo had spread as far as Baltimore. With the approval of John C. Calhoun, who did not desire insiders alone to benefit, Quincy, James Emott of New York, Senator Lloyd of Massachusetts, and others immediately sent word northward. Their warning reached port cities ahead of official announcements of the act.[17] The deputy collector of customs at Boston kept his office open until nine in the evening so that all who desired could secure papers for their ships, and, despite a fog that delayed some departures, more than eighty ships escaped. Revenue cutters caught only three or four. At New York four were arrested of a total of a hundred or more. Foster reported officially that the embargo had misfired; less seriously, he wrote to his mother, "The Embargo has put us all in a fuss. Great Quantities of corn & flour have gone off so I hope Spain & Portugal will not suffer. Theres hardly enough left at New York for the bakers." [18] Grain shipments to Lisbon and Cadiz postponed to a distant day the impact of shortages. Anticipation of the embargo cast onto the seas and even into British ports hundreds of merchant vessels which risked capture when war came. The massive exodus, largest since Erskine's agreement three years before, destroyed the intentions of the embargo's authors.

In the secret debates on the embargo, its supporters repeatedly declared it an administration measure aiming at war. Had this position been taken publicly, the nation might have believed it.

[16] *Ibid.*, pp. 1601–1614. Philip B. Key told Foster he regretted Quincy's intemperate language, without which the House would probably have rejected extension of the embargo to ninety days. Journal entry, April 8, 1812, Foster MSS.

[17] *Annals*, 12th Cong., 1st sess., pp. 1263–1265; Quincy memo, n.d., Edmund Quincy, *Life of Josiah Quincy* (Boston, 1867), pp. 256–257; *New-York Evening Post*, April 2, 1812.

[18] John Borland to Lloyd, April 25, 1812, James Lloyd MSS, Houghton Library, Harvard University; *Columbian Centinel* (Boston), April 8, 11, 1812; *New-York Evening Post*, April 6, 1812; Foster #28 to Castlereagh, April 23, 1812, FO 5/85; Foster to Duchess of Devonshire, April 5, 1812, Foster MSS.

Had Monroe and Madison impressed it upon Foster, the Englishman might conceivably have warned his government that Britain faced a choice between concession and war. The President, however, never explained his motives to the country, and the declarations of known War Hawks could be discounted. Many Republicans, both the orthodox and the independents like Samuel Smith, visited Foster to tell him they did not consider the embargo a war measure. Both the President and the Secretary of State deliberately informed Foster that they felt the same way, and in his diary the British envoy recorded Madison as saying, "One Embargo might be inoculated on another." [19]

At first the *National Intelligencer* called the embargo a measure of precaution rather than of war preparation, and Monroe praised Joseph Gales for this emphasis. "The great object," said Monroe, "is to suggest nothing at the present moment that may . . . compromit the govt., as to the future with either power, or on the other hand check the ardour of the nation." Copying many of Monroe's phrases, Gales then declared that "the spirit of the nation is up," that war with one or both belligerents must follow unless speedy arrangements were made, but that the embargo "is not war, nor does it inevitably lead to war." Only on April 14, ten days after passage of the embargo, did the *Intelligencer* abandon this cautious line, saying, "Let war . . . be forthwith proclaimed against England." [20] Although the administration appeared to have joined the War Hawks, Madison's hesitations were not forgotten. Alert eyes watched for signs of a changed course.

For the next six weeks, while Congress dawdled, ostensibly to permit recruiting and to await the *Hornet*, Federalists sought desperately for some clear indication of what the future held in store. "Never did a set of rulers in any country so completely succeed as ours have done," the *United States Gazette* complained, "in setting at defiance all the calculations of friends and foes, as to the

[19] Campbell to Jackson, April 10, 1812, Andrew Jackson MSS, Library of Congress; *Reporter* (Lexington, Ky.), April 11, 1812; Davis, *op. cit.*, p. 93; journal entries, April 2, 3, 1812, Foster MSS.
[20] Monroe to Gales, [April 3, 1812?], Monroe MSS, NYPL; *National Intelligencer* (Washington), April 7, 9, 14, 1812; Mayo, *Henry Clay*, p. 506.

course of policy intended to be pursued." Federalist analysts divided into three groups. Some believed that, the plan of bluff having failed, "our Government has no choice left but either to recede from the ground they have taken or proceed to the last resort. . . . The high sense of honour which the advocates of the present measures profess forbid a retreat[;] there is therefore no alternative only to fight." Others simply confessed themselves baffled. An important part of the party, including the two leaders, Quincy and Bleecker, still refused to believe the Republicans were in earnest. "The levies do not progress, no important strength is proposed to the fortification of our seaboard, no addition to our navy, no plan for arming our merchantmen is . . . suggested," Quincy wrote. "Can any man believe . . . an Embargo, accompanied by such a state of things is preparatory to war?" On the floor of the House, a month after the embargo, Bleecker declared, "No, sir, rely upon it there will be, there can be, no war . . . within sixty days. Whatever may be thought of it here, the people know that we cannot go to war, at the expiration of the embargo. . . . They think . . . that for the Government to go to war in our present unprepared state, would be little short of an act of treason." [21]

The Federalists had no cohesive policy of their own. Senator Chauncey Goodrich wanted the party to announce its own plan for protecting commerce. Others accepted the prospect of war, certain that it would ruin Republicanism and at least bring to an end the detested policy of commercial restrictions. Quincy convinced himself that the administration had, all along, simply sought to smuggle a permanent embargo in through the back door, and he abandoned the policy of self-restraint for open opposition. "I think," he wrote, "the present state of things, which administration will continue, if they can, worse, both to morals, & to liberty than war with any nation." Still others, most notably Philip B.

[21] *United States Gazette* (Philadelphia), April 15, 1812; Taggart to Pickering, April 3, 1812, Pickering MSS, Vol. XXX; Quincy to Wolcott, April 15, 1812, Wolcott Family MSS, Connecticut Historical Society, Vol. XXIV; *Annals*, 12th Cong., 1st sess., pp. 1380–1381.

Key, thought a quiet course least likely to provoke the Republicans into war. Federalists agreed only to refuse to subscribe to the loans Gallatin sought. Wealthy Bostonians, the *Columbian Centinel* explained, "lend no money to the ruling faction, for the same reason that they would not lend swords to the tenants of a lunatic hospital." [22] This decision apart, Federalists milled in confusion as deep as that within Republican ranks.

Augustus John Foster listened to Federalists of all opinions, continued to entertain even the most determined War Hawks, and frequently visited Madison and Monroe. The embargo did not trouble him, and at the end of April he reported, "My hopes of a favourable issue . . . continue to increase." (In this same dispatch he even went so far as to ask for a six-month leave of absence, since business was at a stand!) Not until May 3 did he suggest that Madison might support the use of force. Almost immediately afterward he hazarded a guess that "the Bubble will soon burst. I am assailed on every side with tremendous Stories but the ruling party seems to be in a State of Desperation & if we refuse them pabulum to their rage they must burst with the Violence of it."

Until the very end Foster stuck to a belief that even minor changes in British policy would end all chances of war. He repeatedly wrote that Madison and Monroe, particularly the latter, had pleaded for some gesture that would permit them to turn back. "Mr. Monroe in a conversation which I lately had with him," Foster reported in May, "expressed his wish that we would exchange our orders for blockades which might answer the same purpose." One week before Madison finally completed his war message, the Englishman advised his government that even the most nominal change in the Orders in Council would have a striking effect. Foster correctly divined the administration's hope

[22] Goodrich to Roger Griswold [?], April 7, 1812, William G. Lane Collection, Yale University Library; Tallmadge to McHenry, April 11, 1812, Bernard C. Steiner, *The Life and Correspondence of James McHenry* (Cleveland, 1907), p. 576; Quincy to Wolcott, April 15, 1812, Wolcott MSS, Vol. XXIV; *Columbian Centinel*, May 6, 1812.

for peace, but woefully underestimated the price it would ask. Like the Federalists, he found it hard to believe that a new day had dawned.[23]

Foster's hope for peace was badly served by America's interpretation of parliamentary news that arrived during these critical months, for the United States clung as stubbornly to a dated interpretation as he did. At London, Jonathan Russell completely ignored hints that the orders would fall. He steadily reported that they would last as long as the Perceval ministry, and he interpreted the declaration of April, 1812, as a sign of firmness. In a letter received by Monroe shortly before the final crisis Russell wrote: "Indeed I am convinced that whoever wishes for the respect of this highminded people must occasionally fight them." American papers considered the initial defeat of Brougham's motion for an investigation the death knell of American hopes, totally overlooking the uncertainty of government speakers and the strength of the Opposition tally. In March the *Columbian Centinel*, Boston's Federalist bellwether, expected the orders to collapse within three months, but in April and May it declared that no chance of repeal existed. On May 5, learning that Perceval's tenure had been confirmed, Monroe directed Russell to warn American merchants in London that a rupture impended; ominously, he also asked Russell to stay in Britain as an agent for prisoners when war broke out.[24] Neither the President nor Congress saw an easy exit from the position in which preparedness legislation and the embargo had placed them.

Late in March, as the first, discouraging parliamentary reports arrived from England, news of renewed French outrages reached Washington. This pillaging of American commerce, primarily grain ships bound for the Peninsula, became more dramatic when an indiscreet French commander explained apologetically, after putting

[23] These paragraphs rest upon Foster #17–#23 to Wellesley, March 22–April 3, 1812, and Foster #24–#38 to Castlereagh, April 20–May 23, 1812, FO 5/85–86. The quotations are from #30, secret, April 24, 1812; unnumbered, private, May 5, 1812; #31, most secret, May 3, 1812; #37, May 22, 1812.
[24] Russell to Monroe, April 22, 1812, Despatches, Great Britain, Vol. XVIII; Russell to Monroe, private, March 28, 1812, *ibid.*; *Columbian Centinel*, March 7, April 4, May 16, 1812; Monroe to Russell, May 5, 1812, Instructions, Vol. VII.

a merchantman to the torch, that "he had orders from the Government to burn all American vessels sailing to or from an enemy's port." Georges de Caraman, an attaché at the imperial legation, thought this news prevented a declaration of war almost immediately after the embargo. Certainly it checked ardent congressmen. Nathaniel Macon declared, "The Devil himself could not tell, which Govt England or France is the most wicked," and Congress rang with what Sérurier described as "the most lively speeches against France." Monroe raised the specter of a declaration of war against both major belligerents, and the President led Sérurier from one of Dolley's receptions to his private office to hear a long diatribe against the "numberless vexations" America suffered. Complaints continued until and beyond the declaration of war against England, and in August Madison warned France, through Barlow, that Congress might declare war against France in the fall whether or not the conflict with England continued.[25] Violent feeling against Napoleon made many congressmen doubt the wisdom of war with Britain.

War's perils might seem an inconsequential thing, a trifle compared to the nation's honor, to insouciant congressmen who enjoyed Foster's libations, his chess set and playing cards, and then rode off to the Capitol to support war measures. For the nation at large, particularly after Napoleon's fiery torch had revealed

---

[25] *Annals*, 12th Cong., 1st sess., p. 1235; Georges de Caraman, "Les États-Unis Il Y a Quarante Ans," *Révue Contemporaine*, 1st Series, III (1852), 233; Macon to Nicholson, March 23, 1812, Joseph H. Nicholson MSS, Library of Congress; Sérurier #52, #54, #61 to Minister of Foreign Relations, April 9, 24, July 12, 1812, AAE, CP, E-U, Vol. LXVII. Although urged by Bassano, Napoleon did not even condescend to appoint a plenipotentiary to negotiate with Barlow until the end of April, and a month later this worthy reported that "in conformity with the spirit of my Instructions, the work is not much advanced." Bassano to Napoleon, April 17, 1812, *ibid.*, Vol. LXIX; Bassano to Barlow, April 20, 1812, *ibid.*; Duc Dalberg to Bassano, May 28, 1812, *ibid.*

Just before the American declaration of war, too late to affect happenings at Washington, Bassano presented Barlow with the spurious decree of April 28, 1811. Designed primarily to inveigle England into repeal of the Orders in Council, this document, as has been noted, did not fool Barlow and certainly could not be expected to mislead the American government. Barlow #12 to Monroe, May 12, 1812, and enclosures, Despatches, France, Vol XIII. Napoleon was fortunate that this transparent trick did not become known in the American capital soon enough to increase the hatred of France which delayed the declaration of war.

the emptiness of hopes for French sympathy during a war with Britain, the hazards seemed far more important. Late in the spring the first election returns began to come in. Ultimately, although Madison won reëlection and some antiwar congressmen were retired, only the feebleness and the lack of cohesion of the Federalist-Clintonian opposition prevented a Republican disaster. Such War Hawks as William Widgery, John Adams Harper, and Burwell Bassett went down to defeat. Of course, most elections took place after the incapacity of Madison's war leadership had become patent, and after, too, it could be seen that the nation had been thrust unprepared into a war. Certainly, however, the people of the United States did not share the gay bellicosity of leaders who by guile, threats, patriotic appeals, and the favor of fortune managed to carry the nation into war in June, 1812. The War Hawks were not borne forward by a rising tide of public sentiment. Rather did they seize the last possible moment before an ebb should leave them exposed on the beach.

At no time, even when war sentiment was at its peak, did enthusiasm sweep the nation. In January Louis Sérurier wrote: "This war promises well; it is not made with enthusiasm; it is coldly undertaken. Honor may decide the Chiefs of the Nation; but the Citizens make up their minds according to their interest. . . . They regretfully take up arms; they take them up sluggishly; but they will not easily put them down and not without being satisfied on points which England may find it difficult to abandon." A foreigner might be able to afford such a cool view, but the lack of enthusiasm did not please War Hawks. Some hoped that England could be provoked into an attack which would inflame the country. For the most part, war men hoped their own perfervid speeches would raise "the (too sluggish) people to their own standard of Insanity," as an acid Federalist put it. They hoped that patriotic emotions would rally Americans behind them, once armed conflict had actually begun.[26]

[26] Sérurier #42 to Minister of Foreign Relations, Jan. 12, 1812, AAE, CP, E-U, Vol. LXVII; Reed to Pickering, April 25, 1812, Pickering MSS, Vol. XXX. In one of his many brilliant passages, Henry Adams (*History of the United States during the Administrations of Jefferson and Madison* [9 vols.; New York, 1889–1891], VI,

Some war sentiment existed. Congressmen were not so foolish as to proceed without any public support at all. Nearly a dozen state legislatures passed resolutions for the defense of American rights, and mass meetings endorsed equally bellicose sentiments. Circumstances sometimes vitiated their impact, as the Virginia example shows. In January the House of Delegates resolved that "the period has now arrived when *peace, as we now have it,* is disgraceful, and war is honorable." But Taylor of Caroline said none of his neighbors desired war, and the best Jefferson could report was that "all regret that there is cause for war, but all consider it as now necessary." The Valley, stronghold of anti-Republicanism, opposed war. In April Norfolk's congressman, a frequent truant from Washington, found his home town hoping for peace. In June Senator Giles brought forward Richmond and Manchester petitions declaring that, if unfortunately the nation's honor made war imperative, it should be declared against France as well as England.[27]

Sentiment for a double war (or "triangular war," as it came to be called) was widespread. The Kentucky legislature specifically attacked both major belligerents, and four other legislatures referred to France by implication. A mass meeting at Charleston, South Carolina, attended by Federalists (with Charles Cotesworth Pinkney in the van) and Republicans, declared that both Britain and France had given adequate cause for war.[28] Almost

---

210–211) observes: "The experiment of thrusting the country into war to inflame it, as crude ore might be thrown into a furnace, was avowed by the party leaders, from President Madison downward, and was in truth the only excuse for a course otherwise resembling an attempt at suicide. Many nations have gone to war in pure gayety of heart; but perhaps the United States were first to force themselves into a war they dreaded, in the hope that the war itself might create the spirit they lacked."

[27] *Annals*, 12th Cong., 1st sess., pp. 112–114; Taylor to Monroe, Jan. 2, March 12, May 10, 1812, William E. Dodd, ed., "Letters of John Taylor, of Caroline County, Virginia," *John P. Branch Papers*, II (Richmond, 1908), 327–339; Jefferson to Nelson, April 2, 1812, Andrew A. Lipscomb and Albert E. Bergh, eds., *The Writings of Thomas Jefferson* (Memorial ed.; 20 vols.; Washington, 1903–1904), XIII, 138; Charles H. Ambler, *Sectionalism in Virginia from 1776 to 1861* (Chicago, 1910), pp. 92–93; Davis, *op. cit.*, p. 94; Dice R. Anderson, *William B. Giles* (Menasha, Wisc., 1914), pp. 181–182.

[28] *Annals*, 12th Cong., 1st sess., p. 1020; John H. Wolfe, *Jeffersonian Democracy in South Carolina*, James Sprunt Studies in History and Political Science, Vol. XXIV, no. 1 (Chapel Hill, 1940), p. 247.

every set of resolutions emphasized American honor. "We are a Humbled & degraded Nation," a Baltimorean wrote Henry Clay, "and If the Stand that is now Taken is departed from, Without bringing England to Justice, we may as well give up our Republican Government & have a Despot to rule over us." [29] The Speaker doubtless agreed, but he and his colleagues knew that many of their supporters found it difficult to understand why British insults, but not French, required war.

The opponents of war outnumbered its supporters, whether troubled or untroubled. Lowndes, former Congressman Jackson, old John Adams (now Republican in his sympathies), and many other backers of war admitted this. Joseph Nicholson warned his brother-in-law, Albert Gallatin, that the "apathy of the Nation is not yet thrown off and never will be," and Jefferson's former minister to Paris, Robert R. Livingston, became nearly apoplectic in describing the crisis into which Congress had thrust the Republican party by insisting upon war.[30] There were stirrings in North Carolina, Maryland, and other Republican states. Josiah Bartlett, who approved of war in principle, found his New Hampshire constituents hopeful that a declaration could be postponed until fall, and he came to share their sentiments. In Pennsylvania, whose congressional delegation provided the largest group of war men, public opinion turned sharply. Petitions flooded Congress, and just before the declaration of war Dr. Benjamin Rush predicted that the state would go Federalist in the fall elections. Aside from the West (and even here Ohio was a notable exception) and perhaps Georgia, not a single state, even the traditionally Republican ones, failed to provide evidence of antiwar feeling.[31]

[29] Thomas McKim, Jr., to Clay, May 13, 1812, Henry Clay MSS, Library of Congress.
[30] Lowndes to Elizabeth Lowndes, March 23, 1812, Harriott H. Ravenel, *Life and Times of William Lowndes* (Cambridge, 1901), pp. 102–103; Jackson to Madison, April 13, 1812, Madison MSS; John Adams to Jefferson, May 3, 1812, Jefferson MSS; Nicholson to Gallatin, May 7, 1812, Albert Gallatin MSS, New-York Historical Society; Robert R. Livingston to Edward Livingston, May 26, 1812, Robert R. Livingston MSS, New-York Historical Society.
[31] *Wilmington Gazette* (Wilmington, N.C.), May 12, 1812; journal entry, May 14, 1812, Foster MSS; Bartlett to Ezra Bartlett, May 30, 1812, Bartlett MSS; Rush to John Adams, May 19, 1812, Lyman H. Butterfield, ed., *Letters of Benjamin Rush,*

The most serious defections from the Republican cause came in Massachusetts and New York, where the party suffered crippling losses in state elections because their opponents exploited the war issue. Elbridge Gerry, the old friend of Adams and Jefferson, was thrust from the gubernatorial chair at Boston in April, and in May the Federalists recaptured the legislature. By a majority of 166, 58 more than the Federalists could command by their own votes, the new legislature passed a resolution opposing "offensive war." [32] In New York opinion flowed steadily against the administration after the turn of the year. "Old [Thomas] Sammons," as Randolph called his colleague although Sammons was only fifty, "returned from the Mohawk river [and his constituents] as decided an advocate for peace as he was a partizan of war at the commencement of the Session." In May, in the usual tangled contest with Clintonians and orthodox Republicans, the Federalists made a gain of nineteen seats and secured a clear majority in the assembly.[33] The Republicans had lost their major strongholds in the North, the Pennsylvania bridgehead seemed to be tottering, and they appeared about to be driven to their old citadels south of the Potomac.

In May, somewhat overoptimistically, Samuel Taggart estimated that a majority in every state opposed war. The *New-York Herald* declared that "nothing was ever so universally execrated as is the projected war," although the paper felt forced to add, in good Federalist style, "by every man . . . who possesses the means of earning a decent subsistence." Randolph taunted the Republicans for risking a contest the people did not want, and Harmanus Bleecker predicted that war would bring to an end "the reign of theory, sophistry, and false philosophy." At the time of the declaration of war, the *Herald* estimated that 90 per cent of

---

II, American Philosophical Society, *Memoirs*, Vol. XXX (1951), p. 1134; Alfred B. Sears, *Thomas Worthington: Father of Ohio Statehood* (Columbus, 1958), pp. 174–177.

[32] Gerry to Madison, private, May 19, 20, 1812, Madison MSS; Henry D. Sedgwick to Bleecker, June 6, 1812, Sedgwick MSS, Part II, Massachusetts Historical Society; *Annals*, 12th Cong., 1st sess., pp. 259–261.

[33] Randolph to Garnett, April 21, 1812, John Randolph MSS, Library of Congress; *New-York Herald*, May 23, 1812.

the American people opposed it; Foster more cautiously settled on 80 per cent.[34] Doubtless Foster and the Federalists exaggerated. During the spring, however, and particularly after the Massachusetts election, no Republican had the temerity to claim that the American people demanded war.

Unfortunately for the irenic, most protests against war did not come until the die had in effect been cast. Until the embargo, opponents of war did not feel it worth the energy to protest against a course expected to be abandoned in the end. "We are told," Hugh Nelson complained to Jefferson, "the people do not believe we mean war. Is this possible. If our countrymen do not believe us, how can we expect that foreign govts will." The country showed comparatively little alarm, John Randolph stated in the war debates, only "because the public are totally unaware of the high price at which this House holds its own consistency—that the ruin of the nation weighs nothing in the scale against it." James A. Bayard sought to delay the Senate's vote on war because "the general opinion abroad was, that there would be no war." [35] Had Congress convinced the people of its determination, had not the Republican past created an indelible impression of weakness, by an ironic turn of chance the War Hawks would have been deluged with such forceful expressions of public anger that they probably could not have carried a declaration of war. Unwittingly Madison had served the cause better than he knew.

Congress did consider the embargo a major step toward war. The War Hawks spent the ensuing six weeks defending their position against the attacks of Federalists and wavering Republicans rather than in active legislation. Some were tempted to support a proposal to suspend nonimportation, a plan perhaps put forward as a move toward escape but attractive to Clay, Lowndes, Cheves, and Calhoun since it would permit prewar stockpiling.

[34] Taggart to Rev. John Taylor, May 13, 1812, George H. Haynes, ed., "Letters of Samuel Taggart, Representative in Congress, 1803–1814," American Antiquarian Society, *Proceedings*, n.s., XXXIII (1923), 399; *New-York Herald*, May 19, 1812; *Annals*, 12th Cong., 1st sess., pp. 1388–1389, 1405–1406; *New-York Herald*, June 17, 1812; Foster #48 to Castlereagh, secret, June 21, 1812, FO 5/86.

[35] Nelson to Jefferson, April 27, 1812, Thomas Jefferson MSS (Coolidge Collection), Massachusetts Historical Society; *Annals*, 12th Cong., 1st sess., pp. 288, 1388.

Wiser men pointed out that the proposal would encourage England to believe that America was totally dependent upon her, and Monroe, "tremblingly alive to any *appearance* of relaxation," strenuously opposed it.[36] The plan died.

Toward the end of March congressmen began to talk of adjournment. This talk became widespread after the embargo, when war men thought legislative preparation complete. Some realized that the country would interpret a recess as further evidence that Congress desired to escape a crisis, and John A. Harper threatened to present a war manifesto to the House of Representatives and dare members to go home without debating it.[37] Other War Hawks expected citizens to urge their congressmen to war, while the Federalists, wiser than their enemies, supported an adjournment for precisely the opposite reason. Republican waverers wanted to take the temperature of their constituents and delay the final vote on war.

On April 10 the House of Representatives approved a recess in principle by a vote of seventy-two to forty. Thirty-one who later voted for war, including such stanch War Hawks as Calhoun, Williams, Johnson, and Widgery, voted for the resolution. A joint committee of both chambers agreed to adjourn until May 18, and this proposal would almost certainly have gone through had not the Senate voted to extend the date to June 8. This smacked too much of evasion, and War Hawks rallied to oppose it. Jonathan Roberts cleverly proposed that the members of Congress give up pay and travel money during the recess, thus saving the Treasury $40,000. Rather than accept Roberts' proposal, many of the majority that sought a recess joined with War Hawks to shelve the subject by a vote of sixty-two to fifty-five. Thus, Foster observed,

the advocates for Peace tho' a Majority, in all Probability, were defeated . . . by the address of the more decided advocates for war, who shewed the others that although they might have an adjournment, yet it should be to their Cost. . . . To the Faction who were swayed by such motives we

---

[36] *Annals*, 12th Cong., 1st sess., pp. 237–239, 1288–1290; Randolph to Garnett, April 14, 1812, Randolph MSS.

[37] Harper to Plumer, April 29, 1812, William Plumer MSS, Library of Congress.

perhaps may have to attribute more importance than they deserve: for they were taken off their Guard and being confident of adjournment voted against the Resolution as amended thinking they should be able subsequently to regain the lost Ground.

This confidence proved ill advised. Although the Senate agreed to a shorter period, the House now rejected by eight votes a proposal it would have whooped through a week earlier. By this extremely narrow margin, a margin that could have been reversed had not a number of antiwar men gone home without waiting for a recess, the war movement avoided a fatal check. Jonathan Roberts had a right to be proud of what he described in his memoirs as "an artful stroke." [38]

The desire for a recess was often coupled with a scheme to send a special mission to Europe. By clearing the air in France a mission might conceivably have broadened support for war against England if it did not arrive in London (as the event proved would have happened) in time to receive repeal of the Orders in Council. On the other hand, like an adjournment, the appointment of a mission would have discouraged the war spirit that did exist, and all Washington believed the chances of a settlement slim indeed. Nevertheless, the mission was widely discussed and was thought to have the President's blessing. The details of this affair are obscure, and Senator Worthington's story that Grundy and Clay threatened to oppose Madison's reëlection if he persisted in this plan cannot be accepted. There is no reason to doubt that congressional leaders reminded Madison that a special mission would, by demolishing the government's already scanty reputation for determination, jeopardize Republican electoral prospects. [39]

Fully as challenging to the war spirit and even more fantastic was the suggestion, much bruited about in Washington, that the United States should mete the same measure to France as to Brit-

[38] *Annals*, 12th Cong., 1st sess., pp. 1314–1316, 1334–1342; journal entry, April 26, 1812, Foster MSS; memoirs (photostat), II, 19–21, Jonathan Roberts MSS, Historical Society of Pennsylvania.

[39] *Courier* (London), May 14, 1812; Abraham Shepherd to Pickering, Feb. 20, 1814, Henry Adams, *The Life of Albert Gallatin* (Philadelphia, 1879), pp. 457–458; Mayo, *Henry Clay*, pp. 509–513.

ain. Some ardent War Hawks wanted to fight both nations. These men approached war in a cavalier spirit, detested Napoleonic perfidy, and hoped to destroy their own reputation for Francophilia. Opponents of war hoped to turn the entire project into a *reductio ad absurdum*. Madison found it difficult to make a clear decision, although on balance he inclined to believe a double declaration unwise. He wrote to Jefferson, "To go to war with Eng^d and not with France arms the federalists with new matter, and divides the Republicans some of whom with the Quids make a display of impartiality. To go to war ag^st both, presents a thousand difficulties." Jefferson replied that triangular war was absurd, and Jonathan Roberts talked of it as the joint product of "the weak and the mad." Sérurier jestingly remarked that if it really came about he would have to solicit an interview with Foster to concert measures of resistance. Nonetheless, in April and May there was a great deal of talk about triangular war, and this undermined the drive toward a declaration of war against England.[40]

Had any one of these projects—adjournment, a new mission, resistance to both powers—received the open endorsement of the administration, which was tempted by each of them, war would have been delayed. Delay almost certainly would have meant peace. From early April until the end of May the War Hawks fought a defensive battle against fear, second thoughts, weakness, and the pressure of public opinion. They argued that only firm consistency could regain the nation's honor. But no one could be sure that Porter's Report, preparedness legislation, and the embargo would not go the way of past Republican manifestoes. No one could be sure that the War Hawks would be able to work their will before Congress got totally out of hand.

By common consent, answers awaited the return of the *Hornet*, which had sailed for Europe in December laden with "paper bullets, bloody messages, war resolutions and frightful speeches." On

[40] Madison to Jefferson, May 25, 1812, Hunt, *op. cit.*, VIII, 191; Jefferson to Madison, May 30, 1812, Lipscomb and Bergh, *op. cit.*, XIII, 153–154; Roberts to Matthew Roberts, May 23, 1812, Roberts MSS; journal entry, April 11, 1812, Foster MSS; Sérurier #57 to Minister of Foreign Relations, May 27, 1812, AAE, CP, E-U, Vol. LXVII.

May 22, weeks after she was expected and after, too, false reports of her arrival had thrown sessions of Congress into confusion, the *Hornet* arrived. Monroe's office became suffocatingly crowded as officials and citizens sought to learn if she brought any news that would enable America to escape gracefully from a war. The dispatches disappointed everyone. As Minister Sérurier received no instructions to guide him, and Joel Barlow's reports made it clear that Napoleon continued irascible, hope had to be abandoned for a settlement with France which would ease the path to war with Britain. Although unofficial accounts aplenty showed that the Orders in Council were being heavily attacked, Russell's reports held out no prospect of repeal. Anger, confusion, and gloom spread through Washington. Sérurier had an uncomfortable conversation with Monroe when they met at Speaker Clay's, the Secretary complaining that the administration had been betrayed by France. There were reports that the Cabinet, which met on two consecutive days to discuss future policy, contained almost as many opinions as members. The *National Intelligencer*, however, insisted that England was the chief enemy—"let it not be said that the misconduct of France neutralizes in the least that of Great Britain"—and Monroe's conversations with Foster made it seem that there was nothing to hope from England.[41]

Although not hostile in tone, Castlereagh's instructions to Foster, which formed the most important part of the *Hornet*'s budget of information, showed how little Britain understood America. Basing his argument largely on a recent report by the Duke of Bassano, the Foreign Secretary declared it was now obvious, as England had maintained all along, that France had not repealed her decrees. America had been tricked.

It is impossible America should not feel under these Circumstances that She has not only an Act of Justice to perform by Great Britain, but that France has deliberately attached Conditions to the Repeal of Her Decrees which she knew Great Britain could never accept, hoping thereby to fo-

---

[41] *Federal Republican* (Baltimore), March 13, 1812; Sérurier #57 to Minister of Foreign Relation., May 27, 1812, AAE, CP, E-U, Vol. LXVII; Foster #38 to Castlereagh, May 23, 1812, FO 5/86; *National Intelligencer*, May 30, 1812.

ment Disunion between Great Britain and America. America can never be justified in continuing to resent against Us that failure of Relief, which is alone attributable to the insidious Policy of the Enemy. . . . we are entitled to claim at Her Hands, as an act not less of Policy, than Justice, . . . that She should cease to treat Great Britain as an Enemy.

The truth of this analysis of French policy seemed so obvious to Castlereagh that he expected the Americans to share it. He hoped the evidence of imperial perfidy would provide the United States with "an opportunity of receding without disgrace from the precipice of War. . . . To rescue America from the influence of France, is of more importance, than committing Her to War with that Power." To sweeten the pill for America, Castlereagh offered to regulate licenses so that the two countries might share European trade, or even to abandon them entirely.[42] "At any other time," as Theodore C. Smith has observed, "this would have at least opened the way for renewed negotiations, but not in 1812."[43] Castlereagh and his colleagues totally misread the situation in America. The instructions, far more pleading than threatening, actually determined Madison to abandon his hedging for peace.

On May 27 and 28 Foster discussed the British argument and proposed concession with Monroe and Madison. The Americans ignored the proposal on licenses, to which they had formerly attached so much importance. They stubbornly reiterated that the Berlin and Milan decrees had been repealed. Seizing upon Castlereagh's declaration that England would insist upon complete, unconditional French repeal and abandonment of the municipal regulations shutting off British commerce with Europe, they declared this an extension of England's demands. "With this formal notice," Madison recalled fifteen years later, "no choice remained but between war and degradation, a degradation inviting fresh provocation & rendering war sooner or later inevitable." The Foreign Secretary's instructions, Madison told Jared Sparks in 1830, were "intended to show an utter disregard of the complaints

[42] Castlereagh #8, #9 to Foster, April 10, 1812, Mayo, ed., *Instructions*, pp. 353–367. Foster was authorized to read to Monroe the first of these instructions, containing Castlereagh's arguments on French repeal, and he did so.
[43] *Op. cit.*, p. 338.

of the United States. This letter seemed to shut out the prospects of conciliation, & the president considered war as the next necessary step to vindicate the rights and honor of the nation." [44] The failure of understanding was reciprocal.

For more than a month eager members of the Foreign Affairs Committee had been drafting a manifesto for use as a reply to the presidential war message, and Monroe also prepared one for friendly congressmen.[45] On May 13, when nearly a sixth of the membership was absent, the House of Representatives voted to re-call absentees. On May 18 eighty Republicans caucused to ar-range their plans, and three days later the President was reported at work on his war message. Apparently a congressional delegation headed by Clay visited the White House to assure Madison that Congress awaited his message, and later, on a morning ride to Georgetown, the Speaker told a colleague that the war message could be expected on June 1. On May 29 John Randolph delivered a bitter attack on the project. After he had accused the Republican leaders of seeking to make Americans "the tools, the minions, sycophants, parasites of France," he was silenced by the Speaker and Calhoun. Visitors began to examine Foster's livestock and even the marquee under which he held his famous parties, with an eye to purchasing them when he departed. Congress adjourned for the week end, knowing that on Monday the long-awaited cli-max of the battle between honor and interest would begin.[46]

During these hectic days, last-minute misgivings plagued the

[44] Foster #41 to Castlereagh, June 6, 1812, FO 5/86; Foster to Castlereagh, private and secret, June 6, 1812, *ibid.*; Madison to Henry Wheaton, Feb. 26–27, 1827, Hunt, *op. cit.*, IX, 272–273; journal entry, April 18[–23], 1830, Jared Sparks MSS, Houghton Library, Harvard University.

[45] Harper to Plumer, April 29, 1812, Plumer MSS; journal entry, May 27, 1812, Foster MSS; Charles M. Wiltse, "The Authorship of the War Report of 1812," *American Historical Review*, XLIX (1943–1944), 253–259. While hazarding a guess that John C. Calhoun may have been the author of this paper, Wiltse declares that the authorship cannot be safely ascribed to any individual. Harper's letter makes it likely that the final version combined passages prepared by a number of men.

[46] *Annals*, 12th Cong., 1st sess., pp. 1424–1427; journal entry, May 19, 1812, Foster MSS; George M. Bibb to John J. Crittenden, May 21, 1812, Wiltse, *op. cit.*, p. 256; Smith, *op. cit.*, pp. 340–344; *Annals*, 12th Cong., 1st sess., p. 1477n; journal entries, May 31, June 3, 1812, Foster MSS.

administration. The President, who knew that he must go ahead and was prepared to do his duty, faced it without enthusiasm. On May 25 he sent Congress the discouraging correspondence from Barlow, and on the same day he considered the possibility of a triangular war. On Monday morning Monroe, who said he was too busy to undertake the task himself, asked Gallatin to inform Senator Crawford of the two secretaries' wish for a limited war. "I am convinc'd," Monroe wrote, "that it is very important to attempt, at present, the maritime war only. I fear however that difficulty will be experienced in the committee, which may extend itself to the gentlemen, or some of them, at least, at Mrs. Dawsons." [47] The President kept his own counsel.

James Madison did not feel that the times called for any unusual departure from Republican forms, and his deference to Congress was fitting since the war impulse had come from its members rather than the White House. As always, the President left the reading of his message to a clerk who droned it out for almost half an hour. Nor did Madison directly endorse any particular course. The decision between peace and war, a war "avoiding all connections which might entangle . . . [the United States] in the contest or view of other powers" and prosecuted only until an opportunity for peace occurred, "is a solemn question which the Constitution wisely confides to the legislative department of the

[47] James D. Richardson, ed., *A Compilation of the Messages and Papers of the Presidents* (Washington, 1897), I, 499; Madison to Jefferson, May 25, 1812, Hunt, *op. cit.*, VIII, 191–192; Monroe to Gallatin, June 1, 1812, Gallatin MSS. Lowndes, years after the event, put some scattered memories onto paper. "One of the most curious anecdotes" he recalled was "the effort of the Executive to prevent a declaration of war. . . . after the Presidents message was sent in . . . considerable effort was made to substitute something & less—letters of marque &c. . . . as far as I know none of the Cabinet unless it were Hamilton were adverse. Grundy was brought over. I remember being one of a good many Sen$^s$. & Rep$^s$. at this time (Crawford was one) talking it over. We determined to adjourn & go home doing nothing, or have a War in common form." William L. Lowndes, Historical Anecdotes, and Observations, MSS, Library of Congress. Assuming that Lowndes could not have made up this story out of whole cloth, it appears to intimate that Gallatin carried out Monroe's suggestion. It will be noted, however, that the President's name is not specifically mentioned by Monroe or Lowndes. Two possible conclusions are that the President prudently concealed his attitude or that his secretaries felt it possible to ignore his wishes.

Government." The President unnecessarily asked "early delibera-
tions" on the question.[48] All he professed to do was to recapitulate
the evidence and, in his final paragraph, to suggest that a decision
on French relations be postponed until further word came from
Barlow. Sometimes Madison was eloquent, sometimes labored and
intricate, as when he declared that by impressment "a self-redress
is assumed which, if British subjects were wrongfully detained and
alone concerned, is that substitution of force for a resort to the
responsible sovereign which falls within the definition of war." On
the whole, the message compared unfavorably with the annual
message presented seven months before.

The President attempted to show that Great Britain was already
prosecuting an undeclared war against the United States: "We
behold . . . on the side of Great Britain a state of war against the
United States, and on the side of the United States a state of peace
toward Great Britain." Impressment, particularly of native Americans, was an act of war that neither "remonstrances and expostula-
tions" nor friendly offers to regulate the employment of seamen
had been able to bring to an end. Indian warriors attacked the
West, presumably at Britain's behest. English warships violated
American territorial waters. "Pretended blockades," particularly
Fox's of 1806,[49] permitted American commerce to be "plun-
dered in every sea." Most important of all, the British Cabinet,
"not content with these occasional expedients for laying waste our
neutral trade, . . . resorted . . . to a sweeping system of blockades, under the name of orders in council, which has been molded
and managed as might best suit its political views, its commercial
jealousies, or the avidity of British cruisers." Justified as retaliation, although long since "deprived of this flimsy veil" by French
repeal, the Orders in Council and the ancillary license trade were
really a war upon American commerce. Economic pressure on the

[48] See Richardson, *op. cit.*, I, 499–505, for the entire message.
[49] The President's argument that the British showed their inveterate hostility by
declaring Fox's Blockade to be "comprehended" in the orders, and by refusing to
encourage Napoleonic repeal of the allegedly retaliatory Berlin Decree by repealing
the blockade, was a particularly weak passage in the address. The President well
knew, from Monroe's conversations with Foster, what the British position really
meant.

one hand, and, on the other, offers to join Britain if she withdrew her regulations while France remained stubborn, had failed to bring the Cabinet to its senses. "Such," said the President, "is the spectacle of injuries and indignities which have been heaped on our country, and such the crisis which its unexampled forbearance and conciliatory efforts have not been able to avert."

The use of hyperbole did not destroy the essential truth of Madison's indictments of England. In Henry Adams' words, "For five years, the task of finding excuses for peace had been more difficult than that of proving a *casus belli*." [50] That impressment and hovering off American shores had scarcely been mentioned in recent diplomatic correspondence, until the former was pushed to the fore at the very end, proved only that the American government had lost hope of peaceful arrangements, not that the acts were less criminal. The British restrictive system was, as Madison stated, heavily tinctured with selfishness. Had Madison emphasized the harmfulness of the orders, he would have been on more solid ground. To connect their justice with French repeal, and to assert in the face of the evidence that French repeal was a fact, simply invited criticism, although the administration's policy since 1810 made emphasis on this theme almost inevitable.

In later years Madison came fairly close to apologizing for his decision to present a war message in June, 1812. "The circumstances under which the war commenced on our part," he wrote in 1813, "require that it should be reviewed with a liberality above the ordinary rules and dispositions indulged in such cases. It had become impossible to avoid or even delay war, at a moment when we were not prepared for it, and when it was certain that effective preparations would not take place, whilst the question of war was undecided." The moment, Madison observed in retrospect, appeared propitious. Napoleon's Grand Army lay poised for an attack on Russia. "Had the French Emperor not been broken down as he was, to a degree at variance with all human probability, and which no human sagacity could anticipate, can it be doubted," the President asked, "that G.B. would have been constrained by her

[50] *History*, VI, 221.

own situation and the demands of her allies, to listen to our reasonable terms of reconciliation." [51] In this spirit James Madison joined the War Hawks.

Both House and Senate considered Madison's message behind closed doors. Although common in the upper house, executive sessions were rare in the House, and three times the opponents of war sought to lift the injunction of secrecy. Thrice beaten, Federalists declined to debate the question and began to prepare an appeal to the nation stating their reasons for opposing war.[52] Theoretically, secrecy speeded legislative action and concealed American intentions from the enemy. Actually, it took Congress more than two weeks to pass a declaration of war, and nobody—certainly not Foster—failed to learn that war was being discussed. Secrecy did deprive Federalists of the opportunity to assail Republican inconsistencies before a public audience and delayed exposure of the majority's misgivings.

Most observers expected the House to follow the War Hawks' lead without difficulty, although Macon wrote, the day after the message, "It is doubtful this morning . . . whether Congress are as firm, for war as they have been thought." [53] The Republicans had an overwhelming majority, and in a presidential year considerations of party unity bulked larger than normally. Many felt that after the bellicose speeches of the past seven months it would be an open confession of weakness to reject the war bill. The arrival, on June 3, of the Prince Regent's declaration, mistakenly interpreted as a sign of stubborn devotion to the orders, aided the War Hawks. Still, a large number of Republicans did not want war and knew their constituents opposed it. A visit home noticeably cooled David R. Williams. Samuel Ringgold of Maryland, previously the object of Federalist mirth for allegedly "hav-

[51] Madison to John Nicholas, April 2, 1813, Hunt, *op. cit.*, VIII, 242; Madison to Wheaton, Feb. 26–27, 1827, *ibid.*, IX, 273–274. The President emphasized that by mere coincidence, and not because the United States wanted to aid Napoleon, the climax with England came at the same time that the invasion of Russia began.

[52] Bleecker to Theodore Sedgwick, Sr., June 27, 1812, Sedgwick MSS; Taggart to Rev. John Taylor, June 23, 1812, Haynes, *op. cit.*, p. 405. *Annals*, 12th Cong., 1st sess., pp. 1629–1637, covers the House proceedings at this time.

[53] Macon to Nicholson, June 2, 1812, Nicholson MSS.

ing had a project of the declaration of war so long in his pocket that it was at length worn out," lost his enthusiasm and reportedly told Monroe that war would ruin his political future. William Richardson, who held Varnum's old seat, returned from a six weeks' visit to the Bay State opposed to war. All these men ultimately voted for the declaration, but they supported it reluctantly. Many hoped the Senate would save the nation from the consequences of their own votes in the House. "I think the business was too hasty," Dr. Josiah Bartlett wrote, "& did not give the Bill my assent in first stage [but] after it had passed with no material alteration I was against its postponement as it would look like retracing the steps & shew a vacillating disposition which the times totally forbid but I did hope the Senate would have so altered the Bill at their house as to give it the character of Reprisals by granting restrictive letters of Marque but they did not see fit." [54] Had the members of Congress voted as they wished in their hearts, the bill would not have passed.

Nevertheless, the declaration of war moved rapidly through the House of Representatives. On June 3 John C. Calhoun, who replaced Porter at the head of the Foreign Affairs Committee when the New Yorker scampered off to the easier and more lucrative task of selling supplies to the army, presented the committee's manifesto and a bill declaring war on England. The Federalists, deprived of the opportunity to debate publicly, remained silent, and the House adjourned at an unexpectedly early hour. On June 4 the representatives met at eleven o'clock. Information that Madison wished them to delay until he could send a new message threw them temporarily into consternation, raising fears that the President intended to recede from the ground he had taken. When the message arrived it proved to contain only an exchange of correspondence between Foster and Monroe. After beating back three attempts at delay, the House passed the war bill by a vote of seventy-nine to forty-nine. One of the majority had been sworn

[54] Taggart to Rev. John Taylor, May 9, 1812, Haynes, *op. cit.*, p. 399; Davis, *op. cit.*, pp. 95–96; journal entry, May 29, 1812, Foster MSS; Taggart to Pickering, May 11, 1812, Pickering MSS, Vol. XXX; Bartlett to Ezra Bartlett, June 18, 1812, Bartlett MSS.

in only the day before, and another, who had taken an extended French leave, returned to the Capitol one hour before the vote. In the next few days seven other absentees arrived, among them Ezekiel Bacon, Richard Cutts, and Abijah Bigelow, who had been delayed together on the packet between Rhode Island and New York. The votes of the returnees would not have altered significantly the margin by which the declaration of war passed.[55]

The sectional aspect of the vote is often overstressed. Except for three North Carolinians—Quid Stanford, Federalists Joseph Pearson and Archibald McBryde—congressmen from the states south of Virginia voted as a bloc. The nine members from beyond the mountains all voted for war, and Henry Clay of course would have done so had he not been in the chair. Although solid, the real South and the West provided slightly less than one-third of the affirmative votes. A few members from upstate New York, Vermont, New Hampshire, and the Maine district may possibly be considered frontiersmen, but they scarcely affect the generalization. The core of the war coalition, thirty-five in all, came from Pennsylvania, Maryland, and Virginia, squarely in the middle of the nation. In each state there had been grumblings. Nevertheless, all but one Pennsylvania Republican and the six from Maryland (out of a state delegation of nine) remained firm. In Virginia, Randolph and the Valley Federalists opposed the declaration, but four Republicans who had been rumored ready to do so [56] rallied behind their party's cause, and the state delegation split thirteen to five in favor of war. Although in most ways a Southern state, the Old Dominion had little direct interest in the conquest of Florida or Canada and in Indian warfare, and party loyalty and the need for an export market explain the support given to the bill. Finally, it must be noted that congressmen from north of the Dela-

---

[55] *Annals,* 12th Cong., 1st sess., pp. 1546–1554; Charles M. Wiltse, *John C. Calhoun, Nationalist, 1782–1828* (Indianapolis, 1944), pp. 64–65; *Annals,* 12th Cong., 1st sess., p. 1637; Taggart to Rev. John Taylor, June 5, 1812, Haynes, *op. cit.,* pp. 401–403.

[56] Taggart to Rev. John Taylor, May 9, 1812, Haynes, *op. cit.,* p. 398, listed five Republican deserters who were expected to join the seven Federalists and Quids. They were Taliaferro, Burwell, Smith, Nelson, and Matthew Clay, but the latter was absent on the final roll call.

ware River provided the war resolution with its majority. Their seventeen votes, cast in opposition to majority sentiment in the area, could not have been spared, and the six Massachusetts votes for war were outnumbered by those from only three other states. Although it is difficult to cast the prowar Northerners in any particular pattern (is William Widgery, of Portland, Maine, to be

CONGRESSIONAL ACTION ON THE DECLARATION OF WAR, 1812

△ Residence of congressmen voting for war
• Residence of congressmen voting against war
(Congressmen absent and not voting are omitted.)

considered a frontiersman or the representative of a seaport?), a preponderance of them came from areas interested in overseas commerce. Since many of these places had been centers of disaffection under the Embargo, it is possible that, like some Federalists, their congressmen considered any alternative better than commercial self-restriction. Since the representatives of other port towns from Philadelphia and Baltimore to Charleston and Savannah also voted for war, one might only half-facetiously declare that hostilities commanded the support of a great crescent along the seaboard. In any event, the sectional pattern will not do as an explanation of the vote for war.

Far more important was party regularity. The Republicans had a tradition of incredible factionalism, but June, 1812, obviously was a special occasion. Although the dangers of going to war against the country's wishes were obvious, to back down at this late date would expose the Republicans to ridicule almost certain to cost them their political hold. Even if the declaration passed by a narrow margin over substantial Republican defections, the political consequences might be unfortunate. Far better to vote for war and trust the country to rally behind its leadership. Hezekiah Niles gave Republican strength in the House of Representatives as 106.[57] Ten were absent on June 4; a few, like Randolph and Stanford, had long since been Republicans in name only; and most of the six New York Republicans who voted against war were Clintonians hopeful of unseating James Madison in the election of 1812. Ninety per cent of the real, available Republican membership backed the bill. Some twenty were veterans who had supported the Embargo four and a half years before, and a few, including Macon's nephew, Willis Alston; Jefferson's old secretary, William A. Burwell; Ohio's lone congressman, Jeremiah Morrow; and the antique Pennsylvania duo, John Smilie and William Findley, had voted steadily for every Republican measure since that time. Others, the timid, the disputatious, and the wavering, were mobilized for the last trial.

As everyone knew, the Senate would dispose of what the House

[57] *Niles' Register*, Dec. 5, 1812.

proposed, and the margin promised to be extremely narrow. On June 4, when the representatives passed the war bill, six senators—Giles, Lloyd, Hunter of Rhode Island, Franklin of North Carolina, Bradley of Vermont, and Alexander Campbell of Ohio—were away from Washington. All were expected to oppose the bill passed by the House.[58] The failure of a committee, named on June 1 and composed in equal parts of war men, waverers, and Federalists, to report a bill speedily seemed a good omen for peace. Not until June 8, when all the absentees except Bradley and Alexander Campbell had returned, raising attendance to thirty-two, did the committee report out the war bill.[59]

Its opponents could count on twelve votes, including all the Federalists and Nicholas Gilman, a maverick Republican now virtually a Federalist, reëlected from Vermont in 1810 over the opposition of William Plumer and orthodox Republicans. Two Republicans, Worthington of Ohio and Pope of Kentucky, were firmly in their camp. As early as April, on the strength of news from France, Pope, who had formerly supported the administration, told Foster that "the dispute between our two Countries was now only one upon paper. The Trade to France was null, and besides our Situation was to be considered as well as the State of the whole World." Pope opposed war knowing that it would cost him his political future in bellicose Kentucky. Worthington, who had been impressed briefly while a young man, nevertheless thought it "folly and madness to get into the war for abstract principles when we have not the power to enforce them." He hated France and knew the Ohio frontier was nearly defenseless.[60] If

[58] Bayard to Andrew Bayard, June 4, 1812, Elizabeth Donnan, ed., *Papers of James A. Bayard, 1796–1815,* American Historical Association, *Annual Report, 1913,* II (Washington, 1915), 198. Bayard himself had only just returned to Washington. Campbell, kept in Ohio by illness in his family, would have voted against war. Sears, *op. cit.,* p. 177.

[59] *Annals,* 12th Cong., 1st sess., pp. 265–298, follows the Senate proceedings. Only two speeches are reported in detail.

[60] Journal entry, April 9, 1812, Foster MSS; journal entry, May [12 or 13], 1812, Thomas Worthington MSS, Library of Congress. Foster praised Worthington as "a very worthy man" and went on: ". . . although he had once been impressed himself . . . and was consequently against our doctrine on the subject of impressment, saying he would rather live on a crust than be so disgraced, yet it was without the smallest

Stephen Bradley, who explained in interviews as he posted southward that opinion in New England had convinced him to oppose war, arrived in time, the opponents would number thirteen. They had good reason to hope for the support of Joseph Howell of Rhode Island, a weak man (as even his father admitted) under heavy pressure from his constituents.[61] Those who wished to ratify the House decision could count on only ten votes, even assuming that Senator Brent, to whom Foster had assigned an aide to keep him drunk or convert him with alcohol, did his duty.

No fewer than eight senators, Republicans all, were thought to entertain doubts in varying degrees. Anderson of Tennessee had been a sturdy War Hawk and in the end voted like one. In May his comments at a dinner given by Foster led the Englishman to write in his journal that Anderson "is much softened down, speaks of young Men having wished to go into violent Measures & thinks the news being bad from France, favorable, & that an Union of Interests between England & America would be a good Thing." Franklin of North Carolina also surprised Foster by voting steadily for war. John Smith of New York and John Condit were considered at least partially committed to the antiwar cause. Alexander Gregg, a professional Pennsylvania politician for whom, apparently, nobody had much respect, had lost the bellicosity shown when he introduced Gregg's Resolutions in 1806. As a published letter of his stated, he wanted the Senate to substitute letters of marque, possibly against both belligerents, for a declaration of war, leaving the ultimate decision until fall when the nation would be better prepared and the foreign situation clearer.[62]

Even if these five of the eight waverers voted with their Repub-

---

rancour that he gave his opinion, and he voted against the declaration of war . . . from pure conviction that there was not sufficient ground for it, as well as the persuasion that we were really fighting for our existence and at the same time for the cause of liberty and independence all over the world against military despotism and irreligion." Davis, *op. cit.*, pp. 192–194.

[61] *Poulson's American Daily Advertiser* (Philadelphia), June 19, 1812; David Howell to Gallatin, Oct. 20, 1811, Gallatin MSS.

[62] Journal entry, May 23, 1812, Foster MSS; Gregg to ———, June 4, 1812, *True American and Commercial Advertiser* (Philadelphia), June 16, 1812.

lican colleagues, the decision still rested with the three great schismatics, William Branch Giles, Samuel Smith, and Michael Leib. Jonathan Roberts detested Leib so much that he threatened to kick him where it would do the most good. Giles had always advocated vigor, at least in theory. Sounding him out, John A. Harper hoped for the best, but he admitted that Giles "is however deadly hostile to Mr. Munroe, and not much in *love* with Mr. Madison." Nobody dared guess how Samuel Smith would finally vote. After talking both ways, on June 2 he refused to reveal his intentions to Augustus Foster. None of these men cared a snap for party support, Republican success, and particularly Madison's reputation. No wonder Monroe complained, during the Senate's debates, that nominal Republicans were a much greater problem than avowed Federalists! [63]

On June 10 Gregg moved to substitute naval reprisal and letters of marque for full war. The motion passed by seventeen to thirteen, with all the doubters except Samuel Smith and Franklin voting for it. Even if Bradley did not arrive in time, the opponents of war appeared to have a safe majority. On June 12, however, they failed by fifteen to seventeen to carry a resolution placing England and France upon the same footing, gaining the votes of Pope, its author, and Samuel Smith, but losing those of four timid men who thought that one enemy at a time—even if only a half enemy—was enough. Gregg's resolution, called up again, lost on a tie vote. Senator Giles's vote was the key; for reasons that can only be explained as the fruit of his own eccentricity, he abandoned the position he had taken a couple of days before. With these two narrow defeats, the peace movement passed the peak, although the antiwar men still had the support of exactly half the Senate and could pray for the speedy arrival of Bradley's coach. "I know you are anxious to be informed what we are doing, or what we will do," Macon wrote to his friend, Judge Nicholson, "to tell this would

[63] Roberts to Matthew Roberts, June 17, 1812, Roberts MSS; Harper to Plumer, June 14, 1812, Plumer MSS; journal entry, June 2, 1812, Foster MSS; Monroe to Taylor, June 13, 1812, James Monroe MSS, Library of Congress.

require a greater man, than I ever saw, and though this is telling nothing, yet it is telling all, it is telling what is literally true." Hunter told Foster that "they were all in the wind again." [64]

Although rain fell in torrents on the fifteenth, all the senators in town attended the session at the Capitol. They voted down two attempts at delay and, by the narrow margin of two votes, defeated Michael Leib's proposal to issue letters of marque and reprisal, the same to take effect against France as well as England if positive proof of repeal of the Berlin and Milan decrees was not forthcoming. Then, by a vote of nineteen to thirteen, the Senate passed the war bill to a third reading. All the waverers, disappointed in their hopes for a limited war, swung over to join the majority. The next day Bayard could mobilize only eleven votes behind his proposal to delay a final decision until November, and only nine for a delay until July. Pope and Worthington informed Foster that the game was up, but outside observers were tortured by doubt. Roberts wrote that "all that is diabolical is is at work in the Senate. . . . It is shrewdly suspected some of Fosters bills of exchange has dropped in the Senate. . . . the suspense we are in is worse than hell!!!!" [65]

After beating aside a last attempt to limit the war to the ocean, proposed this time by the unpredictable Giles, the Senate finally approved a declaration of war on June 17. Since Pope, although opposed, declined to vote against a great national decision, the tally was nineteen to thirteen. According to Jonathan Roberts, Gregg voted for war only to assure War Hawk support for his gubernatorial candidacy, and certainly neither Gregg nor his colleague, Leib, wanted war. Foster said that two or three senators shifted only when they saw that their negative votes would not prevent a declaration of war,[66] and, as the votes on letters of marque

[64] Macon to Nicholson, June 12, 1812, Nicholson MSS; journal entry, June 14, 1812, Foster MSS.

[65] Journal entry, June 17, 1812, Foster MSS; Roberts to Matthew Roberts, June 17, 1812, Roberts MSS.

[66] *Annals*, 12th Cong., 1st sess., p. 297; Davis, *op. cit.*, p. 100. Timothy Pickering composed two memoranda, dated 1822 and 1828 (Pickering MSS, Vol. LII, fol. 77; Vol. XLVII, fol. 84), in which he stated that Madison, who did not want war, counted on Samuel Smith, John Smith of New York, Leib, and Gregg to oppose it. According

showed, a majority obviously would have preferred to avoid one. If Giles had remained firm, or if Bradley had arrived earlier—he first appeared in the Senate two days after the declaration—the majority might have held together. In the pinch, with letters of marque defeated on a tie vote, Republican waverers preferred a declaration of war to postponement or surrender, for either of these courses would expose the hollowness of the vigor which so many of them professed to support. Doubtless Giles, Smith, and Leib (who, with Leib's friend, William Duane, had ostensibly supported positive action for some years) consoled themselves, too, with the thought that if the war went badly the accounting could be laid at Madison's door, not theirs.

Thus, after a struggle of seven and a half months, the War Hawks worked their will. Epithets aside, the *Federal Republican* spoke accurately in saying that the country had been dragged "by the blind and senseless animousity of a few 'new-hatched unfledged comrades,' who are but boys in public affairs, and who, in fact, have not been seen before by the American people on the public stage." The true War Hawks were a minority, even of the Republican party. The mistakes of their opponents and the apparent stubbornness of Great Britain had created a situation in which Congress was at last *"driven, goaded, dragged, forced, kicked"* into war, as the always impatient Lexington *Reporter* put it. "I have to remark on this extraordinary measure," wrote Foster, "that it seems to have been unexpected by nearly the whole Nation; & to have been carried in opposition to the declared sentiments of many of those who voted for it, in the House of Representatives, as well as in the Senate, in which latter body there was known to have been at one time, a decided Majority against it." [67]

At three in the afternoon on June 18, Monroe called Foster to

---

to Pickering, Smith told a friend that the President even called him in to urge him to vote against war, only to be scornfully rejected. Such a storÿ, filtered through at least two bitter enemies of Madison, must be entirely discredited, but, allowing for extreme distortion, it perhaps gives a shred of presidential support to Monroe's scheme for limited war, mentioned above in note 47.

[67] *Federal Republican,* June 18, 1812; *Reporter,* June 27, 1812; Foster #47 to Castlereagh, June 20, 1812, FO 5/86.

the State Department to inform him officially of the declaration of war. Foster understood Monroe to suggest that compromise might still be possible. Two days later they met again and "endeavoured to frighten one another for a whole Hour by descanting on the Consequences of War." Then Monroe asked Foster and his secretary to take tea with him. Since bad weather delayed the departure of Madison, who at this moment of climax had decided on a vacation at Montpelier, Foster was able to pay a final call at the White House on June 23. The two men exchanged regrets that war had come. Hinting that he hoped for a limited war, Madison stated that he opposed "pushing matters to extremes." In instructions sent to Russell three days later, however, the American government made it virtually certain that this would be neither a limited nor a short war. Impressment as well as the Orders in Council had to cease if the war were to come to a speedy end, Monroe declared. Speed was imperative, for if much time passed the invasion of Canada might force the United States into "compromitment" with its inhabitants and "the effect, which success, (which could not fail to attend it) might have on the public mind here" would make it "difficult to relinquish Territory which had been conquered." The administration had convinced itself that Canada was a simple matter of marching, that a mere declaration of war might well bring down the British government. "My candid opinion is," Monroe had recently written to his old friend, Taylor of Caroline, "that we shall succeed in obtaining what it is important to obtain, and that we shall experience little annoyance or embarrassment in the effort." [68]

At noon on June 25, having shaken the last friendly congressional hand, Augustus Foster rode out of the capital in which he had served gaily but without success. After a leisurely and unmolested journey overland, he sailed from New York on July 12. Already General Hull had set in motion the army that was expected to sweep through Canada, and Commodore Rodgers in the

[68] Foster minute of June 23, 1812, enclosed in Foster #49 to Castlereagh, June 24, 1812, FO 5/86; Monroe to Russell, June 26, 1812, Instructions, Vol. I; Monroe to Taylor, June 13, 1812, Monroe MSS.

*Constellation* had sought to bring to battle H.M.S. *Belvidera,* a British warship sighted off New York. Scores of vessels now nearing the American coast with word that the Orders in Council had been repealed were to become the first important prizes of the war. For a second and last time, through mutual misunderstanding, America and Britain had failed to find the road to peace.

# XII

## "THIS UNNATURAL WAR"

Although America's declaration of war came only after seven years of controversy and as many months of noisy congressional action, it surprised Great Britain and the United States. The English, who did not want war, were serenely confident of the result. "We cannot fear a war with any power in the world," the *Times* commented, " . . . but it is not unmanly to say, that we regret the sad necessity . . . of carrying the flame and devastation of war to a part of the world which has not seen a hostile foot for thirty years." [1] After repeal of the Orders in Council, Britain discounted all bad news from the United States, sure that America would abandon notions of a quixotic struggle when she learned of her great victory over the chief symbol of discord.

Even news of the declaration of war caused only muted debate in Britain. Henry Brougham expected a speedy armistice, and Alexander Baring advised him to support the government on existing issues, confident that Madison could not continue the war for two weeks after news of repeal arrived. The *Sun* unreasonably

[1] *Times* (London), June 5, 1812.

418

complained that, in his war message, "Mr. MADDISON recapitulates all the subjects of complaint against this country, . . . but he cautiously avoids answering any of the charges that have been preferred against the American Government." In an editorial lacking its usual splenetic fire, the *Courier* answered Madison point by point and warned that war might continue despite England's surrender of the orders. The *Morning Chronicle*, while complaining that the Americans had acted precipitately and objecting that "there is, in Mr. MADISON's paper, a querulous spirit, which betrays more of the littleness of the lawyer than the enlarged and national indignation of a Statesman," let its chief criticism fall upon the ministry. The *Chronicle* asserted "that our mode of proceeding towards America has been most irritating to her, as well as most injurious to ourselves—that the charge against us, of obstinate perseverance in error, from pride rather than conviction, is just . . . —and that we have, in truth, more reason to impute to our own imbecile Councils, all the calamities that may spring from this unnatural war, than to the influence of the French on the councils of America." The *Caledonian Mercury* and the *Times* agreed that, with the orders repealed, impressment was too "paltry an affair for two great nations to go to war about." Madison's message, the *Times* stated, "sums up all her grievances against us; and to speak candidly, she makes a fair shew." [2] Only later did humiliating naval defeats, the threat to Canada, and America's refusal to make peace after learning of the revocation of the orders ignite British anger against President Madison.

No such mildness characterized the American reaction to the declaration of war. Many moderates, whatever their desires prior to June 18, quietly supported the war once it had come. The joyful celebration of war men and the strident complaint of Federalists made up for their silence. A drunken celebrant, driving Winfield Scott's gig, twice tipped the young officer into the ditch. Republican

---

[2] Brougham to Grey, Aug. 2, 1812, Henry Brougham, *The Life and Times of Henry Lord Brougham* (2 vols.; Edinburgh, 1871), II, 27–28; Baring to Brougham, Aug. 1, 1812; *ibid.*, II, 36–39; *Sun* (London), July 31, 1812; *Courier* (London), July 31, 1812; *Morning Chronicle* (London), July 31, 1812; *Caledonian Mercury* (Edinburgh), Aug. 3, 1812; *Times*, July 31, 1812.

centers like Richmond congratulated themselves on the impending "new harvest of political advantage and national glory." A Virginian, assigning too much personal credit to the President, wrote him: "You have politically regenerated the nation, and washed out the stain in their national character, inflicted on it by England." A mass meeting at Germantown resolved to support the war, since "it hath pleased the Almighty Ruler of the universe to suffer the perfidious outrages of the British government to render it necessary, once more, for the American people to struggle for their 'sovereignty and independence.'" In many New England seaports church bells tolled a dirge, shops closed, and ships' flags flew at half-mast. Bostonians hissed two prowar congressmen, and another was mobbed at Plymouth. The *Connecticut Courant* summed up the Federalist reaction, saying the war "was commenced in folly, it is proposed to be carried on with madness, and (unless speedily terminated) will end in ruin." [3] Many found consolation only in the conviction that it made Republican defeat certain.

The mixed reaction in New York perhaps best characterized the national mood. The *Evening Post* bitterly criticized the administration, and Moses Austin's wife wrote him that war "has come like an Electrick shock upon the great part of the people who have been two sanguine, in regard to peace Measures." Mrs. Austin added that most people were prepared to unite behind the government, and another observer, after noting that the city overwhelmingly opposed war, added, "but there are not wanting those who rejoice." "Pepal here are more reasonable about the war measure than what I esspected," John Jacob Astor wrote to his friend Gallatin, "& alltho many disapprove of the manner and time it was declared all agree that we have plenty cause." [4] The silent, nega-

[3] Wirt to Monroe, June 21, 1812, James Monroe MSS, Library of Congress; William Pope to Madison, July 10, 1812, James Madison MSS, Library of Congress; *Aurora* (Philadelphia), Aug. 12, 1812; *Connecticut Courant* (Hartford), June 30, 1812.

[4] *New-York Evening Post*, June 20, 1812; Maria A. Austin to Moses Austin, June 23, 1812, Eugene C. Barker, ed., *The Austin Papers*, I, American Historical Association, *Annual Report, 1919*, Vol. II (Washington, 1924), p. 214; Arthur E. Roorbach to Livingston, June 24, 1812, Robert R. Livingston MSS, New-York Historical Society; Astor to Gallatin, June 27, 1812, Albert Gallatin MSS, New-York Historical Society.

tive support extended to the government spoke volumes for the ineptitude of Congress and the President during the winter.

Five weeks after the declaration of war America learned that the Orders in Council had been repealed. Noting particularly that Castlereagh had reserved the right to restore the system in May, 1813, if French or American conduct so required, Madison interpreted the development as a trick to turn America from war. War Hawk journals quickly shifted to impressment and indemnities for past seizures. Attacking Alexander Baring, one of America's best English friends, for saying the orders were America's only major complaint, the Lexington *Reporter* wrote that "we will take the liberty to inform him that whenever peace is made, he will find that the SCALPS and lives of the FARME[R]S in the western world will not again be abandoned to British savages, and that the liberty of our seamen will have some weight in the scale." The *National Intelligencer* soon quieted the *Reporter*'s fears that the administration would be "deceived by this trap of our eternal enemies." On August 25 it contrasted conditional British repeal with the absolute revocation of the French edicts and added, "A public act of one belligerent, *so deliberately framed, so worded*, is in derogation from and *violation* of our standing neutral rights. A war against such inadmissible pretensions . . . is a war for the freedom, sovereignty and independence of . . . the American Union." "It should take more to make peace than to prevent war," Jefferson declared. "The sword once drawn, full justice must be done." [5] A concession which, if known in time, would have prevented war, utterly failed to move the two nations toward peace. The Americans raised their terms, and England angrily rejected what seemed an attempt at extortion.

The war continued for two and a half years, and for nearly 150 years it has challenged those who seek to explain its coming. Contemporary Federalists found a simple explanation in alleged Re-

[5] Madison to Gallatin, Aug. 8, 1812, Henry Adams, ed., *The Writings of Albert Gallatin* (3 vols.; Philadelphia, 1879), I, 523; *Reporter* (Lexington, Ky.), Aug. 23, 1812; *National Intelligencer* (Washington), Aug. 25, 1812; Jefferson to Robert Wright, Aug. 8, 1812, Andrew A. Lipscomb and Albert E. Bergh, eds., *The Writings of Thomas Jefferson* (Memorial ed.; 20 vols.; Washington, 1903–1904), XIII, 184.

publican subserviency to France. A New York dominie declared God had brought on war so that the young republic might chastise the British government, "a *despotic usurpation—A superstitious combination of civil and ecclesiastic power—A branch of the grand antichristian apostacy—Erastian in its constitution and administration—*and *Cruel in its policy.*" [6] Actually, neither God nor Napoleon seems an adequate explanation for the war, and historians have sought to establish the importance of more mundane influences.

Most nineteenth-century historians emphasized British outrages against American commerce. Admiral Mahan said that the orders "by their enormity dwarfed all previous causes of complaint, and with the question of impressment constituted a vital and irreconcilable body of dissent which dragged the two states into armed collision." Henry Adams apparently considered this maritime emphasis inadequate, but, as Warren Goodman suggests in an able historiographical article, he modified rather than abandoned the traditional view, although he did hint that Canadian-directed imperialism played a part.[7] Despite a dislike of Jefferson and Madison so bitter that he sometimes doctored the evidence, Adams' volumes remain the most complete, often the best written, and, when used with proper caution, the most useful survey of the entire period. After a lapse of some years, A. L. Burt reëmphasized maritime causes in a graceful summary of the era.

For two decades before the appearance of Burt's work in 1940, scholars sought to explain the motives of the West, the section that most unanimously supported war. Louis M. Hacker, then in a Marxist phase, suggested that a greedy desire for fertile Canadian farm land lay behind the façade of arguments for national honor. Julius W. Pratt contradicted Hacker's position, largely by disproving the central hypothesis, that there was no longer good agricul-

[6] Alexander McLeod, *A Scriptural View of the Character, Causes and Ends of the Present War* (New York, 1815), p. 97.

[7] Alfred T. Mahan, *Sea Power in Its Relation to the War of 1812* (2 vols.; Boston, 1905), I, 2; Warren H. Goodman, "The Origins of the War of 1812: a Survey of Changing Interpretations," *Mississippi Valley Historical Review*, XXVIII (1941–1942), 173. Including texts and general histories, Goodman examined forty-three treatments of the subject.

tural land on the American side of the frontier.[8] Then, following a line already sketched by Dice R. Anderson, Pratt in his turn suggested a bargain between frontiersmen and Republicans of the North, who desired Canada, and Southerners, who wanted to absorb Florida. Sectional jealousies, Pratt concluded, broke down this alliance only after it had brought on war. Pratt found it difficult to demonstrate a real bargain, and there is reason to believe that the South did not almost universally desire the acquisition of Florida, as he maintained. But not without merit is Pratt's thesis that Western Anglophobia was stirred by the menace of Indian warfare believed to be inspired by Canadian authorities.[9] Finally, George R. Taylor put forward the argument that the West, economically overextended and suffering from depression from 1808 onward, blamed its troubles on the restrictive edicts of Europe and advocated war to break down this barrier to prosperity. In April, 1812, Augustus J. Foster anticipated this interpretation: "The Western States having nothing to lose by war, . . . [are] clamorous for it, . . . being likely even to gain in the Exports of their produce while the exportation of that of the Atlantic shall be impeded." [10] Moreover, there was always the chance that war, or even the threat of war, would drive England to surrender the orders.

Hacker billed his suggestion "a conjecture," and Pratt and Taylor specifically noted that they were dealing, in the former's words, "with one set of causes only." Still, despite Pratt's coördinate interest in Southern ambitions for Florida, the researches of these scholars concentrated attention upon the West. The war came to bear the mark of the West, although only nine congressmen—a mere one of each nine voting for war—came from Western states. Taylor's suggestion that the West sought war to regain an export

[8] Louis M. Hacker, "Western Land Hunger and the War of 1812: a Conjecture," *Mississippi Valley Historical Review*, X (1923–1924), 365–395 *passim;* Julius W. Pratt, "Western Aims in the War of 1812," *ibid.*, XII (1925–1926), 45–50 and *passim.*

[9] Dice R. Anderson, "The Insurgents of 1811," American Historical Association, *Annual Report, 1911*, I (Washington, 1913), 167–176; Julius W. Pratt, *Expansionists of 1812* (New York, 1925), pp. 12–14 and *passim.*

[10] George R. Taylor, "Agrarian Discontent in the Mississippi Valley Preceding the War of 1812," *Journal of Political Economy*, XXXIX (1931), 471–505 *passim;* Foster #28 to Castlereagh, April 23, 1812, Foreign Office Archives, Public Record Office, FO 5/85.

market might just as legitimately have been applied to other agricultural areas of the country, particularly the South, as Goodman, Burt, and Margaret K. Latimer have recently noted.[11] Studies of Western motivation, despite the caveats of their authors, have distorted the image of events leading to the War of 1812.

In his biography of the President, Irving Brant attempts to refurbish Madison's reputation. Attention is so narrowly concentrated on the President and on events with which he dealt that many important developments in Europe and America are slighted. Brant clearly shows the President's technical diplomatic ability. He does not equally clearly disprove Henry Adams' contention that, by emphasizing America's right to demand repeal of the orders as a consequence of alleged French repeal,

Madison had been so unfortunate in making the issue that on his own showing no sufficient cause of war seemed to exist. . . . Great Britain was able to pose before the world in the attitude of victim to a conspiracy between Napoleon and the United States to destroy the liberties of Europe. Such inversion of the truth passed ordinary bounds, and so real was Madison's diplomatic mismanagement that it paralyzed one-half the energies of the American people.[12]

As Brant claims, Madison recognized that peace might become impossibly costly, but in 1812 he abandoned with great reluctance what Samuel Flagg Bemis has perceptively called his "strategy of auctioning the great belligerents out of their respective systems of retaliation."[13] Perhaps Napoleon and Perceval acted foolishly in rejecting the bids Madison put forward during the auction; perhaps the President calculated more accurately the mutual benefits of accommodation. Still, it is one of the supreme functions of

[11] Goodman, *op. cit.*, p. 184; Alfred L. Burt, *The United States, Great Britain, and British North America from the Revolution to the Establishment of Peace after the War of 1812* (New Haven, 1940), pp. 306–307; Margaret K. Latimer, "South Carolina—a Protagonist of the War of 1812," *American Historical Review*, LXI (1955–1956), 914–929 *passim*.

[12] Henry Adams, *History of the United States during the Administrations of Jefferson and Madison* (9 vols.; New York, 1889–1891), VI, 398–399.

[13] Samuel F. Bemis, *John Quincy Adams and the Foundations of American Foreign Policy* (New York, 1949), p. 181.

the statesman to weigh the intangibles as well as the tangibles, to expect illogical and prejudiced reactions along with coolly calculated ones. When Irving Brant declares that "President Madison to be successful . . . needed to deal with men whose understanding matched his own," [14] he really confesses the political failure of his hero.

Madison never firmly controlled the Congress; he often lost command of his own Cabinet; frequently he seemed to drift rather than to direct policy. John Adams, fiercely challenged during the disintegration of Federalism, at least remained firm. In the spring of 1812 the congressional delegate from Mississippi Territory wrote that "the Executive is much censured by all parties for the tardiness of its advances to meet the *tug of war,* and the tenure of Mr. Madison's continuance in the presidential chair, in my opinion, depends upon the success of our hostile preparations." Yet the President did not forcefully support the cause of those whose loyalty had to be preserved for the impending election, nor did he speak out in favor of a course that might have maintained the peace he cherished. He reigned but he did not rule. After the declaration of war Jonathan Roberts wrote: "The world are pleased to suppose I am on good terms at the White House which by the way is no advantage for the cry of mad dog is not more fatal to its victim than the cry of executive connexion here." [15] Madison won reëlection, but he was the least respected victor the country had yet known.

The war came, not because of the President, but despite him. The war came, not for any single reason, but from the interplay of many. The nation did not want war, and surely it did not embark gleefully on a great crusade. Tired of the self-flagellation and the disgrace that had marked the years since 1805, propelled by the fear of ridicule for inconsistency and by an honest interest in the nation's honor, a sufficient number of congressmen allowed themselves to support war. Justification for a declaration of war was

[14] Irving Brant, *James Madison: the President* (Indianapolis, 1956), p. 483.

[15] George Poindexter to William C. Mead, April 10, 1812, Bernard Mayo, ed., *Henry Clay, Spokesman of the New West* (Boston, 1937), p. 512; Roberts to Matthew Roberts, July 1, 1812, Jonathan Roberts MSS, Historical Society of Pennsylvania.

not wanting, and the long-term results were probably beneficial. Still, the war came just when the United States might have enjoyed without a struggle the immense benefits of the neutrality in which so much Christian forbearance (or cowardice) had been invested. Neither side sought the War of 1812, and in the short run it was tragically unnecessary.

The United States did not go to war to add new states to the Union. A very few ebullient men from the North may have desired this. For sectional reasons the South and the West opposed it. A few advance agents of manifest destiny believed, as the Reverend McLeod put it in 1815, that the war was "a contest, not only to prevent the recolonization of these states, but also in the Providence of God for extending the principles of *representative democracy*— the blessings of liberty, and the rights of self-government, among the colonies of Europe." Even McLeod counted more on the imperialism of ideas than on military conquest. For most Americans Canada was but a means to an end, "a blow that might have given a speedier termination to the controversy," as Niles put it. At most, the occupation of the British provinces seemed the best means to reduce the enemy's power. A loyal Republican paper in Virginia commented:

The great advantages to be derived from the acquisition of those possessions will not accrue so much from the tenure of them as a conquest, . . . but from the very important consequences which their loss will occasion to Britain; and among these consequences we may reckon the suppression of a great deal of smuggling, the curtailment . . . of the British fur trade and the disseverance of the West India Islands from Great Britain.[16]

So feeble was the desire for permanent incorporation of Canada within the Union that within six weeks after the destruction of British power in Upper Canada at the battle of the Thames in 1813, the Western militia had returned to their homes.

From the opening of the war session, both supporters and enemies of war proclaimed that an attack upon Canada would be the

16 McLeod, *op. cit.*, p. 220; *Niles' Weekly Register* (Baltimore), March 28, 1812; *Virginia Argus* (Richmond), Nov. 11, 1811.

principal American offensive. Congress ostensibly tailored the new army to the requirements of this campaign. All the Republicans, at least, believed that even the slightest effort would result in victory. "In four weeks from the time that a declaration of war is heard on our frontier," John C. Calhoun declared, "the whole of Upper and a part of Lower Canada will be in our possession." When Federalists complained that their opponents sought to establish a standing army that might menace American liberties, Trenton's *True American* replied, "It will be a *moving, fighting, conquering,* army—and as soon as its duty is done, it will be disbanded." [17] Had Bermuda or Jamaica been vulnerable to attack by a flotilla of Jefferson's gunboats, the War Hawks would have been equally satisfied to invade them.

Even Indian warfare did not inspire important demands for Canadian conquest in the winter of 1811–12. "Much of that resentment against the British, which prevailed so strongly in the western states," a Kentucky historian of the war stated, ". . . may fairly be attributed to this source." Even this Western chronicler, however, declared that the Orders in Council became more intolerable than any other source of complaint against England.[18] After Tippecanoe desultory warfare took place along the frontier, but most Indian tribes remained at peace until General Hull surrendered his army to Isaac Brock in the summer of 1812. Although Grundy and the Lexington *Reporter* remained irate, the Indian menace played a comparatively minor part in congressional debates until the very end of the session, when all complaints against Britain were being brought together to support a declaration of war. At that time congressmen emphasized Britain's interference in American affairs rather than the material consequences to one section.

The most important, most justified American complaints against England sprang from Britain's exercise of her maritime power.

[17] *Annals,* 12th Cong., 1st sess., p. 1397; *True American* (Trenton), May 18, 1812. Later in the war, however, many Americans, including Madison and Monroe, were tempted by the dream of incorporating Canada into the United States.
[18] Robert McAfee, *History of the Late War in the Western Country* (Lexington, Ky., 1816), pp. 2, 7.

Substantively, through the loss of seamen, ships, and cargoes, America suffered greatly from impressment, blockades, and the Orders in Council. The sovereign spirit and the self-respect of the American nation suffered perhaps even more every time a seaman was removed from beneath the Stars and Stripes or a merchant vessel was haled to trial before an admiralty court that paid scant heed to international law. The penalties of neutrality are often dear, and perhaps only the weak, the phlegmatic, or the noble are capable of enduring them. Jefferson and Madison might fit into one or the other of these categories. Ultimately the nation felt taxed beyond endurance. However necessary to British prosecution of the contest with Napoleon impressment and attacks upon neutral commerce might be, they finally brought war with America. Fortune rather than justice postponed the outbreak of war beyond the gloomiest days of Britain's struggle, when American entry might well have played an important part.

Impressment, Frank A. Updyke has observed, was "the most aggravating and the most persistent" American grievance. By 1812 the press gangs had been at work for twenty years. In many instances—probably even the majority—the British forcibly recalled a king's subject to his allegiance rather than kidnapped an American. More often than was generally admitted, the Admiralty released mariners mistakenly seized. Still, impressment formed an ultimately intolerable insult to national sovereignty. When, during the war, the Federalist legislature of Massachusetts undertook an investigation to show that very few seamen had been impressed, John Quincy Adams angrily and accurately declared the question irrelevant:

No Nation can be Independent which suffers her Citizens to be stolen from her at the discretion of the Naval or military Officers of another. . . . The State, by the social compact is bound to *protect* every one of its Citizens, and the enquiry how many of them a foreign Nation may be allowed to rob with impunity is itself a humiliation to which I blush to see that the Legislature of my native state could defend. . . . The principle for which we are now struggling is of a higher and more sacred nature than any question about taxation can involve. It is the principle of personal liberty, and of every social right.[19]

Failures of American arms and a European peace that halted impressment caused Adams, along with Madison and Monroe, to accept a peace silent on impressment. In principle, however, he was correct. America might well have gone to war on this issue, perhaps at the time of the *Chesapeake* affair.

Although officially the American government made very little of impressment from 1808 onward, the people could not forget it. During the war session, and particularly in the spring, impressment aroused more and more heat. *Niles' Register*, which began publication in 1811, rallied opinion on this issue. "Accursed be the American government, and every individual in it," an imprecation ran, "who . . . shall agree to make peace with Great Britain, until ample provision shall be made for our impressed seamen, and security shall be given for the prevention of such abominable outrages in the future." A Quid and a Republican who hoped to avoid war told Foster this was the most ticklish problem to explain to their constituents, and even the stanchly antiwar senator, Thomas Worthington, found impressment almost impossible to tolerate. "He says," Foster wrote in his diary, "he would rather live on a Crust in the Interior than live degraded." Foster, who repeatedly suggested that modification of the orders would prevent a declaration of war, nevertheless recognized the renewed importance accorded to impressment. On April 23 he wrote, "Very inflammatory paragraphs and letters on the subject . . . have lately been circulated in the American papers, and as the causes of war become more closely canvassed, that arising out of the practice of impressment seems to be dwelt upon with considerable vehemence."[20] When war approached, the War Hawks had a singularly effective propa-

---

[19] Frank A. Updyke, *The Diplomacy of the War of 1812* (Baltimore, 1915), p. 3; Adams to Plumer, Aug. 13, 1813, Adams Family MSS (microfilm), Massachusetts Historical Society, Vol. CXXXIX.

[20] *Niles' Register*, April 18, 1812 (italics omitted); journal entries, April 19, 22, May 24, 1812, Foster journal, Augustus J. Foster MSS, Library of Congress; Foster #28 to Castlereagh, April 23, 1812, FO 5/86.

ganda point in this violation of the rights of individual Americans who deserved better of their country.

Both the British government and the Federalists later complained that the President only resuscitated the impressment issue after the Orders in Council had disappeared. They pointed out that, particularly in the Erskine negotiations, the administration had allowed impressment to pass in silence. In 1813 Lord Castlereagh described it as "a cause of war, now brought forward as such for the first time." [21] These criticisms showed only that the administration had been backward in defending the rights of citizens, or that the President and Congress had been willing for a time to exchange the kidnaping of Americans for the benefits of neutrality. Neither Lord Castlereagh nor Timothy Pickering, who as secretary of state had himself vehemently protested the practice, should have been surprised that the American people considered impressment an insult.

Even more than impressment, with which congressmen and newspaper editors often coupled them, the Orders in Council showed Britain's contemptuous disdain for American protests against her use of sea power. The forcible enlistment of seamen could be expressed in dramatic human terms. The Orders in Council more massively and more selfishly assaulted the United States. Their material cost was impressive. Although the number of seizures actually fell after 1808, the year beginning in October, 1811, saw an increase of nearly 50 per cent. The orders and the *Essex* case had long since reduced the reëxport trade to a shadow of its former size. After a spurt stimulated by Macon's Bill #2 and the Cadore letter, the export of native American produce fell drastically after the spring of 1811. By far the greatest proportion of this decline came in exports to Britain, particularly because return cargoes were forbidden and the United Kingdom suffered from glut.[22] Agriculturists and plantation owners, some shipowners, and the average congressman ascribed the decline to Britain's

[21] *Hansard*, XXIV, 371.
[22] Adam Seybert, *Statistical Annals . . . of the United States of America* (Philadelphia, 1818), pp. 79–80, 93, 112–113.

Orders in Council, which prevented Americans from developing the presumably lucrative Continental market. At the same time, particularly because the British permitted their own subjects to trade with Europe under license, the Orders in Council seemed humiliating. Since at least November, 1807, the English had presumed to legislate not only for their own people but also for the commercial world. Economic necessity and national right alike cried out against the Orders in Council.

Everyone in Washington during the months from November to June placed the Orders in Council at the head of the list of American grievances. Louis Sérurier and Augustus Foster, Federalists and Republicans were in agreement. When the British minister asked Chauncey Goodrich, a Federalist senator, "what was required of us by Men of fair Views, he replied, take off the Orders in Council and come to some Arrangement about Impressment." In November President Madison considered British maritime policy the transcendent issue between the two countries. Porter's report declared that the orders "went to the subversion of our national independence" and were "sapping the foundation of our prosperity." [23] Throughout the winter congressmen assailed the orders, drowning out the "whip-poor-will cry" for Canada of which John Randolph spoke. Repeal, Madison noted years later, would have postponed war and led to renewed negotiations on impressment "with fresh vigor & hopes, under the auspices of success in the case of the orders in council." The orders, he told Jared Sparks in 1830, were the only issue sturdy enough to bear a declaration of war.[24]

The strength of this issue depended in part upon the reinforcement provided by impressment and other grievances, the flying buttresses of the central structure. Had the orders stood alone as a British challenge, war would probably not have come in 1812. But they became the key to the drive for war. No other factor,

[23] Journal entry, May 18, 1812, Foster MSS; Madison to Adams, private, Nov. 15, 1811, Gaillard Hunt, ed., *The Writings of James Madison* (9 vols.; New York, 1900–1910), VIII, 166–167.

[24] Madison to Wheaton, Feb. 26–27, 1827, Hunt, *op. cit.*, IX, 273; journal entry, April 18[–23], 1830, Jared Sparks MSS, Houghton Library, Harvard University.

not even impressment, which most directly affected Northeasterners, struck all sections so impartially. Not even impressment exceeded the orders as a threat to America's position as a sovereign power. The Orders in Council were four years old when the Twelfth Congress met, going on five when America declared war. Why this delay? A natural desire to escape war partly explains it. Unreal faith in the power of trade boycotts, more justified expectations from the Erskine agreement, optimism engendered by the Cadore letter, hope that the Prince of Wales would replace his insane father's ministers with more friendly men, the anticipated impact of American measures of preparedness in Great Britain—all these counseled delay. When war ultimately came in June, 1812, the Orders in Council were the central issue. The requirements of consistency and a growing realization that American honor had been nearly exhausted were the immediate precipitants.

Since at least 1806 the United States government, and more particularly Republican congressmen, had proclaimed that America would not settle for whatever neutral trade the belligerents chose to let her enjoy. Profitable as such trade might be (and it often was extremely rewarding), the United States would demand its rights. Of course Jefferson, and especially Madison, did not demand utter surrender from their opponents, and they did not press certain claims they considered comparatively insignificant. In principle, however, they insisted that Britain and France recognize American rights and tailor their policies to them. Commercial pressure failed, political bargaining did not succeed, pleas for justice rebounded hollowly across the Atlantic. Still America maintained her claims, and the only remaining weapon to secure them was military power. The War Hawk Congress initiated preparedness, and the administration discreetly encouraged it, in the hope that England would surrender to this weapon what she had denied to boycotts, bargaining, and complaint.

Once embarked upon this course it became almost impossible to turn back. Many who voted for military measures without wanting war found it difficult to recede from the ground they had taken.

The 10,000-man army proposed by the House of Representatives had an ostensible military purpose, but its supporters valued it chiefly as a demonstration of American determination. "We are not at war yet tho' David R. Williams hopes in god we soon shall be. Till we are at war I shall not go above 10,000 additional troops," Jonathan Roberts wrote in December. As time passed, Roberts became more and more bellicose. In February he wrote, "There seems to be no disposition to relax our war measures but I believe every body would be exceeding glad to remain at peace." A month later he stated, "I am well convinced we have no hope of peace but by vigorous preparations for War," but he added that he was ready to vote for war.[25] As the spring passed, Roberts found his Quaker principles weakening, and he attended meetings very infrequently. In May and June this man, who had come to Washington determined that affairs should be forced to a solution and yet still hopeful war could be avoided, found himself more and more firmly committed to the cause of the War Hawks. The logic of the situation carried the Pennsylvanian and many of his colleagues forward.

In May John Randolph declared that, although many members of the majority would not follow the same course if they had it to do over again, "they have advanced to the brink of a precipice, and not left themselves room to turn." John Smilie admitted as much, arguing that while he would have preferred a further attempt at commercial coercion he now felt it necessary to go on toward war, since "if we now recede we shall be a reproach among nations." Willis Alston of North Carolina told Foster in March that Congress "should have originally taken another Course, now too late. it would have been better to protest against the belligerents & let Commerce thrive, this should have been done from the Beginning." Alston voted with the War Hawks on every important roll call. Speaker Clay and his supporters counted on and made frequent, effective reference to consistency in the closing months of the session. "After the pledges we have made, and the stand we have

[25] Roberts to Matthew Roberts, Dec. 20, 1811, Feb. 3, March 2, 1812, Roberts MSS.

taken," Clay asked his colleagues, "are we now to cover ourselves with shame and indelible disgrace by retreating from the measures and ground we have taken?" Remembering the reputation of the Tenth Congress, many representatives felt that the answer was as obvious as Clay pictured it. Thus legislators who were really "scarecrow men" came to support a declaration of war. James A. Bayard, one Federalist who had foreseen this danger from the beginning, chided a friend for his shortsightedness, saying, "You have thought the thing all along a jest & I have no doubt in the commencement it was so, but jests sometimes become serious & end in earnest." [26] So it was in 1812.

Consistency in congressmen, in a party, or in an administration became national honor when applied to the country as a whole. Since the acquisition of Louisiana in 1803, America had endured a steady diet of diplomatic humiliation. Jefferson, Madison, and the Congresses of their time attempted to reverse European policy by applying economic pressure. This tactic failed because Congress lacked staying power and Republican leaders underestimated the strength of emotions abroad. Defeats continued. Napoleon's announcement of repeal merely worsened the situation, for his cynical contempt and the gullibility of the American administration soon became apparent. Republicans had jeopardized the national character and the reputation of the United States; they had created a situation from which war was almost the only honorable escape; they had encouraged England, where unfortunately such encouragement was too little needed, to act almost as though Lord Cornwallis had won the battle of Yorktown. "We have suffered and suffered until our forbearance has been pronounced cowardice and want of energy," a friend wrote Jonathan Roberts. Although talk of honor perhaps came too easily to the lips of some patriotic orators, the danger was real. When John C. Calhoun asserted that "if we submit to the prentensions of England, now openly avowed, the independence of this nation is lost. . . . This is the second strug-

---

[26] *Annals*, 12th Cong., 1st sess., pp. 1403, 1592; journal entry, March 18, 1812, Foster MSS; Calhoun to Virgil Maxcy, May 2, 1812, Robert L. Meriwether, ed., *The Papers of John C. Calhoun*, I (Columbia, S.C., 1959), 101; *Annals*, 12th Cong., 1st sess., p. 1588; Bayard to Rodney, June 11, 1812, James A. Bayard Letterbook of Letters to Caesar A. Rodney, New York Public Library.

gle for our liberty," he scarcely exaggerated. When a Republican Fourth of July meeting at Boston toasted "The War—The second and last struggle for national freedom—A final effort to rescue from the deep the drowning honor of our country," the sentiment was apt.[27]

In his first annual message after the outbreak of war, President Madison declared:

To have shrunk under such circumstances from manly resistance would have been a degradation blasting our best and proudest hopes; it would have struck us from the high rank where the virtuous struggle of our fathers had placed us, and have betrayed the magnificent legacy which we hold in trust for future generations. It would have acknowledged that on the element which forms three-fourths of the globe we inhabit, and where all independent nations have equal and common rights, the Americans were not an independent people, but colonists and vassals.

A year after the war ended, Henry Clay similarly stressed the theme of national honor and self-respect. "We had become the scorn of foreign Powers, and the contempt of our own citizens," he said. " . . . Let any man look at the degraded condition of this country before the war; the scorn of the universe, the contempt of ourselves. . . . What is our present situation? Respectability and character abroad—security and confidence at home. . . . our character and Constitutions are placed on a solid basis, never to be shaken." Years later, Augustus J. Foster philosophically wrote: "This war was certainly productive of much ill-blood between England and America, but in the opinion of the Speaker, Mr. Clay, and his friends it was as necessary to America as a duel is to a young naval officer to prevent his being bullied and elbowed in society. . . . Baleful as the war has been, I must confess that I think in this respect something has been gained by it."[28] The President, the Speaker, and the envoy, who stood at the center of affairs during the war session, effectively summarized the one unanswerable

---

[27] Thomas J. Rogers to Roberts, March 22, 1812, Roberts MSS; *Annals*, 12th Cong., 1st sess., p. 1399; *Independent Chronicle* (Boston), July 6, 1812.

[28] James D. Richardson, ed., *A Compilation of the Messages and Papers of the Presidents* (Washington, 1897), I, 520; *Annals*, 14th Cong., 1st sess., pp. 777, 783; Richard B. Davis, ed., *Jeffersonian America: Notes on the United States of America . . . by Sir Augustus John Foster, Bart.* (San Marino, 1954), pp. 4–5.

argument for war. All the insults suffered by the United States, even the most important of them all, the Orders in Council, posed a greater threat in the realm of the spirit than in the world of the accountant and the merchant, the seaman and the frontiersman.

That war became imperative in June, 1812, does not mean that the American people desired it or that it could not have been avoided by greater wisdom in earlier years. Castlereagh's statement, in 1813, that "Great Britain has throughout acted towards the United States of America, with a spirit of amity, forbearance, and conciliation," [29] was simply preposterous. While the policy of England was far less rigid than Americans often suggested, the self-righteous spirit of messianism engendered by the Napoleonic wars and a woeful underestimation of the price of American good will combined to prevent a reconciliation Jefferson and Madison eagerly desired. In America, most of the Federalists served their country ill, for, blinded by their own hatred of Napoleon and their inveterate contempt for the politicians who had displaced them, they sabotaged peaceful American resistance to British outrages and repeatedly declared that the Republicans lacked the fortitude to go to war. Roberts wrote in his memoirs, "There had all along been an idea cherish'd by the opposition, that the majority would not have nerve enough to meet war. This I believe, mainly induc'd Britain to persist in her aggressions. If she could have been made to believe . . . that we were a united people, & would act as such, war might have been avoided." The *Independent Chronicle* complained with a good deal of justice, "In every measure of government, the federal faction have rallied in opposition, and urged the Ministry to persist in their Orders. They forced the United States to the alternative, either to *surrender their independence,* or *maintain it by War.*" [30] American disunion was clear enough, the desire to avoid war quite obvious. Despite the temporary and transparent policy advocated by Quincy, the Federalists contributed to that disunion and to British stubbornness.

<hr>

[29] *Hansard,* XXIV, 364.
[30] Memoirs (photostat), II, 14, Roberts MSS; *Independent Chronicle,* July 16, 1812.

Still, the Republican chieftains must bear primary responsibility for the war and the factionalism that made it an almost fatal test of the sturdiness of the nation they themselves had done so much to build. Whereas Washington and Adams kept objectives and means in harmony with one another, their successors often committed the United States to seek absolute right with inadequate weapons. Compromise, when sought, was usually offered at an impossible time. The justice of American demands is nearly undeniable, but the two Virginians, who prided themselves on the coolness of their logic, failed to perceive that justice was not a weapon in itself. They provided it with insufficient support, and they expected warring powers to view collateral problems with the same coolness that America exhibited. Economic warfare rested upon a rigid, mechanical conception of international trade. Although it was, of course, felt by the belligerents, it proved far more harmful to America, economically and morally, and served chiefly to convince Europe of the cowardice of the United States.

The two presidents secured not one important diplomatic objective after 1803. They scarcely challenged the development of factionalism within the Republican party, factionalism that deprived Congress of any real sense of direction. They provided public opinion with far too little leadership. They and their followers often spoke loudly and carried no stick at all. When at last a small group of congressmen declared that the time for half measures had ended and carried a majority with them down the road toward war, neither Great Britain nor the American people believed the destination would be reached. Thus British concession was discouraged and national union made impossible. In a state of military and psychological unpreparedness, the United States of America embarked upon a war to recover the self-respect destroyed by Republican leaders. Old John Taylor of Caroline wrote to the Secretary of State on the day of the declaration of war, "May God send you a safe deliverance." [31]

---

[31] Taylor to Monroe, June 18, 1812, William E. Dodd, ed., "Letters of John Taylor, of Caroline County, Virginia," *John P. Branch Papers*, II (Richmond, 1908), 342.

# NOTE ON THE SOURCES

This work examines a controversial period in American history as well as aspects of the major European war of the nineteenth century. Available materials are so multitudinous that a mere listing might conceal the most important. American and British manuscripts and contemporary publications are the principal foundations of this work, and the most important new contributions have come from these primary sources. Finally, the student of Anglo-American relations in this period is particularly fortunate in the bibliographical aids available to him. The excellent basic guide edited by Samuel F. Bemis and Grace G. Griffin (*Guide to the Diplomatic History of the United States* [Washington, 1935]) has been supplemented and in a sense brought up to date, at least so far as secondary materials are concerned, by the masterful bibliographical article of Warren H. Goodman ("The Origins of the War of 1812: a Survey of Changing Interpretations," *Mississippi Valley Historical Review*, XXVIII [1941–1942], 171–186) and the more recent *Harvard Guide* (Oscar Handlin *et al.*, eds., *Harvard Guide to American History* [Cambridge, 1954]). Consequently this note attempts no historiographical essay and singles out only those materials, principally contemporary, which have been especially useful. The footnotes indicate books and articles helpful at particular points, either for fact or interpretation.

The three most important studies of the entire period from 1805 to 1812 are those of Henry Adams, Alfred L. Burt, and Irving Brant. No student of these years can fail to owe a great debt to Henry Adams, *History of the United States during the Administrations of Jefferson and Madison* (9 vols.; New York, 1889–1891), especially Vols. III–VI. Adams is almost unreservedly hostile toward the Republican leaders and, as Irving Brant has shown, is not above shading the evidence in a fashion modern historians would consider improper. Although Adams worked more deeply among British manuscripts than any who have followed after him, his attitude toward England is colored with the nationalism of the period in which he wrote. Nevertheless, in the vigor of his judgments, in his capacity for magnificent prose (amidst, may it be said, extremely lengthy quotations and paraphrases), and in the breadth of his vision, Henry Adams still challenges those who follow him. Alfred L. Burt, *The United States, Great Britain, and British North America from the Revolution to the Establish-*

*ment of Peace after the War of 1812* (New Haven, 1940), covers a longer period in far less space than Adams. Burt's work, with a few exceptions on the British side, rests primarily upon printed materials, both primary and secondary. His judgments are judicious, but Burt perhaps fails to capture the emotional fire of the period. The same criticism cannot be made of Irving Brant, *James Madison: Secretary of State* (Indianapolis, 1953) and *James Madison: the President* (Indianapolis, 1956), for Brant is a strong partisan of the Republicans and particularly of Madison himself. Like those of Adams, Brant's verdicts are provocative, and many of them are particularly useful in forcing a reconsideration of the usual assumption that Madison was a weak or even incompetent secretary and president. Based as they are upon an intensive study of primary materials available in the United States, including copies of British diplomatic correspondence, Brant's volumes provide a great deal of information available nowhere else; on the British side, because of the intensive focus upon Madison, they are less satisfactory. I frequently disagree with Brant, but his viewpoint, like that of Adams, cannot be ignored by anyone attempting to untangle the threads of this period.

Because of serious errors and omissions in *American State Papers, Foreign Relations*, Vols. II–III (Washington, 1832–1833), the Department of State's official correspondence must be consulted in the original or on microfilm available from the National Archives. The following departmental files have been used: Diplomatic Instructions, All Countries, Vols. VI–VIII; Despatches, Great Britain, Vols. XII–XVIII (including one unnumbered volume); Despatches, France, Vols. X–XIII; and Consular Letters, London, Vol. IX. The latter contains much information on impressment and the campaign against the Orders in Council. *Annals of Congress*, 9th Congress–12th Congress (Washington, 1852–1853), do not fully reflect congressional sentiment because they were pasted together years later from newspaper accounts, Senate debates often went unreported, and the Federalists too often fluctuated between extravagant criticism and tactical silence. Nevertheless, they are an invaluable source.

Fortunately, the papers of the leading Republicans—Jefferson, Madison, Monroe, and Gallatin—are all readily available. The chief collections of the correspondence of the first three are at the Library of Congress, much Madison material being in the William C. Rives Collection. In addition there is Jefferson correspondence in the Massachusetts Historical Society (Coolidge Collection), extremely valuable Monroe manuscripts (particularly for the negotiation of 1806) in the New York Public Library, and a small and unimportant Madison collection at the same place. Gallatin's papers are in the New-York Historical Society. These collections displace the printed selections, particularly because the incoming correspondence is often especially useful. No major collection of Robert Smith's papers is available or has been published, although the Maryland Historical Society has a small Robert and William Smith collection.

Although William Pinkney's papers have disappeared, the other American representatives at London left valuable collections. In addition to the Monroe MSS, there is an important series of John Spear Smith letters in the Samuel Smith MSS, Library of Congress, and useful material in the Jonathan Russell MSS, Brown University Library.

The Library of Congress has the manuscripts of at least a score of Republican figures. Some, notably the papers of Joseph H. Nicholson, Wilson C. Nicholas, and William Plumer, are extremely helpful. Unfortunately, other collections (for example, those of Henry Clay, George W. Campbell, and Thomas Worthington) are extremely small. Two recent publications, Robert L. Meriwether, ed., *The Papers of John C. Calhoun,* Vol. I (Columbia, S.C., 1959), and James F. Hopkins, ed., *The Papers of Henry Clay,* Vol. I (Lexington, Ky., 1959), bring together the very limited political correspondence of these two men. The DeWitt Clinton MSS at Columbia University and the Thomas McKean Papers at the Historical Society of Pennsylvania help explain local Republican politics, and the memoirs (photostats) and especially the correspondence of Jonathan Roberts in the latter repository reveal as well as any single collection the ebbs and flows in the War Hawk Congress. The Adams Family MSS, Massachusetts Historical Society, now available on microfilm, help to show the drift of John and John Quincy Adams toward Republicanism. The younger Adams' particularly trenchant comments have been printed in Worthington C. Ford, ed., *The Writings of John Quincy Adams,* Vols. III–IV (New York, 1914), and Charles F. Adams, ed., *Memoirs of John Quincy Adams,* Vols. I–II (Philadelphia, 1874).

Federalists left even more plentiful manuscript materials than their political opponents. Comparatively moderate, loyal Federalism may be followed in James A. Bayard, Letterbook of Letters to Caesar A. Rodney, New York Public Library; in Elizabeth Donnan, ed., *Papers of James A. Bayard, 1796–1815,* American Historical Association, *Annual Report, 1913,* Vol. II (Washington, 1915); and in the Rufus King MSS, New-York Historical Society, although King's correspondents were usually more immoderate than he was. The Wolcott Family Papers, Connecticut Historical Society, reveal the attitude of Oliver Wolcott, not yet a convert to Republicanism. For more strident Federalist criticism of the Republican regime and its policies, one should see the Harrison Gray Otis MSS (the most valuable portions are printed in Samuel E. Morison, *The Life and Letters of Harrison Gray Otis* [2 vols.; Boston, 1913]) and the extremely voluminous papers of Timothy Pickering, both in the Massachusetts Historical Society. Many high Federalists corresponded with Francis James Jackson, whose papers are in the Public Record Office, FO 353/58–61. The *Catalogue of James McHenry Papers for Auction by Parke-Bernet Galleries* (New York, 1944) makes one regret that the small Maryland Historical Society and Library of Congress collections are, aside from an equally tiny Alexander C. Hanson collection at the former place, the only readily available sources for Federalism south of Delaware. Helpful Federalist commentaries on particular sessions of Congress may be found in the Hillhouse Family MSS and, for Senator Chauncey Goodrich, the William G. Lane Collection, both in the Yale University Library; the Abijah Bigelow MSS, American Antiquarian Society (published in Clarence S. Brigham, ed., "Letters of Abijah Bigelow, Member of Congress, to His Wife, 1810–1815," American Antiquarian Society, *Proceedings,* n.s., XL [1931], 305–406); and George H. Haynes, ed., "Letters of Samuel Taggart, Representative in Congress, 1803–1814," American Antiquarian Society, *Proceedings,* n.s., XXXIII (1923), 113–226, 197–438. Several extremely important letters are printed in Edmund Quincy, *Life of Josiah Quincy* (Boston, 1867).

Historians of Anglo-American relations have far less frequently exploited British manuscripts. For their use, an indispensable preliminary is Charles O. Paullin and Frederick L. Paxson, *Guide to the Materials in London Archives for the History of the United States since 1783* (Washington, 1914). It is now possible, particularly with the aid of the National Register of Archives, to discover many manuscript collections unavailable at the time Paullin and Paxson appeared.

Official British records are at the Public Record Office. There will be found the FO 5 series, the Foreign Office file on American affairs, as well as FO 95, the archives of the legation at Washington. (The instructions have been published in Bernard Mayo, ed., *Instructions to the British Ministers to the United States, 1791–1812,* American Historical Association, *Annual Report, 1936,* Vol. III [Washington, 1941].) In addition, there are various Foreign Office records that bear upon American relations, notably FO 95/515, entitled Treaty and Papers Relating There to, Signed at

London Decem$^r$. 31 1806, and FO 83/2204–2205, Law Officers Reports. The papers of the Admiralty have been searched with the aid of the Ind series; they are extremely cumbersome but often very important. Greenwich Hospital Miscellanea, Adm 80/116–117, contains important material on trade and the negotiations of 1806. The minutes of the Board of Trade (BT 5/15–21) throw some light on British policy toward the United States, as do the records of the Colonial Office, particularly CO 43/22–23, Secretary of State's Despatches. The position taken by admiralty courts is indicated in Christopher Robinson, ed., *Reports of Cases Argued and Determined in the High Court of Admiralty*, Vols. V–VI (London, 1806–1808); Thomas Edwards, ed., *Reports of Cases Argued and Determined in the High Court of Admiralty* (London, 1812); and John Dodson, ed., *Reports of Cases Argued and Determined in the High Court of Admiralty*, Vol. I (London, 1815). *Hansard,* though more satisfactory than the *Annals,* still must be supplemented by the *Journals of the House of Commons, Journals of the House of Lords,* and *Parliamentary Papers.* The Royal Archives, Windsor Castle, have been particularly useful for political background and for specific references to American affairs. The correspondence of George III for this period has not been published, and that of his son (Arthur Aspinall, ed., *The Letters of King George IV*, Vol. I [Cambridge, 1938]) is not particularly helpful, but the manuscripts in the Royal Archives contain evidence previously ignored.

Of the British ministers to the United States, Anthony Merry and David M. Erskine left no known manuscripts, and George H. Rose's papers, recently acquired by the British Museum, were not available for this study. Francis James Jackson's papers are in the Public Record Office, FO 353/58–61. Those of Augustus John Foster are in the Library of Congress. Selections from Foster's writings are in Vere Foster, ed., *The Two Duchesses* (London, 1898), and Richard B. Davis, ed., *Jeffersonian America: Notes on the United States of America . . . by Sir Augustus John Foster, Bart.* (San Marino, 1954). For the correspondence of a perceptive British representative in the United States, see George L. Rives, ed., *Selections from the Correspondence of Thomas Barclay* (New York, 1894).

The position of those generally known in Britain as "the Opposition," although they controlled the government in 1806–1807, is perhaps best seen in the papers of William Wyndham Grenville, Baron Grenville, now in the possession of George Grenville Fortescue, Boconnoc, Lostwithiel, Cornwall; William Eden, Baron Auckland, MSS, British Museum, Add.

MSS 34412–34471, 45728–45730; and the papers of Charles Grey, Second Earl Grey, The Prior's Kitchen, Durham University. The Charles James Fox MSS, British Museum, Add. MSS 47559–47601, are disappointing, as are the papers of Henry Brougham, now at University College, London. The Samuel Whitbread MSS, owned by Major Simon Whitbread, Southill Park, Biggleswade, Bedfordshire, contain important letters to Whitbread but little of his own writings. Thomas Grenville's papers, British Museum, Add. MSS 41851–41859, include scattered important letters.

The two foreign secretaries forced from the Cabinet were Marquis Wellesley and George Canning. The Wellesley MSS, Series II, British Museum, Add. MSS 37274–37318, have material on negotiations with William Pinkney. Canning's papers, now in the possession of H.R.H. the Princess Royal, have not yet been opened to scholars, but I have been assured that they do not contain substantial material for this period. Another independent, Viscount Sidmouth, left an extensive collection now on deposit at the County Record Office, The Castle, Exeter, Devon. The papers of his lieutenant, Nicholas Vansittart, are in the British Museum, Add. MSS 31229–31237.

The position of Spencer Perceval and his allies has recently become much more understandable with the gathering of the premier's papers. The Dudley Perceval Papers and the Holland Perceval Papers, examined while temporarily on deposit at the Register of National Archives, will soon be available at the British Museum. The Liverpool Papers, British Museum, Add. MSS 38190–38489, 38564–38581, containing the manuscripts of the first and second Earls of Liverpool, are frequently helpful. So too are the manuscripts of the Earl of Sheffield, Earl Melville, and John W. Croker, William L. Clements Library, Ann Arbor; of the first Earl of Harrowby, now in the possession of the Earl of Harrowby, Sandon Hall, Staffordshire; and of Viscount Castlereagh, now in the possession of the Marchioness Dowager of Londonderry, Mount Stewart, Newtownards, County Down, Northern Ireland. Francis Bickley, ed., *Report on the Manuscripts of Earl Bathurst* (London: Historical Manuscripts Commission, 1923), contains valuable material on the Order in Council of 1809.

Although I do not presume to deal exhaustively with Franco-American relations, French sources have aided development of the central theme. Most notable are the Archives des Affaires Étrangères, available in photostat form at the Library of Congress. Other useful materials include *Correspondance de Napoléon I$^{er}$*, Vols. XI–XXVII (Paris, 1862–1869); Léon Lecestre, ed., *Lettres Inédites de Napoléon I$^{er}$* (2 vols.; Paris, 1897); and

Louis M. Turreau de Garambouville, *Aperçu sur la Situation Politique des États-Unis d'Amérique* (Paris, 1815).

Forty American newspapers and an equal number of pamphlets have been used in the research for this study, all of them available in the extremely broad collection of the American Antiquarian Society. Although all have been valuable in fixing the temperature of American politics from time to time, attention need here be called to only a few of the most representative newspapers. The *National Intelligencer* (Washington) spoke clearly for the administration. More bellicose were the *Aurora* (Philadelphia), the *Independent Chronicle* (Boston), the *Enquirer* (Richmond), and, for the West, the *Reporter* (Lexington, Ky.). *Niles' Weekly Register* (Baltimore), first published in 1811, supported the War Hawks. The *Columbian* (New York), founded in 1809, put forward the Clintonian position. The Federalist position was stated in the various pamphlets of John Lowell, the *Columbian Centinel* (Boston), the *New-York Evening Post*, and, so stridently that it later provoked mob action, by Alexander C. Hanson's *Federal Republican* (Baltimore), founded in 1808. An impressive contemporary summary of the positions of both parties, combined with an appeal for unity in the face of Britain, is Matthew Carey, *The Olive Branch, or Faults on Both Sides, Federal and Democratic* (3d ed.; Boston, 1815).

British periodicals similarly cover the political spectrum. The arguments against restricting American trade were most strenuously put by the *Edinburgh Review*, the *Morning Chronicle* (London), and various provincial journals. Representing two quite distinct portions of the middle ground, and particularly useful because they reveal a shift among the uncommitted, are *Cobbett's Political Register* (London) and the *Times* (London). The defense of the Orders in Council was most energetically prosecuted by the semiofficial *Courier* (London) and, from its founding in 1809, the *Quarterly Review* (London). James Stephen, *War in Disguise; Or, the Frauds of the Neutral Flags* (London, 1805), and Alexander Baring, *An Inquiry into the Causes and Consequences of the Orders in Council; and an Examination of the Conduct of Great Britain towards the Neutral Commerce of America* (London, 1808), clearly set forth the rival positions. The Goldsmiths' Collection (University College, London), the British Museum and its newspaper branch at Colindale contain all the above material and much more which is cited only in the footnotes. For a discussion of British opinion based upon some of these materials, see Reginald Horsman, "British Opinion and the United States of America, 1806–1812," unpublished M.A. thesis, University of Birmingham, 1955.

Although this note has attempted to minimize references to readily available or obvious printed materials, a few new studies must be mentioned. Herbert Heaton, "Non-Importation, 1806–1812," *Journal of Economic History*, I (1941), 178–198, is one of the few articles to suggest the important legal loopholes in Jeffersonian commercial legislation. François Crouzet, *L'Economie Britannique et le Blocus Continental* (2 vols.; Paris, 1958), adds greatly to information previously elucidated by Heckscher, Melvin, and Cunningham. As for the central theme of this volume—the coming of the War of 1812—little need be added to the able comments in Goodman, "Origins of the War of 1812," for Irving Brant's volumes are the only full-scale treatment to appear since 1941. George Dangerfield, *The Era of Good Feelings* (New York, 1952), pp. 15–41, is a strongly written synthesis of existing scholarship. Harry C. Allen, *Great Britain and the United States* (New York, 1955), contains a number of judicious and penetrating comments, and Samuel F. Bemis, *John Quincy Adams and the Foundations of American Foreign Policy* (New York, 1949), has many helpful suggestions. Margaret K. Latimer, "South Carolina—a Protagonist of the War of 1812," *American Historical Review*, LXI (1955–1956), 914–929, convincingly extends to South Carolina and, by implication, to the entire South the thesis first put forward in George R. Taylor, "Agrarian Discontent in the Mississippi Valley Preceding the War of 1812," *Journal of Political Economy*, XXXIX (1931), 471–505. Reginald Horsman, in various articles, most notably "Western War Aims, 1811–1812," *Indiana Magazine of History*, LIII (1957), 1–18, and Patrick C. T. White, "Anglo-American Relations from 1803 to 1815," unpublished Ph.D. dissertation, University of Minnesota, 1954, have dealt with the general topic of this volume. The important political study by Roger H. Brown, "A Republic in Peril; the Crisis of 1812," unpublished Ph.D. thesis, Harvard University, 1960, was completed too late to be used in this volume, as was the forthcoming article in the *William and Mary Quarterly*, Norman K. Risjord's "1812: Conservatives, Warhawks, and the Nation's Honor," which shares some of the conclusions I have reached. But in the past twenty years no one has published either an extensive synthesis or a complete restudy of the coming of the War of 1812.

# INDEX

Adams, Henry: on war threat, 321, 353; on Madison's war message, 405; on causes of war, 422; criticizes Madison, 424

Adams, John, 33, 45, 64–65, 197

Adams, John Q.: critical of United States, 9, 173; assesses Jefferson, 38; on Continental System, 69–70, 367; on Orders in Council, 77, 149, 340–341; on impressment, 84, 290, 428–429; favors Non-Importation Act, 113; and Embargo, 149, 151, 153–154, 179; retires from Senate, 158–159; approves Macon's Bill #2, 242

Adjournment of Congress, proposed (1812), 397–398

*Alexandria Gazette*, 60, 353

Alston, Willis, 433

American Intercourse Act, British, 104

Ames, Fisher, 57, 77

Anderson, Dice R., on causes of war, 423

Anderson, Joseph, 412; bill to suspend Embargo, 174–175

*Annual Register* (London), 325

Archer, Stevenson, 373

*Argus* (Richmond), 150

Armed forces, American: Republican policy toward, 50–52, 174; Madison asks increase, 297–298; Porter report urges increase, 356. *See also* Army, United States; Navy, United States

Armstrong, John, mission to France, 68, 215, 237–238, 244–245, 248. *See also* Cadore, Duke of

Army, United States: legislation on, 360–361

Astor, John J., 421

Atcheson, Nathaniel: defends Orders in Council, 29, 303

Auckland, William, Lord: on ignorance of British opinion, 6, 205; favors lenience toward American trade, 16–17; regrets *William* decision, 84; introduces American Intercourse Bill, 104; and Fox's Blockade, 105–106; scoffs at Non-Importation Act, 113; defends Monroe-Pinkney treaty, 134;

explains pledge on impressment, 189; warns of American war, 319. *See also* Monroe-Pinkney treaty

*Aurora* (Philadelphia): opposes Jefferson, 36; and balance of power, 56; anti-British, 55, 65, 284; pro-French, 63, 248; urges war, 107; defends Embargo, 157; praises Madison message, 298; hails repeal of Orders in Council, 341; on American cowardice, 355; fears congressional weakness, 375, 378

Austin, Maria A., 420

Bacon, Ezekiel: and Embargo repeal and Non-Intercourse Act, 179–180, 182, 227–229, 231; on administration policy, 239; in War Hawk Congress, 344–345, 362, 362–364, 371

Balance of power, American interest in, 54–58

Barclay, Thomas, 107, 143

Baring, Alexander, 28–29, 324, 421; analyzes Anglo-American trade, 18–20; criticizes admiralty courts, 76; on *War in Disguise*, 79; approves impressment, 87; opposes Orders in Council, 202, 302, 323, 332; praises Order in Council of 1809, 209; *An Inquiry into the Orders in Council*, 303–304; defends America, 314; supports Liverpool ministry, 418

Barlow, Joel, 68; and search for cultural independence, 97–98; mission to France, 294, 335, 367–368, 400, 403; answers Robert Smith, 269

Barron, James. See *Chesapeake*, U.S.S.

Bartlett, Josiah, 394, 407

Bassano, Hugues-Bernard, Duke of, 254. *See also* France

Bassett, Burwell, 392

Bathurst, Henry, Earl, 12; and Embargo, 177; and *Chesapeake*, 191, 193; and Orders in Council, 200, 205–207, 309, 328

Bayard, James A.: favors Non-Importation Act, 112–113; criticizes Monroe-

447

*Of Related Interest*

## THE ENGLISH CIVIL WAR AND AFTER, 1642-1658
*Edited by R.H. Parry*

Original essays on the Civil War and its aftermath by R.H. Parry, Brian Manning, D.H. Pennington, Dame Veronica Wedgwood, Austin Woolrych, Ivan Roots, and Robert Ashton. "Seven celebrated historians . . . a remarkably balanced picture of the Great Rebellion."—*Thomas G. Barnes*

paper, $2.45
cloth, $7.00

## AN ANTHROPOLOGIST LOOKS AT HISTORY
**Selected Essays**
*by A.L. Kroeber*
*Edited, with an Introduction, by Theodora Kroeber*
*With a Foreword by Milton Singer*

"These fourteen essays, all written when A.L. Kroeber was past 70, combine the wide-spreading speculations of one of the most knowledgeable anthropologists of our time with 'next assignments' for his younger colleagues."—*Journal of Modern History*

cloth, $4.50

## GUNS ON THE EARLY FRONTIERS
**A History of Firearms from Colonial Times, Throughout the Years of the Western Fur Trade**
*by Carl P. Russell*

"It approaches understatement to call *Guns on the Early Frontiers* an outstanding contribution to firearms literature. It sets its own standard."
—*New York Times*
paper, $2.45

*UNIVERSITY OF CALIFORNIA PRESS*

# PROLOGUE TO WAR
## England and the United States, 1805-1812

The first full-scale study of the coming of the War of 1812 since the work of Henry Adams. Mr. Perkins contends that diplomatic disasters cannot always be explained in rational terms and that emotional factors more often than not dictate the course of history. He shows how the hotheads of the two countries made folly beget folly, until a war that neither side wanted became a reality.

"The 'second war for American independence' is dealt with by Bradford Perkins... with a breadth and comprehensiveness that make it a landmark of diplomatic history. . . . With exactitude and discrimination he deals with the whole complex of circumstances that led to a battle neither of the nations wanted. . . . This account may have relevance for our own time."
—Sidney Warren in *The Saturday Review*

"As a result of his patient examination, British statemanship during this period acquires, not so much a new shape, as a new texture. . . . Merely from this point of view, and there are others, 'Prologue to War' has many of the signs of a masterpiece. This is not a word one uses lightly. . . ."
—George Dangerfield in *The New York Times Book Review*

"Perkins traces, step by step, the coming of this 'unnatural war.' Fresh insights and new interpretations are so well supported and so persuasively set forth that it would indeed be difficult not to be at least half convinced. *Prologue to War,* like its predecessor *The First Rapprochement,* is a major contribution to diplomatic history, and a book that no scholar, whatever his specialty, who hopes to understand the age of Jefferson, dare overlook."
—Charles M. Wiltse in *The American Historical Review*

BRADFORD PERKINS, Professor of History at the University of Michigan, began his trilogy of Anglo-American relations with *The First Rapprochement: England and the United States, 1795-1805* and ended it with *Castlereagh and Adams: England and the United States, 1812-1823,* which was awarded the 1965 Bancroft Prize for the best work in American Diplomacy. The complete trilogy is published by the University of California Press.

## UNIVERSITY OF CALIFORNIA PRESS
### Berkeley, California 94720